MOZART SPEAKS

Views on Music, Musicians, and the World

Drawn from the Letters of Wolfgang Amadeus Mozart
and Other Early Accounts

Selected and with Commentary by

ROBERT L. MARSHALL

SCHIRMER BOOKS
A Division of Macmillan, Inc.
New York
Maxwell Macmillan Canada
Toronto
Maxwell Macmillan International
New York   Oxford   Singapore   Sydney

Schirmer Books
A Division of Macmillan, Inc.
866 Third Avenue, New York, N. Y. 10022

Maxwell Macmillan Canada, Inc.
1200 Eglinton Avenue East, Suite 200
Don Mills, Ontario M3C 3N1

Macmillan, Inc. is part of the
Maxwell Communication Group of Companies

Library of Congress Catalog Card Number: 91-3250

Printed in the United States of America

printing number

1   2   3   4   5   6   7   8   9   10

Library of Congress Cataloging-in-Publication Data

Mozart, Wolfgang Amadeus, 1756–1791.
    Mozart speaks: views on music, musicians, and the world: drawn from
the letters of Wolfgang Amadeus Mozart and other early accounts/selected
and with commentary by Robert L. Marshall.
    p.   cm.
Includes bibliographical references (p.   ) and index.
ISBN 0-02-871385-0
    1. Mozart, Wolfgang Amadeus, 1756-1791—Correspondence.
2. Composers—Austria—Biography.   3. Music—Europe—18th century—
History and criticism.   I. Marshall, Robert Lewis.   II. Title.
ML410.M9A285   1991
780'.92—dc20
[B]   91-3250
                                              CIP
                                              MN

The paper used in this publication meets the minimum requirements of
American National Standard for Information Sciences—Permanence of Paper
for Printed Library Materials. ANSI Z39.48-1984.   ∞™

"Be so good as to reread my letters now and then and to follow my advice."
WAMozart
Paris, 30 July 1778 (To Aloysia Weber)

Contents

Illustrations

Frontispiece. Wolfgang Amadeus Mozart at the keyboard, ca. 1789. Unfinished oil painting by Josef Lange. Salzburg: Internationale Stiftung Mozarteum, Mozart Museum.

Figure 2.1. Archbishop Hieronymus Colloredo. Engraving by Franz Xaver König, 1772. Salzburg: Erzabtei St. Peter.

Figure 2.2. Emperor Joseph II. Engraving by Friedrich John after Friedrich Heinrich Füger. Augsburg: Stadtarchiv.

Figure 4.1. Salzburg. Engraving by Anton Amon after Franz von Naumann, 1791. Salzburg: Internationale Stiftung Mozarteum, Mozart Museum.

Figure 4.2. View of Vienna. Engraving by Jacob Alt. Private Property, Vienna.

Figure 4.3. Prague. Colored etching by L. Peukert, as reproduced in Alexander Koval, *Mozart and Prague*. Prague: Artia, 1962.

Figure 4.4. Nuremberg. Photograph of the Burg vicinity before the Hallertor by Max Hermann, as reproduced in Eugen Kusch, *Nürnberg: Lebensbild einer Stadt*. Nürnberg: Verlag Nürnberger Presse.

Figure 5.1. Doodle portrait of Maria Anna Thekla Mozart ("Bäsle") from Wolfgang Amadeus Mozart's Letter of 10 May 1779. By permission of the British Library.

Figure 5.2. Multilingual inkblot from Mozart's letter to his father of 4 January 1783. Berlin: Staatsbibliothek Preußischer Kulturbesitz, Musikabteilung.

Figure 5.3. Anonymous pencil drawing of Maria Anna Thekla Mozart ("Bäsle"). Salzburg: Internationale Stiftung Mozarteum, Mozart Museum.

Figure 5.4. From Mozart's letter of 10 May 1779 to his cousin Maria Anna Thekla. By permission of the British Library.

Figure 5.5. Constanze Mozart, née Weber, 1782. Oil painting by Josef Lange. Glasgow: Hunterian Art Gallery.

Figure 5.6. Mozart's Mother, Anna Maria née Pertl, ca. 1775. Anonymous oil painting. Salzburg: Internationale Stiftung Mozarteum, Mozart Museum.

Figure 5.7. Mozart's father, Leopold Mozart, ca. 1765. Anonymous oil painting. Salzburg: Internationale Stiftung Mozarteum, Mozart Museum.

Figure 7.1. Pianoforte built by Johann Andreas Stein, Augsburg, 1773. Leipzig: University of Leipzig, Musical Instrument Museum.

Figure 7.2. Mozart's pianoforte, built by Anton Walter, Vienna, ca. 1780. Salzburg: Internationale Stiftung Mozarteum, Mozart Museum.

Figure 13.1. Muzio Clementi. Engraving by T. Hardy, ca. 1794, after an original owned by J. Bland. New Haven: From the Wilshire Collection in the Music Library of Yale University.

Figure 13.2. Abbé Georg Joseph Vogler. Engraving by Johann Michael Schramm. Augsburg: Stadtarchiv.

Figure 13.3. Antonio Salieri. Anonymous oil painting. Vienna: Gesellschaft der Musikfreunde.

Figure 14.1. Anton Raaff. Engraving by G. F. Touchemolin. Formerly in the possession of the Graphische Sammlung, Munich.

Figure 14.2. Aloysia Weber, 1784. Oil painting by J. B. von Lampi. Private Collection.

The portraits and illustrations have been reproduced with the kind permission of their owners.

Musical Examples

CHAPTER 14. PERFORMERS

A Most Necessary Introduction

"I should like to write a book, a short introduction to music, illustrated by examples." Thus wrote Mozart to his father from Vienna on the 28th of December 1782. Although he never got to write that book, Mozart did get to express his views—rather copiously—not only on musical issues but on a colorful variety of other topics as well. His comments are preserved primarily in his letters, also in the first-hand (occasionally, second-hand) reports and recollections of eye witnesses. And they are enough to fill a book.

It seems that Mozart had always felt a desire to share with others his insights and experiences as a musician, and to declare himself on topics ranging from a particular singer's miserable acting, to the practical matter of the proper tempo of a fugue, to the fundamental issue of the nature and limits of musical representation in opera. Some of these remarks may have been made as much for his own benefit as for others. They seem to have helped him clarify his thoughts about essentials. It is significant, for example, that he declared his intention to write a book just three days before completing the first of the string quartets dedicated to Haydn, works which, in Mozart's words, were the "fruit of a long and laborious endeavor."

For most of the previous year, in fact, Mozart had been preoccupied with an even longer and more laborious endeavor: the composition of *Die Entführung aus dem Serail*. After almost a full year of gestation, *Die Entführung* finally had its premiere in July 1782. Work on the opera had been accompanied by a series of letters home, in which Mozart described in remarkable detail the rationale behind his approach to several numbers in the evolving opera. Perhaps it was the writing of those letters—that is, the experience of giving expression to his thoughts, in writing, about substantial musical issues (along, of course, with the experience of having written those landmark compositions)—that had precipitated Mozart's desire to "write a book, a short introduction to music." For in the process he had managed to set forth the basic elements of his artistic credo. Such passages in the letters could easily have served as preliminary notes for

Mozart's book. Only the promised musical examples were lacking; but they could be found, of course, in the opera.

To put it a bit fancifully (and, admittedly, rather immodestly), the purpose of the present book is to help Mozart not only to complete but to expand upon his "short introduction." There is every reason to believe, after all, that many passages in the letters and other contemporary documents in fact offer a reasonable clue as to what Mozart would have said in a book on music. Assuming that is so, then it should be a matter of collecting and organizing the pertinent material into topical categories and thereupon, in accordance with Mozart's intentions, illustrate his points with appropriate musical examples: examples drawn from his own works and specified by the composer himself. Even the categories would in effect be dictated by Mozart, since they would necessarily be derived from the topics he had chosen to address.

But the present book has another, even more immodest purpose. There is, after all, really no need, once we have begun, to limit the scope to purely musical matters. In principle, the subject matter of our book need be nothing less than Mozart's mind: that is to say, his opinions, perceptions, intentions, ambitions about a large variety of topics—music chief among them—but only to the extent, of course, that he (or others) took the trouble to write them down. The fact is that Mozart recorded his views on a host of issues, which taken together form the outline of a richly furnished spiritual universe. Among other things, Mozart was inevitably a witness to his time; and it is no surprise that his observations shed invaluable light, for example, on the nature of life, especially a musician's life, in the late eighteenth century. This, too, then, can properly fall within our province. But rather than write another "life of Mozart," the emphasis in this respect will be more on social history than biography in the conventional sense. That is to say, relating the particular events of Mozart's life for their own sake will not be our objective. Certain topics that loom large in the letters—and in most editions of Mozart's letters—will loom small here: for example, the circumstances leading to his break with Salzburg, the murky negotiations surrounding his marriage with Constanze Weber, the infinite complexity of his relationship with his father.

Even so, there is no paucity of material. For Mozart's letters, like his music, contain a superabundance of ideas, of "themes": playful or serious, comic or tragic, learned or simple. In this respect the letters are quite Mozartean in style—but not in technique. One of the miracles of Mozart's greatest music is that it mysteriously succeeds, despite its often seemingly wasteful extravagance of themes, in forming a compelling whole. This is rarely true of his correspondence. There the wealth of material can be bewildering. Themes often appear in maddening and confusing juxtaposition; some may be introduced too parenthetically to be fully appreciated at first or even properly noted, or they may be developed insufficiently before being supplanted by others. In profound contrast to his music, complete and effective exposition is not usually Mozart's paramount concern in his letters. Nor need it be. As a literary genre, letters are more like fantasias than fugues or sonatas. They have the privilege of being open-ended, of returning to earlier themes, if at all, only in a later "work." One of our tasks, then, will be to make sure that we have identified the principal themes, to decide on an appropriate form for them, and, after doing so, to accord them suitable exposition (for example, by means of an epigraph), development, and, often enough, recapitulation. The reader should be alerted at once that the same passage may return, abbreviated or expanded, in more than one context, if it appears that it will gain or contribute new or enriched significance thereby.

The volume that has finally emerged from such considerations consists of fourteen chapters organized into three Parts. The five chapters of Part One, "Self-Portrait with Landscape," are concerned, as the title suggests, with Mozart the man, the historical figure, set, at least in the first four chapters, against an ever-larger background. Chapter 1, "The Musician," narrows the focus to the constituent elements of his genius, beginning with the inborn, natural talent (the ear, the memory, the sensitivity), proceeding to a description of his multiple manifestations as a performer, and finally contemplating the stigmata of the supremely endowed composer: the recognition of the calling, the nature of the gift, the approach to the task. Since much of the material of this chapter relates to Mozart's childhood, it was necessary here, more than elsewhere, to draw on the accounts of contemporaries.

Chapter 2, "The Career," is concerned with the relatively mundane matter of Mozart's day-to-day experiences as a practicing musician. This is inevitably the most purely biographical, or rather, autobiographical, chapter in the volume. Mozart reports here on his plans and ambitions, his daily routines, his awareness of his worldly success. In Chapter 3, "The Profession," however, Mozart is cast less in the role of protagonist than of witness. The emphasis here is on the musical profession per se, as it was practiced in late eighteenth-century Europe. We experience, through Mozart's eyes, the contemporary world of patrons, publishers, and copyists, of concert programs and opera contracts. A full-scale social history of music in Mozart's time addressing such issues has yet to be written. Mozart himself, however, has provided a substantial first draft.

The larger world is the subject, and the title, of Chapter 4—or at least that part of the larger world that was of interest to Wolfgang Amadeus Mozart. What was his relation to the other arts? What literature did he read? Was he interested in politics? current events? As one of the most widely traveled individuals of his time, finally, what was his opinion of the peoples and places he had got to know: Italians, French, English, Jews,

Germans? Part One concludes by returning to Mozart, not the musical phenomenon this time, but rather the all-too-mortal man: his amusements and pastimes, his human foibles and failings of greater and lesser magnitude, his philosophy of life and death.

The subject of music occupies the center of the volume. Taking our clue from the composer, Part Two begins with "A Short Introduction." Chapter 6 attempts to identify the basic premises of Mozart's aesthetic philosophy —illustrating them with musical examples—before proceeding to describe his method of teaching composition. This has been accomplished by drawing not only on his letters but on some of his surviving lessons as well. Chapter 7, too, deals with basic issues: this time the basics of proper performance, gathering together Mozart's advice on tempo, on expression and interpretation, on ornamentation, ensemble size, keyboard playing (and keyboard instruments), on singing, on playing the violin.

The five remaining chapters of Part Two address the music itself, exploring in turn the realms of opera, church music, and instrumental music. Since Mozart had more to say about opera than any other musical topic, it is the subject of three chapters. Chapter 8 discusses the principal dramatic, national, and stylistic categories of opera; Chapter 9 investigates the multifaceted issue of opera as drama; Chapter 10, finally, provides information on the origins and early reception of individual operas. Mozart's observations on church music in general and on individual compositions are collected in Chapter 11. In Chapter 12, "Instrumental Music," the composer explains the stylistic and performance options available in the concerto, and identifies the prevailing national styles in orchestral music, before turning his attention to certain modish "forms of fashion" and recounting the origins, purposes, and destinies of a number of particular works.

Part Three, "On Musicians," forms the finale, with one chapter devoted to Mozart's comments on individual composers—divided into "the good," "the bad," and "the indifferent"—and one chapter on performers —classified this time, with the exception of the singers, not by their abilities but by their medium of tone production. Mozart's opinions of his fellow musicians—whether composers or performers—embrace their moral as well as their musical virtues and vices. These judgments can be abundantly generous or absolutely merciless, highly indignant or simply hilarious.

The vast majority of material in this volume is drawn from Mozart's letters. They are presented here, with permission, in the classic translation of Emily Anderson, *The Letters of Mozart and his Family*, first published in 1938. (Page references to the third edition, published in 1985, appear at the end of each cited passage.) The readability and reliability of Anderson's translation have been confirmed time and again over the course of the past half-century. It is reproduced here with minimal change. The spelling has been rendered according to American practice, and the punctuation normalized in order to harmonize with the rest of the volume. At times Anderson chose to retain the original language in longer passages written in French or Italian; these have been translated here but printed in italics with the original language identified in brackets. Italics are used here also to identify passages originally written by Mozart in code. (The Mozart family had resorted to a code based on a system of letter substitutions—*a* for *m, e* for *l, s* for *o*, etc.—in order to evade the curiosity of censors. The passages had already been deciphered, with the resolutions entered into the originals, by Georg Nikolaus Nissen, an early Mozart biographer and the second husband of his widow, Constanze.) Where the translation is problematic, or where it seems desirable as a point of information to have the original German (as in the case of certain technical terms), this is provided (occasionally with a literal or an alternative translation) either in brackets, for single words and brief expressions, or in an endnote, for longer passages. For Mozart's word games, doggerel poems, and scatological writings, Anderson's translations are, reasonably enough, more faithful to the spirit than to the letter of the originals. For the benefit of those able to read the original, therefore, the complete German text of such material is printed in an appendix.

The earliest letter surviving in Mozart's hand is a brief note, undated and addressed to an unknown girl friend. It is thought to have been written no earlier than the year 1769, that is, when Mozart was thirteen years old and already an accomplished, indeed world famous, musician. By 1769, after all, he had already composed some seventy works and spent three-and-a-half years traveling as a Wunderkind on a spectacularly successful grand tour through Northern Europe that had taken him to the leading towns and courts of France, England, Belgium, Holland, and Switzerland. (Mozart's first dated letter was written to his sister Nannerl from Verona on 7 January 1770.) For information, then, not only about what Mozart may have said but even about what he had done and seen during his eventful and formative years as a child prodigy, it is necessary to consult second-hand sources. These include contemporary newspaper announcements and reviews of concert appearances, and especially the numerous and highly informative letters written on these early journeys by Leopold Mozart to his landlord, the Salzburg merchant, Lorenz Hagenauer. Leopold's main objective in writing these extensive and detailed accounts, incidentally, was to create a documentary record for use in his own biography of his son.

Additional reliable information on Mozart's childhood and early career is preserved in the reminiscences of a close friend of the Mozart family, one Johann Andreas Schachtner, trumpeter at the Salzburg Court, and sometime librettist and translator for Mozart. Schachtner recorded his recollections in April 1792 in a letter addressed to Mozart's sister, Nannerl. In the spring of 1792 Nannerl set down her own reminiscences at the request of an historian, Friedrich von Schlichtegroll, who was preparing an obituary of Mozart. (The obituary was published in 1793.) Further memoirs of Nannerl were published several years later in the *Allgemeine Musikalische Zeitung* (Leipzig, 22 January 1800). These documents, and numerous others, have been collected in *Mozart: Die Dokumente seines Lebens,* by Otto Erich Deutsch. The volume is published in English under the title *Mozart: A Documentary Biography,* from which the selections printed here have been reproduced. (Page references to the Deutsch *Documentary Biography* are preceded by DDB.)

Paradoxically, Mozart's own account is relatively thin at the latter end of his career, as well. Of the more than 300 letters that survive in Mozart's hand, fully one-fifth were written during the sixteen-month period of Mozart's journey to Munich, Mannheim, and Paris: the period from September 1777 to January 1779. The number of Mozart's letters falls off significantly during Mozart's Vienna period. But this development, upon reflection, is readily understandable. During the last ten years of his life Mozart largely remained at home; as he did not travel extensively, he had little occasion to maintain an extensive correspondence. After all, his colleagues, his friends, and, since 1782, the most significant member of his family, his wife Constanze, were all nearby. It is symptomatic that not a single first-hand letter exists between Mozart and the librettists of his greatest operas: Lorenzo Da Ponte, the librettist of *The Marriage of Figaro, Don Giovanni,* and *Così fan tutte,* and Emanuel Schikaneder, the author of *The Magic Flute.* Mozart had even less occasion to write letters after the death of his father on 28 May 1787. Fewer than seventy letters by Mozart survive from the last four-and-a-half years of his life—a disproportionate number of them (almost one-fourth) consisting of desperate pleas for money addressed to his fellow Mason Michael Puchberg.

Not only for Mozart's childhood, then, but for his later years as well we must augment his own words with the accounts of others. Among the most important of these are the reminiscences of Constanze, as related to the English couple Vincent and Mary Novello and published as *A Mozart Pilgrimage: Being the Travel Diaries of Vincent & Mary Novello in the Year 1829.* The diaries also record the Novellos' interviews with other individuals who knew Mozart, for example, Abbé Maximilian Stadler, a family friend, who helped catalogue Mozart's music. In addition we can consult the early biography of Franz Xaver Niemetschek, *Life of Mozart (Leben des K. K. Kapellmeisters Wolfgang Gottlieb Mozart,* Prague, 1798). Niemetschek, a Czech professor of philosophy, made Mozart's acquaintance in Prague, presumably in 1787. Ten years later he published a revised and expanded edition under the title *Biography of Mozart (Lebensbeschreibung des K. K. Kapellmeisters Wolfgang Amadeus Mozart,* Prague, 1808).

Reasonably credible reports of Mozart's activities and attitudes during the Vienna years are transmitted as well in the following accounts written by individuals who either knew the composer personally, or seem to have known others who did:

Jean-Baptiste-Antoine Suard, "Anecdotes sur Mozart," *Mélanges de Littérature* (Paris, 1804). Unfortunately, Suard's connection to Mozart is obscure.

The reminiscences (1808) of Mozart's brother-in-law, Joseph Lange, the husband of Aloysia, née Weber.

The *Reminiscences of Michael Kelly of the King's Theatre and Theatre Royal Drury Lane* (London, 1826). The Irishman Kelly, who was a tenor in the Vienna Court Theater from 1783 to 1787, sang the roles of Don Curzio and Basilio in the first performance of *Figaro* under Mozart's direction.

The memoirs of Mozart's sister-in-law, Sophie Weber Haibel, as published in Georg Nikolaus Nissen, *Biographie W. A. Mozart's* (Leipzig, 1828).

The *Memoirs of Lorenzo Da Ponte*. Da Ponte published this colorful document in New York in 1829 and 1830.

The memoirs of one Joseph Frank, published in *Deutsches Museum* (Leipzig, 1852). Frank was a prominent Viennese physician who knew Beethoven and Haydn as well as Mozart.

The original intention was to allow the documents assembled here to speak for themselves, with a minimum of editorial explanation. This policy, however, threatened to render the volume of limited use to readers not already rather thoroughly familiar with the facts bearing both on Mozart's life and works and on much of eighteenth-century musical history, as well. Moreover, the minimalist approach was also inherently less than elegant: there was clearly a structural and an aesthetic need to provide a thread of continuity to connect the often brief passages. In the end, the proportion of space allocated to editorial commentary, compared with the original intention, had grown significantly.

With the exception of biographical information, explanatory remarks appear directly before or following the pertinent passage. In order to avoid excessive repetition, biographical material for writers and musicians appears only in conjunction with the alphabetically arranged entries devoted to them variously in Chapter 4 (writers), Chapter 13 (composers), or Chapter 14 (performers). For all other individuals, brief identifications are included in Appendix I, "Biographical Glossary." Page references for biographical entries are printed in italics in the index.

A note about the musical examples. Since musical examples are not only costly but also consume considerable space, both their number and extent necessarily had to be limited. Nonetheless, the very rationale of the present book—to carry out in some fashion an explicit but unfulfilled intention of Mozart's—dictated that a substantial number of examples would be included here. Their main function is to illustrate or clarify discussions of aesthetic, stylistic, or interpretive points, usually by drawing on a work or passage specifically mentioned by Mozart himself. Other examples serve the more modest purpose of "identifiers," calling to mind the principal theme or opening measures of a cited compostion. Some, finally, are included because they were already present in the documents. In all instances, for the musically literate reader the specificity and vividness provided by a musical example can only serve to enhance the musical discussion in much the same way that a pictorial reproduction enhances the discussion of a painting.

Passages from the following volumes have been reproduced with the kind permission of the copyright holders. Davenport, Marcia. *Mozart.* Reprinted with permission of Charles Scribner's Sons, an imprint of Macmillan Publishing Company, and Brandt & Brandt, Literary Agents, Inc. for the estate of Marcia Davenport. Copyright 1932 by Charles Scribner's Sons, renewed 1960 by Marcia Davenport. Deutsch, Otto Erich. *Mozart: A Documentary Biography*, translated by Eric Blom, Peter Branscombe, and Jeremy Noble. Published in 1965 by A & C Black, London; also Stanford University Press, Stanford, California. *Mozart Briefe and Aufzeichnungen.* Edited by the Internationale Stiftung Mozarteum. Published 1962–1975 by Bärenreiter-Verlag, Kassel.

I wish, finally, to express my gratitude to the following individuals for helpful comments and information of various sorts: Thomas Bauman, Mark Kroll, Brenda Marshall, Michael Ochs, Leon Plantinga, Maynard Solomon, Harrison J. Wignall, and Robert S. Winter; to Robert Axelrod and Maribeth Anderson Payne of Schirmer Books and to my wife, Traute, for their interest and for encouraging me to add ever more editorial commentary; to Roberta Marvin for her assistance in the preparation of the manuscript and the index; to the Mazer Fund for Faculty Research of Brandeis University for its generous research support.

Mozart's Life: An Outline

The following chronological outline of the principal events in Mozart's career should suffice to set the selections into their biographical context.

EARLY CHILDHOOD: 1756–1763

Salzburg. 27 January 1756: Wolfgangus Theophilus Mozart is born to Leopold and Anna Maria Pertl Mozart. January/February 1761: Mozart writes his first compositions: Andante and Allegro for Keyboard, K. 1a, 1b.

Vienna. 18 September 1762 to 5 January 1763. October 1762: Performance before Emperor Francis I and Empress Maria Theresa.

GRAND TOUR TO PARIS, LONDON, HOLLAND: 9 JUNE 1763 TO 29 NOVEMBER 1766

Paris. 18 November 1763 to 10 April 1764. Versailles. 1 January 1764: An audience with King Louis XV.

London. 23 April 1764 to 1 August 1765. 27 April 1764: A performance before King George III.

19 May 1764: A meeting with Johann Christian Bach. November/December 1764: Vocal instruction from the celebrated castrato Giovanni Manzuoli.

Holland. ca. 9 September 1765 to April 1766. April to 29 November 1766: Return to Salzburg through Belgium, France, and Switzerland.

SALZBURG RESIDENCY: 1766–1769

14 November 1769: Mozart is appointed unpaid member (third Konzertmeister) of the Salzburg court orchestra.

FIRST ITALIAN JOURNEY: 13 DECEMBER 1769 TO 29 MARCH 1771

1770

Verona. 5 January: Mozart's first concert performance in Italy.

Bologna. 25/26 March: Mozart composes fugues for Padre Giambattista Martini.

Rome. 11/12 April: Hears and copies Gregorio Allegri's *Miserere* in the Sistine Chapel. 5 July: Receives the Order of the Golden Spur. 8 July: An audience with Pope Clement XIV.

Bologna. October: Daily counterpoint lessons with Padre Martini. 9 October: Mozart passes the examination for membership in the Accademia filarmonica.

Milan. 26 December: The premiere of *Mitridate, Rè di Ponto*, K. 87/74a.

SECOND ITALIAN JOURNEY: 13 AUGUST 1771 TO 15 DECEMBER 1771

Milan. 17 October: The premiere of *Ascanio in Alba*, K. 111.

Salzburg, 16 December: Archbishop Schrattenbach dies.

1772

Salzburg. 29 April: Hieronymus Colloredo is installed as Prince-Archbishop. July: Mozart is appointed a regular salaried member of the Salzburg court orchestra. 21 August: Promotion to Konzertmeister.

THIRD ITALIAN JOURNEY: 24 OCTOBER 1772 TO 13 MARCH 1773

Milan. 26 December: The premiere of *Lucio Silla*, K. 135.

SALZBURG RESIDENCY: 1773 TO 1781

5 December 1773: Symphony in G minor, K. 183/173dB. 6 April 1774: Symphony in A major, K. 201/186a. Munich. 13 January 1775: The premiere of *La finta giardiniera*, K. 196. June to October 1775: Four violin concerti, K. 211, 216, 218, 219.

SOJOURNS IN MANNHEIM AND PARIS: 23 SEPTEMBER 1777 TO MID JANUARY 1779

1777

Augsburg. 11 October: Mozart meets his cousin Maria Anna Thekla, "Bäsle." 12 October: A visit to the piano maker Johann Andreas Stein.

Mannheim. 30 October 1777 to 14 March 1778. Numerous visits to Christian Cannabich, conductor of the Mannheim court orchestra.

1778

Paris. 23 March to 26 September 1778. April: Sinfonia Concertante for Four Wind Instruments (lost). June: Symphony in D (*Paris*), K. 297. 3 July: Mozart's mother dies. Return to Salzburg: 26 September 1778 to 17 January 1779 via Strasbourg (15 October to 3 November) and Mannheim (6 November to 9 December).

1779

Salzburg. 17 January 1779: Appointment as court organist. Summer 1779: Sinfonia Concertante for Violin and Viola, K. 364/320d.

1780

Sojourn in Munich: 6 November 1780 to 16 March 1781. 29 January: The premiere of *Idomeneo*, K. 366.

VIENNA: 1781 TO 1791

1781

16 March: Mozart's arrival in Vienna. 9 May: Final break with Archbishop Colloredo. 6 June: A kick in the pants from Count Arco, Salzburg court chamberlain. 30 July: Commencement of work on *Die Entführung aus dem Serail*. 24 December: Piano contest with Muzio Clementi before Joseph II.

1782

April: Sundays to the Baron van Swieten to play the music of Bach and Handel. 16 July: The premiere of *Die Entführung aus dem Serail*, K. 384. Late July: Symphony in D, K. 385 (*Haffner*). 4 August: Mozart marries Constanze Weber in St. Stephen's Cathedral. 31 December: Completion of the String Quartet in G, K. 387, the first of the six quartets dedicated to Haydn.

1783

17 June: The birth of the Mozarts' first child, Raimund Leopold (d. 19 August 1783).

Sojourn in Salzburg: July to November. 26 October: Performance of the C-minor Mass, K. 427/417a. 4 November: Symphony in C, K. 425 (*Linz*).

1784

9 February: First entry in Mozart's thematic *Catalog of all my Works:* Piano Concerto in E-flat, K. 449. 21 September: Birth of the Mozarts' second child, Karl Thomas (d. 1858). 14 December: Initiation into the Masonic lodge "Zur Wohltätigkeit."

1785

11 February to June: Leopold visits Mozart in Vienna. February and March: Composition of the piano concertos in D minor, K. 466, and C, K. 467. 2 April: Performance of the six string quartets dedicated to Haydn. Autumn: Commencement of work on *Le nozze di Figaro.* 16 December: Completion of the Piano Concerto in E-flat, K. 482.

1786

19 February: Mozart distributes the "riddles and proverbs of Zoroaster" at a masked ball. March: Composition of the piano concertos in A, K. 488, and C minor, K. 491. 1 May: The premiere of *Le nozze di Figaro,* K. 492. Autumn: Mozart plans a journey to England. December: Piano Concerto in C, K. 503.

1787

First journey to Prague: 8 January to mid February. 19 January: Symphony in D, K. 504 *(Prague).* 22 January: The Prague performance of *Le nozze di Figaro.* Mid February: Return to Vienna. 7–20 April: Beethoven arrives in Vienna to study with Mozart. 28 May: Leopold Mozart dies in Salzburg.

Second Journey to Prague: 1 October to mid November. 29 October: The premiere of *Don Giovanni.* Mid November: Return to Vienna. 7 December: Mozart receives an appointment as Imperial Chamber Compositeur.

1788

7 May: The Viennese performance of *Don Giovanni.* Summer: Mozart begins to borrow money from Michael Puchberg. 26 June: Symphony in E-flat, K. 543. 25 July: Symphony in G minor, K. 550. 10 August: Symphony in C, K. 551 *(Jupiter).*

1789

Journey to Dresden, Leipzig, and Berlin: 8 April to 4 June. Leipzig. 22 April: Mozart plays on the organ in the Thomaskirche.

1790

26 January: The premiere of *Così fan tutte*, K. 588. 20 Feburary: Joesph II dies.

Journey to Frankfurt: 23 September to November. Frankfurt. 9 October: The coronation of Leopold II. 10 November: Return to Vienna.

1791

25 April: Mozart applies for the position of unpaid Assistant Kapell-meister of St. Stephen's Cathedral. 4 June to mid July: Constanze sojourns in Baden. Summer: Composition of *Die Zauberflöte*. Mid July: Mozart receives the commission for *La Clemenza di Tito*. 26 July: Birth of the Mozart's sixth child, Franz Xaver Wolfgang (d.1844).

Third Journey to Prague: Mid August to mid September. September: Coronation of Leopold II. 6 September: The premiere of *La Clemenza di Tito*, K. 621. Mid September: Return to Vienna. 30 September: Premiere of *Die Zauberflöte*, K. 620. Early October: Mozart completes the Clarinet Concerto in A, K. 622. Mid October to mid November: Work on the *Requiem*, K. 626. 20 November: Mozart takes to bed. 5 December. Mozart dies at 12:55 a.m. 6 December: Burial in St. Marx Cemetery.

The basic unit of currency in eighteenth-century Austria was the silver gulden or florin (fl). It would seem that in the 1780s one gulden was worth approximately $20.00 in 1990 dollars. 1 kreuzer = $\frac{1}{60}$ gulden = $0.33. 1 gold ducat = 4.50 gulden = $90.00.

The French louis d'or, also mentioned in the selections printed here, was worth about 10 gulden, or $200.00.

Abbreviations

A: Emily Anderson. *The Letters of Mozart and His Family.* Chronologically arranged, translated and edited with an Introduction, Notes and Indexes. 3rd edition. London: Macmillan Press, 1985.

DDB: Otto Erich Deutsch. *Mozart: A Documentary Biography.* Translated by Eric Blom, Peter Branscombe, and Jeremy Noble. Stanford: Stanford University Press, 1965.

K: Identifying number in the "Köchel catalogue" of Mozart's works. Many of Mozart's compositions carry more than one identifying number. This reflects a change in the presumed date of composition between the publication of the first edition of Köchel's catalogue in 1862 ("K1") and the most recent, sixth, edition ("K6"). Redated works will be cited here, in accordance with prevailing practice, by the more familiar, and official, "K1" number followed, in parentheses, by the "K6" number. For example, the number for the Mass in C minor is K. 427 (417a). Some works have been redated more than once, resulting in more complex designations (e.g., in the case of the early Symphony in G minor, K. 183 (173dB).

K6: Ludwig Ritter von Köchel. *Chronologisch-thematisches Verzeichnis sämtlicher Tonwerke Wolfgang Amadé Mozarts.* 6th edition. Edited by Franz Giegling, Alexander Weinmann, Gerd Sievers. Wiesbaden: Breitkopf & Härtel, 1964.

MBA: *Mozart Briefe und Aufzeichnungen.* Complete edition. Published by the Internationale Stiftung Mozarteum, Salzburg. 7 Volumes. Volumes 1–4: text, edited by Wilhelm A. Bauer and Otto Erich Deutsch; volumes 5–7: commentary and index, prepared by Joseph Heinz Eibl. Kassel, 1962–1975.

NMA: Wolfgang Amadeus Mozart. *Neue Ausgabe Sämtlicher Werke (Neue Mozart-Ausgabe).* Edited by the Internationale Stiftung Mozarteum, Salzburg, in cooperation with the Mozart cities Augsburg, Salzburg, and Vienna. Kassel, 1954–1991.

MOZART
SPEAKS

Part One

Self–Portrait
with Landscape

1

The Musician

I cannot write in verse, for I am no poet. I cannot arrange the parts of speech with such art as to produce effects of light and shade, for I am no painter. Even by signs and gestures I cannot express my thoughts and feelings, for I am no dancer. But I can do so by means of sounds, for I am a musician.

Mannheim, 8 November 1777

NATURAL TALENT

► That geniuses are born, not made, is, of course, a cliché dating back to antiquity. While its universal validity may be questioned, a quite compelling argument for the proposition can certainly be made in the case of Mozart. And so it has been ever since his own time. When, on his sojourns in Paris and London in the years 1763 and 1764, the seven- (or eight)-year-old displayed his abilities to identify pitches, to improvise, to read at sight, to play the violin, to perform on the keyboard—with a hand that could barely stretch a sixth—the most difficult compositions, and, finally, to compose on command without recourse to an instrument, he was described as "a wonderchild," "a prodigy of nature," "an extraordinary phenomenon." His talent was similarly characterized as "incredible," "unheard of," "a veritable miracle," "surpassing all understanding or imagination," an "extraordinary gift" "bestowed" by God. The numerous eyewitness accounts of Mozart's public appearances leave no doubt that he was already an accomplished performer and composer by the age of seven.

Before the achievement, of course, there was the disposition. The first manifestation of the prodigious talent, as the passages selected below reveal, was a pronounced sensitivity to musical sounds per se. By the age of three Mozart had already developed a literally irresistible attraction to euphonious harmonic sonorities—specifically, to the rich consonances of thirds. On the other hand, he soon displayed an equally powerful aversion to certain sounds: specifically, loud or high-pitched instruments—the trumpet, then the flute, later on the mechanical clock (but allegedly the harp, as well).

For the crucial period of Mozart's early childhood we have no choice but to rely on the accounts of others. But we can pay particular attention to those reports that not only relate some sensational musical exploit by the Wunderkind but manage also to shed some light on the boy's awareness and attitude toward his phenomenal gifts. ◄

SOUND SENSE

The Reminiscences of Nannerl Mozart, 1792

The son was three years old when the father began to instruct his seven-year-old daughter in the clavier.

The boy at once showed his God-given [and] extraordinary talent. He often spent much time at the clavier, picking out thirds, which he was always striking, and his pleasure showed that it sounded good. (DDB, 455)

The Reminiscences of Johann Andreas Schachtner, 1792

Until he was almost nine he was terribly afraid of the trumpet when it was played alone, without other music. Merely to hold a trumpet in front of him was like aiming a loaded pistol at his heart. Papa wanted to cure him of this childish fear and once told me to blow [my trumpet] at him despite his reluctance, but my God! I should not have been persuaded to do it; Wolfgangerl scarely heard the blaring sound, then he grew pale and began to collapse, and if I had continued, he would surely have had a fit. (DDB, 453)

To Leopold Mozart   *Mannheim, 14 February 1778*

You know that I become quite powerless whenever I am obliged to write for an instrument which I cannot bear [viz., the flute]. (A, 481)

The Memoirs of Joseph Frank, 1852

Once when we were speaking about instruments Mozart said that he loathed the flute and the harp. (DDB, 561)

To Constanze   *Frankfurt am Main, 3 October 1790*

The works consist solely of little pipes, which sound too high pitched and too childish for my taste. (A, 943–944)

► Not only individual sounds, of course, but music per se—both good and bad music—had an unusually powerful physical effect on Mozart. ◄

To Leopold Mozart   *Mannheim, 13 November 1777*

[Ignaz von Beecke] then went on to say (something which is quite true) that music is performed in the imperial apartments [in Vienna] which would drive a dog away. I remarked that whenever I heard that kind of music and could not get away from it, it always gave me a headache. (A, 369)

To Leopold Mozart   *Mannheim, 10 December 1777*

Thereupon Mlle. Rosa [Cannabich] played my sonata very seriously. I assure you, I couldn't keep from weeping. (A, 414)

MEMORY

► Along with his innate, exquisite sensitivity to sounds, Mozart also possessed a phenomenal musical memory, perhaps the most formidable in history; his gift went far beyond "perfect pitch" (i.e., the ability to remember and identify individual notes or clusters of notes) to encompass the ability to hear and remember entire compositions—motets, concertos, even operas—to such an extent that he was able to write them down subsequently.

The most famous anecdote concerning Mozart's memory is surely the one about the Miserere setting by the late Renaissance composer Gregorio Allegri (1582–1652), which he heard in Rome at the age of fourteen. Leopold's original report and Nannerl's later recollection of the event follow. ◄

Leopold Mozart to his Wife   *Rome, 14 April 1770*

You have often heard of the famous Miserere in Rome, which is so greatly prized that the performers in the chapel are forbidden on pain of excommunication to take away a single part of it, to copy it or to give it to anyone. *But we have it already.* Wolfgang has written it down and we would have sent it to Salzburg in this letter, if it were not necessary for us to be there to perform it. But the manner of its performance contributes more to its effect than the composition itself. So we shall bring it home with us. Moreover, as it is one of the secrets of Rome, we do not wish to let it fall into other hands, *so that we shall not incur the censure of the Church now or later* [Latin]. (A, 127)

The Reminiscences of Nannerl Mozart, 1792

On Wednesday afternoon during holy week in Rome they went at once to the Sistine Chapel, to hear the famous Miserere. And as according to tradition it was forbidden under ban of excommunication to make a copy of it from the papal music, the son undertook to hear it and then copy it out. And so it came about that when he came home, he wrote it out; the next day he went back again, holding his copy in his hat, to see whether he had got it right or not. But a different Miserere was sung. However, on Good Friday the first was repeated again. After he had returned home he made a correction here and there, then it was ready. It soon became known in Rome, [and] he had to sing it at the clavier at a concert. (DDB, 459)

► For all the fame of this legendary piece—legendary today owing to Mozart's having copied it out by memory—its musical content, as example 1.1 reveals, is by no means extraordinary or complex, consisting as it does of rather rudimentary repeated harmonies and simple textures. Nonetheless, the entire work is over 120 measures long— quite a bit, then, after all, for anyone to commit to memory after essentially but one hearing. ◄

EXAMPLE 1.1. Gregorio Allegri: Miserere, Opening and Closing Sections

► But did Mozart accomplish this feat precisely in the manner implied by his father and his sister? That is, did he write out Allegri's Miserere in its entirety, having never heard it before? The piece in fact was known outside Rome. It had even been performed in Vienna during Mozart's childhood; moreover, both the Austrian Emperor Leopold I and the venerable musical pedagogue Padre Giovanni Battista Martini at Bologna—with whom Mozart had taken instruction in counterpoint just three weeks before his visit to Rome—had copies of it. In short, Mozart could have had occasion to hear—and also to see—Allegri's Miserere before he had ever set foot in the Sistine Chapel. The possibility, then, cannot be dismissed that Leopold, at the least, may have been exaggerating Wolfgang's achievement.[1]

At all events, we have Mozart's own testimony as to the power of his musical memory. One such account dates from just about a year-and-a-half after the Miserere incident, when Mozart, once again, was back in Italy. ◄

To his Mother and Nannerl   *Milan, 2 November 1771*

There is a performance of Hasse's opera today, but . . . I cannot be there. Fortunately I know nearly all the arias by heart and so I can see and hear it at home in my head. (A, 205)

► The opera was *Ruggiero,* the last opera seria of Johann Adolf Hasse's long career. Hasse's opera and Mozart's serenata, *Ascanio in Alba,* K. 111, incidentally, were composed for the same occasion: the marriage of Archduke Ferdinand of Austria and Princess Maria Ricciarda Beatrice of Modena.

Seven years later he reports the following from Paris. ◄

To Leopold Mozart   *Paris, 3 October 1778*

[Joseph] Le Gros purchased from me the two overtures and the sinfonia concertante [for four wind instruments and orchestra, K. 297B]. He thinks that he alone has them, but he is wrong for they are still fresh in my mind and, as soon as I get home, I shall write them down again. (A, 622)

TRANSCRIBING

► The ability to transcribe works from one medium to another with ease is another of the "mechanical" musical abilities which, as the following reveals, not every talented composer necessarily possessed. ◄

To Leopold Mozart   *Mannheim, 6 December 1777*

Papa is right in his guess as to the chief reason *for Herr Cannabich's friendship.* But there is one other little matter for which *he can make use of me.* He has to produce selections of all *his ballet music,* but these must be arranged for *the clavier.* He is quite unable to transcribe them in such a way as to render them effective and at the same time easy. So he finds me very handy *for this,* as he did on one occasion already when I arranged a contredanse for him [italicized words in code]. (A, 408)

► Mozart was a virtuoso of the highest order on the piano, the organ, and the violin. His successful career as a pianist throughout Europe and especially during his first five years in Vienna is well known. But he was also distinguished enough as a violinist to have served in Salzburg as Konzertmeister of the court orchestra and as an organist to have been appointed court organist there as well. In addition to his technical prowess Mozart was particularly proud of his ability to improvise in various styles and to sightread. As a pianist he was celebrated for the expressive power of his playing and for his exceptional left hand technique; as a violinist it was his "purity of tone." Mozart was also active as a conductor—at least in performances of his own music.

Needless to say, Mozart's technical capabilities as an instrumentalist drew on that uncanny natural talent described above—specifically, in this connection, on an evidently inborn instinct that enabled him to play certain instruments even before he was taught how. We learn that Mozart as a child was able to play the organ pedals after having received a mere verbal explanation, and the violin with even less guidance than that.

Apart from the time it took from composing, no doubt the greatest frustration associated with his existence as a virtuoso was the need to play for uninterested, uncomprehending audiences. Conversely, it seems that a single appreciative listener sufficed to create the favorable conditions for him to offer his best effort as a performer. ◄

KEYBOARD PLAYER

For I am a born wood-hitter and all I can do is to strum a little on the clavier.

Mannheim, 22 February 1778

PLAYING CONDITIONS

► In order for Mozart to perform at his best, the playing conditions had to be right. This meant, above all, that the audience had to be right: attentive and appreciative. ◄

To Leopold Mozart   *Paris, 1 May 1778*

At last the Duchesse de Chabot appeared. She was very polite and asked me to make the best of the clavier in the room, as none of her own were in good condition. Would I perhaps try it? I said that I would be delighted to play something, but that it was impossible at the moment, as my fingers were numb with cold. . . . I had the honor to wait. The windows and doors were open and not only my hands but my whole body and my feet were frozen and my head began to ache. . . . At last . . . I played on that miserable, wretched pianoforte. But what vexed me most of all was that Madame and all her gentlemen never interrupted their drawing for a moment, but went on intently, so that I had to play to the chairs, tables, and walls. Under these detestable conditions I lost my patience. I therefore began to play the Fischer variations[2] and after playing half of them I stood up, whereupon I received a shower of éloges. Upon which I said the only thing I had to say, which was, that I could not do myself justice on that clavier; and that I should very much like to fix some other day to play, when a better instrument would be available. But, as the Duchess would not hear of my going, I had to wait for another half hour, until her husband came in. He sat down beside me and listened with the greatest attention and I—I forgot the cold and my headache and in spite of the wretched clavier—I played, as I play when I am in good spirits. Give me the best clavier in Europe with an audience who understand nothing, or don't want to understand and who do not feel with me in what I am playing, and I shall cease to feel any pleasure. (A, 531–532)

The Reminiscences of Constanze Mozart, 1829

Nor did he like playing to strangers, except when he knew them to be *good judges*, when he would exert himself to the outmost for their gratification. (Novello, 77)

STYLE AND TECHNIQUE

► When Mozart had the right audience (and preferably the right instrument, too), his exertions were designed to display not only a formidable, and apparently effortless, digital technique but a command of the full spectrum of contemporary keyboard styles. ◄

To Leopold Mozart   *Augsburg, 24 October 1777*

[The piano maker Johann Andreas Stein] used to be quite crazy about [Ignaz von] Beecke; but now he sees and hears that I am the better player. . . . Count Wolfegg and several other passionate admirers of Beecke publicly admitted at a concert the other day that I had wiped the floor with him. (A, 340)

To Leopold Mozart   *Paris, 18 July 1778*

Here . . . the chopping-board is good. . . . So, as you may imagine, I preluded in the manner of Fischietti, played off a galanterie sonata in the style and with the fire, spirit, and precision of [Michael?] Haydn, and then played fugues. . . . My fugal playing has won me everywhere the greatest reputation. (A, 570)

To Leopold Mozart   *Vienna, 28 April 1784*

When I played to [Georg Friedrich Richter] he stared all the time at my fingers and kept on saying: "Good God! How hard I work and sweat—and yet win no applause—and to you, my friend, it is all child's play." "Yes," I replied, "I too had to work hard, so as not to have to work hard any longer." (A, 875)

▶ Following are some assessments of Mozart's keyboard playing by his contemporaries.

    The first documented account of Mozart's specifically playing a fortepiano appeared in the Augsburg-based journal, *Deutsche Chronik*. The reviewer is anonymous. ◀

Deutsche Chronik   *Augsburg, 27 April 1775*

In Munich last winter I heard two of the greatest clavier players, Herr *Mozart* and Captain *von Beecke;* my host Herr [Franz] Albert, who is enthusiastic about all that is great and beautiful, has an excellent fortepiano in his house. It was there that I heard these two giants in contest on the clavier. Mozart's playing had great weight, and he read at sight everything that was put before him. But no more than that; Beecke surpasses him by a long way. (DDB, 153)

Franz Xaver Niemetschek, Life of Mozart, 1798

In Vienna, above all, his piano playing was admired. . . . His admirable dexterity, which particularly in the left hand and the bass were considered quite unique, his feeling and delicacy, and beautiful expression of which only a Mozart was capable, were the attractions of his playing. (Niemetschek 1798, 31)

The Reminiscences of Michael Kelly, 1826

His feeling, the rapidity of his fingers, the great execution and strength of his left hand particularly, and the apparent inspiration of his modulations astounded me. (Kelly, 1:222)

Muzio Clementi

Until then I had never heard anyone play with so much spirit and grace. Especially did an Adagio and several of his extemporized variations surprise me, for which the Emperor chose the theme on which we, accompanying each other by turns, had to play variations.[3]

▶ Clementi is referring to his legendary piano playing contest with Mozart that took place at Emperor Joseph's command in December

1781.[4] A rather less enthusiastic opinion of Mozart's pianism was rendered by none other than Ludwig van Beethoven. Beethoven, who had come to Vienna in April 1787 to take lessons from Mozart, must have heard him play during the three weeks, 7–20 April, whereupon he suddenly had to return to Bonn to attend to his sick mother. ◄

Beethoven

He had a fine but choppy [*zerhacktes*] way of playing, no *ligato.*[5]

IMPROVISING

► A centerpiece of any Mozart piano performance was the demonstration of his prowess as an improviser. The reminiscences of Kelly and Clementi just cited attest to that. And we may be reasonably sure that the preludes, fugues, and the "galanterie sonata" he mentions in his letter of 18 July 1778 from Paris were improvised, as well. ◄

To Leopold Mozart   *Augsburg, 24 October 1777*

Afterwards they brought in a small clavichord and I improvised and then played a sonata. . . . Then the others whispered to the Dean [of the Holy Cross Monastery] that he should just hear me play something in the organ [i.e., fugal] style. I asked him to give me a theme. He declined, but one of the monks gave me one. I put it through its paces. . . . The Dean was absolutely staggered. "Why, it's simply phenomenal, that's all I can say," he said. "I should never have believed what I have heard. You are a first-rate fellow." (A, 339)

► Early in 1785 Mozart had his piano equipped with a pedal board, like an organ pedal board, with about a two-octave range extending from contra C. He introduced the device at his public concert at the Burgtheater on 10 March 1785 (for which the handbill survives). Henceforth, improvisations on the pedal piano were a frequent feature of Mozart's public performances. ◄

Information

On Thursday, 10th March 1785, Herr Kapellmeister Mozart will have the honor of giving at the I[mperial] & R[oyal] National Court Theater a Grand Musical Concert for his benefit, at which not only a new, just finished *Forte piano Concerto* [in C major, K. 467] will be played by him, but also an especially *large Forte piano pedal* will be used by him in *improvising.* (DDB, 239)

Leopold Mozart to Nannerl   *Vienna, 12 March 1785*

Since my arrival your brother's fortepiano has been taken at least a dozen times to the theater or to some other house. He has had a large fortepiano pedal made, which is under the instrument and is about two feet longer and extremely heavy. It is taken to the Mehlgrube every Friday and has also been taken to Count Zichy's and to Prince Kaunitz's. (A, 888–889)

The Reminiscences of Constanze Mozart, 1829

He did not play much in private, but would occasionally extemporize when he was sitting alone with [me]. (Novello, 77)

SIGHTREADING

► Throughout his Wunderkind years, especially when on his grand tour to London, Paris, and Holland in the mid 1760s, Mozart invariably displayed, along with his powers of improvisation, his ability to play *prima vista*, that is, to perform at sight—as the contemporary reports and advertisements put it: "whatever is submitted to him," including "the most difficult pieces." Leopold provides a description of a typical occasion: a performance at court before the King and Queen of England. ◄

Leopold Mozart to Lorenz Hagenauer, Salzburg   London, 18 May 1764

King [George III] placed before him not only works of Wagenseil, but those of [Johann Christian] Bach, [Karl Friedrich] Abel, and Handel, and he played off everything *prima vista*. . . . Then he accompanied the Queen [Sophie Charlotte] in an aria which she sang and also a flautist who played a solo. Finally he took the bass part of some airs of Handel (which happened to be lying there) and played the most beautiful melody on it and in such a manner that everyone was amazed. (A, 47)

► But in later years, too, Mozart frequently deigned to amaze his audience—and amuse himself—by offering to play "anything" at sight. We return once more to Mozart's account of his performance at the Monastery of the Holy Cross in Augsburg. ◄

To Leopold Mozart   Augsburg, 24 October 1777

They brought in a small clavichord. . . . At last someone produced a sonata in fugal style and wanted me to play it. But I said: "Gentlemen, this is too much. Let me tell you, I shall certainly not be able to play that sonata at sight." "Yes, that I can well believe," said the Dean very pressingly, for he was my strong supporter. "It is too much to expect. No one could tackle that." "However," I said, "I should like to try it." I heard the Dean muttering behind me all the time: "Oh, you little villain, oh, you rascal, oh, you——!" (A, 339)

To Leopold Mozart   *Mannheim, 22 February 1778*

I, too, prostitution though it be, shall ask them to give me something to strum and shall contrive to thump it out *prima fista*. (A, 488)

To Leopold Mozart   *Vienna, 6 October 1781*

[Ignaz Umlauf] invited me to his house in the most polite manner (*c'est à dire*, in his own manner) that I might hear his opera, adding: "You must not think that it is worth your while to hear it—I have not got as far as you have, but indeed I do my best." I heard afterwards that he said: "It's quite certain that Mozart has a devil in his head, his limbs, and his fingers— why, he played off my opera (which I have written out so disgracefully that I myself can hardly read it) as if he had composed it himself." Well, adieu. (A, 772)

▶ As for his attitude toward sight-reading, Mozart's view, at least as expressed in his maturity, could hardly have been more uncompromising. ◀

To Leopold Mozart   *Mannheim, 17 January 1778*

Wherein consists the art of playing *prima vista*? In this: in playing the piece in the time in which it ought to be played, and in playing all the notes, appoggiaturas and so forth, exactly as they are written and with the appropriate expression and taste, so that you might suppose that the performer had composed it himself. (A, 449)

▶ There is reason, however, to think that in reality Mozart's sight-reading—at all events during his childhood appearances, and when confronted with truly difficult music—was not quite so scrupulous. It was marked, rather by what every musician knows, *pace* Wolfgang, is the true essence of the art of sight-reading: the ability to "fake." The French opera composer Grétry, who met Mozart in Geneva in 1766, recalled the following incident in his memoirs, published in Paris in 1795: ◀

André Grétry, Memoirs, 1795

Once in Geneva I met a child who could play everything at sight. His father said to me before the assembled company: "So that no doubt shall remain as to my son's talent, write for him, for tomorrow, a very difficult sonata movement." I wrote him an Allegro in E flat; difficult but unpretentious; he played it, and everyone, except myself, believed that it was a miracle. The boy had not stopped; but following the modulations, he had substituted a quantity of passages for those which I had written. (DDB, 477)

ORGANIST

► On 17 October 1777 Mozart proclaimed the organ to be not only his "passion" but indeed "the king of instruments" (a sobriquet whose authorship is often attributed to Robert Schumann). Exactly fifteen months later, on 17 January 1779, this passion was consummated with his appointment as Salzburg court organist at an annual salary of 450 gulden. Some ten years thereafter, on 22 April 1789, Mozart's by then fairly abandoned career as an organist attained another consummation, this time more symbolic than material, when he improvised on the organ of the Thomaskirche in Leipzig, the venue of J. S. Bach. ◄

Leopold Mozart to Hagenauer   *Wasserburg (Bavaria), 11 June 1763*

The latest news is that in order to amuse ourselves we went to the organ and I explained to Woferl the use of the pedal. Whereupon he tried it *stante pede* [i.e., at once], shoved the stool away and played standing at the organ, at the same time working the pedal, and doing it all as if he had been practicing it for several months. Everyone was amazed. (A, 20)

To Leopold Mozart   *Augsburg, 17 October 1777*

When I told [Johann Andreas] Stein that I should like very much to play on his organ, as that instrument was my passion, he was greatly surprised and said: "What? A man like you, so fine a clavier player, wants to play on an instrument which has no douceur, no expression, no piano, no forte, but is always the same?" "That does not matter," I replied; "in my eyes and ears the organ is the king of instruments." . . . I noticed at once from what he said that he thought that I would not do much on his organ; that I would play, for instance, in a thoroughly pianistic style. . . . We reached the choir and I began to improvise, when he started to laugh; then I played a fugue. "I can well believe," he said, "that you like to play the organ, when you play so well." (A, 329)

To Leopold Mozart   *Augsburg, 24 October 1777*

[After Mozart had improvised a fugue on the clavichord, see above, the Dean said:] "My Abbot told me, it is true, that he had never in his life heard anyone play the organ so smoothly and so soundly." (For he had heard me a few days before, when the Dean was away.) (A, 339)

To Leopold Mozart   *Mannheim, 13 November 1777*

Last Sunday I tried the organ in the chapel for fun. I came in during the Kyrie and played the end of it, and, when the priest had finished intoning the Gloria, I played a cadenza. As my performance was so different from what they are accustomed to here, they all looked round. . . . Now and then the music was marked pizzicato and each time I just touched the keys very lightly. I was in my very best spirits. Instead of a Benedictus the organist has to play here the whole time. So I took the theme of the Sanctus and developed it as a fugue. Whereupon they all stood gaping. Finally, after the Ita missa est, I played a fugue. . . . The pedal there is different from ours, which put me out a bit at first; but I soon got the hang of it. (A, 370)

To Leopold Mozart   *Mannheim, 27 December 1777*

I went the other day with M. De La Potrie, the Dutch officer, who is my pupil, to the Reformed Church, and played on the organ for an hour and a half. I put my whole heart into it. Sometime soon we . . . are going to the Lutheran church, where I shall have some good fun on the organ. I tried the full organ before during that test, about which I wrote to you, but didn't play much, only a prelude and a fugue. (A, 435)

The Reminiscences of Constanze Mozart, 1829

Mozart's favorite Instrument was the organ—upon which . . . he played with the most incomparable skill. (Novello, 95)

STRING PLAYER

VIOLINIST

► We may be sure that hearing the sound of the violin constituted one of Mozart's earliest musical experiences. He was, after all, the son of one of the preeminent violin pedagogues in Europe. We may be just as sure that he received his first, and probably only, instruction on the instrument from his father, as was the case with his lessons on the keyboard. But, if the family friend, Johann Andreas Schachtner, can be believed, Mozart had not yet received his first violin lesson until January 1763, at the earliest—after he and his sister Nannerl had already undertaken two concert tours (to Munich in January 1762 and to Vienna the following autumn) as clavier virtuosi, and only after Mozart had already seized the initiative and virtually taught himself to play the instrument by little more than observation and the sheer force of will alone. By November 1769 Mozart was (unpaid) Third Konzertmeister in the Salzburg court orchestra. On 21 August 1772 he was officially promoted to Konzertmeister at an annual salary of 150 gulden, a post he retained for some five years, composing during that time, among other things, five violin concertos (four in 1775), very likely for his own use. In 1777 Mozart set out for Munich, Augsburg, Mannheim, and Paris, where he frequently appeared as a violin soloist. It does not seem, though, that he maintained his technique as a virtuoso violinst after he settled in Vienna; but he continued to enjoy playing violin and viola in chamber music. ◄

Schachtner to Nannerl Mozart, 1792

In the days after your return from Vienna [i.e., in autumn, 1762] Wolfgang having a little violin that he got as a present in Vienna, our former very good violinist, the late Herr Wenzl, came to us. He was a beginner in composition, and brought six trios with him, which he had written while your father was away and asked your father for an opinion on them. We played the trios, Papa playing the bass with his viola, Wenzl the first violin and I was to play the second violin. Wolfgang had asked to be allowed to play the second violin, but Papa refused him this foolish request, because he had not yet had the least instruction in the violin, and Papa thought that he could not possibly play anything. Wolfgang said: "You don't need to have studied in order to play second violin," and when Papa insisted that he should go away and not bother us any more, Wolfgang began to weep bitterly and stamped off with his little violin. I asked them to let him play with me; Papa eventually said: "Play with Herr Schachtner, but so softly that we can't hear you, or you will have to go"; and so it was. Wolfgang played with me; I soon noticed with astonishment that I was quite superfluous. I quietly put my violin down, and looked at your Papa; tears of wonder and comfort ran down his cheeks at this scene, and so he played all six trios. When we had finished, Wolfgang was emboldened by our applause to maintain that he could play the first violin too. For a joke we made the experiment, and we almost died for laughter when he played this [part] too, though with nothing but wrong and irregular positioning, in such a way that he never actually broke down. (DDB, 453)

To Leopold Mozart   *Munich, 6 October 1777*

As a finale I played my last Cassation [i.e., Divertimento] in B-flat [K.287,

EXAMPLE 1.2. Divertimento in B-flat (*Lodron,* K. 287 (271H), Opening Theme for Movements 1 and 2

for string quartet and two horns., ex. 1.2]. They all opened their eyes! I played as though I were the finest fiddler in all Europe. (A, 300)

To Leopold Mozart   *Augsburg, 23 October 1777*

During the meals we had some music. . . . I performed a symphony and played Vanhal's violin concerto in B-flat, which was unanimously applauded. . . . In the evening at supper I played my Strasbourg concerto [i.e., the Violin Concerto in D, K. 218, ex. 1.3], which went like oil. Everyone praised my beautiful pure tone. (A, 338).

EXAMPLE 1.3. Violin Concerto in D, K. 218, Opening Themes

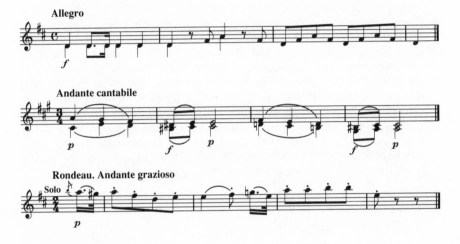

CHAMBER PLAYER

► Mozart's activities as a chamber player during the Vienna years are recorded in the reminiscences of two acquaintances: the singer Michael Kelly and the Abbé Maximilian Stadler. ◄

The Reminiscences of Michael Kelly, 1826

[Stephen] Storace gave a quartet party to [Mozart's] friends. The players were tolerable; not one of them excelled on the instrument he played, but there was a little science among them, which I dare say will be acknowledged when I name them:

The First Violin . . . . Haydn.
"   Second Violin. . . . . . Baron Dittersdorf.[6]
"   Violoncello. . . . . Vanhall.
"   Tenor [i.e., Viola]. . . . . Mozart.

The poet Casti and Paesiello formed part of the audience.[7] I was there, and a greater treat or a more remarkable one, cannot be imagined. (Kelly, 1: 237–238)

The Reminiscences of Maximilian Stadler, 1829

Mozart and Haydn frequently played together with [Maximilian Stadler] in Mozart's Quintettos; [Stadler] particularly mentioned the 5th in D major [K. 593] . . . the one in C major [K.515], and still more that in G minor [K.516]. . . . 1st Viola either Haydn or Mozart in turn. (Novello, 170, 347)

CONDUCTOR

▶ During the eighteenth century the task of leading ensemble performances was carried out either by the Kapellmeister—i.e., the principal administrator and director of the musical establishment (as well as resident composer)—conducting from the keyboard, or by the Konzertmeister, conducting from the first violin stand. We know that Mozart directed performances of his early symphonies in London and of his operas—in Italy as well as Vienna—from the keyboard. As Konzertmeister in Salzburg he could have directed the court orchestra either from the violin desk or from the keyboard. In the church, however, where he is known to have performed the music of others as well as his own, he would have used a baton. ◀

Announcement in the Public Advertiser

Mr. Mozart, the Father of the celebrated young Musical Family . . . proposes . . . a CONCERT. Which will chiefly be conducted by his Son . . . with all the Overtures [i.e., symphonies] of his own Composition. (DDB, 44)

Leopold Mozart to Hagenauer   *Vienna, 30 July 1768*

His Majesty asked our Wolfgang whether he would not like to write an opera and said that he would very much like to see him at the clavier conducting it. (A, 88)

Leopold Mozart to Hagenauer   *Vienna, 12 November 1768*

The new church of Father Parhammer's orphanage will be blessed on the Feast of the Immaculate Conception. For this Feast Wolfgang has composed a solemn mass, an offertorium, and a trumpet concerto for a boy, and has dedicated them to the orphanage. Presumably Wolfgang himself will conduct this music. [*tactieren,* i.e., literally, "beat time."] (A, 94)

► Of the compositions mentioned, the mass was probably the *Waisenhaus-Messe*, the Missa Solemnis in C minor, K. 139 (47a)—a genuine masterpiece by the twelve-year-old composer; the offertory K. 47b, has not been identified; and the trumpet concerto, K. 47c, is lost. ◄

The Reminiscences of Nannerl Mozart, 1792

[In Milan, Wolfgang] had conducted the first three performances of his opera [*Mitridate*, 1770] from the clavier, as is the custom in Italy. (DDB, 460)

To Leopold Mozart   *Vienna, 19 October 1782*

My opera [*Die Entführung*] was performed for [the Russian Royalty] the other day, and on this occasion I thought it advisable to resume my place at the clavier and conduct it. I did so partly in order to rouse the orchestra who had gone to sleep a little, partly (since I happen to be in Vienna) in order to appear before the royal guests as the father of my child. (A, 828)

To Anton Stoll, Baden bei Wien   *Vienna, 12 July 1791*

I have a request to make, and that is, that you would be so kind as to send me by the first mail coach tomorrow my mass in B-flat, which we performed last Sunday,[8] and Michael Haydn's Graduale in B-flat, "Pax Vobis," which we also performed. I mean, of course, the parts, not the scores. I have been asked to conduct [*dirigiren*] a mass in a church. (A, 965–966)

The Reminiscences of Constanze Mozart, 1829

Occasionally [Mozart] would stamp with his foot when impatient, or things did not go correctly in the orchestra. [I was] with him at the opera *Il Seraglio* when they took the time of one of the movements too fast—he became quite impatient and called out to the orchestra without seeming to fear or to be aware of the presence of the audience. (Novello, 113).

► There was, however, some limit even to Mozart's talents as a performer: He was no singer—although he could sing. ◄

The Reminiscences of Constanze Mozart, 1829

His voice was a tenor, rather soft in speaking and delicate in singing, but when anything excited him, or it became necessary to exert it, it was both powerful and energetic. (Novello, 113)

COMPOSER

I am a composer and was born to be a Kapellmeister.

Mannheim, 7 February 1778

The Calling

▶ By the time Mozart embarked on his journey to Mannheim and Paris in the fall of 1777—his first systematic search for employment—he well knew that he was not just an extraordinarily talented and versatile musician but a composer. His letters from this period contain repeated affirmations of this fundamental realization. Moreover, he was in no doubt about the unique magnitude of his gift for composition and clearly understood the implications of this fact for his future. Nothing —not even other musical activities such as performing (much less teaching), as necessary as they might be for his physical survival— could be allowed to interfere with his pursuit and fulfillment of this calling. ◀

To Leopold Mozart   *Munich, 11 October 1777*

And I am happier when I have something to compose, for that, after all, is my sole delight and passion. (A, 305)

To Leopold Mozart   *Mannheim, 7 February 1778*

I am a composer and was born to be a Kapellmeister. I neither can nor ought to bury the talent for composition with which God in his goodness has so richly endowed me (I may say so without conceit, for I feel it now more than ever). (A, 468)

To Leopold Mozart   *Munich, 26 September 1777*

I remarked . . . that a first-rate composer was badly needed here. (A, 276)

To Leopold Mozart   *Munich, 2 October 1777*

[The Elector, Karl Theodor] has no idea what I can do. Why do these gentlemen believe what anyone tells them and never try to find out for themselves? Yes, it is always the same. I am willing to submit to a test. Let him get together all the composers in Munich, let him even summon a few from Italy, France, Germany, England, and Spain. I undertake to compete with any of them in composition. (A, 290)

To Leopold Mozart   *Mannheim, 31 October 1777*

Some who knew me by repute were very polite and fearfully respectful; others, however, who had never heard of me, stared at me wide-eyed, and certainly in a rather sneering manner. They probably think that because I am little and young, nothing great or mature can come out of me; but they will soon see. (A, 350)

THE NATURE OF THE GIFT

► Just as Mozart's general musicality and his gifts as a performer built on innate competencies all present in him to a degree perhaps unmatched in all of history—the "ear," the aural memory, the "digital instinct" at the keyboard and fingerboard (and pedalboard, as well)—so too, as we can infer from his own descriptions of his talent, his gift for composition represented a uniquely powerful combination of natural abilities and acquired or considered attitudes and insights. Specifically, an inborn facility and versatility were inevitably enlarged and strengthened over time by constantly accumulating experience, but also enriched by an ever more profound and conscious concern for originality in style and expression. Indeed, these qualities are introduced into the correspondence in chronological succession. ◄

Leopold Mozart to Hagenauer   *Munich, 10 November 1766*

Wolfgang had at once to compose, standing beside the Elector, a piece for which His Highness hummed the beginning, or rather a few bars of the theme, and he then had to play it for him after dinner in the music room. (A, 68).

Leopold Mozart to Hagenauer   *Vienna, 30 July 1768*

I asked someone to take any portion of the works of Metastasio, open the book and put before little Wolfgang the first aria which he should hit upon. Wolfgang took up his pen and with the most amazing rapidity wrote, without hesitation and in the presence of several eminent persons, the music for this aria for several instruments. He did this at the houses of Kapellmeister Bonno, Abbate Metastasio, Hasse, and the Duke de Braganza and Prince von Kaunitz. (A, 89)

To Leopold Mozart   *Munich, 29/30 September 1777*

I have been three times to Italy already, I have written three operas,[9] I am a member of the Bologna Academy, where I had to pass a test, at which many maestri have labored and sweated for four or five hours, but which I finished in an hour.[10] Let that be a proof that I am competent to serve at any court. (A, 286)

► Nannerl recalled the examination at the Bologna academy. ◄

The Reminiscences of Nannerl Mozart, 1792

Father Maestro [Giovanni Battista] Martini, that great contrapuntist, was, with all the other Kapellmeisters, quite beside himself when the son provided the correct countersubject, according to the rules of the mode, to the fugue theme which Padre Martini wrote down for him and at once performed the fugue on the clavier. (DDB, 459)

To Leopold Mozart   *Mannheim, 7 February 1778*

The Wendlings, one and all, are of the opinion that my compositions would be extraordinarily popular in Paris. I have no fears on that score, for, as you know, I can more or less adopt or imitate any kind and style of composition. (A, 468)

► Ultimately, and perhaps inevitably, the emphasis falls on originality. ◄

To Leopold Mozart   *Munich, 19 December 1780*

The orchestra and the whole audience discovered to their delight that the second act [of *Idomeneo*] was actually more expressive and original than the first. (A, 692)

To Leopold Mozart   *Vienna, 10 February 1784*

What I have composed has been put away safely. I guarantee that in all the operas which are to be performed until mine [*L'Oca del Cairo*] is finished, not a single idea will resemble one of mine. (A, 867)

► There was, however, another, shadow attribute associated with Mozart's genius (his own word) for composition—one of which he was also acutely aware: its fragility. A most necessary precondition for his creative work was, in brief, peace of mind, a condition readily undone by adverse circumstances. As we shall see shortly, he needed tranquility at least as much as a clavier, in order to be able to function effectively as a composer. ◄

To Leopold Mozart   *Paris, 18 July 1778*

I intend, in God's name, to persevere in my life *here*, which is totally opposed to my genius, inclinations, knowledge, and sympathies.[11] . . . God grant only that I may not impair my talents by staying here; but I hope that it won't last long enough for that. God grant it! (A, 573)

To Leopold Mozart *Paris, 11 September 1778*

A fellow of mediocre talent will remain a mediocrity, whether he travels or not; but one of superior talent[12] (which without impiety I cannot deny that I possess) will go to seed, if he always remains in the same place. . . . I can assure you that this journey has not been unprofitable to me, I mean from the point of view of composition, for, as for the clavier, I play it as well as I ever shall. (A, 612)

To Leopold Mozart *Vienna, 9 June 1781*

I implore you, dearest, most beloved father, for the future to spare me such letters. I entreat you to do so, for they only irritate my mind and disturb my heart and spirit; and I, who must now keep on composing, need a cheerful mind and a calm disposition. (A, 742)

► Leopold had been subjecting Mozart for the past two months (in a series of letters now lost) to apparently merciless pressures and recriminations about his decision to resign from the service of the Prince-Archbishop of Salzburg. Ten years later toward the end of his life, Mozart reiterated his need for tranquility—and for hard work. ◄

To Constanze, Baden *Vienna, 8 October 1791*

If I had had nothing to do, I should have gone off at once to spend the week with you; but I have *no facilities for working at Baden,* and I am anxious, as far as possible, to avoid all risk of *money difficulties.* For the most pleasant thing of all is to have a mind at peace. To achieve this, however, one must work hard; and I like hard work. (A, 968)

THE PROCESS

I prefer to work slowly and with deliberation.

Vienna, 5 July 1783

► How in fact did Mozart approach the task of composition? The principal tangible evidence bearing on this question is to be found, naturally enough, in the autograph manuscripts of the music itself: in Mozart's own original notation of his works.[13] But his letters, and also the observations of contemporaries, shed valuable light on the question, as well. They testify, once again, to the composer's need and desire for congenial circumstances, peace of mind, and adequate time—time to plan and to contemplate. The documents testify also that he rarely had these amenities—time least of all. Mozart, it turns out, composed at his legendarily breathtaking speed out of necessity, not inclination. ◄

Conditions and Preconditions: The Need for a Keyboard, the Pressures of Time

► The first precondition, the *sine qua non*, it seems—as fundamental as peace and quiet—was the availability of a clavier. ◄

To Leopold Mozart   *Vienna, 1 August 1781*

The room into which I am moving is being got ready. I am now going off to hire a clavier, for until there is one in my room, I cannot live in it, because I have so much to compose and not a minute to be lost. . . . You know that usually I go on composing until I am hungry. (A, 756)

► Mozart, of course, did not literally need a piano to compose. As Constanze reported to the Novellos: ◄

The Reminiscences of Constanze Mozart, 1829

He seldom went to the instrument when he composed. . . . When some grand conception was working in his brain he was purely abstracted, . . . but when once arranged in his mind, he needed no pianoforte. (Novello, 78)

► Clarification is provided by Mozart's first biographer, Franz Xaver Niemetschek. ◄

Franz Xaver Niemetschek, Life of Mozart, *1798*

Mozart . . . never touched the piano while writing. When he received the libretto for a vocal composition, he went about for some time, concentrating on it until his imagination was fired. Then he proceeded to work out his ideas at the piano; and only then did he sit down and write. That is why he found the writing itself so easy. (Niemetschek, 1798, 62–63)

► Mozart, to be sure, would have *"preferred* to work slowly and with deliberation." Reality dictated, however, that he was frequently constrained to compose under almost unimaginable pressures of time, often combined, for good measure, with external commotion. Mozart usually could accept these far less than ideal conditions, often with good humor. At other times he could not; or the *internal* conditions, the "mood" was not right. ◄

To Nannerl   *Milan, 24 August 1771*

Upstairs we have a violinist, downstairs another one, in the next room a singing master who gives lessons, and in the other room opposite ours an oboist. That is good fun when you are composing! It gives you plenty of ideas. (A, 194)

To Leopold Mozart   *Mannheim, 14 February 1778*

I have not been able to finish [several commissions], for I never have a single quiet hour here. I can only compose at night, so that I can't get up early as well; besides, one is not always in the mood for working. I could, to be sure, scribble off things the whole day long, but a composition of this kind[14] goes out into the world, and naturally I do not want to have cause to be ashamed of my name on the title page. (A, 481)

To Leopold Mozart   *Vienna, 27 July 1782*

You will be surprised and disappointed to find that this contains only the first Allegro [of the *Haffner* Symphony, K. 385]; but it has been quite impossible to do more for you, for I have had to compose in a great hurry a serenade, but only for wind instruments (otherwise I could have used it for you too).[15] (A, 809)

To Leopold Mozart   *Linz, 31 October 1783*

On Tuesday, November 4, I am giving a concert in the theater here and, as I have not a single symphony with me, I am writing a new one at breakneck speed, which must be finished by that time.[16] (A, 859)

Conception and Execution

► Before Mozart could begin to plan a new composition even in the broadest musical terms, there was frequently a preliminary stage of preparation. In the case of an opera or other vocal work this stage was represented by the selection of the text or libretto. Similarly, it was obviously necessary first to select a tune before one could write a set of variations. While Mozart was extremely careful about the choice of an opera libretto (an issue that will be explored in detail in Chapter 9), with songs and concert arias, evidently his only concern in this regard was to please the intended singer who was, in fact, encouraged to make the selection of the text him–or herself. ◄

To Leopold Mozart   *Mannheim, 28 February 1778*

Yesterday at Wendling's I sketched the aria I had promised his wife, adding a short recitative.[17] She had chosen the words herself—from *Didone*, "Ah, non lasciarmi, no." (A, 497–498)

To Nannerl   *Vienna, 21 July 1784*

Please give my greetings to Gretl [Margarethe Marchand] . . . As for the aria she must exercise a little patience. But what I do advise her to do, if she wants to have the aria soon and without fail, is to choose a text which suits her and send it to me, as it is impossible for me to find time to wade through all sorts of operas. (A, 881)

► Apart from the choice of texts or tunes to serve as the basis of a composition, Mozart often chose a work by another composer to serve as a model or stimulus for a composition of his own. This of course represents "precompositional" activity of an altogether different order. ◄

To Leopold Mozart   *Vienna, 24 November 1781*

I have been looking about for Russian popular songs, so as to be able to play variations on them.[18] (A, 780)

► For the most part, our knowledge of Mozart's use of such compositional models is really a deduction based on the discovery or recognition of the likely model: for example, Haydn's string quartets, op. 20, and Mozart's string quartets, K. 168–173, or Haydn's string quartets, op. 33, and Mozart's quartets dedicated to him. It is, therefore, especially fascinating to learn from Mozart himself that he once took a work by another composer—Johann Christian Bach's aria, "Non sò, d'onde viene" (ex. 1.4)—as a model for his own setting of the same text (ex. 1.5)—with the unusual twist that his self-imposed challenge was not to emulate his model but rather to try to compose a setting that would differ from it as much as possible. ◄

To Leopold Mozart   *Mannheim, 28 February 1778*

For practice I have also set to music the aria "Non so d'onde viene," [K. 294] which has been so beautifully composed by [J. C.] Bach. Just because I know Bach's setting so well and like it so much, and because it is always ringing in my ears, I wished to try and see whether in spite of all this I could not write an aria totally unlike his. And, indeed, mine does not resemble his in the very least. At first I had intended it for [Anton] Raaff; but the beginning seemed to me too high for his voice. Yet I liked it so much that I would not alter it; and from the orchestral accompaniment, too, it seemed to me better suited to a soprano. So I decided to write it for Mlle. [Aloysia] Weber . . . and made up my mind to compose it exactly for Mlle. Weber's voice. (A, 497)

► The differences Mozart had in mind, however, are concerned primarily with matters of form and structure. Indeed, as examples 1.4 and 1.5 reveal, the principal melodies of both arias, while hardly identical, are equally indebted to long-standing operatic conventions as to how to set the "tender feelings" described in the text: namely, in the gentle, lyric mode known at the time as the *aria cantabile*, a style normally characterized, as here, by a triple meter, a moderately slow tempo, and

EXAMPLE 1.4. J. C. Bach: "Non so d'onde," Principal Theme

TRANSLATION: I know not whence comes | This tender feeling, | This strange sensation, | Which awakens in my breast.

a song-like melody in the major mode. Similarly, the restless accompaniment figure introduced by Mozart in connection with the words "moto ignoto" (strange sensation or stirring) also makes its appearance in J.C. Bach's aria and numerous other settings of this popular text. Whereas Bach, however, has cast his aria in an old-fashioned *da capo*

EXAMPLE 1.5. Mozart: "Non so d'onde," K. 294, Principal Theme

form (in which the music of the opening section of the aria is repeated literally (but with additional vocal embellisments) after a contrasting middle section, Mozart employs a far more complex, more modern design, in which the final section is substantially new.[19]

We can be reassured that Mozart's compositions did not spring forth spontaneously from the head of their creator—certainly not as a rule. They had to be conceived, planned, and executed. On his own testimony, Mozart's most significant works were the product of a shorter or longer period of intense gestation: much of it—perhaps most of it—internal rather than on paper, but no less intense for that. The grander the conception, the more intensive the planning. ◄

To Leopold Mozart   *Paris, 31 July 1778*

You know that I am, so to speak, soaked in music, that I am immersed in it all day long and that I love to plan works, study, and meditate. (A, 587)

To Leopold Mozart   *Vienna, 1 August 1781*

Well, the day before yesterday Stephanie junior gave me a libretto to compose. . . . The subject is Turkish and the title is *Belmonte and Konstanze,* or *Die Verführung aus dem Serail.* I intend to write the overture, the chorus in act 1 and the final chorus in the style of Turkish music. (A, 754–755)

► Two days after receiving the libretto for *Die Entführung aus dem Serail,* then, Mozart had embarked on the planning of the work beginning with large strokes: setting, as it were, the formal and stylistic pillars of an entire act in place before proceeding to details.[20] ◄

To Leopold Mozart   *Vienna, 27 July 1782*

You will be surprised and disappointed to find that this contains only the first Allegro [of the *Haffner* Symphony, K. 385]. . . . On Wednesday the 31st I shall send the two minuets, the Andante, and the last movement. (A, 810)

► The *Haffner* symphony, it seems, was not originally planned as a symphony at all. After completing the first movement, Mozart still intended for it to have the two minuets typical of a serenade. ◄

To Leopold Mozart   *Vienna, 5 July 1783*

As for the opera [*L'oca del Cairo*] . . . as I prefer to work slowly and with deliberation, I thought that I could not begin too soon. (A, 855)

To Joseph Haydn   *Vienna, 1 September 1785*

[These string quartets] are, indeed, the fruit of a long and laborious study.[21] (A, 891)

The Reminiscences of Joseph Lange, 1808

Never was Mozart less recognizably a great man in his conversation and actions than when he was busied with an important work. At such times he not only spoke confusedly and disconnectedly, but occasionally made jests of a nature which one did not expect of him; indeed he even deliberately forgot himself in his behavior. But he did not appear to be brooding and thinking about anything. Either he intentionally concealed his inner tension behind superficial frivolity, for reasons which could not be fathomed, or he took delight in throwing into sharp contrast the divine ideas of his music and these sudden outbursts of vulgar platitudes, and in giving himself pleasure by seeming to make fun of himself. I can understand that so exalted an artist can, out of a deep veneration for his Art, belittle and as it were expose to ridicule his own personality. (DDB, 503)

The Reminiscences of Constanze Mozart, 1829

When some grand conception was working in his brain he was purely abstracted, walking about the apartment, and knew not what was passing around. (Novello, 78)

► When the creative challenge was relatively unproblematic—as, for example, in the composition of simple recitatives (or ballroom dances) —then the act of conception and the activity of writing were virtually simultaneous. At such times, Constanze reported, Mozart composed music "as if he were writing a letter."[22] ◄

To his Mother   *Milan, 20 October 1770*

I cannot write much, for my fingers are aching from composing so many recitatives. (A, 166)

To Nannerl   *Milan, 21 September 1771*

I cannot write much, first, because I have nothing to say, and second, because my fingers ache from composing. (A, 199)

► But we learn from Mozart's own report that when the conception, in Constanze's words, was "grand," then composing and writing music were two entirely distinct activities—distinct to the extent that he could compose one work while writing down another. Moreover, the mechanical act of writing was not only more tedious but actually took longer than the spiritual and intellectual act of composition. ◄

To Leopold Mozart   *Munich, 30 December 1780*

Well, I must close, for I must now write at breakneck speed. Everything has been composed, but not yet written down [viz., portions of act 3 of *Idomeneo*]. (A, 702)

To Leopold Mozart   *Vienna, 26 May 1781*

It is true that during the last few days [before the premiere of *Idomeneo*] I had to compose the greater and most difficult part of my opera; yet this was not from laziness or negligence—but because I had spent a fortnight without writing a note, simply because I found it *impossible to do so.* Of course I composed a lot, but wrote down nothing. I admit that I lost a great deal of time in this way, but I do not regret it. (A, 737)

To Leopold Mozart   *Vienna, 8 April 1781*

Today (for I am writing at eleven o'clock at night) we had a concert, where three of my compositions were performed—new ones, of course; a rondo for a concerto for [Antonio] Brunetti [the Rondo for Violin and Orchestra in C, K. 373]; a sonata with violin accompaniment for myself [in G, K. 379/373a, ex. 1.6], which I composed last night between eleven and twelve (but in order to be able to finish it, I only wrote out the accompaniment for Brunetti and retained my own part in my head); and then a rondo for [Francesco] Ceccarelli [the aria "Or che il cielo a me ti rende," K. 374], which he had to repeat. (A, 722)

EXAMPLE 1.6. Sonata for Piano and Violin in G, K. 379 (373a). Opening Themes

► Mozart's account of the composition of the violin sonata was later elaborated upon by another. ◄

Jean-Baptiste-Antoine Suard, "Anecdotes sur Mozart," 1804

It came about one day that, having to do a piece for a court concert, he had no time to write out the part that he was to play. The Emperor Joseph, happening to glance at the music paper which Mozart appeared to be following, was astonished to see on it nothing but staves without notes, and [he] said to him: "Where is your part?"—"There," said Mozart, putting his hand to his forehead. (DDB, 499)

To Leopold Mozart   *Vienna, 6 October 1781*

I am beginning to lose patience at not being able to go on writing my opera

[*Die Entführung*]. True, I am composing other things in the meantime—yet all my enthusiasm is for my opera, and what would at other times require fourteen days to write I could now do in four. I composed in one day Adamberger's aria in A ["O wie ängstlich"], Cavalieri's in B-flat ["Doch wie schnell schwand meine Freude"] and the trio ["Marsch, marsch, marsch," all in act 1], and copied them out in a day and a half. (A, 771)

To Nannerl   *Vienna, 20 April 1782*

I send you herewith a prelude and a three-part fugue [in C major, K. 394, ex. 1.7]. The reason I did not reply to your letter at once was that, on account of the wearisome labor of writing these small notes, I could not finish the composition any sooner. And, even so, it is awkwardly done, for the prelude ought to come first and the fugue to follow. But I composed the fugue first and wrote it down while I was thinking out the prelude. (A, 800)

EXAMPLE 1.7. Prelude and Fuge in C, K. 394 (383a), Opening Themes

The Reminiscences of Constanze Mozart, 1829

When once arranged in his mind, he needed no pianoforte but would take music paper and while he wrote he would say to [me], "Now, my dear wife, have the goodness to repeat what has been talked of," and [my] conversation never interrupted him, he wrote on—which is more . . . than I can do with the commonest letter. (Novello, 78)

► The heading on the autograph manuscript of the Twelve Duos for Two Wind Instruments, K. 487: ◄

"By Wolfgang Amadé Mozart . . . Vienna, the 27th of July 1786, while bowling."

► Mozart's musical manuscripts provide the most complete testimony about the various stages in the genesis of a composition. They reveal, among other things, that Mozart did not necessarily "begin at the beginning"—certainly not in the case of an opera, where the overture was typically the very last element to be composed. We know also that Mozart frequently composed the recitatives first, then the ensemble numbers, and only later the solo arias—after he had had an opportunity to hear the singers in person and become familiar with the peculiarities of their voices (often enough this was at the time of the first rehearsals). Within an individual number, Mozart normally first set down the principal melodic parts and the bass line before completing the accompaniment or orchestration during a later stage. The letters shed relatively little light on these matters but enough to corroborate the evidence of the musical sources. ◄

Leopold Mozart to his Wife   *Bologna, 29 September 1770*

Wolfgang began the recitatives for the opera [*Mitridate*, first performed 26 December 1770] today. (A, 163)

To Leopold Mozart   *Munich, 19 December 1780*

The work [*Idomeneo*] is almost finished. Only three arias, the last chorus of act 3, the overture and the ballet are still lacking—and then—adieu partie! (A, 693)

To Leopold Mozart   *Vienna, 6 December 1783*

I have only three more arias to compose and then the first act of my opera [*L'Oca del Cairo*] will be finished. I can really say that I am quite satisfied with the aria buffa, the quartet, and the finale. (A, 861)

To Constanze, Baden   *Vienna, 2 July 1791*

Please tell that idiotic fellow Süssmayr to send me my score of the first act [of *Die Zauberflöte*], from the introduction to the finale, so that I may orchestrate it. (A, 959)

The Reminiscences of Constanze Mozart, 1829

Madame confirmed the truth of her sitting up all night with him whilst he wrote the overture to *Don Giovanni*. (Novello, 95–96)

► If we may extrapolate from a single case (that of *Die Entführung aus dem Serail*), Mozart evidently derived benefit from playing through completed portions of longer works in progress—acts of operas, at all events—for a discerning listener and eliciting a preliminary judgment. At the same time, however, he protested that he paid no attention at all to the verdict. ◄

To Leopold Mozart   *Vienna, 8 August 1781*

I lunched yesterday with Countess Thun . . . and played to her what I have finished composing [of *Die Entführung*] and she told me afterwards that she would venture her life that what I have so far written cannot fail to please. But on this point I pay no attention whatever to *anybody's praise or blame*—I mean, until people have heard and seen the work *as a whole*. (A, 756)

To Leopold Mozart   *Vienna, 8 May 1782*

I was at Countess Thun's yesterday and played through my second act to her, with which she seems no less pleased than she was with the first. (A, 804)

To Leopold Mozart   *Vienna, 29 May 1782*

My dear Constanze and I are lunching tomorrow with Countess Thun and I am to play over my third act to her. (A, 807)

► An inevitable part of the compositional process is that of revision. Mozart was quite prepared to revise what he had written, especially when it was a matter of satisfying a singer. Interestingly enough, Mozart informs us in this connection that he preferred to cut than to lengthen.

Not only was Mozart willing to make relatively minor revisions, he was also prepared to recast compositions quite substantially—often as a time- or labor-saving device. The most notable example was his reworking of the unfinished Mass in C minor, K. 427 (417a), composed in 1782/1783, some two years later into the Italian cantata *Davidde Penitente*, K. 469, completed in March 1785. He was similarly prepared in 1784, as we learn below, to cannibalize his early sacred drama *La*

Betulia liberata, K. 118 (74c), composed in 1771, in order to produce a new oratorio. Mozart obviously did not subscribe to the Romantic view of the inviolability of artworks. ◄

To Leopold Mozart   *Mannheim, 28 February 1778*

I was at Raaff's yesterday and brought him an aria which I composed for him the other day. The words are: *"Se al labbro mio non credi, bella nemica mia,"* and so on. . . . I asked him to tell me candidly if he did not like it or if it did not suit his voice, adding that I would alter it if he wished or even compose another. "God forbid," he said; "the aria must remain just as it is, for nothing could be finer. But please shorten it a little, for I am no longer able to sustain my notes." "Most gladly," I replied, "as much as you like. I made it a little long on purpose, for it is always easy to cut down, but not so easy to lengthen." (A, 496–497)

To Leopold Mozart   *Vienna, 12 September 1781*

The translator of [Gluck's] *Iphigenie* into German is an excellent poet, and I would gladly have given him my Munich opera to translate. I would have altered the part of Idomeneo completely and changed it to a bass part for Fischer. In addition I would have made several other alterations and arranged it more in the French style. (A, 765)

► Mozart, in fact, had originally intended to cast the title role of his opera *Idomeneo* as a bass before he learned in Munich that the part was to be sung by the tenor, Anton Raaff. (See Chapter 8.) ◄

To Leopold Mozart   *Vienna, 20 July 1782*

When I have no intention of going out I always remain en négligé. . . . I gave free rein to my ideas and then made my alterations and cuts at the last moment. (A, 808)

To Nannerl   *Vienna, 21 July 1784*

I beg Papa not to forget to send me by the next mail coach what I asked him for. I should be delighted if he could send me my old oratorio *La Betulia liberata* [K. 118], too. I have to compose the same oratorio for the Society in Vienna and possibly I might use bits of it here and there. (A, 881)

2

The Career

I should very much like a good appointment, but it must be a Kapellmeister's and a well-paid one too.

Paris, 3 July 1778

My desire and my hope is to gain honor, fame and money.

Vienna, 16 May 1781

PLANS AND AMBITIONS

► Behind Mozart's desire for honor, fame, money, and position was his abiding desire to be able to spend his time composing, preferably composing operas, free of distraction and free of material need. But Mozart also knew his worth and wanted others to know it, and to acknowledge it according to the traditional measures of success in this world. The most direct and efficient means to all these ends would have been to obtain the position of Kapellmeister at a court with a substantial and prestigious musical establishment. But before there would be such an appointment Mozart understood that he first had to establish his credentials as a first-rate composer, especially as a composer of opera, and to bring that fact to the attention of the appropriate individuals. In the meantime he would still have to find a way to support himself, by teaching, performing, securing commissions. His early travels had indeed brought him fame and honor, and even some money. But that was the ephemeral, and even questionable, fame of a Wunderkind—a sort of circus performer—not the reputation of a mature, serious artist. In setting out in the fall of 1777, at the age of twenty-one, for the powerful musical centers of Munich, Mannheim, and Paris, young man Mozart was at last setting out in earnest to make his career, that is, seeking a position: on his own, though with his mother at his side and his father at his back (to whom he duly reported his ever-changing plans and calculations). ◄

EARLY OBJECTIVES

► Mozart's first station, after departing with his mother from Salzburg at six o'clock on the morning of 23 September 1777 was Munich, where two years earlier he had produced his comic opera, *La finta giardiniera*, K. 196, and made a number of important acquaintances, among them Count Joseph Anton Seeau, the influential director of theatrical events for the Bavarian court. Mozart's initial plan was to try to secure at the least a commission, preferably a long-term contract, for one or more operas, either in Munich or elsewhere. ◄

To Leopold Mozart   *Munich, 2 October 1777*

If I were here alone, it would not be impossible for me to manage somehow, for I should ask for at least three hundred gulden from Count Seeau. As for food, I should not have to worry, for I should always be invited out, and whenever I had no invitation, Albert [the innkeeper] would be only too delighted to have me at table. . . . I should draw up a contract with Count Seeau (all on the advice of my good friends) on the following lines: to compose every year four German operas, some *buffe*, some *serie;* and to be allowed a *sera* or benefit performance of each for myself, as is the custom here. That alone would bring me in at least five hundred gulden, which with my salary would make up eight hundred gulden. But I should certainly make more. (A, 290)

To Leopold Mozart   *Munich, 11 October 1777*

Myslivecek . . . told me that Signor Gaetano Santoro, the Naples impresario, had been obliged . . . to give the carnival opera this season to a certain Maestro Valentini, but that next year he would have three to distribute, one of which would be at his [Myslivecek's] disposal. "So," said Myslivecek, "as I have already composed six times for Naples, I have not the slightest objection to taking on the less important opera and giving you the better one. . . . The cast for next year is excellent. . . . I implore you," he urged, "go to Italy. There one is really esteemed and valued." I am sure he is right. . . . I have an inexpressible longing to write another opera. It is a long way to go [to Naples], it is true, but it would be a long time before I should have to write it. Many things may happen before then. But I think I ought to accept it. If in the meantime I fail to secure an appointment, eh bien, then I can fall back on Italy. I shall still have my certain one hundred ducats at the carnival and once I have composed for Naples, I shall be in demand everywhere. . . . I should not make very much, it is true, but, all the same, it would be something; and they would bring me more honor and credit than if I were to give a hundred concerts in Germany. And I am happier when I have something to compose, for that, after all, is my sole delight and passion. And if I secure an appointment or if I have hopes of settling down somewhere, then the scrittura [i.e., the opera commission] will be an excellent recommendation, will give me prestige and greatly enhance my value. (A, 303–305)

► On that same day, 11 October 1777, the Mozarts left Munich. After spending some two weeks in Augsburg, they set out for Mannheim, arriving there on 30 October. They remained in Mannheim until the following March. ◄

To Leopold Mozart   *Mannheim, 11 January 1778*

I know for a fact that *the Emperor* is proposing to *establish German opera in Vienna* and that he is making every effort *to find a young Kapellmeister* who understands the *German language,* is talented, and is capable of striking out a new line. . . . I think it would *be a good thing for me*—provided, of course, that *the pay* is good. *If the Emperor will give me a thousand gulden, I will write a German opera for him; if he won't have me,* it's all the same to me [italicized words in code]. (A, 444)

► In Mannheim Mozart met Aloysia Weber, the talented soprano, then seventeen years old, to whom he gave vocal lessons, for whom he composed a number of arias, and with whom he soon fell passionately in love. Mozart first mentioned Aloysia in a letter of 17 January 1778. Thereafter, she figured in his plans—most notably the idea (violently opposed by Leopold) of going to Italy with her and her family, rather than to Paris with his Mannheim colleagues. ◄

To Leopold Mozart   *Mannheim, 4 February 1778*

It is unlikely that I shall be able to travel with them [the Mannheim colleagues, Ramm and Wendling] to Paris. . . . Perhaps I shall follow them—or perhaps go elsewhere. . . . My idea is as follows:

I propose to remain here and finish entirely at my leisure that music for DeJean. . . . In the meantime Herr Weber [Aloysia's father] will endeavor to get engagements here and there for concerts with me, and we shall then travel together. . . . My advice is that [the Weber family] should go to Italy. So now I should like you . . . to enquire what are the highest terms given to a prima donna in Verona. . . . Perhaps too it would be possible to obtain the Ascensa[1] in Venice. . . . I beg you to do your best to get us to Italy. You know my greatest desire is—to write operas. I will gladly write an opera for Verona for fifty zecchini, if only in order that [Aloysia Weber] may make her name; for if I do not compose it, I fear that she may be victimized. By that time I shall have made so much money on the other journeys we propose to undertake together that I shall not be the loser. I think we shall go to Switzerland and perhaps also to Holland. . . . Do not forget how much I desire to write operas. I envy anyone who is composing one. I could really weep for vexation when I hear or see an aria. But Italian, not German; seriosa, not buffa. (A, 461–462)

► In the end Mozart followed Leopold's insistent advice and went to Paris, not Italy, arriving in the French capital in March 1778. Mozart continued to make contacts and to make plans. On the day of his mother's death—which he would not reveal to Leopold for another six days—Mozart described the current state of his career prospects and objectives as follows: ◄

To Leopold Mozart   *Paris, 3 July 1778*

As for Versailles, I never thought of going there. I asked Baron Grimm and some other good friends for their advice and they all thought as I did. The salary is small and I should have to pine for six months of the year in a place where nothing else can be earned and where my talent would be buried. Whoever enters the King's service is forgotten in Paris—and then, to be an organist! I should very much like a good appointment, but it must be a Kapellmeister's and a well-paid one too. (A, 559)

► Although Mozart was to remain in Paris until September, it was clear by July that he would not find a good permanent position there. He continued to explore his options, including the possibility of an opera commission in Paris, and a position at Munich. ◄

To Leopold Mozart   *Paris, 9 July 1778*

You know that there is nothing I desire more than a good appointment, good in its standing and good in money—no matter where—provided it be in a Catholic country. (A, 563)

To Leopold Mozart   *Paris, 18 July 1778*

Padre Martini's letter to Raaff, in which he praises me, must have gone astray. . . . Now since the Elector [Karl Theodor of Munich] rightly thinks a lot of the Padre Maestro's opinion, I believe it would be a very good thing if you would be so kind as to ask him to send another letter about me to Raaff. It would surely be of good use; and good Padre Martini would not hesitate to do me this kindness twice over, as he knows well that in so doing he might make my fortune.[2] It is to be hoped that he will write in such a manner that Raaff can show the letter, if need be, to the Elector. (A, 572)

To Leopold Mozart   *Paris, 31 July 1778*

I cannot help it—I must write a grand opera or none at all; if I write a small one, I shall get very little for it (for everything is taxed here). And should it have the misfortune to displease these stupid Frenchmen, all would be over; I should never get another commission to compose, I should have gained nothing by it, and my reputation would have suffered. If, on the other hand, I write a grand opera, the remuneration will be better; I shall be doing the work in which I delight—and I shall have better hopes of success, for with a big work you have a better chance of making your name. I assure you that if I am commissioned to write an opera, I shall have no fears whatever. (A, 587)

► Mozart left Paris on 26 September 1778. After spending a month in Mannheim (6 November to 9 December), he returned to Salzburg where, on 17 January 1779, he assumed the position of court organist. He remained in Salzburg until November 1780 when he left for Munich to work on the commissioned opera *Idomeneo* and to resume his quest for a good appointment. ◄

To Leopold Mozart   *Munich, 13 November 1780*

Be so kind as to send me the scores of the two masses³ which I brought away with me—and also the mass in B-flat [K. 275 (272b)] for Count Seeau will be telling the Elector something about them shortly. I should also like people to hear some of my compositions in this style. (A, 663)

VIENNA

► The premiere of *Idomeneo* took place on 29 January 1781. Mozart remained in Munich until March 12. On that day he left for Vienna at the command of Prince-Archbishop Colloredo in order to join his entourage there. He arrived in the city on March 16. Over the course of the next three months Mozart became enamored of the musical life of the imperial capital, established contact with the principal musical patrons and institutions among the court and the aristocracy, and soon determined to settle there, expecting to make his way by teaching, giving concerts, and securing an occasional commission. In May he disobeyed the Archbishop's command to return to Salzburg and, on 10 May attempted to submit his resignation to the Court Chamberlain Count Arco. On 8 June 1781 Mozart finally secured his release from the Salzburg services in the form of a kick in the pants from the Count. ◄

To Leopold Mozart   *Vienna, 24 March 1781*

My chief object here is to introduce myself *to the Emperor* [code] in some becoming way, for I am absolutely determined that he shall *get to know me*. I should love to run through my opera [*Idomeneo*] for him and then play a lot of fugues, for that is what he likes. (A, 718)

To Leopold Mozart   *Vienna, 8 April 1781*

I am thinking of asking the Archbishop to allow me to remain in Vienna. Dearest father, . . . *were it not for you, I swear to you on my honor that I should not* hesitate for a moment *to leave the Archbishop's service.* I should *give a grand concert, take four pupils, and in a year I should have got on so well in Vienna that I could make at least a thousand thalers a year* [italicized words in code]. (A, 722)

To Leopold Mozart   *Vienna, 11 April 1781*

When I think that I must leave Vienna without bringing home *at least* [emphasis in original] a thousand gulden, my heart is sore indeed. So, for the sake of a *malevolent Prince* who *plagues me* every day and only pays me a *lousy salary of four hundred gulden,*[4] I am to *kick away a thousand?* For I should *certainly* make that sum if I *were to give a concert.* . . . *I neither can nor will remain here unless I give a concert.* Still, even if I have only two *pupils,* I am better off here than in Salzburg. But if I had one thousand or twelve hundred gulden *in my pocket, I should be a little more solicited* and therefore *exact better terms.* . . . *Oh, how I hope to hear by the next post whether I am to go on burying my youth and my talents in Salzburg, or whether I may take my fortune as best I can, and not wait until it is too late.* It is true *that I cannot make my fortune* in a fortnight or three weeks, any more than I *can make it in a thousand years in Salzburg.* Still, it is more pleasant to wait *with a thousand gulden a year* than with *four hundred.* For if I wish to do so, I am quite certain of making that sum . . . and I am not *including in my calculations what I may compose.* Besides, think of the contrast—*Vienna and Salzburg!* When *Bonno dies, Salieri will be Kapellmeister,* and then *Starzer* will take the place of *Salieri* in conducting the practices [i.e., the rehearsals]; and so far *no one* has been mentioned to take the place of *Starzer.* Basta [italicized words in code]. (A, 723–724)

To Leopold Mozart   *Vienna, 9 May 1781*

I am so sure of my success in Vienna that I would have resigned even without the slightest reason. . . . I want to hear nothing more about Salzburg. I hate the Archbishop to madness. (A, 729)

► For the past two hundred years Hieronymus von Colloredo (fig. 2.1), Prince-Archbishop of Salzburg and hence the city's supreme ruler and Mozart's patron, has been cast in the role of supreme arch-villain in the composer's life. Born in Vienna in 1732, Colloredo had succeeded Sigismund von Schrattenbach in the post of Prince-Archbishop on 14 March 1772. An admirer of Voltaire and Rousseau as well as Joseph II, Colloredo had instituted a number of Enlightened reforms, among

FIGURE 2.1. Archbishop Hieronymus Colloredo

them a significant reduction in the role of music in the church service.[5] Considerably more irritating to the Mozart family (especially to Wolfgang), though, was Colloredo's relatively restrictive policy regarding leaves of absence and above all his extreme frugality—a stinginess motivated at least in part by a principled disdain of luxury that nonetheless had disastrous consequences for his musical establishment. Given Mozart's ambitions and his obvious need, among other things, for first-rate colleagues and a functioning opera, his relationship with his native Salzburg and its reigning Prince-Archbishop was clearly doomed. ◄

To Leopold Mozart *Vienna, 16 May 1781*

My desire and my hope is to gain honor, fame, and money, and I have every confidence that I shall be *more useful to you in Vienna than if I were to return to Salzburg* [italicized words in code]. (A, 733)

To Leopold Mozart *Vienna, 2 June 1781*

It is perfectly true that the Viennese are apt to change their affections. . . . And, even granted that they do get tired of me, they will not do so for a few years, certainly not before then. In the meantime I shall have gained honor and money. (A, 739)

► Six months after the permanent break with Salzburg, Mozart's fortunes —apart from having received the commission for *Die Entführung aus dem Serail*—had not yet taken off, and he continued to formulate career plans. ◄

To Leopold Mozart *Vienna, 23 January 1782*

I want to give you my opinion as to my prospects of a small permanent income. I have my eye here on three sources. The first is not certain, and, even if it were, would probably not be much; the second would be the best, but God knows whether it will ever come to pass; and the third is not to be despised, but the pity is that it concerns the future and not the present. The first is young Prince [Alois Josef] Liechtenstein, who would like to collect a wind instrument band [Harmonie Musick][6] (though he does not yet want it to be known), for which I should write the music. This would not bring in very much, it is true, but it would be at least something certain, and I should not sign the contract unless it were to be for life. The second (in my estimation, however, it is the first) is the Emperor himself. Who knows? I intend to talk to Herr von Strack about it and I am certain that he will do all he can, for he has proved to be a very good friend of mine; though indeed these court flunkeys are never to be trusted. The manner in which the Emperor has spoken to me has given me some hope. . . . The third is the Archduke Maximilian. Now of him I can say that he thinks the world of me. He shoves me forward on every occasion, and I might almost say with certainty that if at this moment he were Elector of Cologne, I should be his Kapellmeister. It is, indeed, a pity that these great gentlemen refuse to make arrangements beforehand. I could easily manage to extract a single promise from him, but of what use would that be to me now? . . . I can write, it is true, at least one opera a year, give a concert annually, and have some things engraved and published by subscription. There are other concerts too where one can make money, particularly if one has been living in a place for a long time and has a good reputation. But I should

FIGURE 2.2. Emperor
Joseph II

prefer not to count on such takings but rather to regard them as windfalls. However, if the bow will not bend, it must break, and I will rather take the risk than go on waiting indefinitely. My affairs cannot get worse; on the contrary, they must continue to improve. (A, 794–795)

► Following the success of his first public concert on March 3 at the Burgtheater, there were rumors that the Emperor (fig. 2.2) was prepared to take Mozart into his service. This led him to consider the alternative of prestige, on the one hand, and money and security, on the other. ◄

To Leopold Mozart   *Vienna, 10 April 1782*

If [the Emperor] wants me, he must pay me, for the honor alone of serving him is not enough. Indeed, if he were to offer me one thousand gulden and some Count two thousand, I should decline the former proposal with thanks and go to the Count—that is, of course, if it were a permanent arrangement. (A, 799–800)

► The premiere of *Die Entführung* took place on 16 July 1782; on 4 August,

Mozart married Constanze Weber. Despite the success of the Singspiel no further auspicious prospects were currently in the offing in Vienna. ◄

To Leopold Mozart   *Vienna, 17 August 1782*

My idea is to go to Paris next Lent, but of course not simply on chance. I have already written to Le Gros about this and am awaiting his reply. I have mentioned it here too—particularly to *people of position*—just in the course of conversation. For you know that often in conversation you can throw out a hint and that this is more effective than if the same thing were announced in the tones of a dictator. I might be able to get engagements for the Concert Spirituel and the Concert des Amateurs[7]—and besides, I should have plenty of pupils—and now that I have a wife I could superintend them more easily and more attentively—and then with the help of compositions and so forth—but indeed I should rely chiefly on opera commissions. (A, 815)

► Mozart had occasionally entertained the idea of going to England. In the autumn of 1786 the prospect of joining his English friends Ann (Nancy) and Stephen Storace, Michael Kelly, and Thomas Attwood on their planned return to London the following February seemed to lend the notion some plausibility, and Mozart raised the idea with Leopold. ◄

Leopold Mozart to Nannerl   *Salzburg, 17 November 1786*

Your brother actually suggested that I should take charge of his two children, because he was proposing to undertake a journey through Germany to England in the middle of next carnival. . . . Not at all a bad arrangement! They could go off and travel—they might even die—or remain in England—and I should have to run off after them with the children. (A, 901–902)

► Mozart's professional fortunes in Vienna reached their nadir in the years 1788 and 1789. In search of a remedy he undertook a concert tour to Dresden, Leipzig, and Berlin in the spring of 1789. In the fall of 1790, he undertook another—this time to Frankfurt am Main in connection with the coronation of Leopold II as Emperor. By then, however, Mozart had learned to prefer the life of an independent musician in Vienna. ◄

To Constanze   *Frankfurt am Main, 8 October 1790*

If I work very hard in Vienna and take pupils, we can live very happily;

and nothing but a *good engagement at some court* can make me abandon this plan. (A, 945)

TEACHING — PERFORMING — COMPOSING

▶ Mozart stated his preferences concerning the three mainstays of his life as a professional musician on many occasions and always with unmistakable clarity. His paramount objective was to be a composer. In order to make a living, however, he was certainly willing to perform — preferably as a conductor and pianist than as a violinist. The least desirable, indeed altogether undesirable but unavoidable, option was teaching — especially giving piano lessons. ◀

To Leopold Mozart   *Mannheim, 7 February 1778*

I could not get on at all without pupils, which is a kind of work that is quite uncongenial to me — and of this I have an excellent example here. I could have had two pupils. I went three times to each, but finding one of them out, I never went back. I will gladly give lessons as a favor, particularly when I see that my student has talent, inclination, and anxiety to learn; but to be obliged to go to a house at a certain hour, or to have to wait at home for a pupil, is what I cannot do, no matter how much money it may bring me in. I find it impossible, so must leave it to those who can do nothing else but play the clavier. I am a composer and was born to be a Kapellmeister. I neither can nor ought to bury the talent for composition with which God in his goodness has so richly endowed me . . . ; and this I should be doing were I to take many pupils, for it is a most unsettling metier. I would rather, if I may speak plainly, neglect the clavier than composition, for in my case the clavier with me is only a sideline, though, thank God, a very good one. (A, 468)

To Leopold Mozart   *Paris, 31 July 1778*

I shall do my utmost to get along here by teaching and to earn as much money as possible, which I am now doing in the fond hope that my circumstances may soon change; for I cannot deny, and must indeed confess, that I shall be delighted to be released from this place. For giving lessons here is no joke. Unless you wear yourself out by taking a *large number of pupils*, you cannot make much money. You must not think that this is laziness on my part. No, indeed! It just goes utterly against my genius and my manner of life. (A, 587)

To Leopold Mozart   *Paris, 11 September 1778*

I will no longer be a fiddler. I want to conduct at the clavier and accompany arias. (A, 613)

DAILY ROUTINES

AT HOME

▶ Practically and prosaically considered, how did Mozart go about his career and organize his time, day for day, as a professional musician? Not surprisingly, his daily routine varied according to circumstances: whether he was at home or on tour, in Salzburg or Vienna. In Salzburg Mozart held salaried positions in the service of the court: from 1772 as Konzertmeister, from 1779 as organist. He was accordingly obliged to observe regular schedules of rehearsals and performances which, for all their tedium, no doubt provided a reassuringly predictable framework for his daily activities.

Since Mozart lived at home with his family in Salzburg, with all his close friends nearby, there was little occasion for him to write to anyone about his activities there. Of course, he may well have written to acquaintances he had met during his travels; but—except for a letter to Padre Martini in Bologna, containing some valuable observations on the state of music in Salzburg (particularly its church music)[8]—no such letters survive. A letter home from Italy, however, makes an intriguing reference to an exotic tradition of domestic music-making in the Mozart household and thereby provides a solitary reference by Mozart to any aspect of his Salzburg routine. ◀

To Nannerl   *Bologna, 6 October 1770*

I hope that I shall soon hear those Pertl chamber symphonies [Pertelzkammersinfonien] and perhaps blow a little trumpet [trommpetterl] or play on a little pipe [pfeifferl] by way of accompaniment. (A, 164–165)

▶ Pertl was the maiden name of Mozart's mother. But "Pertelzkammer" at the same time seems to be a pun on "Berchtesgaden," the town in the Bavarian alps which was the home of a famous toy industry where toy symphonies, such as Leopold Mozart's *Toy* Symphony and "Musical Sleigh Ride", were traditionally performed. This would explain Mozart's reference here to toy instruments.[9] ◀

▶ In Vienna—at least until December 1787, when he was appointed Imperial Chamber Compositeur (a position, however, entailing only a token salary)—Mozart was a free agent, obliged, first of all, to recruit students, performances, and commissions; to organize his various commitments into a reasonable schedule; and finally to try to make them all add up to a living. Given the finite number of hours in a day, significant changes in any of these activities led to changes in the daily routine. The number of concerts and students Mozart had at any given time, incidentally, was not a simple reflection of the status of his particular fortunes and popularity but was also significantly affected by such mundane factors as the season of the year. For example, since the nobility left Vienna for the country in the summer time, there were fewer students, and fewer concerts, but more time for composing. In short, Mozart's "normal" daily schedule in Vienna was repeatedly subject to revisions which, at least so long as Leopold lived, were duly reported back to Salzburg.[10] ◄

To Leopold Mozart   *Vienna, 16 June 1781*

The present season is, as you know, the worst for anyone who wants to make money. The most distinguished families are in the country. So all I can do is to work hard in preparation for the winter, when I shall have less time to compose. (A, 744)

► Here follow some dozen references to Mozart's Viennese schedule, most of them dating from his first few years in the city. His initial concern, after finally settling in Vienna in June 1781—the famous kick in the pants from Count Arco occurred on the 6th of June—was to recruit a stable number of regularly paying pupils. His hope was to have four whose lessons would fill the mid-morning hours and whose payments would keep him afloat. Mozart tried to reserve the early morning (from 7 to 9 or 10 A.M.), along with as many evenings as possible, for composition—often working, by his own account (with or without interruptions, such as a concert or a visit to his fiancée)—to 1 or 1:30 A.M. (In later years, according to Constanze, he would compose often enough to 2:00 A.M.) The afternoons, following lunch, were evidently occupied with a variety of changing tasks such as proofreading parts, conducting rehearsals, or, presumably (although it is not specifically mentioned), practicing at least a little, especially during the winter and spring concert seasons. With variations, this was to remain Mozart's pattern of activity throughout the Vienna years. ◄

To Leopold Mozart   *Vienna, 16 June 1781*

At present I have only one pupil, Countess Rumbeck. . . . I could have many more, it is true, if I chose to lower my terms, but by doing so, I should lose repute. My terms are six ducats for twelve lessons. . . . I would rather have three pupils who pay me well than six who pay badly. With this one pupil I can just make *both ends meet*, and that is enough for the present. (A, 744–745)

► Six months later the number of students had doubled—to two. ◄

To Leopold Mozart   *Vienna, 22 December 1781*

Every morning at six o'clock my friseur arrives and wakes me, and by seven I have finished dressing. I compose until ten, when I give a lesson to Frau von Trattner and at eleven to the Countess Rumbeck, each of whom pays me six ducats for twelve lessons and to whom I go *every day*, unless they put me off, which I do not like at all. I have arranged with the Countess that she is never to put me off; I mean that, if I do not find her at home, I am at least to get my fee; but Frau von Trattner is too economical for that. (A, 789)

► By January there were three. ◄

To Leopold Mozart   *Vienna, 23 January 1782*

I have three pupils now [Countess Rumbeck, Frau von Trattner, and Fräulein Josepha Auernhammer], which brings me in eighteen ducats a month; for I no longer charge for twelve lessons, but monthly. I learned to my cost that my pupils often dropped out for weeks at a time; so now, whether they learn or not, each of them must pay me six ducats. I shall get several more on these terms, but I really need only one more, because four pupils are quite enough. With four I should have 24 ducats, or 102 gulden, 24 kreuzer. (A, 795)

To Leopold Mozart   *Vienna, 13 February 1782*

My hair is always done by six o'clock in the morning and by seven I am fully dressed. I then compose until nine. From nine to one I give lessons. Then I lunch, unless I am invited to some house where they lunch at two or even three o'clock. . . . I can never work before five or six o'clock in the evening, and even then I am often prevented by a concert. If I am not prevented, I compose until nine. I then go to my dear Constanze, though the joy of seeing one another is nearly always spoiled by her mother's bitter remarks. . . . At half past ten or eleven I come home—it depends on her mother's darts and my capacity to endure them! As I cannot rely on being able to compose in the evening owing to the concerts which are taking place and also to the uncertainty as to whether I may not be summoned now here and now there, it is my custom (especially if I get home early) to compose a little before going to bed. I often go on writing until one—and am up again at six. (A, 797)

To Leopold Mozart   *Vienna, 8 May 1782*

In the mornings . . . not only do I never go out, but I do not even dress, as I have such a lot of composing to do. (A, 804)

To Leopold Mozart   *Vienna, 29 May 1782*

At the moment I have nothing but very tiresome work—that is, correcting [i.e., proofreading parts for *Die Entführung aus dem Serail*]. We are to have our first rehearsal next Monday. (A, 807)

► Following the premiere of *Die Entführung* on 16 July, 1782, its extraordinarily successful run throughout the following months, and the growing calendar of concert dates for the upcoming season, Mozart's prospects, at least temporarily, looked rather rosy. This inevitably reduced (but did not eliminate) his need for more pupils. ◄

To Leopold Mozart   *Vienna, 12 October 1782*

I am not looking for pupils, for I can have as many as I please. (A, 828)

To Leopold Mozart   *Vienna, 28 December 1782*

I have asked some people to come here at six for a little concert. Altogether I have so much to do that often I do not know whether I am on my head or my heels. I spend the whole forenoon giving lessons until two o'clock, when we have lunch. After the meal I must give my poor stomach an hour for digestion. The evening is therefore the only time I have for composing and of that I can never be sure, as I am often asked to perform at concerts. (A, 833)

► Three days after writing this letter Mozart completed the score of the first of the string quartets ultimately dedicated to Haydn, the Quartet in G, K. 387. ◄

To Leopold Mozart   *Vienna, 8 January 1783*

I have to finish a rondo ["Ah, non sai, qual pena," K. 416] this evening for my sister-in-law Aloysia Lange, which she is to sing on Saturday at a big concert in the Mehlgrube.[11] (A, 836)

To Leopold Mozart   *Vienna, 10 February 1784*

Well, I must close, for I must really compose. I spend the whole morning giving lessons, so I have only the evening for my beloved task—composition. (A, 867)

To Leopold Mozart   *Vienna, 3 March 1784*

You must forgive me if I don't write very much, but it is impossible to find time to do so, as I am giving three subscription concerts . . . beginning on March 17. . . . Well, as you may imagine, I must play some new works—and therefore I must compose. The whole morning is taken up with pupils and almost every evening I have to play. (A, 869–870)

To Leopold Mozart   *Vienna, 6 May 1784*

We ourselves do not go to bed until midnight and we get up at half past five or even five, as we go to the Augarten[12] almost every morning. (A, 878)

To Constanze, Baden   *Vienna, 8 October 1791*

This morning I worked so hard at my composition that I went on until half past one. So I dashed off in great haste to Hofer, simply in order not to lunch alone, where I found Mamma too. After lunch I went home at once and composed again until it was time to go to the opera. Leutgeb begged me to take him a second time and I did so. I am taking *Mamma* tomorrow. (A, 969)

The Reminiscences of Constanze Mozart, 1829

He frequently sat up composing until two and rose at four, an exertion which assisted to destroy him. (Novello, 96)

▶ Baron Gottfried van Swieten (1733–1803), prefect of the Imperial Library in Vienna, was largely responsible for introducing Mozart to the music of J. S. Bach and Handel. Mozart arranged a number of fugues from the *Well-Tempered Clavier* presumably for performance at van Swieten's musicales. (Van Swieten later commissioned Mozart to arrange several of Handel's oratorios for performance by a music society he had founded expressly for the purpose of reviving that repertoire.) ◀

To Leopold Mozart   *Vienna, 10 April 1782*

I go every Sunday at twelve o'clock to the Baron van Swieten, where nothing is played but Handel and Bach. (A, 800)

To Leopold Mozart   *Vienna, 4 January 1783*

There are a few counterpoint works by Eberlin . . . and some things of [Michael] Haydn, which I should like to have for the Baron van Swieten, to whose house I go every Sunday from twelve to two. (A, 835)

ON TOUR

▶ Mozart's schedule of activities when away from home depended, of course, on the purpose—and the duration—of his tours. The grand tour of his childhood years (1763–1766) to Paris, London, and Holland, was mostly taken up with concert performances and other public appearances, although he also managed to take lessons in London and to compose. The first journey to Italy (1769–1771) began as a concert tour but ended with a major commission for an opera seria. The two remaining journeys to Italy (1771, 1772–1773) were largely spent composing commissioned works. Mozart himself wrote nothing about his "way of life" on any of these trips until June 1770, during the first Italian journey. But one suspects that he was more interested in being amusing than informative in this first communication to Nannerl. ◀

To Nannerl   *Naples, 5 June 1770*

Now I shall begin to describe my way of life. *I wake up at nine, sometimes even at ten, and then we go out, and then we lunch at an eating house, and after lunch we write, and then we go out, and then we have supper, and what do we eat? On ordinary days, half a chicken or a small slice of roast meat; on fast days a little fish; and then we go to bed* [Italian]. (A, 142)

To Nannerl   *Bologna, 4 August 1770*

My fiddle has now been restrung and I play every day. But I add this simply because Mamma wanted to know if I still play the fiddle. More than six times I have had the honor of going alone to a church and to some magnificent function. (A, 153)

► The extended sojourns in Mannheim and Paris between 1777 and 1779 had been undertaken with a different purpose altogether: to try to secure a regular court appointment. Owing to the relatively long periods of time Mozart was to spend in these two cities, his life there could settle into something of a routine consisting, again, of teaching, performing, and composing, but also of innumerable visits: social calls—often of a job-seeking nature. ◄

To Leopold Mozart   *Mannheim, 7 December 1777*

At 6:30 I am going on to Cannabich's to give my usual daily lesson on the clavier. (A, 409)

To Leopold Mozart   *Mannheim, 20 December 1777*

I am writing this at eleven o'clock at night, for it is the only time I am free. We can't get up before eight o'clock, for until half past eight there is no daylight in our room, which is on the ground floor. I dress in haste and at ten I sit down to compose until about twelve or half past twelve. Then I go to Wendling's, where I again compose a little until half past one, when we have lunch. Thus the time passes until three, when I go off to the Mainzischer Hof (an inn) to a Dutch officer to give him a lesson in galanterie and thoroughbass,[13] for which I receive, if I am not mistaken, four ducats for twelve lessons. At four I must be home again to instruct the daughter of the house. We never begin our lesson before half past four, as we have to wait for the lights. At six I go to Cannabich's and give Mlle. Rosa her lesson. I stay there to supper, after which we talk or occasionally someone plays. (A, 429)

To Leopold Mozart   *Mannheim, 14 February 1778*

I can only compose at night, so that I can't get up early as well. (A, 481)

To Leopold Mozart   *Paris, 31 July 1778*

You know that I am, so to speak, soaked in music, that I am immersed in it all day long and that I love to plan works, study, and meditate. Well, I am prevented from all this by my way of life here. I shall have a few free hours, it is true, but these few hours I shall need more for rest than for work. (A, 587)

To Leopold Mozart   *Paris, 11 September 1778*

I can then leave on the 6th, for I am not in a hurry; nor is my stay here vain or fruitless, as I shut myself up and work in order to make as much money as possible. (A, 616)

► Between November 1780 and March 1781 Mozart was in Munich for the composition, rehearsal, and performance of *Idomeneo*. ◄

To Leopold Mozart   *Munich, 22 November 1780*

Every minute is precious; and, as it is, I can generally only compose in the evenings, as the mornings are so dark; then I have to dress. . . . When the castrato[14] comes, I have to sing with him, for I have to teach him his whole part as if he were a child. (A, 669)

To Leopold Mozart   *Munich, 13 December 1780*

I have only been to the theater once, as I have no time, since the evening is always my favorite time for working. (A, 686)

To Leopold Mozart   *Vienna, 26 May 1781*

Until the first performance of my opera [*Idomeneo*, in Munich] I had never been to a theater, or gone anywhere but to the Cannabichs'. (A, 737)

► Finally, while on his last concert tour, the journey to Frankfurt am Main for the coronation of Leopold II, in the fall of 1790, Mozart described his routine in a letter home. ◄

To Constanze   *Frankfurt am Main, 3 October 1790*

Up to the present I have been living here altogether in retirement. Every morning I stay indoors in my hole of a bedroom and compose. My sole recreation is the theater, where I meet several acquaintances from Vienna, Munich, Mannheim, and even Salzburg. . . . This is the way I should like best of all to go on living—but—I fear that it will soon come to an end and that I am in for a restless life. Already I am being invited everywhere—and however tiresome it may be to let myself be on view, I see nevertheless how necessary it is. (A, 944)

RECOGNITION AND REPUTATION

► Despite the fluctuations of his material fortunes, Mozart had the gratification of knowing that his talent was recognized and appreciated as something unique. It should be no surprise that he did not hesitate to record and report the enthusiastic opinions of his admirers. ◄

To Leopold Mozart   *Munich, 1 December 1780*

I cannot tell you how delighted and surprised they all were. But indeed I never expected anything else, for I assure you that I went to that rehearsal [of *Idomeneo*] with as easy a mind as if I were going to a lunch party somewhere. Count Sensheim said to me: *"I assure you that though I expected a great deal from you, I really did not expect that."* . . . Ramm said to me . . . : *"I must honestly confess that no music has ever made such an impression on me, and I can assure you that I thought fifty times of your father and of what his delight will be when he hears this opera."* (A, 677)

To Leopold Mozart   *Munich, 30 December 1780*

I have heard too from a very good source that on the same evening after the rehearsal [the Elector Karl Theodor] spoke of my music to everyone with whom he conversed, saying: *"I was quite surprised. No music has ever made such an impression on me. It is magnificent music."* (A, 701)

To Leopold Mozart   *Vienna, 2 December 1781*

At table the other day the Emperor gave me the very highest praise, accompanied by the words: *"C'est un talent, décidé!"* (A, 789)

To Leopold Mozart   *Vienna, 31 July 1782*

So the whole world declares that by my boasting and criticizing I have made enemies of the professors of music and of many others! *What* world, pray? Presumably the world of Salzburg, for everyone in Vienna can see and hear enough to be convinced of the contrary. (A, 811)

To Leopold Mozart   *Vienna, 17 August 1782*

[Count] Kaunitz said the other day to the Archduke Maximilian, when the conversation turned on myself, that *"such people only come into the world once in a hundred years and must not be driven out of Germany, particularly when we are fortunate enough to have them in the capital."* (A, 814)

Leopold Mozart to Nannerl   *Salzburg, 3 November 1785*

The journalist [Professor Lorenz Hübner of Munich] met me a few days

ago and said: "It is really astonishing to see what a number of compositions your son is publishing.[15] In all the announcements of musical works I
see nothing but Mozart. The Berlin announcements, when quoting the
quartets, merely add the following words: 'It is quite unnecessary to
recommend these quartets to the public. Suffice it to say that they are the
work of Herr Mozart'" (A, 893)

► The poignant fact remains, however, that in the final year of his life,
Mozart still felt the need to cite his international fame in application for
the most humble—indeed unpaid—position of Assistant Kapellmeister of St. Stephen's cathedral. ◄

To the Municipal Court of Vienna   *Vienna, April 1791*

When Kapellmeister [Johann Leopold] Hofmann was ill, I thought of
venturing to apply for his post, seeing that my musical talents, my works,
and my skill in composition are well known in foreign countries, my name
is treated everywhere with some respect, and I myself have the honor to be
employed as composer to the Court of Vienna. I trusted therefore that I
was not unworthy of this post and that I deserved the favorable consideration of our enlightened municipal council. (A, 949)

3

The Profession

*A courtier can't do the work of a Kapellmeister, but a Kapellmeister can be a
courtier.*

Paris, 9 July 1778

At least I have the honor of being placed above the cooks.

Vienna, 17 March 1781

EMPLOYMENT AND COMMERCE

PATRONS

► As a composer living in late eighteenth-century Europe Mozart inevitably found himself contending with the social, cultural, economic, and
commercial institutions of the *ancien régime.* This meant above all else
that he had to survive and flourish under an almost feudal system of
patronage where a musician, as Mozart remarked (and meant quite
literally), could expect to occupy a social status not too far "above the
cooks." Mozart's resentment at needing (and not being able to obtain)
the Prince-Archbishop's permission to perform at a concert in Vienna
soon after his arrival there lent urgency to his intention to leave the
Salzburg service.[1] Two years after his break with Salzburg, Mozart
continued to worry about the reach of the Prince-Archbishop's authority over his life and limb, hesitating to return to visit his father there,
since, as he declared, "as I have never been discharged, the Archbishop
might have me arrested." (Vienna, 12 July 1783)
   Nonetheless, one could do far worse as an artist—then or now—
than to find a secure, well-paying, salaried appointment as a Kapellmeister in the employ of an affluent and enthusiastic court or aristocrat.
After all, a Kapellmeister could "be a courtier."
   Although Mozart never received the coveted post of Kapellmeister,
he did apply for and receive other positions. His first regular appoint-

ment, as an unpaid third Konzertmeister in the Salzburg Court Chapel, took effect in November 1769. He was later granted the title of Konzertmeister; but this too remained an unpaid position until 21 August 1772. At that time, upon "the most submissive supplication" to the Archbishop, Mozart was granted an annual salary of 150 gulden[2]— the equivalent, in 1990 dollars of roughly $3,000. Some six years later he applied for another post in the Salzburg service—again most submissively. ◄

To Prince-Archbishop Hieronymus Colloredo   *Salzburg, January 1779*

Your grace,
Most worthy Prince of the Holy Roman Empire! Most Gracious Prince and Lord! After the decease of Cajetan Adlgasser Your Grace was so good as to take me into your service. I therefore humbly beseech you to grant me a certificate of my appointment as Court Organist. I remain,
Your Grace's most humble and obedient servant,
                        Wolfgang Amadé Mozart[3] (A, 651)

► Mozart's petition was granted on 17 January 1779. Archbishop Colloredo's decree specifies that Mozart will "carry out his appointed duties . . . in the Cathedral as well as at Court and in the Chapel, and shall as far as possible serve the Court and the Church with new compositions made by him." (DDB, 182) The annual salary was fixed at 450 gulden—the same as Adlgasser's had been.

   After settling in Vienna, Mozart not only made countless efforts to secure a salaried position at the imperial court, he also continued to seek regular, part-time, employment elsewhere. In 1784 his father had established contact with an old Salzburg acquaintance, Sebastian Winter, who had since become the personal valet of Prince von Fürstenburg of Donaueschingen, and had sent him some of Wolfgang's compositions. In 1786 Winter had approached Mozart directly, evidently with a renewed request. Mozart took the opportunity to propose a salaried position. ◄

To Sebastian Winter, Donaueschingen   *Vienna, 8 August 1786*

I am very glad that you have applied to me in person. I should long ago have sent some specimens of my poor work to your highly respected Prince. . . . I am therefore jotting down at the end of my letter a list of my latest compositions from which His Highness has only to choose, so that I may hasten to serve him. If His Highness should so desire, I shall send him in future all the new works which I compose. Further, I venture to make a little musical proposal to His Highness which I beg you, my friend, to put before him. As His Highness possesses an orchestra, he might like to have works composed by me *for performance solely at his court,* a thing which in my humble opinion would be very gratifying. If His Highness would be so gracious as to order from me every year a certain number of symphonies, quartets, concertos for different instruments, or any other compositions which he fancies, and to promise me a fixed salary yearly, then His Highness would be served more quickly and more satisfactorily, and I, being sure of that commission, should work with greater peace of mind. (A, 897–900)

▶ The list that Mozart appended consisted of the opening themes for four symphonies: the *Haffner* and *Linz* Symphonies, as well as two symphonies from the Salzburg period (K. 319 and 338); five piano concertos: K. 453, 456, 451, 459 (all from 1784), and the Concerto in A, K. 488 (completed in March 1786); and three relatively recent chamber compositions: the Sonata for Piano and Violin, K. 481 (December 1785), the Piano Trio in G, K. 496 (July 1786) and the Piano Quartet in G minor, K. 478 (October 1785).

Finally, in December 1787, Mozart received a permanent, if modest, court appointment which he promptly reported to his sister. ◀

To Nannerl   *Vienna, 19 December 1787*

Of my writing *Don Giovanni* for Prague and of the opera's triumphant success you may have heard already, but that His Majesty the Emperor has now taken me into his service will probably be news to you. (A, 914)

▶ Mozart received the appointment as Imperial Kammermusicus (i.e., chamber musician), with an annual salary of eight hundred gulden, on 7 December (effective 1 December) 1787. Gluck, his predecessor had received two thousand gulden in the same post.[4] ◀

To Nannerl   *Vienna, 2 August 1788*

PS.—In reply to your question about my appointment, I must tell you that the Emperor has taken me into his household. I now have therefore a permanent appointment, *for the time being* at a salary of only eight hundred gulden. However, no one else in the household is drawing *so large a sum*. (A, 918)

Jean-Baptiste-Antoine Suard, "Anecdotes sur Mozart," 1804

He had been named Chamber Composer by the Emperor, and in respect of this position he had a salary of eight hundred florins per year. . . . He was asked one day, in pursuance of a general order from the government, for a statement of the stipend that he received from the court. He wrote in a sealed letter: "Too much for what I have done, too little for what I could have done." (DDB, 499)

► As late as the last two years of his life Mozart was still interested in finding a permanent position at court. He even considered serving as second Kapellmeister (a post which evidently had never existed before) to Antonio Salieri and went so far as to draft a petition (which he evidently never sent) to Archduke Francis, son of the recently crowned Emperor, Leopold II.[5] A year later, he applied for the unpaid post of Vice Kapellmeister at St. Stephen's cathedral in order, quite blatantly, to position himself as the inevitable successor to the title of Kapellmeister. It is notable in both instances that he called attention to his abilities as a composer of church music—a reflection of his renewed interest in church composition during his later years.[6] ◄

To Archduke Francis　　　　　　　　　　　　　　　　*Vienna, May 1790*

Prompted by a desire for fame, by a love of work, and by a conviction of my wide knowledge, I venture to apply for the post of second Kapellmeister, particularly as Salieri, that very gifted Kapellmeister, has never devoted himself to church music; whereas from my youth up I have made myself completely familiar with the style. (A, 938–939)

To the Municipal Court of Vienna　　　　　　　*Vienna, ca. 25 April 1791*

When Kapellmeister [Leopold] Hofmann was ill, I thought of venturing to apply for his post. . . . Kapellmeister Hofmann, however, has recovered his health and in the circumstances—for I wish him from my heart a long life—it has occurred to me that it might perhaps be of service to the cathedral and, most worthy gentlemen, to your advantage, if I were to be attached for the time being as unpaid assistant to this aging Kapellmeister and were to have the opportunity of helping this worthy man in his office, thus gaining the approbation of our learned municipal council by the actual performance of services which I may justly consider myself peculiarly fitted to render on account of my thorough knowledge of both the secular and ecclesiastical styles of music. (A, 949–950)

► The alternative to holding a salaried post was to serve a variety of patrons, that is, employers—who could be royal, aristocratic, or bourgeois—by accepting ad hoc commissions for the composition of particular works. Again the composer's principal obligation was to satisfy the needs, the tastes, the resources—and perhaps the personal abilities, as well—of his patron.

Mozart's experiences—and frustrations (which at one point erupted into scatological rhyme)—in attempting to fulfill a commission for a set of flute compositions are vividly (if perhaps not completely honestly) documented in a series of letters home to Salzburg. The commission, from a German-born Dutch surgeon and amateur, Ferdinand De Jean, was secured for him by his Mannheim colleague, the flautist Johann Baptist Wendling. Mozart, interestingly enough, voices at the same time his intention to compose on his own initiative—that is, without prior commission, but with an eye toward the advancement of his career— other works, as well: a mass (in order to impress a potential employer and patron, Karl Theodor, Elector Palatine) and a set of duets for violin and piano, the latter apparently in emulation of the commercially popular violin divertimenti of Joseph Schuster that he had heard two months before in Munich.[7] ◄

To Leopold Mozart   *Mannheim, 10 December 1777*

The other day I went to lunch at Wendling's as usual. "Our Indian," he said, meaning a Dutchman [Ferdinand De Jean], a gentleman of means and a lover of all the sciences, who is a great friend and *admirer* [code] of mine, "our Indian is really a first-rate fellow. He is willing to give you two hundred gulden if you will compose for him three short, simple concertos and a couple of quartets for the flute. . . . You can compose duets for clavier and violin here and have them engraved *par souscription.*" . . .

I shall have quite enough to write during the next two months, three concertos, two quartets, four or six duets for the clavier.[8] And then I have an idea of writing a new grand mass[9] and presenting *it to the Elector* [code]. (A, 415)

To his Mother   *Worms, 31 January 1778*

> Wendling, no doubt, is in a rage
> That I haven't composed a single page;
> But when I cross the Rhine once more,
> I'll surely dash home through the door
> And, lest he call me mean and petty,
> I'll finish off his four quartetti.
> The concerto for Paris I'll keep,
> 'tis more fitting.
> I'll scribble it there some day when I'm shitting.
> (A, 456–457)

To Leopold Mozart   *Mannheim, 14 February 1778*

M. De Jean is also leaving for Paris tomorrow and, because I have only finished two concertos and three quartets for him, has sent me ninety-six gulden (that is, four gulden too little, evidently supposing that this was the half of two hundred); but he must pay me in full, for that was my agreement with the Wendlings, and I can send him the other pieces later. It is not surprising that I have not been able to finish them, for I never have a single quiet hour here. I can only compose at night . . . besides, one is not always in the mood for working. I could, to be sure, scribble off things the whole day long, but a composition of this kind goes out into the world. . . . Moreover, you know that I become quite powerless whenever I am obliged to write for an instrument which I cannot bear. Hence as a diversion I compose something else, such as duets for clavier and violin, or I work at my mass. (A, 481–482)

► Too many excuses, Mozart! Ultimately, Mozart composed two flute concertos: the G major, K. 313 (285c), and the D major, K. 314 (285d)—the latter actually an arrangement of a previously composed oboe concerto—and (or so he claims) three flute quartets. Of the three flute quartets generally associated with the De Jean commission—in D, K. 285; in G, K. 285a; and C, K. App. 171 (285b)[10]—the G major (and possibly the C major, as well) may not be authentic. At all events, the C major Quartet was not composed before 1781. In fact, Mozart's references to the De Jean commission contain a number of inconsistencies. A recent analysis of the problem suggests that Mozart was most likely commissioned to compose three concertos and no fewer than four quartets (as he had mentioned to his mother) but managed to complete only two concertos and two quartets—for which he then received only half of the agreed-upon commission.[11] ◄

MUSIC REPRODUCTION: COPYING AND PUBLISHING

I myself have everything copied in my room and in my presence.

Vienna, 15 May 1784

► In his relations with patrons, especially those of royal and aristocratic blood, Mozart was obliged to play the role of the humble servant and was made abundantly aware of his place in the prevailing social order. In his efforts to disseminate his music to the general public, on the other hand, Mozart was cast in the role of the entrepreneur. This was especially so when he dealt with copyists; for then it was Mozart who purchased the services of others—and was put on his guard: concerned about comparative costs, about quality, efficiency, and even the honesty of those he engaged for the task.

Mozart required the services of copyists to prepare the performing parts for his operas, his symphonies, indeed, for everything he composed other than solo piano music. For the most part, the composer's concerns centered on accuracy and speed. Rehearsals and performances were often delayed owing to mistakes or delays in the preparation of the parts. But Mozart also made use of copyists to prepare copies for sale. In the late eighteenth century, manuscript publication rather than engraving and printing continued to be the principal vehicle for the publication of music, especially of works for larger ensembles. Here the main risk was that unauthorized copies would be produced and sold beyond Mozart's supervision and behind his back, thereby depriving him of his share of any profits. Mozart demonstrated his precocious awareness of this problem in one of his earliest surviving letters. Yet, if he wished his music to be circulated and performed, and his name and reputation as a major composer to be known widely in the musical world, then he had to deal with copyists. ◄

To Nannerl Rome, 25 April 1770

A symphony[12] *is being copied (my father is the copyist), for we do not wish to give it out to be copied, as it would be stolen.* [Italian]. (A, 131)

To Leopold Mozart Mannheim, 29 November 1777

I send herewith the Allegro and Andante of the sonata for Mlle. Cannabich [the Piano Sonata in C, K. 309 (284b)]. . . . You must put up with the original. You can have it copied for six kreuzer the sheet more easily than I can for twenty-four. Don't you think that's dear? (A, 397)

► There were sixty kreuzers to the gulden. Accordingly, six kreuzers were worth about $2.00, twenty-four kreuzers, $8.00 ◄

To Leopold Mozart Mannheim, 3 December 1777

I may say that I very much regret not having a copy of at least one mass with me. I should have certainly had one performed. . . . If only I had the "Misericordias" copied out.[13] But it cannot be helped now. There's no altering it. I would have decided to have one copied, but copying is much too expensive here and I might not have got as much for the mass as it would have cost me to have it copied. They are not very generous here. (A, 402)

To Leopold Mozart Munich, 16 December 1780

The rehearsal [of act 3 of *Idomeneo*] has been put off again and again on account of the copyist. (A, 690)

To Leopold Mozart Vienna, 4 July 1781

I badly need the three cassations[14]—those in F and B-flat would do me best for the time being—but you might have the one in D copied for me some time and sent on later, for the charge for copying is so very heavy in Vienna; in addition to which they copy most atrociously. (A, 749)

► Problems associated with preparing copies of *Die Entführung* were the topic of several letters to Salzburg written over a three-month period.[15] ◄

To Leopold Mozart Vienna, 20 July 1782

I send you herewith the original score and two copies of the libretto. . . .

The opera was performed just as you now have it; but here and there the parts for trumpets, drums [Paucken, i.e., timpani] flutes, and clarinets, and the Turkish music [i.e., with cymbals, bass drum, and triangle] are missing, because I could not get any music paper with so many lines. Those parts were written out on extra sheets, which the copyist has probably lost, for he could not find them. (A, 808)

To Leopold Mozart   *Vienna, 25 September 1782*

The Prussian Ambassador, Riedesel, has informed me that he has been commissioned by the Berlin court to send my opera *Die Entführung aus dem Serail* to Berlin and has asked me to have it copied, adding that the remuneration for the music will follow in due course. . . . My idea is to have it copied in Salzburg, where it could be done more secretly and more cheaply! I beg you, therefore, to have the score copied out at once—and as quickly as possible. (A, 822)

To Leopold Mozart   *Vienna, 5 October 1782*

I dispatched by the mail coach today five quires of ruled paper with twelve staves to a page. (A, 827)

To Leopold Mozart   *Vienna, 12 October 1782*

If I could have foreseen that the copyists in Salzburg would have so much to do, I should have decided to have the opera copied here in spite of the extra expense. Well, I must go off to the Ambassador and explain the real reason to him. But please do your very best to have it sent to me soon, and the sooner the better. You think that I should not have got it in a shorter time from a Vienna copyist? Why, I could have got it from the theatrical copyist here within a week or at most ten days. (A, 827)

To Leopold Mozart   *Vienna, 26 October 1782*

It is all the same to me whether the opera is stitched together or bound; I should have it bound in blue paper. (A, 829)

► From the point of view of commercial value, not all musical forms were equal. Mozart, for example, was far more concerned about the surreptitious reproduction of his concertos than of his symphonies. The piano concertos, after all, formed the centerpiece of his public appearances as a piano virtuoso, and most of them were composed primarily to serve that end. Some were intended for the use of his students, on whose behalf Mozart was determined to be no less protective of them. Mozart's instructions home regarding the recently-composed *Linz* Symphony, K. 425, on the one hand, and, on the other, the four new piano concertos of the 1784 season—K. 449, 450, 451, and 453—bear witness to the important relationship obtaining between musical form and commerce. ◄

To Leopold Mozart   *Vienna, 20 February 1784*

The symphony is in the original score, which you might arrange to have copied some time. You can then send it back to me or even give it away or have it performed anywhere you like. The concerto [in E-flat, K. 449] is also in the original score and this too you may have copied; but have it done as quickly as possible and return it to me. Remember, do not show it to a *single soul*, for I composed it for Fräulein [Barbara] Ployer, who paid me handsomely.[16] (A, 868)

To Leopold Mozart   *Vienna, 15 May 1784*

I gave to the mail coach today the symphony which I composed at Linz for old Count Thun and also four concertos. I am not particular about the symphony, but I do ask you to have the four concertos copied at home, for the Salzburg copyists are as little to be trusted as the Viennese. I know for a positive fact that Hofstetter[17] made two copies of Haydn's music. For example, I *really* possess the last three symphonies he wrote.[18] And as no one but myself possesses these new concertos in B-flat [K. 450] and D [K. 451], and no one but *myself* and Fräulein von Ployer (for whom I composed them) those in E-flat [K. 449] and G [K. 453], the only way in which they could fall into other hands is by that kind of cheating. I myself have everything copied in my room and in my presence. (A, 876–877)

► Mozart's experiences with music publishers and engravers extended back to his childhood. His first publications, consisting of two pairs of sonatas for piano and violin, K. 6–7, 8–9, were published in Paris in 1764 as opus 1 and 2. Other compositions appeared during the following two years. But all of these juvenilia passed through the press under the supervision of his father. Mozart did not begin to deal directly with engravers and publishers himself until he set out for Mannheim and Paris. As he reveals in his letter from Mannheim, dated 10 December 1777, the idea of composing a set of duets, or sonatas, for piano and violin for publication seems to have originated with his friend Wendling.[19] A month later (11 January 1778), Mozart's mother reports home that "Wolfgang is now composing six new trios and is going to have them engraved by subscription" (A, 445). And Mozart, as we have already seen (p. 62), reported the same on 14 February. In his next reference to them, just two weeks thereafter, Mozart makes it clear that he is already quite familiar with the business end of the publishing world: that he understands the varieties of monetary arrangements that can exist between a composer and his publisher and that he has to negotiate the most favorable terms he can.[20] ◄

To Leopold Mozart *Mannheim, 28 February 1778*

I still have two of the six clavier sonatas to compose,[21] but there's no hurry, for I can't have them engraved here. Nothing is done in this place by subscription; it is a miserly spot, and the engraver will not do them at his own expense, but he wants to go halves with me in the sale. So I prefer to have them engraved in Paris, where the engravers are delighted to get something new and pay handsomely and where it is easier to get a thing done by subscription. (A, 498)

To Leopold Mozart *Paris, 20 July 1778*

My sonatas will soon be engraved.[22] Up to the present everyone has refused to give me what I asked for them, so in the end I shall have to give in and let them go for fifteen louis d'or [ca. 150 gulden]. It is the best way, too, to make my name known here. (A, 573)

► The prospect of publication evidently appealed to Mozart. Even before the appearance of the violin sonatas he contemplated publishing some older, but highly successful compositions: three piano concertos (all written for others), and his own favorite vehicle, the piano sonatas, K. 279–284 (189d-h, 205b). (Neither the concertos nor sonatas, however, were published during Mozart's lifetime.) As Mozart implies, his interest in publishing his works at this time presumably was based more on the consideration of what it could do for his fame and reputation than of the income it promised. Most likely no more than one hundred copies would be printed; and in any event, there were to be no royalties.[23] He either sold his compositions outright to the publisher for a fixed amount or agreed to share the costs of publication along with the profits. ◄

To Leopold Mozart *Paris, 11 September 1778*

As for my three concertos, the one written for Mlle. Jeunehomme [in E-flat, K. 271], the one for Countess Lützow [in C, K. 246] and the one in B-flat [K. 238], I shall sell them to the man who engraved my sonatas [Sieber], provided he pays cash for them. And, if I can, I shall do the same with my six difficult sonatas.[24] Even if I don't get much—it will be surely better than nothing. (A, 615)

► Sometime in early November 1778 the violin sonatas, K. 301–306, were finally published, but under less than optimal conditions. ◄

To Leopold Mozart *Strasbourg, 2 November 1778*

It is entirely due to [Melchior Grimm's] stupidity in hurrying up my departure [from Paris] that my sonatas have not yet been engraved, or have not appeared—or at any rate that I have not yet received them.[25] And when they do come, I shall probably find them full of mistakes. If I had stayed only three days longer in Paris, I could have corrected them myself and brought them with me. The engraver was in despair when I told him that I should not be able to revise them myself, but should have to commission someone else to do so. (A, 628)

► Actually, Mozart's failure to correct the proofs himself became the rule for him. Most of the editions that were published during his lifetime have so many mistakes that it seems unlikely that Mozart read proofs for them.[26] Mozart's first publishing enterprise in Vienna was the printing of the six sonatas for piano and violin, K. 296, 376–380 (374d-e, 317d, 373a, 374f), dedicated to his pupil Josepha von Auernhammer. Mozart had begun the process during his first few months in Vienna. ◄

To Leopold Mozart   *Vienna, 19 May 1781*

The subscription for my six sonatas has been started and then I shall have some money. (A, 734)

► A week later he reported some progress to his father. ◄

To Leopold Mozart   *Vienna, 26 May 1781*

The subscription is going well. (A, 736)

► The sonatas were published in November 1781 by the famous firm of Artaria & Co. In connection with the publication an advertisement was placed in the December 8 issue of the leading newspaper, the *Wiener Zeitung* (formerly known as the *Wienerisches Diarium*).[27]

Another informative, if frustrating, publishing initiative—one that would take over two years to reach fruition—was launched in the winter of 1782–1783. Before it was over Mozart was forced to become a borrower for the first time. In December 1782 Mozart had determined to compose a set of three piano concertos. These turned out to be the first in the great series of seventeen piano concertos composed during the Vienna years: the concertos in F, A, and C, K. 413–415 (387a, 385p, 387b). Although it is likely that Mozart performed them all in public— he certainly played the C-major Concerto, K. 415, at a grand concert at the Burgtheater on 23 March 1783 in the presence of the Emperor—it seems that he intended them in this instance less for his own use than for publication. (The stylistic consequences of this plan are cited and discussed in Chapter 12)

Mozart's first idea, this time, was to publish the concertos himself in the form of manuscript copies of the performing parts and to sell them, on a subscription basis, from his own home, and thus derive the entire income of the sales. The subscription price of four ducats (eighteen gulden) for the three concertos was equivalent to more than $300 in today's currency. After this ambitious and costly plan failed, he offered the concertos to his old Paris publisher, J. G. Sieber. They were finally published in Vienna—in 1785—by Mozart's second choice: Artaria & Co. Mozart reported on their composition and his attempts to have them published in a series of letters written between December 1782 and March 1784. ◄

To Leopold Mozart　　　　　　　　　　*Vienna, 28 December 1782*

There are still two concertos wanting to make up the series of subscription concertos. These concertos are a happy medium between what is too easy and too difficult. (A, 833)

To Leopold Mozart　　　　　　　　　　*Vienna, 4 January 1783*

Only three concertos are being published and the price is four ducats.

To Leopold Mozart　　　　　　　　　　*Vienna, 22 January 1783*

You need have no fear that the three concertos are too dear. I think after all that I deserve a ducat for each concerto—and besides, I should like to know who could get them copied for a ducat! They cannot be copied, as I shall not let them out of my hands until I have secured a certain number of subscribers. They have been advertised three times in the *Wiener Diarium*,[28] and subscription tickets at four ducats each have been on sale since the 20th at my house, where the concertos can be obtained during the month of April. (A, 837)

To the Baroness von Waldstätten　　　　　　　　　　*Vienna, 15 February 1783*

At the moment I cannot pay—not even half the sum! If I could have foreseen that the subscriptions for my concertos would come in so slowly, I should have raised the money on a longer time limit. I entreat your Ladyship for Heaven's sake to help me keep my honor and my good name! (A, 841)

► It would seem that Mozart had borrowed money in connection with the publication of the concertos—presumably in order to pay the copyist— but this is not certain. At all events, two months later, he had decided to sell them to his Paris publisher, Sieber. ◄

To J. G. Sieber, Paris　　　　　　　　　　*Vienna, 26 April 1783*

You have probably heard about my pianoforte sonatas with accompaniment for one violin[29] which I have had engraved here by Artaria & Co. I am not very well pleased, however, with the way in which works are engraved in Vienna and, even if I were, I should like some of my compositions once more to find their way into the hands of my fellow-countrymen in Paris. Well, this letter is to inform you that I have three piano concertos ready. . . . Artaria wants to engrave them. But I give you, my friend, the first refusal. And in order to avoid delay, I shall quote my lowest terms to you. If you give me thirty louis d'or for them, the matter is settled. Since I wrote those piano concertos, I have been composing six quartets for two violins, viola, and cello.[30] If you would like to engrave these too, I will gladly let you have them. But I cannot allow these to go so cheaply; I mean that I cannot let you have these six quartets under fifty louis d'or.[31] (A, 846)

► Mozart also considered publishing his music in engraved form himself. But this raised the same basic concerns that always attended the preparation of manuscript copies: how to protect himself from unauthorized reproduction. Whether Mozart ever received the advice he sought from Leopold is unknown. ◄

To Leopold Mozart *Vienna, 20 February 1784*

Well, I must ask you something about which I know nothing whatever. If I have some work printed or engraved at my own expense, how can I protect myself from being cheated by the engraver? For surely he can print off as many copies as he likes and therefore swindle me. The only way to prevent this would be to keep a sharp eye on him. Yet that was impossible in your own case, for you were at Salzburg and the printer was at Augsburg.[32] Why, I almost feel inclined not to sell any more of my compositions to any engraver, but to have them printed or engraved by subscription at my own expense, as most people do and in this way make good profits. (A, 868)

► At all events, Mozart soon developed a general policy regarding the publication of piano concertos: he would be prepared, on occasion, to release a concerto for sale to the public only after it had served its original purpose as his personal warhorse. The immediate objects of this policy were the four new concertos of the 1784 season: the piano concertos, in E-flat, B-flat, D, and G, K 449–451, and K. 453 which he had sent to his sister Nannerl in Salzburg. ◄

To Leopold Mozart *Vienna, 26 May 1784*

I am quite willing to wait patiently to get them back, so long as no one else is allowed to get hold of them. Only today I could have got twenty-four ducats for one of them, but I think that it will be more profitable for me to hold on to them for a few years more and then have them engraved and published.[33] (A, 878)

CONCERT LIFE

Public and Private Auspices

► During the course of the eighteenth century important commercial concert organizations began to develop in the leading musical centers. One of the earliest, and certainly the most influential and prestigious in France, was the Concert Spirituel, founded in 1725 by the composer André Philidor. Its director during Mozart's sojourn in Paris was Joseph Le Gros.[34] Le Gros commissioned and performed Mozart's *Paris* Symphony with the Concert Spirituel. Although the concert apparently went well, Mozart's observations about the (solitary) rehearsal for the work are particularly noteworthy. Actually, a single rehearsal for a concert was evidently "the usual eighteenth-century practice."[35] ◄

To Leopold Mozart   *Paris, 3 July 1778*

I have had to compose a symphony for the opening of the Concert Spirituel. It was performed on Corpus Christi day [18 June] with great applause. . . . I was very nervous at the rehearsal, for never in my life have I heard a worse performance. You have no idea how they twice scraped and scrambled through it. I was really in a terrible way and would gladly have had it rehearsed again, but as there was so much else to rehearse, there was no time left. (A, 557)

► Le Gros also commissioned, but failed to perform, Mozart's Sinfonia Concertante for four wind instruments (a work now lost).[36]

The counterpart of the Concert Spirituel in Germany was the Grosses Concert in Leipzig, founded in 1743 and known since 1781 as the Gewandhaus Concerts, after the building (completed in that year) in which its concerts were held. Mozart appeared as a soloist with the Gewandhaus on 12 May 1789.

Elsewhere, such commercial concert organizations were virtually nonexistent. Artists either were asked to perform privately at court or at "house concerts" in the homes of the aristocracy or the wealthy bourgeoisie (or colleagues) for an audience of invited guests, in return perhaps for a gratuity; or they organized their own concerts themselves —for their own benefit and at their own expense. Such "Academies," as they were often called, could take place either in a rented theater or in a private home. Tickets were sold on subscription. Even before settling in Vienna Mozart served as his own concert agent on his travels through France and Germany, for example, in Strasbourg, en route home from Paris. ◄

To Leopold Mozart   *Strasbourg, 15 October 1778*

Things here are in a poor state, but the day after tomorrow, Saturday the 17th, I am giving a subscription concert *all by myself* (for the sake of economy) to please some kind friends, amateurs, and connoisseurs. If I engaged an orchestra, it would cost me, with lighting, over three louis d'or, and who knows whether I shall make that sum? (A, 625)

To Leopold Mozart   *Strasbourg, 26 October 1778*

I told you that on Saturday the 17th I was giving a concert of sorts, for to give a concert here is an even worse undertaking than in Salzburg. That, of course, is over now—I played quite alone and I engaged no musicians, so that at least I might lose nothing. Briefly, I took in three louis d'or in all. The chief receipts consisted in the shouts of "Bravo!" and "Bravissimo!" which echoed on all sides. . . . I wanted to leave Strasbourg at once, but they advised me to stay on until the following Saturday and give a grand concert in the theater. I did so and to the surprise, indignation, and disgrace of all the people of Strasbourg, my receipts were exactly the same. . . . I took in a little more money, certainly, but the cost of the orchestra, . . . the lighting, the guard, the printing, the crowds of attendants at the entrances and so forth made up a considerable sum. (A, 627)

► Immediately upon his arrival in Vienna, on 16 March 1781, Mozart was obliged to perform at private concerts on two successive days: the first at the home of the Archbishop's father, Prince Rudolph Joseph Colloredo; the second at the home of the Russian ambassador. ◄

To Leopold Mozart   *Vienna, 17 March 1781*

We had a concert yesterday at four o'clock, and at least twenty persons of the highest rank were present. . . . Today we are to go to Prince Galitzin. (A, 714)

► Within his first week in Vienna Mozart had begun to inform himself (and his father) of the general concert scene, calling attention at first to the local tradition of charity concerts during the Lenten season for the benefit of the widows and orphaned children of musicians, sponsored by the Tonkünstler-Societät, an organization founded in 1771 by the composer Joseph Starzer, among others. The charity concerts took place in the Kärntnertor Theater which, along with the Burgtheater, was one of the two court-sponsored theaters (for both musical and dramatic performance) in Vienna.[37] ◄

To Leopold Mozart   *Vienna, 24 March 1781*

Oh, had I known that I should be in Vienna during Lent, I would have written a short oratorio and produced it in the theater for my benefit, as they all do here. . . . How gladly would I give a public concert, as is the custom here. But I know for certain that I should never get permission [from the Archbishop] to do so—for just listen to this! You know that there is a society in Vienna which gives concerts for the benefit of the widows of musicians, at which every professional musician plays gratis. The orchestra is 180 strong.[38] No virtuoso who has any love for his neighbor refuses to give his services, if the society asks him to do so. Besides, in this way he can win the favor both of the Emperor and of the public. Starzer was commissioned to invite me and I agreed at once, adding, however, that I must first obtain the consent of my Prince, which I had not the slightest doubt that he would give—as it was a matter of charity, or at any rate a good work, for which I should get no fee. *He would not permit me to take part.* (A, 718)

► In the end Mozart did receive permission to perform at the Society concert, which would take place on April 3. This was to be his first public performance in Vienna. But he still was not permitted to play a concert of his own. ◄

To Leopold Mozart   Vienna, 28 March 1781

I can now add that *the Archbishop has given me permission to play at the concert for the widows.* For Starzer went to the concert at *Galitzin's* and he and *all the nobility worried the Archbishop until he gave his consent* [italicized words in code]. (A, 719)

To Leopold Mozart   Vienna, 4 April 1781

I told you in a recent letter that *the Archbishop* is a great hindrance to me here, for he has done me out of at least a hundred ducats, which I would certainly have made by giving *a concert in the theater.* Why, the ladies themselves offered *of their own accord* [emphasis in original] to distribute the tickets. I can say with truth that I was very well pleased with the Viennese public yesterday, when I played at the concert for the widows in the Kärntnertor Theater. I had to begin all over again, because there was no end to the applause. Well, how much do you suppose I should make if I were to give a concert of my own, now that the public has got to know me? [italicized words in code] (A, 720)

► Soon thereafter Mozart learned about the economic and social advantages of performing at the right private concerts in the capital—and the disadvantages of remaining in the service of the Prince-Archbishop of Salzburg. ◄

To Leopold Mozart   Vienna, 11 April 1781

For the sake of a *malevolent Prince* who *plagues me* every day and only pays me a *lousy salary of four hundred gulden,*[39] I am to *kick away a thousand?* For I should *certainly* make that sum if I *were to give a concert.* When we had our first grand concert in this house,[40] *the Archbishop sent each of us four ducats.*

At the last concert for which I composed *a new rondo for Brunetti, a new sonata* for myself, and *also a new rondo for Ceccarelli,*[41] I received *nothing.* But what made me almost *desperate* was that the very same *evening* we had this *foul* concert, I was invited to Countess Thun's, but of course could not go; and who should be there but *the Emperor!* [The singers] Adamberger and Madame Weigl were there and received fifty ducats each! [italicized words in code] (A, 723)

► By the fall of the following season Mozart was no longer in the Salzburg service. He resumed his performances for private audiences in private homes: the first concert was for the Archduke Maximilian, brother of the Emperor; the second at the home of the businessman, Joseph Michael Auernhammer, the father of Mozart's piano pupil Josepha. He also planned to offer a public concert during the upcoming season but rejected the option of sharing the costs and profits with his former Salzburg colleague, the castrato Ceccarelli. ◄

To Leopold Mozart   *Vienna, 17 November 1781*

Yesterday at three o'clock in the afternoon the Archduke Maximilian sent for me. . . . He then told me that he was intending to give a concert that very evening . . . and suggested that I should play and accompany the arias, adding that I was to come back at six o'clock when all the guests would be assembled. So I played there yesterday. (A, 779)

To Leopold Mozart   *Vienna, 24 November 1781*

I happened to be at Auernhammer's concert yesterday. . . . At the concert there were Countess Thun (whom I had invited), Baron van Swieten, Baron Godenus, the rich converted Jew Wetzlar, Count Firmian. . . . We [Mozart and Josepha] played the concerto a due [K. 365 (316a)] and a sonata for two claviers [K. 448 (375a)] which I had composed expressly for the occasion. . . . No doubt Ceccarelli will want to give a concert with me. But he won't succeed, for I don't care about going shares with people. All that I can do, as I intend to give a concert in Lent, is to let him sing at it and then to play for him gratis at his own. (A, 779–780)

► Before the end of the year, on Christmas Eve, Mozart delivered his most famous private performance—the piano contest with Muzio Clementi held at the command and in the presence of Emperor Joseph in the imperial palace, the Hofburg. ◄

To Leopold Mozart   *Vienna, 26 December 1781*

The day before yesterday, December 24, I played at Court. Another clavier player, an Italian called Clementi, has arrived here. He too had been invited to Court. I was sent fifty ducats yesterday for my playing. (A, 789–790)

▶ Mozart resumed planning for his public concert, which ultimately took place on 3 March 1782, inaugurating his tradition of Lenten concerts which continued into the following years. Serving as his own concert manager could only have been an irritant and a distraction from more rewarding endeavors, such as composing. ◀

To Leopold Mozart   *Vienna, 23 January 1782*

There is nothing more disagreeable than to be obliged to live in uncertainty, not knowing what is happening. Such is my case at the moment with regard to my concert; and it is the same with everyone who wishes to give one. Last year the Emperor intended to continue the plays throughout Lent; perhaps he may do so this year. Basta! At all events I have secured the day (if there is no play), namely, the third Sunday in Lent. If I know a fortnight ahead, I shall be satisfied; otherwise my whole plan will be upset, or I shall be obliged to incur expenses for nothing. (A, 794)

SERIES SUBSCRIPTIONS

▶ There were some initiatives to establish commercial concert series by one Philipp Jakob Martin. As Mozart reports, this impresario had inaugurated a winter series in the Mehlgrube, an inn located in the Neuer Markt, a public square. A summer series was to take place in the Augarten, the elegant park in the Leopoldstadt section of Vienna which had been the private property of the Emperors until Joseph II dedicated them to the public in 1775. The first Augarten concert took place on May 26. ◀

To Leopold Mozart   *Vienna, 8 May 1782*

This summer there is to be a concert every Sunday in the Augarten. A certain Martin organized last winter a series of amateur concerts, which took place every Friday in the Mehlgrube. You know that there are a great many amateurs in Vienna, and some very good ones, too, both men and women. But so far these concerts have not been properly arranged. Well, this Martin has now got permission from the Emperor under charter (with the promise too of his gracious patronage) to give twelve concerts in the Augarten and four grand serenades in the finest open places in the city. The subscription for the whole summer is two ducats. So you can imagine that we shall have plenty of subscribers, the more so as I am taking an interest in it and am associated with it. Assuming that we get only a hundred subscribers, then each of us will have a profit of three hundred gulden (even if the costs amount to two hundred gulden, which is most unlikely). The Baron van Swieten and Countess Thun are very much interested in it. The orchestra consists entirely of amateurs, with the exception of the bassoon players, the trumpeters, and the drummers. (A, 804–805)

▶ During the 1783 season Mozart continued to participate in both private and public concerts. The highlights of the season were the recital of his sister-in-law Aloysia Lange on March 11, in which Mozart participated, and his own concert on March 23, at which the Emperor was present and gave Mozart twenty-five ducats. Both concerts took place in the Burgtheater. (The programs are described below, p. 82-83.) For the 1784 season, however, Mozart planned an ambitious and ultimately highly successful series of subscription concerts. ◀

To Leopold Mozart   *Vienna, 6 December 1783*

Please send me as soon as possible my *Idomeneo* . . . I require *Idomeneo* because during Lent I am going to give, as well as my concert in the theater, six subscription concerts, at which I should like to produce this opera. (A, 862)

To Leopold Mozart   *Vienna, 3 March 1784*

I am giving three subscription concerts in Trattner's room on the last three Wednesdays of Lent, beginning on March 17.[42] I have a hundred subscribers already and shall easily get another thirty. The price for the three concerts is six gulden. I shall probably give two concerts in the theater this year. Well, as you may imagine, I must play some new works—and therefore I must compose . . . Below you will find a list of all the concerts at which I am playing. But I must tell you quickly how it has come about that all of a sudden I am giving private concerts. [Georg Friedrich] Richter, the clavier virtuoso, is giving six Saturday concerts in the said room. The nobility subscribed, but remarked that they really did not care much about going unless I played. So Richter asked me to do so. I promised to play three times and then arranged three concerts for myself, to which they all subscribed. Below you will find a list of all the concerts at which I am playing . . .

▶ The list notes twenty-two engagements, all to take place during the five-week period from February 26 to April 3, and to be held variously at the palaces of such distinguished noblemen as the Russian Prince Galitzin and Count Johann Esterházy, as well as the home of the pianist Richter. At one point Mozart was to give six concerts on six consecutive days (between Wednesday, 17 March, and Monday, 22 March). The series included the following highlights:

Wednesday [March] 17, my first *private* concert . . .

Sunday 21, my first concert *in the theater* . . .

Wednesday 24, my second *private* concert . . .

Wednesday 31, my third *private* concert

Thursday April 1, my second concert *in the theater.*
  (A, 869-70)

To Leopold Mozart   *Vienna, 20 March 1784*

I am sending you the list of all my subscribers. I alone have thirty more than Richter and Fischer[43] together. The first concert on March 17 went off very well. (A, 870–872)

► The appended list records 174 names—among them, in addition to untitled individuals, numerous princes, princesses, counts, countesses, barons, a bishop, and the Spanish ambassador. ◄

To Leopold Mozart   *Vienna, 10 April 1784*

I have done myself great credit with my three subscription concerts, and the concert I gave in the theater was most successful. I composed two grand concertos [the Piano Concertos in B-flat and D, K. 450, K. 451] and then a quintet [for piano and winds, K. 452], which called forth the very greatest applause . . . It is greatly to my credit that my listeners never got tired. (A, 873)

MISCELLANEOUS ENTERTAINMENTS

► On more than one occasion Mozart describes music-making sessions that can be euphemistically described as "informal" in character and quality. Among them were performances staged by his fellow musicians in his honor and to his great delight. ◄

To Leopold Mozart   *Munich, 3 October 1777*

About half past nine in the evening a small orchestra of five players, two clarinets, two horns, and one bassoon, came up to the house. Herr Albert [the innkeeper] (whose name-day is tomorrow) had ordered this music in his and my honor. They did not play at all badly together. They were the same people who play in Albert's dining hall during the meals . . . Tomorrow we are going to have a little scratch-concert [schlackakademie] among ourselves, but, I should add, on that wretched clavier. (A, 293)

To Leopold Mozart   *Mannheim, 13 November 1777*

[Ignaz von Beecke, the pianist] expressed great regret that he himself

happened to have a sore throat (which was perfectly true) and that he
could not therefore take me out himself and entertain me. He was sorry
too that he could not arrange some music in my honor, but on that very
day most of the performers had taken a holiday and gone out walking to
some place or other. (A, 368)

To Leopold Mozart   *Mannheim, 22 February 1778*

Tomorrow I must go out, for our house nymph, Mlle. Pierron, my highly
esteemed pupil, is to scramble through my concerto (written for the high
and mighty Countess Lützow)[44] at the French concert which is held every
Monday. I, too, prostitution though it may be, shall ask them to give
me something to strum and shall contrive to thump it out *prima fista*.
(A, 488)

To Leopold Mozart   *Vienna, 3 November 1781*

At eleven o'clock at night I was treated to a serenade [eine NachtMusick]
performed by two clarinets, two horns, and two bassoons—and that too of
my own composition [the Serenade in E-flat, K. 375, ex. 3.1]—for I wrote it
for St. Theresa's Day [October 15] . . . The six gentlemen who executed it
are poor beggars who, however, play quite well together, particularly the
first clarinet and the two horns . . . On St. Theresa's Night it was
performed in three different places; for as soon as they finished playing it
in one place, they were taken off somewhere else and paid to play it. Well,
these musicians asked that the street door might be opened and, placing
themselves in the center of the courtyard, surprised me just as I was about
to undress, in the most pleasant fashion imaginable with the first chord in
E-flat. (A, 776)

EXAMPLE 3.1. Serenade in E-flat for Wind Instruments, K. 375, Opening
Chords

► For the most part, Mozart's compositions for wind instruments belonged to the genre of "occasional music." The various wind divertimenti of the Salzburg period, for example, are thought to have been
  written for banquets at the archiepiscopal court. In short, they were
  intended not for a formal concert performance but as an accompaniment for some other activity—much like "dinner" or "background"

music today. In the eighteenth century it was referred to variously (and for the most part, arbitrarily) as "serenade," "divertimento," "Tafel-musik," "Nachtmusik," and so on. In a letter from Prague to his Viennese friend Gottfried von Jacquin, Mozart describes a variant of the practice, not necessarily confined to wind instruments, and indicates how it could dissolve into a jam session of sorts. ◄

To Gottfried von Jacquin   *Prague, 15 January 1787*

After the meal old Count Thun entertained us with some music, per-formed by his own people, which lasted about an hour and a half. This kind of *real entertainment* I could enjoy every day . . . After lunch [on the following day] the Count's music must always be listened to, and as on that very day an excellent pianoforte had been put in my room, you may readily suppose that I did not leave it unused and untouched for the whole evening; and that as a matter of course we performed amongst ourselves a little *Quatour in caritatis camera*[45] ("und das schöne Bandl hammera")[46] and in this way the whole evening was spent *sine linea* [i.e., without composing a note]. (A, 903)

► As reported in a note to Constanze, during the concert tour of 1789 Mozart experienced in quick succession the two social extremes of an eighteenth-century musician's life: a private musicale with friends followed by a sudden command performance before a crowned head of state—on this occasion the Elector of Saxony, Friedrich August III. The mode of payment for the latter performance is notable. ◄

To Constanze Mozart   *Dresden, 16 April 1789*

While we[47] were at table a message came that I was to play at court on the following day, Tuesday, April 14, at half past five in the evening. That is something quite out of the ordinary for Dresden, for it is usually very difficult to get a hearing, and you know that I never thought of performing at Court here. We had arranged a quartet among ourselves at the Hôtel de Pologne. So we performed it in the Chapel with Anton Teiber (who, as you know, is organist here) and with Herr [Anton] Kraft, Prince Esterházy's cellist, who is here with his son. At this little concert I introduced the trio [i.e., the Divertimento in E-flat, K. 563, for violin, viola, and cello] which I wrote for Herr von Puchberg and it was played quite decently. Madame Duschek sang a number of arias from *Figaro* and *Don Giovanni*. The next day I played at Court my new Concerto in D [K. 537], and on the following morning, Wednesday, April 15, I received a very handsome snuffbox.[48] Then we lunched at the Russian Ambassador's, where I played a great deal. After lunch we agreed to have some organ playing and drove to the church at four o'clock. (A, 923)

CONCERT PROGRAMS

► Mozart's letters provide abundant information on the contents of his concert programs. They are typical for their time in their great length and their great variety. The modern convention of programming is characterized by a uniformity of performance medium, on the one hand (i.e., either a piano recital, or a string quartet, or an orchestral concert—with or without a soloist) but a variety of historical styles (usually offered in chronological sequence: the eighteenth, then the nineteenth, then the twentieth century), on the other. Mozart's programs, in contrast, were historically unified, consisting entirely of contemporary music (often exclusively his own), but otherwise altogether heterogeneous in style, genre, and medium, featuring both improvised and composed music, with the latter often performed by a varied assortment of soloists and ensembles. Equally striking was the tradition of separating the constituent movements of a single large composition—for example, a symphony—from one another, playing the opening movements at the beginning of a concert and the finale at the end. What we may infer from this practice about Mozart's personal understanding of the aesthetic unity of such a work as the *Haffner* Symphony is far from obvious. ◄

To Leopold Mozart   *Munich, 6 October 1777*

Saturday the 4th . . . we had a little concert here [at the inn], which began at half past three and finished at about eight. (A, 299–300)

To Leopold Mozart   *Augsburg, 16 October 1777*

After lunch [at the home of the Augsburg Magistrate Jakob Langenmantel] I played two concertos, improvised something, and then played the violin in one of Hafeneder's[49] trios. I would gladly have done some more fiddling, but I was accompanied so badly that it gave me the colic . . . When we got back from the theater, I played again until we went to supper. (A, 323)

► A week later, Mozart described the program for his public concert held at the Fuggerhaus in Augsburg on October 22. ◄

To Leopold Mozart   *Augsburg, 24 October 1777*

Now what does Papa think that we played immediately after the symphony? Why, the Concerto for Three Claviers [in F, K. 242]. Herr Demmler [the cathedral organist] played the first, I the second, and Herr [Johann Andreas] Stein [the famous piano maker] the third. Then I gave a solo, my last sonata in D [K. 284 (205b)], written for Baron Dürnitz, and after, my concerto in B-flat [K. 238]. I then played another solo, quite in the style of

the organ, a fugue in C minor and then all of a sudden a magnificent
sonata in C major, out of my head, and a Rondo to finish up with. There
was a regular din of applause. Herr Stein was so amazed that he could only
make faces and grimaces. As for Herr Demmler, he couldn't stop laughing.
(A, 340)

▶ At Mannheim Mozart was often the featured artist at house concerts
held in the home of Christian Cannabich, the director of the Mannheim
Court orchestra. ◀

To Leopold Mozart   *Mannheim, 14 February 1778*

Yesterday there was a concert at Cannabich's, where all the music was of
my composition, except the first symphony, which was his own. Mlle.
Rosa [Cannabich] played my concerto in B-flat [K. 238], then Herr Ramm
(by way of a change) played for the fifth time my oboe concerto [in D, K.
314 (285d)] written for Ferlendis, which is making a great sensation here.
It is now Ramm's cheval de bataille. After that Mlle. [Aloysia] Weber sang
most charmingly the aria di bravura of De Amicis ["Ah, se il crudel" from
Lucio Silla.] Then I played my old concerto in D major [K. 175], because it is
such a favorite here, and I also extemporized for half an hour; after which
Mlle. Weber sang De Amicis's aria "Parto, m'affretto" [from *Lucio Silla*] and
was loudly applauded. Finally my overture to *Il Rè pastore* [K. 208] was
performed. (A, 482)

To Leopold Mozart   *Paris, 24 March 1778*

Thursday [12 March] there was an afternoon concert at Cannabich's,
where my Concerto for Three Claviers [K. 242] was played. Mlle. Rosa
Cannabich played the first, Mlle. Weber the second, and Mlle. Pierron
Serrarius, our house nymph, the third. We had three rehearsals of the
concerto and it went off very well. Mlle. Weber sang two arias of mine, the
"Aer tranquillo" from *Il Rè pastore* [K. 208] and my new one, "Non so
d'onde viene" [K. 294] . . . It was the first time I had heard it with
orchestral accompaniment. (A, 517)

▶ En route to Salzburg after the Paris sojourn Mozart gave a financially
unrewarding solo concert on 17 October 1778 in Strasbourg (see above,
p. 71). At the urging of his hosts he scheduled two concerts with
orchestra for the 24th and 31st—again to a small audience and with
little financial return. He reported on the concert of the 24th as
follows. ◀

To Leopold Mozart   *Strasbourg, 26 October 1778*

In order to show these gentlemen of Strasbourg how little I cared, I played a very long time for my own amusement, giving one more concerto than I had promised—and, in the end, extemporizing for quite a while. Well, that is over—and at least I have won honor and glory. (A, 627)

► Mozart's programs and the program plans for his public and private concerts in Vienna are frequently described and discussed in the letters. The following should convey an idea of their imaginativeness and variety. ◄

To Leopold Mozart   *Vienna, 24 March 1781*

You know that there is a society in Vienna that gives concerts for the benefit of the widows of musicians. [See above.] . . . My Prince . . . *would not permit me to take part* . . . I am only sorry for the following reason. I should not have played a concerto, but (as the Emperor sits in the proscenium box) I should have extemporized and played a fugue[50] and then the variations on "Je suis Lindor" [K. 354/299a] on Countess Thun's beautiful Stein pianoforte, which she would have lent me. Whenever I have played this program in public, I have always won the greatest applause—because the items set one another off so well, and because everyone has something to his taste. (A, 718)

To Leopold Mozart   *Vienna, 13 June 1781*

For the Archbishop's concert [on April 8] I composed a sonata for myself [K. 379 (373a)], a rondo for Brunetti [K. 373], and one for Ceccarelli [K. 374] At each concert[51] I played twice and the last time when the concert was over I went on playing variations (for which the Archbishop gave me the theme) for a whole hour. (A, 742)

► Mozart provides a vivid description of the unusual program that was followed during his contest with Clementi on 24 December 1781. ◄

To Leopold Mozart   *Vienna, 16 January 1782*

After we had stood on ceremony long enough, the Emperor declared that Clementi ought to begin. "La Santa Chiesa Cattolica," he said, Clementi being a Roman. He improvised and then played a sonata. The Emperor then turned to me: "Allons, fire away." I improvised and played variations. The Grand Duchess produced some sonatas by Paisiello (wretchedly written out in his own hand), of which I had to play the Allegros and Clementi the Andantes and Rondos. We then selected a theme from them and developed it on two pianofortes. The funny thing was that although I had borrowed Countess Thun's pianoforte, I only played on it when I played alone; such was the Emperor's desire—and, by the way, the other instrument was out of tune and three of the keys were stuck. "Never mind," said the Emperor. Well, I put the best construction on it I could, that is, that the Emperor, already knowing my skill and my knowledge of music, merely wanted to show especial courtesy to a foreigner. Besides, I have it from a very good source that he was extremely pleased with me. He was very gracious, said a great deal to me privately, and even mentioned my marriage. (A, 793)

► The first of Mozart's famous Lenten concerts in Vienna was held on 3 March 1782. Planning of the program began early. ◄

To Leopold Mozart　　　　　　　　　　*Vienna, 23 January 1782*

With regard to my concert . . . I have secured the day . . . namely, the third Sunday in Lent [i.e., March 3]. . . . Countess Thun, Adamberger, and other good friends of mine are advising me to select the best scenes from my Munich opera [*Idomeneo*] and have them performed in the theater, and myself to play only one concerto [K. 175, with a newly composed finale, K. 382] and to improvise at the close. I too had thought of doing this and I have now quite decided to do so, particularly as Clementi is also giving a concert. So I shall have a slight advantage over him, the more so as I shall probably be able to give mine twice. (A, 794)

To Leopold Mozart　　　　　　　　　　*Vienna, 25 May 1782*

Tomorrow our first concert takes place in the Augarten. [See above.] . . . In the evening we are having the rehearsal of the concert. A symphony by Van Swieten and one of mine[52] are being performed; an amateur singer, Mlle. Berger, is going to sing; a boy of the name of Türk is playing a violin concerto; and Fräulein Auernhammer and I are playing my E-flat concerto for two pianos [K. 365 (316a)]. (A, 805)

► The highlights of the 1783 season, as far as Mozart was concerned, were the concerts of Aloysia Lange on March 11, and his own on the 23rd. Both took place in the Burgtheater. ◄

To Leopold Mozart　　　　　　　　　　*Vienna, 12 March 1783*

My sister-in-law, Madame Lange, gave her concert yesterday in the theater and I played a concerto [K. 175 with the rondo K. 382]. The theater was very full and I was received again by the Viennese public so cordially that I really ought to feel delighted. I had already left the platform, but the audience would not stop clapping and so I had to repeat the rondo, upon which there was a regular torrent of applause. It is a good advertisement for my concert which I am giving on Sunday, March 23. I added my symphony, which I composed for the Concert Spirituel.[53] My sister-in-law sang the aria "Non so d'onde viene" [K. 294]. (A, 841–842)

To Leopold Mozart *Vienna, 29 March 1783*

I need not tell you very much about the success of my concert [on the 23rd], for no doubt you have already heard of it. Suffice it to say that the theater could not have been more crowded and that every box was full . . . Our program was as follows:

(1) [The orchestra played] the new *Haffner* Symphony [K.385].
(2) Madame Lange sang the aria "Se il padre perdei" from my Munich opera, accompanied by four instruments [Ilia's aria from *Idomeneo*].[54]
(3) I played the third of my subscription concertos [the Piano Concerto in C major, K. 415 (387b)].
(4) Adamberger sang the scena which I composed for Countess Baumgarten ["Misera, dove son," K. 369.][55]
(5) The short concertante symphonie from my last Finalmusik [Movement 3 from the Serenade in D, K. 320].
(6) I played my concerto in D major [K. 175], which is such a favorite here, and of which I sent you the rondo with variations [K. 382].
(7) Mlle. [Therese] Teiber sang the scena "Parto, m'affretto" out of my last Milan opera [*Lucio Silla*, no. 16].
(8) I played alone a short fugue (because the Emperor was present) and then variations on an air from an opera called *Die Philosophen* [K. 398 (416e)],[56] which were encored. So I played variations on the air "Unser dummer Pöbel meint" from Gluck's *Pilgrimme von Mekka* [K. 455].
(9) Madame Lange sang my new rondo ["Ah, non sai, qual pena," K. 416].
(10) The last movement of the first symphony [K. 385].

Mlle Teiber is giving a concert tomorrow, at which I am going to play. (A, 843)

To Leopold Mozart *Vienna, 12 April 1783*

I was to play at another concert [on March 30th], that is, at Mlle. Teiber's. The Emperor was there too. I played my first concerto which I played at my concert [K. 415 (387b)]. I was asked to repeat the rondo. So I sat down again; but instead of repeating it I had the conductor's rostrum removed and played alone. You should have heard how delighted the public were with this little surprise. (A, 845)

To Leopold Mozart *Vienna, 24 December 1783*

The day before yesterday, Monday, we had another grand concert of the [Tonkünstler] society, when I played a concerto and Adamberger sang a rondo of my composition.[57] The concert was repeated yesterday, but a violinist played a concerto in my place. The day before yesterday the theater was full. Yesterday it was empty. I should add that it was the violinist's first performance. (A, 866)

Leopold Mozart to Nannerl   *Salzburg, 13 January 1786*

Meanwhile to two letters of mine I have had only one reply from your brother, dated December 28, in which he said that he gave without much preparation three subscription concerts to 120 subscribers, that he composed for this purpose a new piano concerto in E-flat [K. 482], in which (a rather unusual occurrence!) he had to repeat the Andante.[58] (A, 895)

THE OPERA WORLD

CONTRACT NEGOTIATIONS

► Opera, as everyone knows, is not only a major art form but a big business, as well. And never, surely, is a composer more obliged to act and think like a businessman than when he is negotiating the terms for an opera commission. Apart from securing the commission in the first place Mozart had to settle a couple of prosaic but substantial concerns before he could turn his attention to such a fundamental artistic issue as, say, the choice of a librettist and a libretto. To begin with, there were, of course, the matter and the manner of his payment. Mozart makes clear that it was not always self-evident that he would receive a fixed fee agreed upon in advance. Second, and no less important, he had to be assured that his opera would in fact be produced and performed. Despite his oft-repeated eagerness to compose operas, Mozart simply did not sit down to write one unless he was satisfied on these points. He was particularly on his guard in Paris and Mannheim; but even in Vienna he did not hesitate to reject operatic proposals. Shortly before his departure from Paris on 26 September 1778 Mozart reported: ◄

To Leopold Mozart   *Paris, 11 September 1778*

Now that I have said that I am going away I could easily get a commission for an opera; but I have told [the ballet master, Jean Georges] Noverre: "If you will guarantee that *it will be performed* as soon as it is finished, and will tell me exactly what I am going to get for it, I will stay on for another three months and compose it." For I could not reject the offer at once, or people would have thought that I distrusted myself. Noverre could not agree to these terms (and I knew beforehand that he couldn't), for they are not the terms that are ordinarily offered here. What happens in Paris, as you probably know, is this: When the opera is finished, it is rehearsed and if these stupid Frenchmen do not like it, it is not performed, and the composer has had all his trouble for nothing. If they think it is good, it is produced and paid for in proportion to its success with the public. There is no certainty whatever. (A, 613)

► Two months later Mozart stated even more precise terms to the manager of the Mannheim national theater. There were evidently two offers on the table: to compose a *monodrama*—more precisely, a *duodrama*, also known as a *melodrama*, a work for spoken voices with musical accompaniment entitled *Semiramis*, on a text by Otto von Gemmingen; and an "opera"—but also apparently with no sung parts—concerning which negotiations had already been initiated with the composers Gluck and Schweitzer.[59] ◄

To Baron Heribert von Dalberg　　　　　*Mannheim, 24 November 1778*

I therefore take the liberty of stating my final conditions, as it is quite impossible for me to remain here any longer in uncertainty. I undertake to compose a monodrama for the sum of twenty-five louis d'or, to stay on here for another two months, to make all the arrangements which will be necessary in connection with it, to attend all the rehearsals and so forth, but on the condition that whatever happens, I shall be paid by the end of January. In addition I shall of course expect free admission to the theater. You see, my dear Baron, that this is all I can do! If you consider it carefully, you will admit that I am certainly acting with great discretion. In regard to your opera I assure you that I should be delighted to compose the music for it; but you yourself must agree that I could not undertake this work for twenty-five louis d'or, as (reckoned at its lowest) it would be twice the labor of writing a monodrama. Again, what would deter me most would be the fact that Gluck and Schweitzer, as you yourself told me, are already composing the music. Yet, even assuming that you were willing to give me fifty louis d'or, I should still as an honest man most certainly dissuade you from the undertaking. An opera without male and female singers! What an extraordinary idea! Still, if in the meantime there is a prospect of its being performed, I shall not refuse to undertake the work to oblige you—but it would be no light task, that I swear to you on my honor. Well, I have now set forth my ideas clearly and candidly and I request your decision as soon as possible. (A, 637)

► In the end nothing became of these Mannheim plans.

　　In Vienna, before taking on an operatic project, Mozart had to be concerned about the censorship power wielded by the imperial director of the court theaters, Count Orsini-Rosenberg. ◄

To Leopold Mozart　　　　　*Vienna, 16 June 1781*

Even if I had a libretto, I would not put pen to paper, since Count

Rosenberg is not here; and if at the last moment he did not approve of it, I should have had the honor of composing for nothing. (A, 746)

▶ In Vienna, too, the terms of payment had to be individually negotiated. After the success of *Die Entführung* in 1782 (for which he received a flat 100 ducats, or 450 gulden), Mozart contemplated producing his next opera buffa at his own expense and for his own benefit. His normal practice during the Vienna years, however, with the possible exception of *Die Zauberflöte* (about which nothing concerning the financial arrangements is known), was to compose operas on commission for a set fee. For *Le nozze di Figaro* (1786) and *Don Giovanni* (1787) he again received one hundred ducats each; for *La Clemenza di Tito* (1791), two hundred. (He presumably was paid the same amount in 1790 for *Così fan tutte*.) ◀

To Leopold Mozart   *Vienna, 5 October 1782*

I am willing to write an opera, but not to look on with a hundred ducats in my pocket and see the theater making four times as much in a fortnight. I intend to produce my opera at my own expense; I shall clear at least 1,200 gulden by three performances and then the management may have it for fifty ducats. If they refuse to take it, I shall have made some money and can produce the opera anywhere. (A, 826)

▶ Several months later Mozart turned to the librettist of *Idomeneo*, the Salzburg cleric Abbate Giambattista Varesco, for an opera buffa libretto. He described the arrangements for payment in a letter to his father as follows. ◀

To Leopold Mozart   *Vienna, 7 May 1783*

Tell [Varesco] too that his share will certainly amount to four hundred or five hundred gulden, for the custom here is that the poet gets the takings of the third performance. (A, 848)

▶ Mozart was exaggerating. Five hundred gulden would have been more than his own normal earning for an opera, whereas the librettist usually received no more than half the fee of the composer. In 1786 Lorenzo Da Ponte would receive just two hundred gulden for the libretto of *Figaro* and two hundred twenty-five gulden (fifty ducats) in 1787 for *Don Giovanni*. Varesco and Mozart soon embarked on an opera buffa project, *L'Oca del Cairo*, which turned out to be doomed. (See Chapter 9.)

In 1785 Anton Klein (1748–1810), a librettist and author of *Günther von Schwarzburg*, a successful singspiel set to music by Ignaz Holzbauer, sent Mozart the text of his drama, *Kaiser Rudolf von Habsburg* and requested that Mozart set it as an opera. Mozart admired Holzbauer's opera but not Klein's libretto. (See Chapter 13.) At all events, Klein's request elicited the following response in which he again emphasizes the need to guarantee a production in advance. Mozart never set Klein's text. ◄

To Anton Klein   *Vienna, 21 May 1785*

As for the opera . . . I beg you to leave the play with me for a little longer. If I should feel inclined to set it to music, I should like to know beforehand whether its production has actually been arranged for a particular place, since a work of this kind, from the point of view both of the poetry and of the music, deserves a better fate than to be composed to no purpose. I trust that you will clear up this point. (A, 890–891)

REHEARSALS: PREPARING THE PREMIERE OF *Idomeneo*

► After the negotiating and the composing but before there could be a performance, there had to be rehearsals. Mozart's letters from Munich describing the preparations for the premiere of *Idomeneo* are most informative on the number and nature of the rehearsals that preceded the staging of an ambitious new opera. In marked contrast to the practice regarding orchestral performances which, as we have seen (p. 70, above), normally had just a single rehearsal, Mozart's account reveals that opera rehearsals were both numerous and intense. They included recitative rehearsals as well as several offstage rehearsals with partial forces before a full-scale dress rehearsal in the theater. ◄

To Leopold Mozart   *Munich, 1 December 1780*

The rehearsal went off extremely well. There were only six violins in all, but we had the requisite wind instruments. No listeners were admitted except Count Seeau's sister and young Count Sensheim. This day week we are to have another rehearsal, when we shall have twelve fiddlers for the first act (which I am having copied for double forces in the meantime), and when the second act will be rehearsed (like the first on the previous occasion). (A, 677)

To Leopold Mozart   *Munich, 16 December 1780*

Acts 1 and 2 are being rehearsed again this afternoon in the Count's [Seeau] apartments; then we shall have a chamber rehearsal of act 3 only, and afterwards go straight to the theater. The rehearsal has been put off again and again on account of the copyist. (A, 690)

To Leopold Mozart   *Munich, 19 December 1780*

The second rehearsal went off as well as the first . . . Next Saturday both acts are to be rehearsed again. But this time the rehearsal is to be held in a large hall at court, and this I have long wished for, because there is not nearly enough room at Count Seeau's. The Elector is to listen incognito in an adjoining room. Well, as Cannabich said to me, "We shall have to rehearse like the deuce." At the last rehearsal he was dripping with perspiration. (A, 692)

Munich, 27 December 1780

The last rehearsal was splendid. It took place in a spacious room at court. The Elector was there, too. This time we rehearsed with the whole orchestra (I mean, of course, with as many players as can be accommodated in the opera house). After the first act the Elector called out to me loudly, "Bravo!" . . .

As he was not sure whether he could remain much longer, we had to perform the aria with obbligatos for wind instruments [Ilia's aria, "Se il padre perdei"] and the thunderstorm at the beginning of act 2 . . . The next rehearsal will probably be in the theater. (A, 698)

To Leopold Mozart   *Munich, 30 December 1780*

The day before yesterday we had a rehearsal of recitatives at Wendling's and we went through the quartet together. We repeated it six times and now it goes well. The stumbling block was [the castrato Vincenzo] dal Prato. (A, 701)

To Leopold Mozart   *Munich, 10 January 1781*

The latest news is that the opera has been postponed again for a week. The dress rehearsal will not take place until the 27th—my birthday, mark you—and the first performance on the 29th. Why? Presumably in order that Count Seeau may save a few hundred gulden. But I am delighted, as it will give us an opportunity of further and more careful rehearsals . . . Next Saturday the three acts are to be rehearsed in private. (A, 706)

To Leopold Mozart   *Munich, 18 January 1781*

Please forgive a short letter, but I must be off to the rehearsal this very moment (it is almost ten o'clock—in the morning, of course). For the first time we are having a rehearsal of recitatives today in the theater . . . The rehearsal of act 3 went off splendidly. It was considered much superior to the first two acts. (A, 708)

INTRIGUES AND CABALS

► No self-respecting opera scene would be complete without its intrigues and cabals. Mozart's first encounter with this time-honored tradition came when he was barely twelve years old. In January 1768, at the behest of Joseph II, Mozart had begun to compose his very first opera, an opera buffa, *La finta semplice*, K 51/46a, based on a text by Carlo Goldoni. By June the work was done and rehearsals had begun. But efforts against the performance of the work had begun as well. Rumors circulated in Vienna insinuating that the boy was not capable of writing an opera: that the actual composer was not Wolfgang but Leopold Mozart. Moreover, it was deemed highly inappropriate in any case for a mere child to be directing an opera at the imperial theater. Despite the Emperor's orders for an investigation into the matter, pressures from the musicians, the singers, and above all, from the impresario, Giuseppe d'Affligio, insured that the work was never produced in Vienna.

Some fourteen years later, in July 1782, Mozart had finally managed to produce a new opera for the imperial city: *Die Entführung aus dem Serail.* This time he himself reported on the hostile reception that was organized to greet the first performances. Another incident ensued the following year. Mozart prepared some arias for insertion into an opera buffa by another composer, the prolific Pasquale Anfossi. This altogether common practice precipitated an even more unpleasant encounter with the cabal, of which the principal victim was not Mozart but rather the leading tenor of the court opera, Johann Valentin Adamberger. ◄

To Leopold Mozart *Vienna, 20 July 1782*

[*Die Entführung*] was given yesterday for the second time. Can you really believe it, but yesterday there was an even stronger cabal against it than on the first evening! The whole first act was accompanied by hissing. But indeed they could not prevent the loud shouts of "bravo" during the arias. (A, 807–808)

To Leopold Mozart *Vienna, 2 July 1783*

Anfossi's opera *Il curioso indiscreto,* in which Madame Lange and Adamberger appeared for the first time, was performed the day before yesterday, Monday, for the first time. It failed completely with the exception of my two arias,[60] the second of which, a bravura, had to be repeated. Well, I should like you to know that my friends were malicious enough to spread the report beforehand that *"Mozart wanted to improve on Anfossi's opera."* I heard of this and sent a message to Count Rosenberg that I would not hand over my arias unless the following statement were printed in the copies of the libretto, both in German and in Italian.

Notice
The two arias . . . have been set to music by Signor Maestro Mozart to suit Signora Lange, because the arias of Signor Maestro Anfossi were not written for her voice but for another singer. It is necessary that this should be pointed out so that honor may be given to whom

it is due and so that the reputation and the name of the most famous Neapolitan may not suffer in any way whatsoever.

Well, the statement was inserted and I handed out my arias, which did inexpressible honor to my sister-in-law and to myself. So my enemies were quite confounded! And now for one of Salieri's tricks, which has injured poor Adamberger more than me. I think I told you that I had composed a rondo for Adamberger.[61] During a short rehearsal, before the rondo had been copied, Salieri took Adamberger aside and told him that Count Rosenberg would not be pleased if he put in an aria and that he had advised him as his good friend not to do so. Adamberger, provoked by Rosenberg's objection and not knowing how to retaliate, was stupid enough to say, with ill-timed pride, *"All right. But to prove that Adamberger has already made his reputation in Vienna and does not need to make a name for himself by singing music expressly written for him, he will only sing what is in the opera and will never again, as long as he lives, introduce any aria."* What was the result? Why, that he was a complete failure, as was only to be expected! Now he is sorry, but it is too late. For if he were to ask me this very day to give him the rondo, I should refuse. I can easily find a place for it in one of my own operas.[62] (A, 854)

AUDIENCES

► Finally, we come to the raison d'être for the entire effort: the audience, indisputably an indispensable element in the musical life of Mozart's or any time. Mozart's sensitivity to the behavior and attentiveness of his audience was documented earlier.[63] He was also fascinated enough by the varieties of audience behavior to raise the subject time and again, classifying the remarkable phenomena both by nationality and social class. Among other things, it is notable that audiences were free to applaud or shout "bravo" between, and even during, the individual movements of a concerto or symphony—not unlike a modern jazz concert—and that Mozart had no objection to this custom at all, so long as they paid attention and understood. ◄

ITALY AND FRANCE

To Nannerl	*Verona, 7 January 1770*

There is so much whispering in the theater that you can't hear anything [Italian] . . . Everyone is masked now and it is really very convenient when you wear your mask, as you have the advantage of not having to take off your hat when you are greeted and of not having to address the person by name. (A, 105)

I have had to compose a symphony for the opening of the Concert Spirituel.[64] . . . Just in the middle of the first Allegro there was a passage which I felt sure must please. The audience was quite carried away and there was a tremendous burst of applause. But, as I knew, when I wrote it, what effect it would surely produce, I had introduced the passage again at the close—when there were shouts of "Da capo."[65] . . . The Andante also found favor, but particularly the last Allegro, because, having observed that all last as well as first Allegros begin here with all the instruments playing together and generally unisono, I began mine with two violins only, piano for the first eight bars, followed instantly by a forte [ex. 3.2]; the audience, as I expected, said "Hush" at the soft beginning, and when they heard the forte, began at once to clap their hands. (A, 557–558) ◄

EXAMPLE 3.2. *Paris* Symphony, K. 297(300a): Movement 3, mm. 1-15

Salzburg and Vienna

To Leopold Mozart   *Vienna, 26 May 1781*

You yourself must admit that in Salzburg . . . there is no stimulus for my
talent! When I play or when any of my compositions are performed, it is
just as if the audience were all tables and chairs. (A, 736)

To Leopold Mozart   *Vienna, 4 April 1781*

I can say with truth that I was very well pleased with the Viennese public
yesterday, when I played at the concert for the widows in the Kärntnerthor
theater. I had to begin all over again, because there was no end to the
applause. (A, 720)

To Leopold Mozart   *Vienna, 8 April 1781*

I told you about the applause in the theater, but I must add that what delighted and surprised me most of all was the amazing silence—and also the cries of "Bravo!" while I was playing. This is certainly honor enough in Vienna, where there are such numbers and numbers of good pianists. (A, 722)

THE ARISTOCRACY

To Leopold Mozart   *Munich, 2 October 1777*

[Count Salern] really understands music, for all the time he kept on shouting "Bravo," where other noblemen would take a pinch of snuff, blow their noses, clear their throats—or start a conversation. (A, 289–90)

To Leopold Mozart   *Paris, 1 May 1778*

I played on that miserable, wretched pianoforte [at the house of Madame la Duchesse de Chabot]. But what vexed me most of all was that Madame and all her gentlemen never interrupted their drawing for a moment, but went on intently, so that I had to play to the chairs, tables, and walls. (A, 531)

4

The World

THE OTHER ARTS

Spoken Theater

If only there were even a tolerably good theater in Salzburg! For in Vienna my sole amusement is the theater.

Vienna, 26 May 1781

► Next to music, the spoken theater, of all the arts, claimed Mozart's greatest enthusiasm and interest. This is hardly surprising, since he was by profession—opera being, after all, only theater of a special kind—a man of the theater himself. Moreover, Mozart was not only intensely concerned about the dramatic effectiveness of his librettos but also set great store on the acting abilities of his singers. During the eighteenth century musical and spoken drama were far more closely related than they are today: in Vienna it was not unusual for the same performer to act in a play one night and sing in an opera the next.[1] Mozart himself enjoyed acting (at least in pantomime performances at carnivals and masques) and even tried his hand as a playwright of sorts, sketching a plot outline for a play entitled *Der Salzburger Lump in Wien* (The Salzburg Boob in Vienna) and also a draft for a comedy in three acts entitled *Die Liebes-Probe* (The Test of Love).[2] Mozart's critical comments on both the theater and on individual plays are typically brief and usually more concerned with the production, especially the quality of the acting but also the handling of stage effects. ◄

To Nannerl   *Munich, 30 December 1774*

I went to the theater yesterday to see the *Mode nach der Haushaltung,*[3] which was very well acted. (A, 256)

To Leopold Mozart   *Munich, 8 November 1780*

The Grand Master of the Teutonic Order arrived yesterday. *Essex*[4] was

95

given at the Court Theater, followed by a magnificent ballet. The whole theater was illuminated. (A, 660)

To Leopold Mozart   *Vienna, 4 July 1781*

My sole entertainment is the theater. How I wish that you could see a tragedy acted here! Generally speaking, I do not know of any theater where all kinds of plays are *really well* performed. But they are here. Every part, even the most unimportant and poorest part, is well cast and understudied. (A, 751)

▶ Occasionally Mozart does comment on the content or import of the plays themselves. Indeed, he permits himself to question the social sensitivity of a Carlo Gozzi and even the dramaturgical wisdom of a William Shakespeare. ◀

To Leopold Mozart   *Munich, 13 December 1780*

The comedy *Wie man sich die Sache denkt* or *Die zwei schlaflosen Nächte*[5] is charming. I saw it here—no, no, I did not see it; I only read it, for it has not yet been performed. (A, 686)

To Nannerl   *Vienna, 15 December 1781*

Do you not think that *Das Loch in der Thür* [by Gottlieb Stephanie] is a good comedy? But you ought to see it performed here. *Die Gefahren der Verführung* [a German adaptation of Georg Lillo's *George Barnwell*] is also a capital piece. *Das öffentliche Geheimnis* [a German translation of Carlo Gozzi's *Il pubblico segreto*] is only endurable if one remembers that it is an Italian play, for the Princess's condescension to her servant is really too indecent and unnatural. The best part of this play is the public secret itself—I mean, the way in which the two lovers, though preserving their secret, still contrive to communicate with one another publicly. (A, 786)

To Leopold Mozart   *Munich, 29 November 1780*

Tell me, don't you think that the speech of the subterranean voice [in act 3 of *Idomeneo*] is too long? Consider it carefully. Picture to yourself the theater, and remember that the voice must be terrifying—must penetrate —that the audience must believe that it really exists. Well, how can this effect be produced if the speech is too long, for in this case the listeners will become more and more convinced that it means nothing. If the speech of the Ghost in *Hamlet* were not so long, it would be far more effective. It is quite easy to shorten the speech of the subterranean voice and it will gain thereby more than it will lose. (A, 674)

▶ Although the following reference is most likely to Georg Benda's monodrama, and not the Greek tragedy,[6] its testimonial to Mozart's enthusiasm for special stage effects in the theater remains undiminished. ◀

To Leopold Mozart   *Vienna, 24 December 1783*

I am not at all alarmed at the notion of a few fireworks, for the arrangements of the Viennese fire brigade are so excellent that there is no cause for uneasiness about having fireworks on the stage. Thus *Medea* is often performed here, at the end of which one-half the palace collapses, while the other half goes up in flames. (A, 865)

▶ While actors could reasonably be called upon to sing (at least in minor roles), there was danger—especially in the touring theatrical companies of the day—that the talents of a brilliant singer might be squandered in such an environment. Mozart makes this clear in a letter to the father of Aloysia Weber, in which he admonishes him not to let Aloysia join the famous traveling theatrical company of Abel Seyler. ◀

To Fridolin Weber, Mannheim   *Paris, 29 July 1778*

For God's sake, don't mention that Seyler company to me, I couldn't bear to think that your daughter [Aloysia]—or even if she were not your daughter, even if she were only a foundling—I should be very sorry indeed that she with her talent should fall among players, which would mean that she is only good enough to be a stop-gap—for the main thing with the Seylers, indeed with all theatrical companies, is always the play; the singspiel is just put in to give occasional relief to the players now and then—indeed, very often in order to give the actors time and room to change—and generally as a diversion. You must always think of your reputation. (A, 578)

▶ At the theater, as in the opera house and concert hall, Mozart was fascinated with audience behavior and misbehavior. A royal response was worth reporting home. ◀

To Leopold Mozart   *Mannheim, 12 November 1778*

You know that the Mannheim company is in Munich. Well, the Bavarians have already hissed there the two best actresses, Madame Toscani and Madame Urban, and there was such an uproar that *the Elector himself leaned over his box* and called out—"Sh" [Italicized words in code]. (A, 630)

▶ On the scene in Vienna, Mozart was hardly less informed about backstage developments at the spoken theater than about the opera. So he well knew why his brother-in-law, Joseph Lange, a professional actor at the Burgtheater since 1770, did not get the role of Hamlet in a command performance at court in honor of the visiting crown prince of Russia. ◄

To Leopold Mozart   *Vienna, 10 November 1781*

The Emperor commanded each of the actors to select a part in which to appear before the Grand Duke [Paul]. Lange applied for that of Hamlet, but Count Rosenberg, who does not like Lange, said that this could not be, because [Hieronymus] Brockmann had been playing that part for ages. When this was repeated to Brockmann, he went to Rosenberg and told him that he could not appear in the part and that the play could not be performed at all. And why? *Because the Grand Duke himself was Hamlet.* (A, 777–778)

► The Grand Duke was compared to Hamlet because he fell into a depression after the death of his father, Peter III, and the assumption (or usurpation) of the throne by his mother Catherine. ◄

BALLS AND BALLETS, MASKS AND SPECTACLES

► Virtually all of Mozart's comments on entertainments such as balls and ballets, masks and spectacles are contained in his letters to Nannerl written from Italy during his adolescent years. Sometimes his observations assume the detached tone of a tour guide, but elsewhere his assessments are as succinct and pungent as his typical evaluations of singers and actors. (Among the dancers who won his approval, his favorite was evidently the ballet master Carlo De Picq.)

As in the spoken theater Mozart's taste in dance and spectacle ran to the colorful and lively. He seems to have been impatient with the slow tempo of Italian dancing and clearly disdained pomposity. The orderliness [*ordnung*] that Mozart discerned in Viennese ballet is presumably to be understood as a favorable judgment—or did he mean to say it was overly formal and "pompous"? ◄

To Nannerl   *Verona, 7 January 1770*

There is a good dancer here called Monsieur Ruesler. He is a German and dances very well. One of the last times we were at the opera (but not the very last time) we asked M. Ruesler to come up to our palco [i.e., box] . . . and there we had a talk with him. (A, 105)

To Nannerl   *Milan, 26 January 1770*

[On the ballet in Cremona:] Ballerino primo, good. Ballerina prima, good but very plain. There was a woman dancer there, who did not dance badly and, what is very remarkable, was not bad looking on the stage and off it. The others were quite ordinary. A grotesco was there too, who whenever he jumped let off a fart . . . Monsieur Pick [De Picq] who danced in Vienna, is dancing here too. (A, 110–111)

To Nannerl   *Milan, 3 March 1770*

I think we have been to the opera six or seven times and then to the festa di ballo [a dance] which, as in Vienna, begins after the opera, but with the difference that there the dancing is more orderly [zu wien mehr ordnung ist]. We have also seen the facchinata and the chiccherata. The facchinata is a mascherata, a beautiful sight, so-called because people dress up as facchini or valets. There was a barca with a number of people in it, and many persons went on foot, and there were four to six bands of trumpeters and drummers and a few companies of fiddlers and of players on the instruments. The chiccerata which we saw today is also a mascherata. Chiccheri is the Milanese word for the people we call petits-maîtres or, let us say, coxcombs [*windmacher*, i.e., a dandy]. They all rode on horseback and it was a charming affair. (A, 117)

To Nannerl   *Bologna, 24 March 1770*

I shall soon send you a minuet which Mr. Pick [Carlo De Picq] danced in the theater and which everyone danced to afterwards at the feste di ballo in Milan, solely in order that you may see how slowly people dance here. (A, 121)

To Nannerl   *Naples, 5 June 1770*

The opera here is one of Jommelli's . . . The dances are wretchedly pompous. (A, 143)

Leopold Mozart to his Wife   *Milan, 13 September 1771*

Today we saw the rehearsal of the dances and we greatly admired the hard work of the ballet masters, Pick and [his colleague Jean] Fabier [Favier].[7] (A 196)

► Some half dozen years later Mozart, on his own in Munich, reaffirms his taste for the lighter, presumably absurd, side. ◄

To Leopold Mozart   *Munich, 11 October 1777*

I have just been to the Lipperl Theater.[8] I only went to see the ballet, or rather pantomime, which I had not yet seen. It was called *Das von der Fée girigaricanarimanarischaribari verfertigte Ei.*[9] It was excellent and very good fun. (A, 308)

► Mozart, finally, was not unaffected by the deterioration of the ballet in Vienna following the departure of the brilliant Jean-Georges Noverre in 1774 (after some seven years in the imperial capital). Mozart had met Noverre, the leading choreographer of his time, in Vienna in 1773. Later he encountered him in Paris and in fact wrote part of the music for Noverre's ballet, *Le petits riens*, K. 299b. ◄

To Leopold Mozart   *Vienna, 12 September 1781*

We are having one rehearsal after another [for *Die Entführung*] in the theater. The ballet-master Antoine[10] has been summoned from Munich, and supers are being recruited throughout Vienna and all its suburbs. There is still a sorry remnant of Noverre's ballet, who, however, have not moved a leg for the last eight years and most of whom are like sticks. (A, 765)

WRITERS AND LITERATURE

The Reminiscences of Constanze Mozart, 1829

Mozart was fond of reading and well acquainted with Shakespeare in translation. One of his favorite authors is at present in [Constanze's] possession and which she most frequently peruses, it is in nine volumes but being a forbidden fruit in the Austrian states she did not name it—I [Novello] suspect some of the French revolutionary works. (Novello, 94–95)

► The inventory of books in Mozart's possession at the time of his death contains exactly 41 titles.[11] In addition to the Bible there are books on history, geography, politics, travel, mathematics, natural science, and philosophy. Among them are the writings of Frederick the Great and also Moses Mendelssohn's *Phädon, oder über die Unsterblichkeit der Seele* (i.e., Phaedo, or On the Immortality of the Soul). The mysterious French revolutionary volumes have not been identified. Just two musical titles are included: Karl Friedrich Cramer, *Magazin der Musik* for the years 1783–1787, and Johann Nikolaus Forkel, *Musikalischer Almanach für Deutschland*, 1782–1784. Significantly, they are journalistic collections, not theoretical treatises. (Not even Leopold Mozart's treatise on violin playing is mentioned.)

It is no surprise that poetic and dramatic works are most strongly represented. We find works by Wieland and Metastasio. There are several titles in English and Italian but, with the exception of the *Biblia Sacra* and a French atlas, none in French or Latin. Mozart's personal copies of Ovid's *Tristia*, Molière's comedies, and even Beaumarchais's *Figaro* are in German translation. The inventory does not list the German Shakespeare translation alluded to by Constanze.[12]

Of course, one's personal library is notoriously a most imprecise guide to what one has actually read. Moreover, we need not take Constanze's word for his familiarity with Shakespeare—at least with *Hamlet*—since, as we have seen, he cites the work twice in his letters. Nonetheless, we have to conclude that Mozart was probably not a particularly avid reader. (It is easy to believe that he did not have the time.) He does not often refer to books or authors in his letters. In fact, as the following alphabetical survey reveals, he hardly mentions literature at all. ◄

Arabian Nights

To Nannerl   *Bologna, 21 July 1770*

Our hostess in Rome gave me as a present the *Arabian Nights* in Italian. It is very amusing to read. (A, 150)

Christian Fürchtegott Gellert (1715–1769)

► Gellert, a professor at the University of Leipzig, and a moral philosopher, was also the successful author of poems, fables, hymns, and comedies. ◄

Leopold Mozart to Lorenz Hagenauer, Salzburg   *Paris, 1 April 1764*

When parting [Versailles], Baron von Bose gave Wolfgang as a remembrance a beautiful book containing spiritual thoughts in verse. (A, 43)

► According to Nissen, the book was Gellert's *Geistliche Oden und Lieder* (1757). Hymns from this famous collection were set by C.P.E. Bach, Haydn, and Beethoven—but not by Mozart. His rather limited esteem for Gellert also emerges from the following. ◄

To Leopold Mozart   *Milan, 26 January 1770*

I have no news except that Herr Gellert, the poet, has died at Leipzig and since his death has written no more poetry. (A, 110)

Pietro Metastasio (1698–1782)

► Metastasio, imperial court poet in Vienna from 1740, was the preeminent Italian poet and librettist of the eighteenth century. ◄

Leopold Mozart to his Wife   *Milan, 10 February 1770*

After lunch [Count von Firmian] presented Wolfgang with the nine volumes of Metastasio's works, the Turin edition, one of the most beautiful, and very handsomely bound. You can well imagine that this present is very welcome to me as well as to Wolfgang. (A, 112)

Molière (1622–1673)

To Leopold Mozart   *Paris, 24 March 1778*

Herr [Fridolin] Weber . . . made me a present of Molière's comedies (as he knew that I had not yet read them) with this inscription: *Accept, my friend, the works of Molière in token of gratitude and think of me sometimes* [Italian]. (A, 518)

Voltaire (1694–1778)

► The death of the anti-Christian deist, social critic, and satirist in Paris on 30 May 1778 elicited the following outburst from the Catholic composer who was there at the time. ◄

To Leopold Mozart   *Paris, 3 July 1778*

That godless arch-rascal Voltaire has pegged out [i.e., "croaked"] like a dog, like a beast![13] That is his reward! (A, 558)

► Mozart's fury here was surely fueled by more than one cause. Least of all was it a mere matter of satisfaction at the demise of some controversial celebrity. The Mozarts thought they had a personal axe to grind with Voltaire. Some twelve years earlier, during their sojourn in Geneva in late summer 1766, and armed with letters of introduction, they had tried to visit the great man; but Voltaire, a recluse in any case, was indisposed and had refused to meet with them.[14] But no doubt the decisive reason for Mozart's passion when he penned his death notice home—over a month after Voltaire's death—was that 3 July 1778 was the day his mother died. Mozart broke that news at once to his Salzburg friend, Joseph Bullinger, but did not communicate it to Leopold for almost a week. (See Chapter 5.) ◄

Christoph Martin Wieland (1733–1813)

► Wieland was an influential man of letters and advocate of Enlighten-ment thought. Apart from his characterization of Wieland's appearance and personality Mozart is more interested in reporting the famous author's opinion of him than in expressing his views of Wieland's work. Traces of Wieland's possible influence, however, have been detected in the librettos of both *Cosi fan tutte* and *Die Zauberflöte*.[15] ◄

To Leopold Mozart   *Mannheim, 22 November 1777*

During the next Carnival *Rosemunde* will be performed, a new text by Wieland with new music by [Anton] Schweitzer. (A, 385)

To Leopold Mozart   *Mannheim, 27 December 1777*

I have now added Herr Wieland to my list of acquaintances. But he doesn't know as much about me as I know about him, for he has never heard any of my compositions. I had imagined him to be quite different from what I found him. He strikes you as slightly affected in his speech. He has a rather childish voice; he keeps on quizzing you over his glasses; he indulges in a sort of pedantic rudeness, combined occasionally with a stupid condescension. But I am not surprised that he permits himself such behavior here, even though he may be quite different in Weimar and elsewhere, for people stare at him as if he had dropped from Heaven. Everyone seems embarrassed in his presence, no one says a word or moves an inch; all listen intently to every word he utters; and it's a pity they often have to wait so long, for he has a defect of speech that makes him speak very slowly and he can't say half a dozen words without stopping. Apart from that, he is what we all know him to be, a most gifted fellow [*ein fortreflicher kopf*]. He has a frightfully ugly face, covered with pockmarks, and he has a rather long nose. In height he is, I should say, a little taller than Papa. (A, 435)

To Leopold Mozart   *Mannheim, 10 January 1778*

Now that he has heard me twice, Herr *Wieland* [in code] is quite enchanted with me. The last time after showering compliments on me he said: "It is a real piece of good fortune that I have found you here," and he pressed my hand. (A, 444)

► Apart from direct references to particular books and authors, a clue to Mozart's taste and experience as a reader may be detected in the indirect literary allusions and quotations that lurk in a number of comments. ◄

Pierre-Augustin Beaumarchais (1732–1799)

► Beaumarchais, dramatist and literary reformer, was author of *Le barbier de Séville* (1772) and *Le mariage de Figaro ou La folle journée* (1781). *Le barbier* was first performed on the French stage in 1775. Although Mozart may have read the play, it seems more likely that he had seen a theatrical performance during his 1778 sojourn in Paris when it was staged several times.[16] ◄

To Leopold Mozart   *Vienna, 19 October 1782*

The barber of Salzburg (not of Seville) called on me[17] and delivered kind messages from you, from my sister, and from Katherl [Gilowsky]. (A, 829)

Charles Burney (1726–1814)

► In addition to his mammoth four-volume *General History of Music* (1776–1789), Burney, an English music historian, had published two valuable accounts of his musical travels through Europe: *The Present*

State of Music in France and Italy (1771), and *The Present State of Music in Germany, the Netherlands, and United Provinces* (1773). These were translated into German under the titles *Tagebuch einer musikalischen Reise* (1772, 1773; literally, Diary of a Musical Journey). The suggestion that Mozart may be alluding to these volumes in the following passage is not implausible.[18] ◄

To Leopold Mozart   *Paris, 18 July 1778*

When [Anton Raaff] arrived [at Le Gros's] we all happened to be at table. This, too, has nothing to do with the case; it is only to let you know that in Paris, too, we sit down to table as we do elsewhere; and, after all, the midday meal at Le Gros's is much more relevant to my tale of friendship than the coffeehouses and drummers to a description of my musical journey [*einer Musikalischen Reisebeschreibung*]. When I went there the following day there was a letter for me from Herr Weber, which Raaff had brought. Now if I wished to deserve the name of historian, I ought to insert here the contents of this letter; and I may say that I am very reluctant to keep them back. But I must not be too long-winded. Brevity is most admirable, as you can see by my letter! The third day I found Raaff at home and thanked him, for, to be sure, it's a good thing to be polite! I have forgotten what we talked about. That historian must be a very clumsy fellow who cannot forthwith supply some falsehood—I mean, romance a bit. (A, 570)

Friedrich Gottlieb Klopstock (1724–1803)

► Klopstock was a celebrated and influential author of religious epics, plays, hymns, and, especially, lyric odes. Mozart's reference to Klopstock actually consists of an almost literal quotation of the amorous *Ode an Edone*—but without mention of the poet's name—in a letter to his cousin "Bäsle."[19] ◄

To Maria Anna Thekla Mozart (Bäsle), Augsburg   *Salzburg, 10 May 79*

A tender ode!

> Thy picture sweet, O cousin,
> Is e'er before my eyes.
> Yet weep I must, forsooth,
> That thou'rt not here thyself.
> I see thee when the evening
> Darkens and when the moon
> Shines forth. Alas! I weep
> That thou'rt not here thyself.

By all the flowering blossoms
Which I would strew for thee,
By all the myrtle branches
Which I would twine for thee,
I conjure thee, fair spirit,
Appear, transform thyself,
Transform thyself, fair spirit,
And be—my little coz! (A, 653)

PAINTING, SCULPTURE, AND ARCHITECTURE

► Mozart's sister and his widow both assure us of his taste and interest in the fine arts. ◄

The Memoirs of Nannerl Mozart, 1800

In Olmütz [November 1767]. Even at this early age he showed a natural affection for all artists. Every composer, painter, engraver, and the like, whose acquaintance we made on our journeys, had to give him some memento of his skill and these he would carefully preserve. (DDB, 494)

The Reminiscences of Constanze Mozart, 1829

[Mozart] was fond of painting—sculpture—and could draw himself. "Indeed" [Constanze] added—"He had superior talents for all the arts."
  She told us that he drew a little and was very fond of all the arts, that he had indeed a talent for all the arts. (Novello, 80)

► Despite these assurances, the subject of the fine arts rarely arises in Mozart's letters. In contrast to Leopold Mozart's numerous comments on the paintings and architectural monuments they had seen on their journeys, Mozart himself offers few judgments of the kind. ◄

To Nannerl   *Rome, 14 April 1770*

I only wish that my sister were in Rome, for this town would certainly please her, as St. Peter's church and many other things in Rome are *regular* [Regulair]. (A, 128)

► We may assume that Mozart shared the taste for the "regular" architecture he attributes to Nannerl. The same may be implied in his comparison of the Gothic Cistercian monastery in the Swabian town of "Kaysersheim"—that is, Kaisheim—with the baroque-style Benedictine abbey at Kremsmünster, outside Linz. (See also his comments on Nuremberg and Würzburg, below.) ◄

To Leopold Mozart   *Kaysersheim, 18 December 1778*

The monastery [in Kaysersheim] itself has made no great impression on me, for once you have seen the Abbey of Kremsmünster, well . . . !—But of course I am only speaking about the exterior and what they call here the court—for I have yet to see the most famous part. (A, 641)

CURRENT EVENTS

▶ Mozart's interest in the news of the day apparently was extremely limited. It certainly plays a remarkably small role in his letters. As is well known, he seems to have paid no attention at all to the greatest political event of his time, the French Revolution. But caution is in order. Mozart's letters also contain nothing about Freemasonry, a topic about which the composer was keenly concerned. Moreover, at the time of the French Revolution, Mozart's principal correspondent about all issues great and small—his father—was dead. Indeed, there are few letters of any kind from July 1789 on, except for the series of desperate requests for money to his Masonic brother Michael Puchberg, which certainly make plain that Mozart had other, far more immediate and pressing matters on his mind at that time. Nor should we expect his letters to Constanze written en route during his 1790 tour to Germany, or during her numerous sojourns in Baden the following year, to have contained any but the personal communications found in them. Mozart, after all, was again enormously busy—this time with the composition of *Die Zauberflöte.*

At times, Mozart does betray a certain lukewarm interest in local news—a Pope's visit, a scandal involving an Emperor, a King, and a Jewess. ◀

LOCAL NEWS

To Leopold Mozart   *Vienna, 9 January 1782*

Meanwhile I must tell you that the Pope is supposed to be coming to Vienna. The whole town is talking about it. But I do not believe it, for Count Cobenzl told me that the Emperor will decline his visit. (A, 790–791)

▶ Mozart's well-placed informant, Count Cobenzl, was ill informed. Pope Pius VI came to Vienna on March 22 and stayed for an entire month. ◀

To Leopold Mozart   *Vienna, 23 March 1782*

I must tell you that the Pope arrived in Vienna yesterday afternoon at half past three—a pleasant piece of news.[20] And now for a sad one. Frau von

Auernhammer has at last worried her poor dear husband to death. He died yesterday evening at half past six. (A, 798)

► Mozart does not seem to have interested himself at all in the reason for the Pope's visit: his concern about the Emperor's church reforms, in particular the recent imperial order to close a large number of "idle" monasteries.[21] ◄

An International Affair

To Leopold Mozart   *Vienna, 11 September 1782*

The Jewess Eskeles has no doubt proved a very good and useful tool for breaking up the friendship between the Emperor and the Russian court, for the day before yesterday *she was taken to Berlin* in order that the King might have the pleasure of her company. She is indeed a sow of the first order. (A, 819)

► Mozart's interest in this sensational news item—a scandal involving the disclosure to the Prussian court of sensitive information bearing on secret meetings between Emperor Joseph II and Russia's Catherine II—was not the product of idle curiosity. A "very good friend" of his, one Johann Valentin Günther, an aide to the Emperor, was implicated in the affair. Mozart shared the prevailing belief that Günther had been betrayed by his mistress, Eleonore Eskeles, who, having elicited the information from him, had passed it on through intermediaries to Berlin. She was exonerated years later.[22] ◄

War News

► At an earlier time—specifically in the summer of 1778, while he was living abroad in Paris (depressed by the recent death of his mother and rather unproductive)—Mozart was evidently more curious about political (at least military) developments in the world than he would be, or have the time for, in later years. The topic of the day was the Bavarian War of Succession which broke out in July 1778, when Frederick the Great of Prussia, in alliance with Saxony, invaded Bohemia. Frederick had been infuriated by the Pact of Vienna—signed the previous January by the Elector Palatine Karl Theodor and the Austrian Emperor Joseph II—which made Karl Theodor the new ruler of Bavaria. The war finally ended by treaty in May of 1779.[23] ◄

To Leopold Mozart   *Paris, 20 July 1778*

Well, what are you hearing about the war? For the last three days I have been dreadfully sad and depressed. True, it doesn't really concern me, but I am so sensitive, that I immediately feel interested in any matter. I hear that the *Emperor* has been defeated. First of all, it was reported that the *King of Prussia* had surprised *him,* or rather that he had surprised the troops commanded by the *Archduke Maximilian;* that two thousand had fallen on the *Austrian* side; that fortunately the *Emperor* had come to his assistance with forty thousand men, but had been forced to retreat. Second, it was said that *the King* had attacked the *Emperor* and completely surrounded him and that if General [Ernst Gideon, Baron von] *Laudon* had not come to his rescue with eighteen hundred cuirassiers, he would have been taken prisoner; that sixteen hundred cuirassiers had been killed and *Laudon* himself shot dead. But I have not seen this in any newspaper. Today, however, I was told that the *Emperor* had invaded Saxony with forty thousand men; but I don't know whether this is true . . . I saw in the papers that in a skirmish between the Saxons and Croats a Saxon Captain of Grenadiers, Hopfgarten by name, had lost his life and was deeply mourned [italicized words in code]. (A, 574)

► In a letter to his Salzburg friend Joseph Bullinger, just a few weeks later, Mozart briefly introduces into the familiar German-speaking arena of Prussia, Bavaria, and Austria an additional episode set on the exotic terrain across the Atlantic where England was engaged with its unruly colonies and their French allies under the Marquis de Lafayette. ◄

To Abbé Joseph Bullinger, Salzburg   *Paris, 7 August 1778*

Now for the war. As far as I know we shall soon have peace in Germany. The King of Prussia is rather alarmed, it seems. I have read in the papers that the Prussians surprised an imperial detachment, but that the Croats and two regiments of cuirassiers were in the neighborhood and, hearing the tumult, came at once to their rescue and attacked the Prussians, placing them between two fires and capturing five cannon. The route by which the Prussians entered Bohemia is now entirely cut up and destroyed, so that they cannot retreat. The Bohemian peasants are making it as hot as they can for the Prussians, who are suffering moreover from constant desertions among their troops. But these are matters of which you must have had earlier and more accurate news than ourselves. But I must now send you some of our news here. The French have forced the English to retreat, but it was not a very hot fight. The most remarkable thing is that of friends and foes, only a hundred men were killed. Nevertheless there is tremendous jubilation here and nothing else is talked of. It is also reported that we shall soon have peace. It is all the same to me as far as this country is concerned. But I should be very glad indeed for many reasons if we were soon to have peace in Germany. (A, 596)

► Mozart's vivid descriptions of the theaters of battle are more than a little reminiscent of his description of the *facchinata* in Milan—or perhaps the stage directions in a complicated opera finale.

Years later (evidently prompted by a remark by Leopold), Mozart had occasion to refer again to British military actions. This time England prevailed, and Mozart was delighted: Lord Richard Howe lifted the siege of Gibraltar and Sir Edward Hughes annihilated the French navy. One suspects that Mozart, the spiritual Englishman, did not particularly sympathize with the cause of the American colonists and their French supporters when he reported on their victory to Bullinger. ◄

To Leopold Mozart   *Vienna, 19 October 1782*

Indeed, I have heard about England's victories and am greatly delighted too, for you know that I am an out-and-out Englishman [*ein ErzEngelländer*]. (A, 828)

A MUSICIAN'S GUIDE TO EUROPE

► It has been precisely calculated that of the 13,097 days of Mozart's life (35 years, 10 months, 9 days), 3,720 (10 years, 2 months, 8 days) were spent traveling. He visited—or at least passed some time in—no fewer than 202 towns and cities, extending alphabetically from Aachen to Zurich, and geographically from Amsterdam in the north to Pompei in the south, London in the west, and Vienna in the east.[24] But, for all its obvious discomforts in the eighteenth century, Mozart confesses to his need to travel—that it was, in fact, a necessary stimulus to his talent. (That this need not be the case is amply illustrated by Joseph Haydn, who attributed his originality as a composer precisely to his isolation at the remote court of Esterháza in Hungary.) ◄

To Leopold Mozart   *Paris, 11 September 1778*

People who do not travel (I mean those who cultivate the arts and learning) are indeed miserable creatures; and I protest that unless the Archbishop allows me to travel every second year, I can't possibly accept the engagement.[25] A fellow of mediocre talent will remain a mediocrity whether he travels or not; but one of superior talent (which without impiety I cannot deny that I possess) will go to seed if he always remains in the same place. (A, 612)

To Leopold Mozart   *Nancy, 3 October 1778*

I am never in a good humor when I am in a town where I am quite unknown. (A, 622)

To Leopold Mozart   *Munich, 8 November 1780*

My arrival here was happy and pleasant—happy, because no mishap occurred during the journey; and pleasant, because we could hardly wait for the moment to reach our destination, on account of our drive, which though short was most uncomfortable. Indeed, I assure you that none of us managed to sleep for a moment the whole night through. Why, that carriage jolted the very souls out of our bodies—and the seats were as hard as stone! . . . It is all over now, though it will serve me as a warning rather to go on foot than to drive in a mail coach. (A, 659)

► Mozart inevitably became something of an authority on the subject with strong views about the peoples and places he had come to know. Needless to say, his opinions about peoples and places were directly related to his personal fortunes and experiences with them, especially his experiences with music and money. What follows is a Mozartean gazetteer. Beginning with some scathing observations on his native Salzburg, we then follow (for the most part) the sequence of Mozart's travels abroad, recording his comments about Italy, France, England, and the German-speaking world. ◄

Salzburg

► Mozart's limitless contempt for his native Salzburg (fig. 4.1) was not bred of familiarity alone. Although he was not entirely sure whether it was only the Archbishop or also the people and their manners, or the vague nature of his duties that made the prospect of remaining there utterly unbearable, he was in no doubt (and perfectly correct) that the city, with its mediocre orchestra and defunct theater and opera—not to mention (the unacknowledged and unmentioned) suffocating presence of his father—was "no place for my talent." ◄

To Padre Martini, Bologna   *Salzburg, 4 September 1776*

I live in a country where music leads a struggling existence, though indeed apart from those who have left us, we still have excellent teachers and particularly composers of great wisdom, learning and taste. As for the theater, we are in a bad way for lack of singers. [Italian]. (A, 266)

To Abbé Bullinger, Salzburg   *Paris, 7 August 1778*

How I detest Salzburg—and not only on account of the injustices which my dear father and I have endured there, which in themselves would be enough to make us wish to forget such a place and blot it out of our memory forever! But let us set that aside . . . I have far more hope of living pleasantly and happily in any other place. Perhaps you will misunderstand me and think that Salzburg is too small for me? If so, you are greatly mistaken. I have already given some of my reasons to my father. In the meantime, content yourself with this one, that Salzburg is no place for my talent. In the first place, professional musicians there are not held in much consideration; and, second, one hears nothing, there is no theater, no opera; and even if they really wanted one, who is there to sing? For the last

FIGURE 4.1. Salzburg

five or six years the Salzburg orchestra has always been rich in what is useless and superfluous, but very poor in what is necessary, and absolutely destitute of what is indispensable; and such is the case at the present moment . . .

It would be more useful and profitable . . . to look around for a Kapellmeister, as they really have none at present . . . Do your best to find an arse for the orchestra, for that is what they need most of all! They have a head indeed, but that is just their misfortune! (A, 594–596)

▶ The official Kapellmeister from 1765–1783 was Domenico Fischietti. But since he was considered ineffective, he was, from 1776 on, Kapellmeister in title only. ◀

To Leopold Mozart   *Paris, 11 September 1778*

There is one place where I can say I am at home, where I can live in peace and quiet with my most beloved father and my dearest sister, where I can do as I like, where apart from the duties of my appointment I am my own master, and where I have a permanent income and yet can go off when I like, and travel every second year. What more can I desire? To tell you my real feelings, the only thing that disgusts me about Salzburg is the impossibility of mixing freely with the people and the low estimation in which the musicians are held there—and—that the Archbishop has no confidence in the experience of intelligent people who have seen the world. (A, 612)

To Leopold Mozart   *Strasbourg, 15 October 1778*

You alone, dearest father, can sweeten for me the bitterness of Salzburg; and that you will do so, I feel convinced. Still, I must frankly confess that I should arrive in Salzburg with a lighter heart, did I not remember that I am to be in the service of the court. It is that thought which is intolerable to me. Consider it yourself—put yourself in my place! At Salzburg I never know how I stand. I am to be everything—and yet—sometimes— nothing! Nor do I ask *so much* nor *so little*—I just want something—I mean to be something! In any other place I should know what my duties were. Everywhere else, whoever undertakes the violin, sticks to it, and it is the same with the clavier. But no doubt all this can be arranged. Well, I trust that everything will turn out fortunately and happily for me. I rely wholly on you. (A, 624–625)

To Leopold Mozart   *Munich, 8 January 1779*

I swear to you on my honor that I cannot bear Salzburg or its inhabitants (I mean, the natives of Salzburg). Their language—their manners are quite intolerable to me. (A, 649)

To Leopold Mozart   *Munich, 16 December 1780*

You know, my dear father, that *it is only to please you* that I am staying on there, since, by Heaven, if I had followed my inclination, *before leaving* the other day *I would have wiped my behind with my last contract,* for I swear to you on my honor that it is not Salzburg itself but the *Prince* and *his conceited nobility* who become every day more intolerable to me. Thus I should be delighted, were he to send me word in writing that he *no longer required my services* [italicized words in code]. (A, 690)

To Leopold Mozart   *Vienna, 26 May 1781*

You yourself must admit that in Salzburg—for me at least—there is not a farthing's worth of entertainment. *I refuse to associate with a good many people there*—and most of the others do not think me good enough. Besides, there is no stimulus for my talent! (A, 736)

ITALY AND ITALIANS

► Mozart hardly complained of any lack of stimulus for his talent when he was in Italy. Between December 1769 and March 1773, that is, between the ages of fourteen and seventeen, Mozart undertook three journeys to Italy and spent some two years there, visiting all the principal cities from Milan and Venice in the North to Rome and Naples in the South.

    During Mozart's two sojourns in Rome in the year 1770—from 11 April to 8 May and again from 26 June to 10 July—he attended numerous receptions in the homes of the nobility and Catholic hierarchy, heard and copied from memory the famous Miserere by Gregorio Allegri (see Chapter 1), received the Order of the Golden Spur, and, at the end, met Pope Clement XIV. ◄

To Nannerl   *Rome, 14 April 1770*

I only wish that my sister were in Rome, for this town would certainly please her, as St. Peter's church and many other things in Rome are *regular* [*Regulair*]. The most beautiful flowers are now being carried past in the street. (A, 128)

► During Mozart's only visit to Naples—from 14 May to 25 June 1770—he gave a couple of house concerts, visited the opera, and engaged in quite a bit of sightseeing, including visits to Vesuvius and Pompeii. His later plans to compose an opera for Naples (for the sake of Aloysia Weber) never materialized. ◄

To Nannerl   *Naples, 19 May 1770*

We saw the King and Queen at Mass in the court chapel at Portici and we have seen Vesuvius too. Naples is beautiful, but it is as crowded as Vienna and Paris. . . . Here the lazzaroni have their own general or chief, who receives twenty-five ducati d'argento from the King every month, solely for the purpose of keeping them in order. (A, 137)

To Nannerl   *Naples, 5 June 1770*

Vesuvius is smoking furiously today. Thunder and lightning and all the rest . . . Naples and Rome are two sleepy towns . . . The theater is beautiful. (A, 142–143)

To Leopold Mozart   *Munich, 11 October 1777*

It is a real distinction to have written operas in Italy, especially for Naples . . . Once I have composed for Naples, I shall be in demand everywhere. Moreover, as Papa is well aware, there are also opere buffe here and there in the spring, summer and autumn, which one can write for practice and for something to do. I should not make very much, it is true, but, all the same, it would be something; and they would bring me more honor and credit than if I were to give a hundred concerts in Germany. (A, 304–305)

► The high points of Mozart's two visits to Bologna—in March and then from July to October 1770—were his counterpoint studies with the venerable composer, scholar, and teacher Padre Giovanni Battista Martini (who numbered Johann Christian Bach as well as Mozart among his more than one hundred pupils) and his successful completion of the notoriously demanding entrance examination for the prestigious Academia filarmonica. Toward the end of his sojourn in Bologna Mozart had occasion to attend the celebration honoring San Petronio, the patron saint of the famous cathedral. ◄

To Nannerl   *Bologna, 6 October 1770*

I have heard and seen the great festival at St. Petronius in Bologna. It was beautiful, but very long. (A, 165)

► During his first journey to Italy, following the successful premiere of his opera *Mitridate* in Milan, Mozart spent a month in Venice: from February 11th to March 12th 1771. In addition to the numerous visits to families of quality, he performed a concert there on March 5. ◄

To Johann Nepomuk Hagenauer, Salzburg   *Venice, 13 February 1771*

I am charmed with Venice. (A, 182)

To Nannerl   *Venice, 20 February 1771*

Tell Johannes [Johann Nepomuk Hagenauer] that . . . he must soon come back to Venice and submit to the *attacco*, that is, have his bottom spanked when he is lying on the ground, so that he may become a true Venetian. They tried to do it to me—the seven women all together—and yet they could not pull me down. (A, 183)

▶ Over the course of his three sojourns in Italy Mozart spent more than a year in Milan. But apart from describing some of its musical and theatrical attractions (cited earlier), he had only one substantial observation to make about the city. ◀

To his Mother and Nannerl   *Milan, 30 November 1771*

I have seen four rascals hanged here in the Piazza del Duomo. They hang them just as they do in Lyons. (A, 207–208)

▶ Finally, Mozart's succinct assessment of Bozen (or Bolzano), the principal city in the German-speaking South Tyrol region of Italy. Mozart passed through Bozen in 1769, 1771, 1772, on his travels to Italy. ◀

To Nannerl   *Bolzano, 28 October 1772*

Bozen—this pigsty. [*Sauloch*, i.e., the "pits"] (A, 213)

▶ As an eighteenth-century musician, Mozart had almost daily contact with Italians wherever he lived or traveled, for Italian artists exercised an effective hegemony over the cultural life of all Europe. This circumstance, and the resentment it inevitably bred, accounts for the striking contrast between Mozart's fundamental enthusiasm for the land and beauties of Italy, on the one hand, and, on the other, his unmistakable distrust at least of its expatriate representatives. It was only years after his Italian journeys, especially after he had settled in Vienna, that Mozart gave expression to these less-than-flattering generalizations. ◀

To Leopold Mozart   *Munich, 11 October 1777*

When I think it over carefully, I have to admit that in no country have I received so many honors, nowhere have I been so esteemed as in Italy; and certainly it is a real distinction to have written operas in Italy, especially for Naples. (A, 304)

To Leopold Mozart   *Paris, 31 July 1778*

[Aloysia Weber] sang two of my arias and had the good fortune to please, in spite of those Italian blackguards, those infamous scoundrels, who keep on spreading the report that her singing is definitely going off. (A, 589)

To Leopold Mozart   *Vienna, 27 June 1781*

The best way to treat Italians is to be extremely rude. (A, 747)

To Leopold Mozart   *Vienna, 7 May 1783*

[Lorenzo da Ponte] has promised . . . to write a new libretto for me. But
who knows whether he will be able to keep his word—or will want to?
For, as you are aware, these Italian gentlemen are very civil to your face.
Enough, we know them! (A, 848)

FRANCE AND ENGLAND

► Mozart had visited Paris twice as a child, spending five months there
from November 1763 to April 1764, and another two months from May
to July 1766. His decisive encounter with the city, however, was his
six-month sojourn from March to September 1778—professionally and
personally a largely frustrating and (measured by Mozartean standards)
a fairly unproductive period, marked above all by the death of his
mother. Apart from his native Salzburg, Mozart reserved his most bitter
sentiments for the French and their capital. ◄

To Leopold Mozart   *Mannheim, 3 December 1777*

[Wendling] maintains that [Paris] is still the only place where one can make
money and a great reputation. He said: . . . Once a man has written a
couple of operas for Paris, he is sure of a settled yearly income . . .
Wendling is . . . a man who knows Paris (present-day Paris, for it has
changed considerably) thoroughly. (A, 401)

To Leopold Mozart   *Paris, 5 April 1778*

I have this moment returned from the Concert Spirituel. Baron Grimm and
I often give vent to our musical rage at the music here, I mean, between
ourselves, of course. For in public we shout: Bravo, Bravissimo, and clap
our hands until our fingers tingle . . . What annoys me most of all in this
business is that our French gentlemen have only improved their *goût* to the
extent that they can now listen to good stuff as well. But to expect them to
realize that their own music is bad or at least to notice the difference—
Heaven preserve us! And their singing! Good Lord! (A, 522)

To Leopold Mozart   *Paris, 1 May 1778*

You say that I ought to pay a good many calls in order to make new
acquaintances and revive the old ones. That, however, is out of the
question. The distances are too great for walking or the roads too
muddy—for really the mud in Paris is beyond all description. To take a

carriage means that you have the honor of spending four to five livres a day, and all for nothing. People pay plenty of compliments, it is true, but there it ends. They arrange for me to come on such and such a day. I play and hear them exclaim: *"Oh, that is a marvel, that is inconceivable, that is surprising!"* [French], and then it is—Adieu . . . If this were a place where people had ears to hear, hearts to feel, and some measure of understanding of and taste for music, these things would only make me laugh heartily; but, as it is (so far as music is concerned), I am surrounded by mere brute beasts. How can it be otherwise? For in all their actions, emotions, and passions they are just the same. There is no place in the world like Paris. You must not think that I exaggerate when I talk thus of the music here. Ask anyone you like—provided he is not a Frenchman born—and, if he knows anything at all of the matter, he will say exactly the same. Well, I am here. I must endure it for your sake. But I shall thank Almighty God if I escape with my taste unspoiled. (A, 532–533)

To Leopold Mozart   *Paris, 9 July 1778*

The French are and always will be asses, and as they can do nothing for themselves, they are obliged to have recourse to foreigners. (A, 564)

To Leopold Mozart   *Paris, 18 July 1778*

I intend, in God's name, to persevere in my life *here*, which is totally opposed to my genius, inclinations, knowledge, and sympathies. Believe me, this is only too true. I am telling you nothing but the truth. If I were to give you all my reasons, I should write my fingers crooked, and it would do no good. For here I am and I must do my best. God grant only that I may not impair my talents by staying here; but I hope that it won't last long enough for that. God grant it! (A, 573)

To Leopold Mozart   *Paris, 31 July 1778*

M. Grimm said to me the other day: "I hardly think that you will make a success of things in Paris." "Why?" I asked. "I see a crowd of miserable bunglers here who are able to get on, and with my talents should I not be able to do so? . . . "Well, I am afraid," said he, "that you have not been sufficiently active here—you do not go about enough." "Well," I replied, "that is just what I find most difficult to do here." . . . M. le Duc [de Guines] hasn't a spark of honor and must have thought, "After all, he's a young man and a stupid German into the bargain—(for all Frenchmen talk like this about the Germans). (A, 586)

To Leopold Mozart   *St. Germain, 27 August 1778*

France is rather like Germany in feeding people with praises. (A, 607)

► Mozart's problems with the French was not limited to the people but extended to their language. ◄

To Leopold Mozart   *Paris, 9 July 1778*

If I am commissioned to compose an opera, I shall have annoyance in plenty, but that I shall not mind very much, for I am pretty well inured to it; if only that confounded French tongue were not so detestable for music. It really is hopeless; even German is divine in comparison. (A, 564)

► Nor was he at all comfortable with what he saw of the French attitude toward morals. ◄

To Leopold Mozart   *Paris, 18 July 1778*

I dropped into conversation with [the bassoonist] Ritter and among other things said that I was not very happy here; and I added: "The chief reason is, of course, the music. Besides, I can find no soulagement here, no recreation, no pleasant and sociable intercourse with anyone, especially with women, for most of them are prostitutes and the few who are not, have no savoir vivre." Ritter could not deny that I was right. (A, 570–571)

To Leopold Mozart   *Paris, 20 July 1778*

Indeed, I would much rather that [Baron von Laudon] died such a glorious death [in battle],[26] than a shameful one—in Paris in bed, for instance, as most young men do in this place. It is almost impossible to find anyone here who has not suffered two or three times—or is not suffering at the moment—from one of these nice diseases. Why, in Paris children are born with them. But this is no news to you. You know it already, but believe me, it is now worse than ever. (A, 574)

► Along with venereal disease Mozart dreaded another French plague: taxes. ◄

To Leopold Mozart   *Paris, 31 July 1778*

I cannot help it, I must write a grand opera or none at all; if I write a small one, I shall get very little for it (for everything is taxed here). (A, 587)

► Mozart left Paris at the end of September 1778 and, en route home to Salzburg, passed through the towns of Nancy and Strasbourg. His experience in the former was rather more pleasant than in the latter. ◄

To Leopold Mozart   *Nancy, 3 October 1778*

If I had friends here, I should like to stay on, for it is indeed a charming place with handsome houses, fine broad streets and superb squares. (A, 622)

▶ Mozart's two weeks in Strasbourg—from October 15 to November 3 1778—were occupied with the three concerts he gave there: on October 17, 24, and 31. ◀

To Leopold Mozart   *Strasbourg, 26 October 1778*

To give a concert here is an even worse undertaking than in Salzburg. . . . I wanted to leave Strasbourg at once, but they advised me to stay on until the following Saturday and give a grand concert in the theater. I did so and to the surprise, indignation, and disgrace of all the people of Strasbourg, my receipts were exactly the same. The Director, M. Villeneuve, cursed the inhabitants of this really detestable town in a way that was delightful to listen to. (A, 627)

To Leopold Mozart   *Strasbourg, 2 November 1778*

Strasbourg is loath to let me go! You cannot think how much they esteem and love me here. They say that everything about me is so distinguished— that I am so composed, and polite, and have such excellent manners. Everyone knows me . . . I have played here on the two best organs built by Silbermann, which are in the Lutheran churches—the New Church and St. Thomas's Church. (A, 629)

▶ As for the English, during the Grand Tour of his childhood, Mozart spent the fifteen months from 23 April 1764 to 1 August 1765 in England, almost the entire time in London. Unfortunately, but understandably, he did not record his impressions at that time. But he made it clear on several occasions in later years that he harbored a fondness for the English, had made an effort to learn the language (see Chapter 5), and had hoped (in vain) to travel there. ◀

To Nannerl   *Naples, 19 May 1770*

Of the two, London and Naples, I do not know whether Naples does not surpass London for the insolence of the people. (A, 137)

To Leopold Mozart   *Vienna, 19 October 1782*

You know that I am an out-and-out Englishman. (A, 828)

THE GERMAN-SPEAKING WORLD

▶ Mozart's sense of German identity and his nationalistic feelings will be explored in Chapter 5. For the present, our focus is on his judgments of the German (or rather, the Germanic) people by region and by town, including, let it be noted, Austrian Vienna and even Czechoslovakian (more properly: Bohemian) Prague: the latter (at least as far as its privileged classes were concerned) a largely German-speaking city in the eighteenth century, located in fact well to the west of Vienna. ◄

To Leopold Mozart   *Munich, 1 December 1780*

When you meet [the oboist Friedrich Ramm], you will call him a true German—for he tells you to your face exactly what he thinks. (A, 677)

► Here is exactly what Mozart thought of the much-resented Prussians (apropos the Bavarian War of Succession mentioned earlier) and the much-despised Bavarians. ◄

To Leopold Mozart   *Paris, 31 July 1778*

Now for some war news! Let me think! Since the information I sent you in my last letter all that I have heard is that the King of Prussia for the time being has had to retreat. It is even rumored that General Wunsch and 15,000 men have been taken prisoner. But I don't believe a word of it, although *I wish it with all my heart.* If only *the Prussian would get a good thrashing!* [italicized words in code] (A, 589)

To Leopold Mozart   *Mannheim, 12 November 1778*

What a language Bavarian is! So coarse!—as is their whole manner of living, too! I really get scared when I think that I shall have to listen to their "hoben" and "olles mit einonder" and their "gestrenger Herr." (A, 630–631)

► Although Mozart, then, obviously held the Bavarian people in rather low esteem, he nonetheless had the highest opinion of its capital. He had visited the Bavarian capital, Munich, on numerous occasions, beginning with a concert tour in January 1762, shortly before his sixth birthday. He was there for the last time in the fall of 1790, when he passed through on his return to Vienna after having attended the coronation of Leopold II in Frankfurt. Munich was the site for the premieres of Mozart's *La finta giardiniera* (1775) and *Idomeneo* (1781). His dispatches home during the composition and production of the latter, in particular, provide extensive commentary on the city's impressive musical and theatrical establishment. They are presented in later chapters. On this occasion a more general observation, by the twenty-one-year-old, is in order. ◄

To Leopold Mozart   *Munich, 29/30 September 1777*

I like Munich and I am inclined to think, as many of my friends do, that if only I could stay here for a year or two, I could win both profit and honor by my work and therefore would be sought after by the court instead of having to canvass them. (A, 284)

► Mozart liked the Palatine city of Mannheim even more than Munich— although it was not unconditional love at first sight. At all events, Mozart's ultimate attraction to his "beloved" Mannheim is readily explained. It was the residence of the incomparable Mannheim court orchestra; it was also where he had met and fallen in love with Aloysia Weber. Mozart stayed there with his mother from 30 October 1777 to 13 March 1778. En route home to Salzburg after his sojourn in Paris, and counter to the express wishes of his father, Mozart returned to Mannheim where he remained from 6 November to 9 December 1778 in the vain hope of securing an appointment there. He visited the city once more in October 1790 on his return home from Frankfurt. ◄

To Leopold Mozart   *Mannheim, 3 December 1777*

They are not very generous here. (A, 402)

To Leopold Mozart   *Mannheim, 28 February 1778*

Nothing is done in this place by subscription; it is a miserly spot. (A, 498)

To Leopold Mozart   *Mannheim, 12 November 1778*

God be praised that I am back again in my beloved Mannheim! . . . [Madame Cannabich] is telling me of all the events and changes that have taken place during my absence. Since I came here, I have not been able to lunch at home once, as there is a regular scramble to have me. In a word, Mannheim loves me as much as I love Mannheim. And I am not positive, but I believe that I may yet obtain an appointment here. (A, 630)

► Mozart, of course, finally settled neither in Munich nor Mannheim but in Vienna (fig. 4.2). Before doing so—on 16 March 1781—he had visited the Habsburg capital on four previous occasions: in 1762, 1767, 1768, and 1773. His numerous descriptions of Vienna's theatrical, operatic, and concert institutions[27] (with the exception of his comments on the fate of the German National Theater) are generally enthusiastic. Mozart also referred on more than one occasion to the city's enthusiasm for him (at least in the beginning) as well as to the particular qualities of Viennese musical taste—its fickleness and its lack of weight. ◄

To Leopold Mozart   *Mannheim, 13 November 1777*

We [Mozart and the pianist Ignaz von Beecke] fell to talking of various things, among others of Vienna, and how the Emperor was no great lover of music . . . He then went on to say (something which is quite true) that

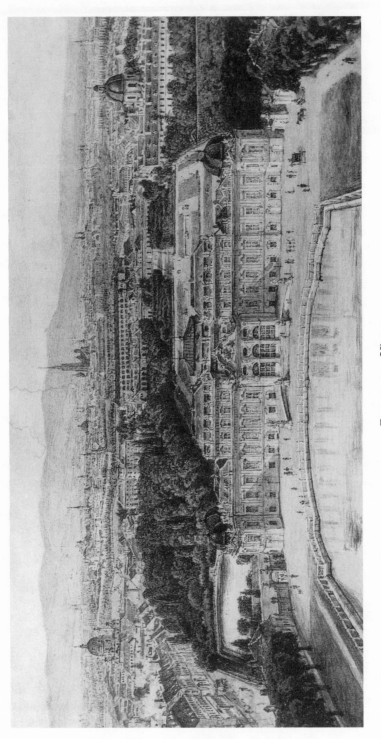

FIGURE 4.2. Vienna

music is performed in the imperial apartments which would drive a dog away. (A, 368–369)

To Leopold Mozart *Vienna, 18 April 1781*

Save for the long dialogues [in the aborted singspiel *Zaide*], which could easily be altered, the piece was very good, but not suitable for Vienna, where people prefer comic pieces. (A, 725)

To Leopold Mozart *Vienna, 26 May 1781*

It is quite certain that when I am in Salzburg I long for a hundred amusements, but here not for a single one. For just to be in Vienna is in itself entertainment enough. (A, 737)

To Leopold Mozart *Vienna, 2 June 1781*

It is perfectly true that the Viennese are apt to change their affections, *but only in the theater;* and my special line is too popular not to enable me to support myself. Vienna is certainly the land of the clavier! And, even granted that they do get tired of me, they will not do so for a few years, certainly not before then. (A, 739)

To Leopold Mozart *Vienna, 19 September 1781*

You know that I am composing an opera [*Die Entführung aus dem Serial*]. Those portions that I have finished have won extraordinary applause on all sides. I know this nation—and I have reason to think that my opera will be a success. If it is, then I shall be as popular in Vienna as a composer as I am on the clavier. (A, 766)

To Leopold Mozart *Vienna, 26 September 1781*

The Janissary chorus [from *Die Entführung*] is . . . all that can be desired, that is, short, lively, and written to please the Viennese . . . The first act was finished more than three weeks ago, as was also the aria in act II and the drunken duet *(per i signori viennesi)* which consists entirely of *my Turkish tattoo.* (A, 770)

To Leopold Mozart *Vienna, 21 May 1783*

Please keep on reminding Varesco about the matter you know of.[28] The chief thing must be the comic element, for I know the taste of the Viennese. (A, 849)

Lorenzo Da Ponte Memoirs, 1830

[In Vienna] *Don Giovanni* did not please! And what did the Emperor say?

He said: "That opera is divine; I should even venture that it is more beautiful than *Figaro*. But such music is not meant for the teeth of my Viennese!" I reported the remark to Mozart, who replied quietly: "Give them time to chew on it." He was not mistaken. On his advice I strove to procure frequent repetitions of the opera: at each performance the applause increased, and little by little even the Vienna of the dull teeth came to enjoy its savor and appreciate its beauties, and placed *Don Giovanni* among the most beautiful operas ever performed on any stage." (Da Ponte, 180)

▶ After he had settled in Vienna, Mozart's itinerant existence largely ended. He returned to Salzburg only once, during the summer and fall of 1783. And it was not until the spring of 1789 that he undertook an extensive concert tour: to Berlin and Leipzig. A year later, in the fall of 1790, he set out again, this time to Frankfurt am Main for the coronation of Leopold II. On the other hand, between January 1787 and September 1791, Mozart visited Prague no fewer than five times, including three longer and triumphant sojourns, connected, respectively, with a concert appearance and a performance of *Figaro* (in January and February 1787), with the premiere of *Don Giovanni* (October–November 1787), and with the premiere of *La Clemenza di Tito* (August–September 1791). ◀

To Gottfried von Jacquin, Vienna   *Prague, 15 January 1787*

I meet with all possible courtesies and honors here and . . . Prague is indeed a very beautiful and pleasant place. (Fig. 4.3). (A, 904)

To Gottfried von Jacquin, Vienna   *Prague, 15 October 1787*

The stage personnel here are not as smart as those in Vienna when it comes to mastering an opera of this kind [*Don Giovanni*] in a very short time. (A, 911)

Franz Xaver Niemetschek, Biography of Mozart, 1808

[Mozart] liked everything in Prague, where he was . . . carried along by an affectionate public and true friends. (DDB, 507)

▶ On the final extended journey of his life—to Frankfurt am Main, in the fall of 1790, for the coronation of Leopold II as Holy Roman Emperor—Mozart rapidly passed through the Bavarian towns of Regensburg, Nuremberg, Würzburg, and Aschaffenburg. In the course of a single letter to Constanze he provided thumbnail sketches for each. It is particularly notable that in virtually the same breath that Mozart condemned the medieval town of Nuremberg as "hideous," he extolled the "fine, magnificent," town of Würzburg, signaling his evident preference for the rococo taste in architecture. ◀

FIGURE 4.3. Prague

FIGURE 4.4.
Nuremberg

To Constanze   *Frankfurt am Main, 28 September 1790*

At Regensburg we lunched magnificently to the accompaniment of divine music, we had angelic cooking and some glorious Moselle wine. We breakfasted at Nuremberg, a hideous town [eine hässliche Stadt] (fig. 4.4).

At Würzburg, a fine, magnificent town, we fortified our precious stomachs with coffee. The food was tolerable everywhere, but at Aschaffenburg, two and a half stages from here, mine host was kind enough to fleece us disgracefully. (A, 942)

► With regard to Frankfurt itself, the proper destination of the adventure, Mozart opined: ◄

To Constanze   *Frankfurt am Main, 8 October 1790*

I am famous, admired, and popular here; on the other hand, the Frankfurt people are even more stingy than the Viennese. (A, 945)

JEWS

► Mozart's few references to Jews, while less than flattering, are also less than hostile. Certainly, in comparison with his opinions on the French and Italians, Mozart's comments about Jews were benign. He was obviously fond of the conceit of the Jews' waiting for their Messiah. Moreover, he did not fail to note the Jewishness of Eleonore Eskeles in the international scandal related earlier. He also chose to associate (at least syntactically) the wealth of his sometime landlord, Raimund Wetzlar, with his Jewishness, even though Wetzlar's father had long since converted to Catholicism.[29] On the other hand, Mozart's relations with Wetzlar were quite close. Indeed, Wetzlar was the godfather of Mozart's first son. (Another converted Jew in Mozart's circle was Lorenzo Da Ponte, whom he first met, incidentally, in Wetzlar's home. Whether Mozart was aware of Da Ponte's Jewish background is not known.) ◄

To Leopold Mozart   *Paris, 7 August 1778*

I know only too well that all these gentlemen [the members of the Salzburg court orchestra] are longing for a Kapellmeister as eagerly and hopefully as the Jews are awaiting their Messiah—but simply because in their present state things are unendurable. (A, 595)

To Leopold Mozart   *Vienna, 26 September 1781*

Fräulein von Auernhammer and I are longing to have the two double concertos.[30] I hope we shall not wait as vainly as the Jews for their Messiah. (A, 770)

To Leopold Mozart   *Vienna, 22 January 1783*

We are now in the small Herberstein house, No. 412, on the third floor. The house belongs to Herr Wetzlar—a rich Jew. (A, 838)

To Leopold Mozart   *Vienna, 21 May 1783*

My wife and I almost lost an honest friend, Baron Raimund Wetzlar, in whose house we used to live. That reminds me, we have been living in another house for some time and have not yet told you. Baron Wetzlar has taken a lady into his home; so, to oblige him, we moved before the time to a wretched lodging in the Kohlmarkt, in return for which he refused to take any rent for the three months we had lived in his house, and also paid the expenses of our removal. Meanwhile, we looked round for decent quarters and at last found them in the Judenplatz, where we are now living. Wetzlar paid for us, too, when we were in the Kohlmarkt. (A, 849)

To Leopold Mozart *Vienna, 18 June 1783*

Now for the godfather question. Let me tell you what has happened. After my wife's safe delivery[31] I immediately sent a message to Baron Wetzlar, who is a good and true friend of mine. He came to see us at once and offered to stand godfather. I could not refuse him and thought to myself: "After all, the boy can still be called Leopold." But while I was turning this round in my mind, the Baron said cheerfully: "Ah, now you have a little Raimund" —and kissed the child. What was I to do? Well, I have had the child christened Raimund Leopold. (A, 852)

5

Personal Affairs

I like to enjoy myself, but rest assured that I can be as serious as anyone else can.

Mannheim, 20 December 1777

► Wolfgang Amadeus Mozart has become in our day the supreme symbol of human creativity, the personification of artistic perfection. But during his lifetime, he was, for all his surpassing musical genius, an all-too-human, all-too-fallible, fellow creature. He was not the "Amadeus" of old or new legend. Indeed, he was not even Amadeus in name. He was baptized Joannes Chrysostomus Wolfgangus Theophilus. In his youth he signed his name simply "Wolfgang." His father often referred to him in letters to third parties as "Wolfgang Gottlieb"—Gottlieb being the German equivalent of Theophilus ("beloved of God"). From about the age of twenty-two on, Mozart regularly signed his name "Wolfgang Amade Mozart"—with or without an accent (going in either direction, grave or acute) over the final *e*. Only twice in his life, in 1774 and in 1779—and both times in a jocular context—did Mozart use the name "Amadeus." The name Amadeus begins to make its appearance literally at the moment of Mozart's death: on the death certificate, on the estate documents, in the newspaper obituaries. It only became established as the standard, indeed official, name of the composer because the publishers Breitkopf & Härtel chose it when they began to publish a complete edition of Mozart's works in 1799.[1] The name "Amadeus," however, is symptomatic. The Latin form seems to clothe the man in the aura of classical purity and universality—more lofty, and more bloodless, than his own choices of "Amade," "Amadeo," or, often enough, no middle name at all. One would be hard put to think of any other composer after 1600 to have been posthumously given a Latinized name.

Mozart, not surprisingly, was in reality a complex but ultimately understandable man: subject to changing moods, capable of holding contradictory opinions, of enjoying numerous amusements both high and low, and burdened with both petty and serious weaknesses and vulnerabilities. What follows is a verbal self-portrait of sorts—really a sketch rather than a portrait—or, if one prefers, a confession: of attitudes, feelings, and convictions ranging from the amusing and trivial to the profound and serious. ◄

AMUSEMENTS AND PASTIMES

► The sources of recreation and amusement that appealed to Mozart seem to have been almost limitless. On the one hand, he delighted in moderate physical activities and stimuli: billiards, bowling, fencing, and horseback riding; dancing and pantomime; beer, wine, tobacco, and colorful clothing. On the other hand—by no means unrelated to the preceding—he was, like many musicians, fascinated by language and languages: by their sounds and, especially, by their capacity for combining and recombining sounds and their attendant meanings, as in poems and puns, and also linguistic games and riddles of all kinds. Common to all these enthusiasms is a strong sensual element. Mozart was a "man, whose world was one of attitudes and feelings, not concepts."[2] In a word, Wolfgang Amadé Mozart was a sensualist. The Mozartean pleasures run the alphabetical gamut from A (Acrostics) to Z (Zoroastran Riddles). ◄

ACROSTICS

► For the Mozart family, recognition of the political realities prevailing in the Europe of autocratic emperors, kings, and prince-archbishops often necessitated the precaution of expressing sensitive or irreverent opinions on paper in code. On at least one occasion Mozart was inspired to elaborate a variation on this prudent but prosaic policy by indulging his penchant for word play. ◄

To Leopold Mozart   *Munich, 24 November 1780*

If only the **a**ss who smashes a **r**ing, and by so doing **c**uts himself a **h**iatus in his **b**ehind so that **I** hear him **s**hit like a castrato with **h**orns, and with his long ear **o**ffers to caress the fox's **p**osterior, were not so . . . (A, 672)

► The boldface letters spell "archbishop."[3] ◄

BILLIARDS

► In his letters Mozart makes only a single reference to billiards, close to the end of his life. But it is clear from the testimony of others that he must have been playing, passionately, for years. The testimony as to whether he could play well, however, is by no means unanimous. ◄

To Constanze, Baden   *Vienna, 7 October 1791*

Immediately after your departure I played two games of billiards with Herr von Mozart, the fellow who wrote the opera [*Die Zauberflöte*] which is running at Schikaneder's theater. (A, 967)

The Reminiscences of Michael Kelly, 1826

He was also fond of billards, and had an excellent billiard table in his house. Many and many a game have I played with him, but always came off second best. (Kelly 1:223)

The Reminiscences of Constanze Mozart, 1829

Billiards he was very fond of, but he composed while he played. (Novello, 95)

► Finally, a colorful, if dubious, account, dated November 1815, from the diary of Sulpiz Boisserée: ◄

[Mozart] was a passionate player of billiards, and played badly. Whenever a famous billiard player arrived in Vienna, it was of more interest to him than the arrival of a famous musician. The latter, he opined, would come to him all right, the former he looked up himself; he played for high stakes, whole nights long. (DDB, 515)

BOWLING

► Mozart learned bowling, or at least the Italian version, *bocce*, by the time he was fourteen. He obviously kept up the game in later years, and even found musical inspiration, it seems, in the percussive clatter of the falling pins. The Trio for Piano, Clarinet, and Viola, K. 498, composed in August 1786, is said to have been written at the "Kegelstatt" (i.e., bowling alley). And Mozart himself attests to that site for the inspiration of at least one other composition. ◄

To Nannerl   *Rome, 25 April 1770*

Immediately after lunch we play boccia. That is a game which I have learned in Rome. When I come home, I shall teach it to you [Italian]. (A, 131)

► On the heading of the autograph manuscript of the Twelve Duos for Two Wind Instruments, K. 487: ◄

"By Wolfgang Amadé Mozart . . . Vienna, the 27th of July 1786, while bowling."[4]

CARD TRICKS

▶ According to Nannerl, when the Mozarts were in the Austrian town of Olmütz, that is, in November 1767, Wolfgang took an interest in card tricks. It is not known whether he maintained this interest later on. ◀

The Memoirs of Nannerl Mozart, 1800

In Olmütz . . . the court chaplain to the Bishop there, Herr Hay . . . visited us daily. He was highly skilled at card tricks. My brother learned them from him with great rapidity. (DDB, 494)

CARNIVALS, MASKS

▶ Mozart was familiar at first hand with the characters and the antics of the age-old *commedia dell'arte*, the ultimate source of opera buffa. Moreover, like his father, apparently, he enjoyed playing in it himself, an experience that presumably helped refine his unsurpassed instinct for stage comedy. ◀

To Leopold Mozart   *Vienna, 22 January 1783*

You are doubtless aware that this is carnival time and that there is as much dancing here as in Salzburg and Munich. Well, I should very much like to go as Harlequin (but not a soul must know about it)—because here there are so many—indeed, nothing but silly asses at the Redoutes. So I should like you to send me your Harlequin costume. But please do so very soon, for we shall not attend the Redoutes until I have it, although they are now in full swing. We prefer private balls. (A, 837)

To Leopold Mozart   *Vienna, 12 March 1783*

On Carnival Monday our company of masqueraders went to the Redoute, where we performed a pantomime which exactly filled the half hour when there is a pause in the dancing. My sister-in-law was Columbine; I, Harlequin; my brother-in-law, Pierrot; an old dancing master (Merk), Pantaloon; and a painter (Grassi), the doctor. Both the plot and the music of the pantomime were mine. Merk, the dancing master, was so kind as to coach us, and I must say we played it charmingly. I am enclosing the program that was distributed to the company by a mask, dressed as a local postman.[5] (A, 842)

CLOTHES

▶ Mozart's early biographer Franz Xaver Niemetschek remarked that "There was nothing special about the physique of this extraordinary man; he was small and his countenance, except for his large, intense eyes, gave no signs of his genius. . . . The ungainliness of his appearance, his small build, was due to the overtaxing of his brain in his youth and the lack of exercise in his childhood." It may be that Mozart suffered from the "ungainliness of his appearance" and that, in compensation for this, he set great store on clothes. But perhaps Mozart's taste for luxurious and colorful clothing was nourished by the same impulse that informed the richness and sensuousness of his orchestrations, on the one hand, and his instinct for the theatrical, on the other. ◄

To Baroness von Waldstätten   *Vienna, 8 May 1782*

A satin or gros de turc silk dress must be trimmed, of course, with silk fringes, and Constanze has a dress of this kind. An ordinary dress of pretty Saxon piqué trimmed with cotton fringes (which, unless you feel them, can hardly be distinguished from silk), looks very well; and the advantage of such a combination is that the fringes can be washed on the dress. (A, 804)

To Baroness von Waldstätten   *Vienna, 28 September 1782*

As for the beautiful red coat, which attracts me enormously, please, please let me know *where it is to be had and how much it costs*—for that I have completely forgotten, as I was so captivated by its splendor that I did not take note of its price. I must have a coat like that, for it is one that will really do justice to certain buttons which I have long been hankering after. I saw them once, when I was choosing some for a suit. They were in Brandau's button factory in the Kohlmarkt, opposite the Milano. They are mother-of-pearl with a few white stones round the edge and a fine yellow stone in the center. I should like all my things to be of good quality, genuine and beautiful. Why is it, I wonder, that those who cannot afford it, would like to spend a fortune on such articles and those who can, do not do so? (A, 823)

DANCING

To Leopold Mozart   *Munich, 6 October 1777*

Yesterday, Sunday, October 5, we had a religious wedding or *altum tempus ecclesiasticum* [a high religious occasion] and there was dancing. I danced only four minuets and by eleven o'clock I was back in my room, for among fifty ladies there was only one who could keep in time. (A, 298–299)

The Reminiscences of Michael Kelly, 1826

After supper the young branches of our host had a dance, and Mozart joined them. Madame Mozart told me that, great as his genius was, he was an enthusiast in dancing, and often said that his taste lay in that art, rather than in music. (Kelly, 1:223)

DARTS (*Bölzlschießen*)

▶ *Bözlschießen*, a marksmanship sport in which darts were shot at a target, was a favorite of the entire Mozart family. The target was normally decorated with pictures and slogans chosen by the players. For example, in the postscript of a letter to his father Mozart expressed his desire for a target to be painted as follows: ◀

To Leopold Mozart   *Mannheim, 4 November 1777*

As for the targets, if it is not too late, this is what I would like. A short man with fair hair, shown bending over and displaying his bare arse. From his mouth come the words: "Good appetite for the meal." The other man to be shown booted and spurred with a red cloak and a fine fashionable wig. He must be of medium height and in such a position that he licks the other man's arse. From his mouth come the words: "Oh, there's nothing to beat it." So, please. If not this time, another time. (A, 358)

▶ There can be little doubt that the short man with fair hair is Mozart and the man in a red cloak the Archbishop. ◀

DOGGEREL[6]

▶ Mozart's love of wordplay extended, not surprisingly, to doggerel verse. He appended the following rhyme to a letter written by his mother. The addressee, Rosalie Joli (1726–1788), a Salzburg friend of the Mozart family and the daughter of the royal confectioner, had sent Mozart good wishes on his name day, October 31. ◀

To Leopold Mozart   *Mannheim, 31 October 1777*

À Mademoiselle Rosalie Joli

A thousand thanks, dear Sally, for your wishes.
Now in your honor I shall drink whole dishes
Of coffee, tea, and even lemonade,
Dipping therein a sticklet of pomade,
And also—Oh! It's striking six o'clock!
Whoe'er denies it, well, he's just a—block. (A, 351)

▶ The following item is fascinating not so much for its scatological crudity as for Mozart's addressing it to his mother. But such modes of expression were not unusual in the Mozart household, and we must conclude that Madame Mozart in particular rather enjoyed such humor. ◄

To his Mother   *Worms, 31 January 1778*

Oh, mother mine!
Butter is fine.
Praise and thanks to be to Him.
We're alive and full of vim.
Through the world we dash,
Though we're rather short of cash.
But we don't find this provoking
And none of us are choking.
Besides, to people I'm tied
Who carry their muck inside
And let it out, if they are able,
Both before and after table.
At night of farts there is no lack,
Which are let off, forsooth, with powerful crack.
The king of farts came yesterday
Whose farts smelt sweeter than the May.
His voice, however, was no treat
And he himself was in a heat.
Well, now we've been over a week away
And we've been shitting every day.
Wendling, no doubt, is in a rage
That I haven't composed a single page;
But when I cross the Rhine once more,
I'll surely dash home through the door
And lest he call me mean and petty,
I'll finish off his four quartetti.
The concerto for Paris I'll keep, 'tis more fitting.
I'll scribble it there some day when I'm shitting.
Indeed I swear 'twould be better fun
With the Webers round the world to run
Than to go with those bores, you know whom I mean,
When I think of their faces, I get the spleen.
But I suppose it must be off we shall toddle,
Though Weber's arse I prefer to Ramm's noddle.
A slice of Weber's arse is a thing
I'd rather have than Monsieur Wendling.
With our shitting God we cannot hurt
And least of all if we bite the dirt.

We are honest birds, all of a feather,
We have summa summarum eight eyes together,
Not counting those on which we sit.
But now I really must rest a bit
From rhyming. Yet this I must add,
That on Monday I'll have the honor, egad,
To embrace you and kiss your hands so fair.
But first in my pants I'll shit, I swear.[7]

Worms, January 1778th
Anno 31.

Your faithful child,
With distemper wild
Trazom
(A, 456–457)

► On the occasion of his sister's wedding, 23 August 1784, to Johann Baptist von Berchthold zu Sonnenburg, Mozart penned an appropriate set of verses. (Henceforth, Nannerl lived in the Austrian town of St. Gilgen until her husband's death in 1801, whereupon she returned to Salzburg.) ◄

To Nannerl   *Vienna, 18 August 1784*

I send you a thousand good wishes from Vienna to Salzburg, and hope particularly that you two will live together as harmoniously as—we two! So take a little piece of advice from my poetical brainbox! Listen:

Wedlock will show you many things
Which still a mystery remain;
Experience soon will teach to you
What Eve herself once had to do
Before she could give birth to Cain.
But all these duties are so light
You will perform them with delight.
Yet no state is an unmixed joy
And marriage has its own alloy,
Lest us its bliss perchance should cloy.
So when your husband shows reserve
Or wrath which you do not deserve
And perhaps a nasty temper too,
Think, sister, 'tis a man's queer way
Say: "Lord, thy will be done by day,
But mine at night you'll do." (A, 882)

DOODLES (A, 653)

▶ Constanze Mozart told the Novellos that Mozart "was fond of painting
—sculpture—and could draw himself." The most ambitious example
of his talent in this regard seems to be a portrait—or anatomical study,
perhaps?—of his cousin Bäsle (fig. 5.1). ◀

To Maria Anna Thekla Mozart (Bäsle),   *Salzburg, 10 May 1709 [sic:*
Augsburg   *actually 1779]*

Fig. I. Kopf [Head]

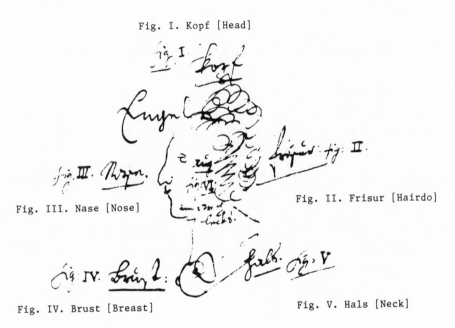

Fig. III. Nase [Nose]

Fig. II. Frisur [Hairdo]

Fig. IV. Brust [Breast]

Fig. V. Hals [Neck]

FIGURE 5.1. Doodle Portrait of "Bäsle"

FENCING

▶ Along with card tricks, the eleven-year-old Mozart learned fencing in
Olmütz. ◀

The Memoirs of Nannerl Mozart, 1800

In Olmütz . . . as the local fencing master . . . visited us, this gentleman
had to teach [Wolfgang] to fence. (DDB, 494)

FOOD, DRINK, AND TOBACCO

▶ The occasional references to his favorite foods reveal that Mozart never renounced his central European palate. At the beginning of the year 1771, for example, after having endured the culinary fare of Italy for more than a year, Wolfgang craved some honest Austrian cuisine. ◀

Leopold Mozart to his Wife   *Milan, 5 January 1771*

We lunched on Thursday with Madame D'Aste, née Marianne Troger, who fed us most magnificently on liver dumplings and sauerkraut, which Wolfgang had asked for. (A, 178)

▶ In Vienna, too, he longed for, and had to import, native dishes. ◀

To Leopold Mozart   *Vienna, 31 August 1782*

May I also ask you to send me some Salzburg tongues . . . (if the customs duty does not make it impossible)? I am under great obligations to the Baroness [von Waldstädten] and when the conversation one day turned on tongues and she said she would very much like to try a Salzburg one, I offered to get one for her. . . . Can you send me some Schwarzreuter [i.e., a trout from the Salzkammergut lakes]? (A, 818–819)

To Leopold Mozart   *Vienna, 11 September 1782*

Many thanks for the tongues. I gave two to the Baroness and kept the other two for myself; and we are to sample them tomorrow. . . . If you can also obtain some Schwarzreuter for me, you will indeed give me much pleasure. (A, 819)

To Michael Puchberg   *Vienna, 20 February 1790*

Had I known that your supply of beer had almost run out, I should certainly never have ventured to rob you of it; I therefore take the liberty of returning herewith the second measure, as today I am already provided with wine. I thank you heartily for the first one, and the next time you have a supply of beer, pray send me a little of it. You know how much I like it. (A, 935)

▶ And for dessert: ◀

To Leopold Mozart   *Paris, 3 July 1778*

I was so happy that as soon as the symphony was over, I went off to the

Palais Royal, where I had a large ice [*ein guts gefrornes* most likely a cold fruit drink], said the Rosary as I had vowed to do—and went home. (A, 557–558)

▶ Finally, to end the repast: ◀

To Constanze, Baden   *Vienna, 8 October 1791*

I told Joseph to get Primus to fetch me some black coffee, with which I smoked a splendid pipe of tobacco.[8] (A, 967)

▶ Posthumous accounts add two further morsels of information. ◀

The Reminiscences of Michael Kelly, 1826

He was remarkably fond of punch, of which beverage I have seen him take copious drafts. (Kelly, 1:223)

The Reminiscences of Constanze Mozart, 1829

Mozart [was] particularly fond of fish, especially trout. (Novello, 213)

HORSEBACK RIDING

▶ The only reference to his horse by Mozart himself was on the occasion of its sale: ◀

To Constanze, Baden   *Vienna, 7/8 October 1791*

Then I sold my nag for fourteen ducats. (A, 967)

▶ But his sister-in-law, Sophie Haibel, attested to his fondness for riding. ◀

The Memoirs of Sophie Haibel, 1828

In his pastimes he was always passionately attached to the latest of them, and so it was with riding, and also with billiards. (DDB, 537)

LANGUAGES: FRENCH, ENGLISH

▶ Mozart was certainly passionately attached to, and fascinated by, foreign languages—a product, no doubt, of both his musicality and the extensive travels of his youth. He was fluent in Italian and French, and particularly interested in English. He claimed to be "an out-and-out Englishman" and had planned on more than one occasion to travel to Britain. ◀

To Bäsle, Augsburg   *Mannheim, 13 November 1777*

Adieu, j'espére que vous aurés deja pris quelque lection dans la langue
française, et je ne doute point que—*Ecoutés:* que vous saurés bientôt mieux
le français, que moi; car il y a certainement deux ans, que je n'ai pas ecrit
un môt dans cette langue. adieu cependant. je vous baise vos mains, votre
visage, vos genoux et votre—afin, tout ce que vous me permettés de
baiser. je suis de tout mon coeur/votre/trés affectioné Neveu et Cousin/
Wolfg: Amadé Mozart (A, 372)[9]

To Leopold Mozart   *Vienna, 17 August 1782*

Latterly I have been practicing my French daily and have already taken
three lessons in English. In three months I hope to be able to read and
understand English books fairly easily. (A, 815)

► On spilling a drop of ink (fig. 5.2). ◄

To Leopold Mozart   *Vienna, 4 January 1783*
(A, 835)

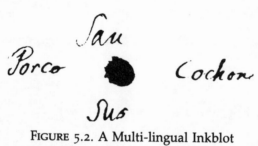

FIGURE 5.2. A Multi-lingual Inkblot

► The English composer Thomas Attwood was a pupil of Mozart's in
theory and composition. His exercises have been preserved and have
been published.[10] Although most of Mozart's verbal comments are in
Italian, some are in English—among them numerous one-word judgments of "bad" or "good," but also the following (preserving Mozart's
spelling). Under a canceled bass harmonization exercise: ◄

"There are many faults in this Exempl[e. You must become more]
attentive"[11]

► After a poorly executed counterpoint assignment: ◄

"you are an ass."

► And, more prosaically: ◄

"This after noon I am not at home, therfore I pray you to come to morrow at three a half—Mozart"

► Mozart wrote the following aphorism, in English, in the family album of a Viennese language teacher and fellow Mason, one Johann Georg Kronauer: ◄

30 March 1787

Patience and tranquillity of mind contribute more tu cure our distempers as the whole art of Medicine.

► It was at about this time that Mozart was seriously contemplating a trip to London. Before Attwood had left for England, in February 1787, Mozart had asked him to try to arrange an opera contract or concert series for him.[12] ◄

NAME GAMES

► The thirty-two-year-old composer was not embarrassed to write the following to his good friend. Mozart's exceptionally high spirits provoked by the Prague successes may have had something to do with the infantile silliness. ◄

To Gottfried von Jacquin, Vienna   *Prague, 15 January 1787*

Now farewell, dearest friend, dearest Hinkiti Honky! That is your name, so that you know. We all invented names for ourselves on the journey. Here they are. I am Punkititi. My wife is Schabla Pumfa. Hofer [a brother-in-law] is Rozka-Pumpa. [Anton] Stadler is Natschibinitschibi. My servant Joseph is Sagadaratà. My dog Gauckerl is Schamanuzky. Madame Quallenberg is Runzifunzi. Mlle. [Marianne] Crux PS. Ramlo is Schurimuri. [Franz Jakob] Freystädtler [one of Mozart's pupils] is Gaulimauli. Be so kind as to tell him his name. . . . Embrace your brother (who by the way could be christened Blatterizi) a thousand times for me; and I kiss your sister's hands (her name is Signora Diniminimi) a hundred thousand times. (A, 904)

NATURE

► Mozart hardly mentions nature in his letters, but he evidently enjoyed it. He specifically refers to the luxurious formal grounds maintained by his patron, Count Cobenzl, and the famous cultivated gardens at Schloss Schwetzingen, near Mannheim. Constanze attests to a similar fondness for the park at Schloss Aigen in Salzburg. ◄

To Leopold Mozart [Reisenberg], 13 July 1781

I am writing to you at an hour's distance from Vienna, at a place called Reisenberg. I once spent a night here, and now I am staying for a few days. The little house is nothing much, but the country—the forest—in which my host [Count Cobenzl] has built a grotto which looks just as if Nature herself had fashioned it! Indeed the surroundings are magnificent and very delightful. (A, 751–752)

To Constanze Mannheim, 23 October 1790

We are going to Schwetzingen tomorrow to see the gardens. (A, 947)

The Reminiscences of Constanze Mozart, 1829

He was very fond of Salzburg's picturesque scenery—especially of the romantic grounds at Aigen. . . . Especially fond of flowers. . . . extremely fond of the country and a passionate admirer of everything that was beautiful in nature—liked little excursions and passed much of their time out of town. (Novello, 109)

Pets

► Mozart, as we have seen, owned a dog in Vienna by the name of Gauckerl. During the Salzburg years the Mozarts had a female fox terrier variously called Pimperl, Bimperl, or Miss Bimbes. ◄

To Nannerl Vienna, 21 August 1773

How is Miss Bimbes? Please give her all sorts of messages from me.

► In addition, there were birds in the Mozart households: a canary in Salzburg and a starling in Vienna. ◄

To Nannerl Naples, 19 May 1770

Tell me, how is Mr. Canary? Does he still sing? And still whistle? Do you know what makes me think of him? Because there is a canary in our front room which makes a noise just like ours. (A, 137)

► The Viennese starling was especially musical. ◄

From Mozart's Account Book Vienna, 27 May 1784

[Purchased:] A Starling 34 kreuzer

EXAMPLE 5.1. The Starling's Tune

That was lovely! (DDB, 225).

► Mozart was obviously delighted that the starling had learned to sing, almost perfectly, the rondo melody from the G-major Piano Concerto, K. 453, composed in April (ex. 5.2). ◄

EXAMPLE 5.2. Piano Concerto in G, K. 453, Opening Theme of Rondo Finale

► On its death on 4 June 1787, exactly one week after Leopold Mozart's death on May 28, Mozart composed an elegy in memory of the starling: ◄

> A little fool lies here
> Whom I held dear—
> A starling in the prime
> Of his brief time,
> Whose doom it was to drain
> Death's bitter pain.
> Thinking of this, my heart
> Is riven apart.
> Oh reader! Shed a tear,
> You also, here.
> He was not naughty, quite,
> But gay and bright,
> And under all his brag
> A foolish wag.
> This no one can gainsay
> And I will lay
> That he is now on high,
> And from the sky,
> Praises me without pay
> In his friendly way.
> Yet unaware that death

Has choked his breath,
And thoughtless of the one
Whose rime is thus well done.

4 June 1787   Mozart[13]

SCATOLOGY[14]

► Mozart seems to have derived particular pleasure from earthy, scatological language. But it is important to realize that language of this sort was by no means taboo in the eighteenth century among the middle class. Body parts and functions were called by their vernacular names, not their Latin euphemisms, and the Mozart family correspondence contains numerous references of this kind. We have seen that the only surviving letter written by Mozart directly and exclusively to his mother consisted of nothing but an awful poem made up of scatological couplets. It would seem that talking about the excretory functions in the late eighteenth century was something of an obsession—a bit like talking about one's diet today, perhaps, or about one's analysis, and no more gauche.

For his part, Mozart's scatological writing is concentrated in the series of letters he wrote to his first cousin, Maria Anna Thekla Mozart, the daughter of Leopold Mozart's brother. They were mainly written in the year 1777–1778, when Mozart was twenty-two years old, and his cousin, whom he called "Bäsle" or "Little Cousin," was turning twenty. Their temporal concentration is significant. This was just the time when Mozart fell deeply in love for the first time in his life—with the singer Aloysia Weber, the sister of his future wife. Perhaps there is a link between the infantile outbursts of crude language in the Bäsle letters and Mozart's infatuation with Aloysia Weber. The letters may have constituted an important outlet for pent-up sexual tensions that must have been almost unbearable for Wolfgang at this time; that is, scatology may have functioned as a substitute—a rather bizarre form of "sublimation"—for the erotic impulses directed toward Aloysia.

It is important to stress two further points about the Bäsle letters—and such similar documents as Mozart's doggerel poem to his mother dating from the same period (January 1778)—and the various vulgar canons. First, their obscenities are almost exclusively scatological. They contain few sexual references.[15] The second point is that their recipients—Bäsle (fig. 5.3)—and Mozart's mother, too—must have been amused by them. Mozart, it seems, was willing to tailor not only his music but his language, as well, to suit his audience. ◄

To Bäsle   *Mannheim, 28 February 1778*

Mademoiselle ma trés chére Cousine!
Perhaps you think or even are convinced that I am dead? That I have pegged out [croaked]? Or hopped a twig [kicked the bucket]? Not at all.

FIGURE 5.3. "Bäsle" Mozart

Don't believe it, I implore you. For believing and shitting are two very different things! Now how could I be writing such a beautiful hand if I were dead? How could that be possible? I shan't apologize for my very long silence, for you would never believe me. Yet what is true is true. I have had so many things to do that I had time indeed to think of my little cousin, but not to write, you see. So I just had to let things be. But now I have the honor to inquire how you are and whether you perspire? Whether your stomach is still in good order? Whether indeed you have no disorder? Whether you still can like me at all? Whether with chalk you often scrawl? Whether now and then you have me in mind? Whether to hang yourself you sometimes feel inclined? Whether you have been wild? With this poor foolish child? Whether to make peace with me you'll be so kind? If not, I swear I'll let off one behind! Ah, you're laughing! Victoria! Our arses shall be the symbol of our peacemaking! I knew you wouldn't be able to resist me much longer. Why, of course, I'm sure of success, even if today I should make a mess, though to Paris in a fortnight or less. So, if you want to send a reply to me from that town of Augsburg yonder, you see, then write at once, the sooner the better, so that I may be sure to receive your letter, or else if I'm gone I'll have the bad luck, instead of a letter to get some muck. Muck!—Muck!—Ah, muck! Sweet word! Muck! chuck! That too is fine. Muck, chuck!—muck! suck!—o charmante! muck, suck! That's what I like! Muck, chuck, and suck! Chuck muck and suck muck! . . . My greetings to every single friend, and whoever doesn't believe me, may lick me world without end, from now to eternity, until I cease to be a nonentity. He can go on licking forever, in truth, why, even I am alarmed, forsooth, for I fear that my muck will soon dry up and that he won't have enough if he wants to sup. Adieu, little cousin. I am, I was, I should be, I have been, I had been, I should have been, oh that I were, oh that I might be, would to God I were, I shall be, if I should be, oh that I should be, I shall have been, oh that I had been, would to God that I had been, what?—a duffer. Adieu ma chère cousine, where have you been? I am your same old faithful cousin

Wolfgang Amadé Mozart

(A, 499–501)

► Clearly pertinent to this edifying topic is the six-part canon, *Leck mich im Arsch*, K. 231/382c, presumably dating from 1782 (ex. 5.3). ◄

EXAMPLE 5.3. Canon: Leck mich im Arsch, K. 231 (382c), for six Parts with Opening of Realization

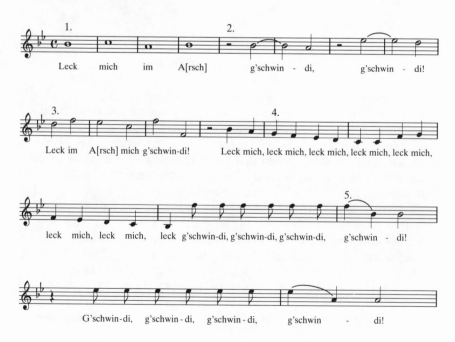

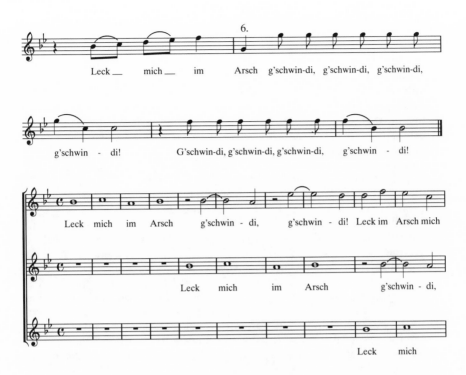

Leck __ mich __ im Arsch g'schwin-di, g'schwin-di, g'schwin-di,

g'schwin - di! G'schwin-di, g'schwin-di, g'schwin-di, g'schwin - di!

Leck mich im Arsch g'schwin - di, g'schwin - di! Leck im Arsch mich

Leck mich im Arsch g'schwin - di,

Leck mich

► Until most recently only the opening four words of the canon were known in their authentic form. (Translation: "Lick my arse.") When the canon was published in the nineteenth century, the words were replaced with "Laßt froh uns sein" (i.e., "Let's be happy"). The remainder of the original text—consisting only of the additional word "g'schwindi" ("hurry"), along with a plethora of repetitions—has now come to light. It was entered in ink into a copy of the nineteenth-century Breitkopf & Härtel edition.[16] ◄

SIGN LANGUAGE

► Mozart was fascinated, too, by yet another kind of language altogether: that of the deaf, which he learned at the age of fourteen in Milan. ◄

To Nannerl   *Milan, 27 October 1770*

At the moment I am talking in signs, as the son of the house is deaf and dumb from birth. (A, 168)

To Nannerl   *Milan, 31 August 1771*

My only amusement is to talk the deaf and dumb language, and that I can do to perfection. (A, 195)

ZOROASTRAN PROVERBS AND RIDDLES

► Mozart's enjoyment of carnival festivals was reported earlier. On 19
February 1786 he attended the Vienna Carnival dressed not as Harlequin this time but as the philosopher Zoroaster, the model for both
Zarathustra and Sarastro. For the occasion he prepared—and went to
the trouble of having printed—a set of eight riddles and fourteen
proverbs entitled *Excerpts from Zoroaster's Fragments*. He sent a copy to
Leopold who placed them at the disposal of the editor of a Salzburg
journal, the *Oberdeutsche Staatszeitung*. Several of the proverbs and one
of the riddles then appeared in the issue of 23 March 1786. Until 1970
the remaining riddles were lost. They have since been published in the
German edition of the Mozart letters and in translation by Maynard
Solomon.[17] With the exception of the first riddle, the official solutions
are still lost. Riddling, as Solomon points out, was a popular social
pastime during the 1780s. Its appeal for Mozart was based on the "play
principle," also "a longing for the secret and forbidden." The Carnival,
for its part, presented Mozart with the opportunity to do "publicly what
he dares not attempt in private: he violates taboos, without conscious
expectation of punishment."[18] Solomon's translation is part of a provoc-
ative psychoanalytical interpretation that attempts to fathom their
autobiographical import. It calls attention, among other things, to the
sexual symbolism, as well as the imagery of mutilation and death that
permeate the riddles. ◄

Vienna, 19 February 1786

[*Proverbs*]

　1. Talk much—and talk badly; but this last will follow of itself: all eyes
　　　and ears will be directed toward you.
　4. I prefer an open vice to an equivocal virtue; it at least shows me
　　　where I stand.
　5. A hypocrite anxious to pretend to virtue can imitate it only with
　　　watercolors.
　10. It is not seemly for everybody to be modest; only great men are able
　　　to be so.
　11. If you are poor but clever, arm yourself with patience, and work. If
　　　you do not grow rich, you will at least remain a clever man.—If you
　　　are an ass, but wealthy, take advantage of your good fortune and be
　　　lazy. If you do not become poor, you will at least remain an ass.
　12. A woman is praised in the surest and most tender fashion by abuse
　　　of her rivals. But how many men are not women in this respect?
　14. If you are a poor dunce, become a C[leric]. If you are a rich dunce,
　　　become a tenant. If you are a noble but poor dunce—become what
　　　you can, for bread. If you are a wealthy noble dunce, become what
　　　you like; only—pray—not a man of sense.

[*Riddles*]

> One can possess me without seeing me.
> One can carry me without feeling me.
> One can give me without having me.
>
> s.h.n.o.r., i.e., "Horns" (*D.e.e.h.i.n.ö.r.r.*, i.e., *Die Hörner*)

1. We are many sisters; it is painful for us to unite as well as to separate. We live in a palace, yet we could rather call it a prison, for we live securely locked up and must work for the sustenance of men. The most remarkable thing is that the doors are opened for us quite often, both day and night, and still we do not come out, except when one pushes us out by force. [Answer: teeth.][19]

2. I am an altogether patient thing; I let myself be used by everyone. Through me the truth, the lie, erudition, and stupidity are proclaimed to the world. He who wants to know everything need only come and ask me, for I know everything. Since everybody needs me I am told everything. Money changers can well use me; I also serve barbers sometimes. I am inevitably necessary to the [illegible word] and [illegible word]. Through me are the most important affairs of state arranged, wars conducted, and lands conquered. Through my endurance the sick receive health, also frequently death. In brief, happiness, unhappiness, life, and death often depend upon me. One would imagine that so many superior qualities would make me happy. O no! My death is generally terrifying—painful, and when it happens gently, base and contemptible. Nevertheless, should I die in the last manner at the hand of a beautiful woman, so shall I take that consolation with me to the grave, that I have seen some things which not everyone gets to see.

3. I am an unusual (*sonderbares*) thing; I have no soul and no body; one cannot see me but can hear me; I do not exist for myself; only a human being can give me life, as often as he wishes; and my life is only of short duration, for I die almost at the moment in which I am born. And so, in accordance with men's caprice, I may live and die untold times a day. To those who give me life I do nothing—but those on whose account I am born I leave with painful sensations for the short duration of my life until I depart. Whatever passions a man finds himself in at the time when he grants me life I will surely bring those along into the world. For the most part, women produce me gently and amiably; many have modestly confessed their love in this way. Many have also saved their virtue through me; in these cases, however, my life can scarcely endure a quarter of an hour. I must come into the world by a singular stroke of fortune: otherwise there is no outlet—the man is deformed. [Answer: a fart.][20]

4. I serve many as an ornament, many as a mutilation. However, I am highly necessary to everyone. Sometimes it would be better if I were not there; sometimes, on the other hand, it is a blessing (Wohltat) that I am there. Frequently even entire [illegible word] are uncovered through me. Frequently many men are even freed of [illegible word] insults through me. Men regard me as a good recommendation to women. I serve old people also, beyond my obligations; on that account [two illegible words] people who become old [illegible word] take care of me, so that I am not spoiled, let alone die before my time.

5. We are created for man's pleasures. How can we help it if an accident befalls by which we become the opposite of them? If he is lacking one of us, then he is—defective.

Postscript

► It is important to recognize that Mozart did not pursue *every* fashionable amusement of the day—for example, the popular flight attempts of the balloonist François Blanchard. ◄

To Constanze, Baden   *Vienna, 7 July 1791*

I did not go to see the balloon, for it is the sort of thing which one can imagine. Besides, I thought that this time, too, nothing would come of it. (A, 963)

► It may be, though, that Blanchard's balloon flights had an influence on the aerial scene following Sarastro's aria, "In diesen heil'gen Hallen," in act 2 of *Die Zauberflöte*.[21] ◄

CONFESSIONS

My chief fault is that—judging by appearances—I do not always act as I should.

13 June 1781

CHILDHOOD: EARLY HABITS, EARLY DREAMS

► The time has come to fill in the blemishes on the self-portrait. We begin at the beginning: in the crucible of childhood—and innocently enough. Mozart's *slightest* fault, no doubt, one for which he self-deprecatingly apologizes more than once, was his poor (text) handwriting: presumably a product of his irregular education, but also of his evidently lifelong impatience with writing mere words. Mozart could, with effort, write in a fair hand, although it was clearly a chore. He was often inclined, like the proverbial poor carpenter, to blame his tools for his unsatisfactory penmanship (fig. 5.4). But the fault, in truth, lay not in his pen; at the age of twenty-two, he had to beg his father, with some impatience (and perhaps desperation), to send him the letters of the alphabet so that he could practice copying them. ◄

To Nannerl *Naples, 5 June 1770*

What a beautiful handwriting mine is, is it not? (A, 143)

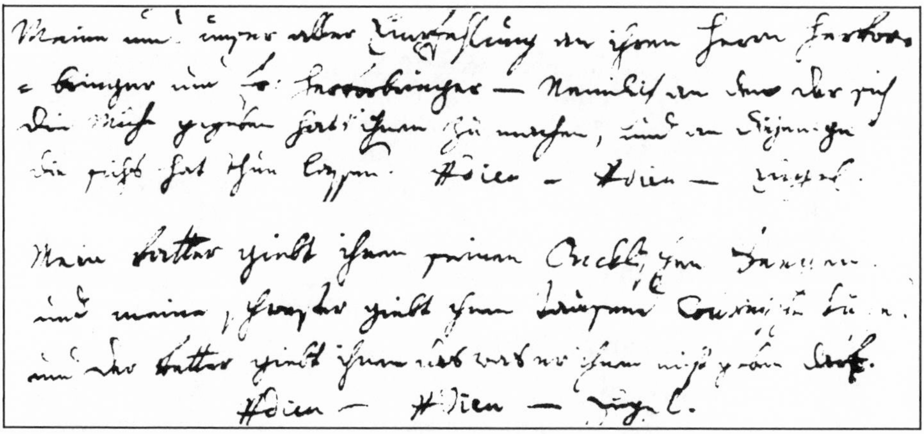

FIGURE 5.4. Mozart's Handwriting

To Nannerl *Bologna, 4 August 1770*

It is impossible for me to write a better hand, for this pen is for writing music and not for letters. (A, 153)

To Bäsle *Mannheim, 3 December 1777*

You see now that I can write just as I like, both fair and untidy, both straight and crooked. The other day I was in a bad humor and wrote a fair, straight, and serious hand; today I am in good spirits and I am writing an untidy, crooked, and jolly one. So all depends now on what you prefer. You must make a choice (I have no medium article to offer you) between fair and untidy, straight and crooked, serious and jolly.[22] (A, 403)

To Leopold Mozart *Mannheim, 11 March 1778*

Please send me something which I asked you for a long time ago, and that is the alphabet, both capitals and small letters, in your handwriting. (A, 509)

To Leopold Mozart   *Paris, 20 July 1778*

A nice scrawl this, isn't it? I haven't the patience to write a beautiful hand; and as long as you can read it, it'll do. (A, 574)

To Leopold Mozart   *Vienna, 24 March 1781*

You must put it down to my pen and this wretched ink, if you have to spell out this letter rather than read it. Basta! It must be written—and the gentleman who cuts my pens, Herr von Lirzer, has let me down this time. (A, 716)

► Mozart's principal childhood occupation, of course, was not practicing writing the letters of the alphabet but practicing the clavier and writing music. But he exercised his imagination in other ways as well. According to Nannerl, Mozart as a child invented an imaginary utopia called The Kingdom of Back which he thought out in the greatest detail. The connection of this activity with Mozart's fundamental creativity is apparent, but it has also been connected with his love for carnivals, secret societies, and secret codes.[23] ◄

The Memoirs of Nannerl Mozart, 1800

Mozart's over-rich imagination was so lively and so vivid, even in childhood, at a time when it still lies dormant in ordinary men, and perfected that which it had once taken hold of, to such an extent, that one cannot imagine anything more extraordinary and in some respects more moving than its enthusiastic creations; which, because the little man still knew so little of the real world, were as far removed from it as the heavens themselves. Just one illustration: As the journeys which we used to make (he and I, his sister) took him to different lands, he would think out a kingdom for himself as we traveled from one place to another, and this he called the Kingdom of Back [Das Königreich Rücken]—why by this name, I can no longer recall. This kingdom and its inhabitants were endowed with everything that could make good and happy—children of them. He was the King of this land, and this notion became so rooted within him, and he carried it so far, that our servant, who could draw a little, had to make a chart of it, and he would dictate the names of the cities, market-towns, and villages to him. (DDB, 493)

THROUGH A LOOKING GLASS: SELF-ESTEEM, SELF-DOUBT

The Reminiscences of Michael Kelly, 1826

He was a remarkably small man, very thin and pale, with a profusion of fine hair, of which he was rather vain. (Kelly, 1: 223)

► On the existential issues that most mattered, Mozart was able to recognize and to carry out what he needed to do: whether to break with Salzburg, for example, or marry Constanze. On issues of lesser import he became uncertain—for example: whether to leave for Paris with his colleagues from the Mannheim court orchestra. ◄

To Leopold Mozart   *Mannheim, 19 February 1778*

The reasons I have not gone off to Paris must be sufficiently evident to you from my last two letters.[24] If my mother had not first raised the point, I should certainly have gone with my friends; but when I saw that she did not like the scheme, then I began to dislike it myself. For as soon as people lose confidence in me, I am apt to lose confidence in myself. (A, 485)

► Or whether to approach a beautiful lady at a ball. ◄

To Gottfried von Jacquin   *Prague, 15 January 1787*

At six o'clock I drove . . . to the . . . ball, where the cream of the beauties of Prague is wont to gather. . . . I neither danced nor flirted with any of them: the former, because I was too tired, and the latter owing to my natural bashfulness. I looked on, however, with the greatest pleasure. (A, 903)

► In a similar vein Mozart was ambivalent, or simply dishonest, as to his need for, or concern about, the opinions of others with regard to his music. He claimed not to care, but he clearly did. ◄

To Leopold Mozart   *Vienna, 8 August 1781*

I played to [Countess Thun] what I have finished composing [from the first act of *Die Entführung*] and she told me afterwards that she would venture her life that what I have so far written cannot fail to please. But on this point I pay no attention whatever to *anybody's praise or blame*—I mean, until people have heard and seen the work *as a whole*. I simply follow *my own feelings*. (A, 756)

To Leopold Mozart   *Vienna, 12 April 1783*

Please send me, if possible, *the reports* about my concert. (A, 846)

► In the face of truly severe criticism, such as he experienced at the time of his break with Salzburg, Mozart not only lost his ability to work but even suffered physical collapse. ◄

To Leopold Mozart   *Vienna, 12 May 1781*

All the edifying things which the Archbishop [Colloredo] said to me during my three audiences, particularly during the last one,[25] all the subsequent remarks which this fine servant of God made to me, had such an excellent effect on my health that in the evening I was obliged to leave the opera in the middle of the first act and go home and lie down. For I was very feverish, I was trembling in every limb, and I was staggering along the street like a drunkard. I also stayed at home the following day, yesterday, and spent the morning in bed, as I had taken tamarind water. (A, 730)

INTERIOR LANDSCAPE: MOZARTEAN MOODS

▶ In recent years Mozart has been diagnosed as having suffered from "cyclothymic disorder," a bipolar affective condition—in effect, a mild form of manic depression. Mozart's symptoms consisted, on the one hand, of "hypomanic swings . . . characterized by elevated or expansive mood, decreased need for sleep, excessive energy, inflated self-esteem, increased productivity, extreme gregariousness, physical hyperactivity, inappropriate joking and punning, and indulgence in frivolous behavior without appreciation of consequences." At some point, however, after days or months, the high spirits inevitably made way for fits of melancholy and depression.[26] At such times Mozart was virtually unable to compose.

Whether Mozart in fact suffered from a congenital pathological condition of this kind may be debated. The composer was hardly unaware of the phenomenal quality of his artistic achievements—achievements repaid, often enough, in the coin of worldly success. And would it really be abnormal, if such "ego reinforcement" at times produced a "manic" state of triumphant elation—and even excessive exuberance? Indeed, it is difficult to imagine how it could fail to do so. As for his sad moods: Mozart himself was convinced that there was "always an [external] cause" for them. And there is evidence that he was not altogether wrong. Most, but not all, of the severe emotional difficulties he experienced can be associated with stressful circumstances of the moment: the death of his mother, loneliness, paternal browbeating, financial worries, separation from his wife. ◀

To Leopold Mozart   *Paris, 31 July 1778*

Now [after his mother's death], thank God, I am perfectly well and healthy. From time to time I have fits of melancholy—but I find that the best way to get rid of them is to write or receive letters, which invariably cheer me up again. But, believe me, there is always a cause for these sad feelings. . . . [When Mozart's mother was ill] I went as if I was bereft of my reason. I had ample leisure then for composing, but I could not have written a single note. (A, 583–585)

To Leopold Mozart   *Munich, 31 December 1778*

What do you mean by "gay dreams"? I do not mind the reference to dreaming, for there is no mortal on the face of this earth who does not sometimes dream! But *gay dreams!* Peaceful dreams, refreshing, sweet dreams! That is what they are—dreams which, if realized, would make my life, which is more sad than cheerful, more endurable. (A, 648)

To Leopold Mozart   *Munich, 24 November 1780*

Pray do not write any more melancholy letters to me, for I really need at the moment a cheerful spirit, a clear head, and an inclination to work, and one cannot have these when one is sad at heart. (A, 672)

To Leopold Mozart   *Munich, 1 December 1780*

When honor and glory are at stake, you naturally get excited—however cool you may be at first. (A, 677)

To Michael Puchberg   *Vienna, 27 June 1788*

I am always at home. During the ten days since I came to live here I have done more work than in two months in my former quarters, and if such black thoughts did not come to me so often, thoughts which I banish by a tremendous effort, things would be even better, for my rooms are pleasant, comfortable, and—*cheap.* (A, 917)

To Constanze, Baden   *Vienna, 7 July 1791*

You cannot imagine how I have been aching for you all this long while. I can't describe what I have been feeling, a kind of emptiness, which hurts me dreadfully, a kind of longing, which is never satisfied, which never ceases, and which persists, nay rather increases daily. When I think how merry we were together at Baden, like children, and what sad, weary hours I am spending here! Even my work gives me no pleasure, because I am accustomed to stop working now and then and exchange a few words with you. Alas! this pleasure is no longer possible. If I go to the piano and sing something out of my opera [*Die Zauberflöte*], I have to stop at once, for this stirs my emotions too deeply. (A, 964)

▶ A particular cause of malaise for Mozart was extensive travel. Few individuals have ever traveled to, or lived in, as many different places over such a short period of time as had he during the first twenty-five years of his life. The emotional cost of the frequent leavetakings and interrupted friendships—and of the ensuing loneliness en route—must have been enormous on the young man as well as the child, despite the resources he evidently developed to cope with them. ◀

To Leopold Mozart   *Nancy, 30 October 1778*

I am never in a good humor when I am in a town where I am quite
unknown. (A, 622)

To Leopold Mozart   *Kaysersheim, 18 December 1778*

My journey from Mannheim to Kaysersheim would have been certainly
most pleasant to a man who was leaving town with a light heart. . . .
But for me, to whom nothing has ever been more painful than leaving Mannheim, this journey was only partly agreeable, and would not
have been at all pleasant, but indeed very boring, if from my youth up
I had not been so much accustomed to leaving people, countries,
and cities, and with no great hope of soon, or ever again, seeing the kind
of friends whom I had left behind. I cannot deny, but must at once
admit, that not only myself, but all my intimate friends, and particularly
the Cannabiches, were in the most pitiable distress during the last few
days, when the time of my sad departure had been finally settled. (A,
640)

► The external manifestation of Mozart's internal emotional and spiritual
   turbulence, not surprisingly, was nervousness: fidgeting and chatter-
   ing. ◄

The Memoirs of Sophie Haibel, 1828

His hands and feet were always in motion, he was always playing with
something, for example, his hat, pockets, watch fob, tables, chairs, as if
they were a clavier. (DDB, 537)

To Nannerl   *Milan, 27 October 1770*

You know what a chatterbox I am—and was, when I left you. (A, 168)

To Gottfried von Jacquin, Vienna   *Prague, 15 January 1787*

We heard *Le gare generose* [by Paisiello]. In regard to the performance of
this opera I can give no definite opinion because I talked a lot; but that
quite contrary to my usual custom I chattered so much may have been due
to . . . Well, never mind![27] (A, 904)

DOING THE WRONG THING

► Mozart well knew that he did "not always act" as he should. Jealous of
   his prerogatives as an artist, Mozart could, when irritated or frustrated,
   be quite sarcastic or simply rude. ◄

To Leopold Mozart   *Munich, 10 January 1781*

I have had a desperate fight . . . about the trombones [in *Idomeneo*]. I call it a desperate fight, because I had to be rude to [Count Seeau] or I should never have got my way. (A, 706)

▶ Mozart's first months in Vienna in particular were an enormously stressful period marked by his attempt to cut his ties to Salzburg. This unpleasant business was immensely aggravated by confrontations not only with the Prince-Archbishop and his emissary, Count Arco, but with Leopold, as well. It is easy to believe that under such circumstances Mozart's self-control may have frayed. But we don't know whether there is any merit to the rumors that reached Leopold concerning boastful irreligion and consorting with ladies of ill repute. ◀

To Leopold Mozart   *Vienna, 13 June 1781*

My chief fault is that—*judging by appearances*—I do not always act as I should. It is not true that I boasted of eating meat on all fast days; but I did say that I did not scruple to do so or consider it a sin, for I take fasting to mean abstaining, that is, eating less than usual. I attend Mass every Sunday and every holy day and, if I can manage it, on weekdays also, and that you know, my father. The only association which I had with the person of ill repute was at the ball, and I talked to her long before I knew what she was, and solely because I wanted to be sure of having a partner for the contredanse.[28] (A, 743)

▶ Mozart's "chief fault," without question, was his well-known difficulty in properly managing his finances. His earnings from commissions and performances were often substantial but typically sporadic; his expenses, on the other hand, were constant. At times, particularly during the year-long period beginning in the summer of 1788, this created acute crises that obliged him to borrow money from friends and associates. But as early as 1783 he had begun to borrow (evidently in connection with a publishing venture at the time);[29] and even in 1785, at the height of his success, he had approached his publisher for a loan. Whether Mozart was merely the victim of fiscal ineptitude, bad luck stemming from unsuccessful investments, the expenses associated with his wife's medical needs, or whether there was perhaps a more sinister cause of his financial worries—such as an addiction to gambling[30]—will probably never be known for certain. ◀

To the Baroness von Waldstätten   *Vienna, 15 February 1783*

Here I am in a fine dilemma! Herr von Trattner and I discussed the matter the other day and agreed to ask for an extension of a fortnight. As every merchant does this, unless he is the most disobliging man in the world, my mind was quite at ease and I hoped that by that time, if I were not in the position to pay the sum myself, I should be able to borrow it. Well, Herr von Trattner now informs me that the person in question absolutely refuses to wait and that if I do not pay the sum before tomorrow, he will *bring an action against me. . . .* At the moment I cannot pay—not even half the sum! If I could have foreseen that the subscriptions for my concertos would come in so slowly, I should have raised the money on a longer time limit. I entreat your Ladyship for Heaven's sake to help me keep my honor and my good name! (A, 841)

To Franz Anton Hoffmeister   *Vienna, 20 November 1785*

Dearest Hoffmeister!

I turn to you in my distress and beg you to help me out with some money, which I need very badly at the moment . . . Forgive me for constantly worrying you, but as you know me and are aware how anxious I am that your business should succeed, I am convinced that you will not take my importunity amiss and that you will help me as readily as I shall help you. (A, 894)

▶ Although the nature of Mozart's distress is not known, it is assumed that he was approaching Hoffmeister for an advance against royalties for the publication of the Piano Quartet in G minor, K. 478, completed in October and published in December of that year.

Between June 1788 and August 1790 Mozart sent at least seventeen letters to his fellow Freemason Michael Puchberg in which he asks for money. Puchberg eventually loaned Mozart a total of about 1,415 gulden. The sum was paid back after Mozart's death. ◀

To Michael Puchberg   *Vienna, Summer 1788*

Dearest Brother!

Your true friendship and brotherly love embolden me to ask a great favor of you. I still owe you eight ducats. Apart from the fact that at the moment I am not in a position to pay you back this sum, my confidence in you is so boundless that I dare to implore you to help me out with a hundred gulden until next week, when my concerts in the Casino are to begin. By that time I shall certainly have received my subscription money and shall then be able quite easily to pay you back 136 gulden with my warmest thanks.

I take the liberty of sending you two tickets which, as a brother, I beg you to accept without payment, seeing that, as it is, I shall never be able adequately to return the friendship which you have shown me.

Once more I ask your forgiveness for my importunity and with greetings to your esteemed wife I remain in true friendship and fraternal love, your most devoted brother.[31] (A, 914–915)

To Franz Hofdemel *Vienna, March 1789*

Dearest Friend!

I am taking the liberty of asking without any hesitation for a favor. I should be very much obliged to you if you could and would lend me a hundred gulden until the 20th of next month. On that day I receive the quarterly installment of my salary and shall then repay the loan with thanks. I have relied too much on a sum of a hundred ducats due to me from abroad. Up to the present I have not yet received it, although I am expecting it daily. Meanwhile I have left myself too short of cash, so that *at the moment* I greatly need some ready money and have therefore appealed to your goodness, for I am absolutely convinced of your friendship.

Well, we shall soon be able to call one another by *a more delightful name!* For your novitiate [in the Order of Freemasons] is very nearly at an end! (A, 919)

Amadeo Amoroso

If I had to marry all those with whom I have jested, I should have two hundred wives at least.

Vienna, 25 July 1781

► Sometimes Mozart acted as . . . he should. We know that his sexuality was strong; he attests to it directly in a letter to his father written at the time of his betrothal to Constanze. ◄

To Leopold Mozart *Vienna, 15 December 1781*

The voice of nature speaks as loud in me as in others, louder, perhaps, than in many a big strong lout of a fellow. (A, 783)

► The fact that the letters to Bäsle, for all their scatological dissonance, contain few overt sexual references, suggests that Mozart observed something of a taboo regarding sexual obscenities.[32] But he did compose several erotic letters. They were written to his wife in 1789 when he was on a concert tour to Dresden and Berlin. The letters were written over the space of a month and a half; and they reveal an interesting evolution in the composer's amorous inclinations—which can perhaps be characterized as a "Divertimento in Four Parts." The tempo markings, needless to say, do not appear in the original. ◄

I
Moderato Affettuoso

To Constanze *Budwitz, 8 April 1789*

How are you? I wonder whether you think of me as often as I think of you? Every other moment I look at your portrait—and weep partly for joy, partly for sorrow. Look after your health which is so precious to me and farewell, my darling! . . . Adieu. I kiss you millions of times most tenderly and am ever yours, true till death. (A, 919–920)

II
Scherzo

To Constanze   *Dresden, 13 April 1789*

If I were to tell you all the things I do with your dear portrait, I think you would often laugh. For instance, when I take it out of its case, I say, "Good day, Stanzerl!—Good day, little rascal, pussy-pussy, little turned up nose, little bagatelle. Schluck and Druck." And when I put it away again, I let it slip in very slowly, saying all the time, "Nu, Nu, Nu!" with the peculiar emphasis which this word so full of meaning demands, and then just at the last quickly, "Good night, little mouse, sleep well." Well, I suppose I have been writing something very foolish (to the world at all events); but to us who love each other so dearly, it is not foolish at all. (A, 922)

III
Serioso

To Constanze   *Dresden, 16 April 1789*

Dear little wife, I have a number of requests to make. I beg you . . . in your conduct not only be careful of *your honor and mine*, but also to consider *appearances*. Do not be angry with me for asking this. You ought to love me even more for thus valuing our honor. (A, 924–925)

IV
Finale

To Constanze   *Berlin, 23 May 1789*

On June 1 I intend to sleep in Prague, and on the 4th—the 4th—with my darling little wife. Arrange your dear sweet nest very daintily, for my little fellow deserves it indeed, he has really behaved himself very well and is only longing to possess your sweetest. . . . Just picture to yourself that rascal; as I write he crawls on to the table and looks at me questioningly. I, however, box his ears properly—but the rogue is simply . . . and now the knave burns only more fiercely and can hardly be restrained.[33] (A, 929)

PERSONAL PHILOSOPHY

To live respectably and to live happily are two very different things.

Paris, 7 August 1778

▶ Mozart had neither the time nor the inclination to indulge in profound intellectual meditations on the great social, political, or metaphysical questions. But he saw fit, from time to time, at least to address them. It is not always clear whether Mozart's "philosophical" declarations were altogether sincere. Some of his comments were obviously designed to impress his reader: most palpably, the pompous declaration to Padre Martini as to why "we live in this world." (That letter, incidentally, is written—in Italian—in Leopold Mozart's hand, and its intellectual posturing is presumably Leopold's as well.) By and large, however, Mozart's opinions were the direct product of his personal experience. And when they are, one is inclined to assume their authenticity: for example, his repeated appeals to his sense of honor which, along with his moral code, seems to have governed his artistic and personal affairs and was evidently informed by lifelong religious convictions. ◀

ON SOCIETY: WEALTH, CLASS, NATION

▶ Mozart by no means despised wealth. His expressed "desire and hope," after all, was to "gain honor, fame, and money." But to be respectable and respected, wealth had, indeed, to be *gained*—that is, *earned* by virtue of one's talent and achievements—and not merely inherited. ◀

To Joseph Bullinger, Salzburg   *Paris, 7 August 1778*

You know well that the best and truest of all friends are the poor. The wealthy do not know what friendship means, especially those who are born to riches, and even those whom fate enriches often become spoiled by their good fortune. But when a man is placed in favorable circumstances not by blind fate but by reasonable good fortune and merit, that is, a man who during his early and less prosperous days never lost courage, remained faithful to his religion and his God, was an honest man and a good Christian and knew how to value his true friends—in short, one who really deserved better luck—from such a man no ingratitude need be feared! (A, 593)

▶ It appears, moreover, from contradictory sentiments contained in a single letter, that Mozart may have been a political democrat in theory but a cultural aristocrat in spirit. ◀

To Nannerl   *Vienna, 15 December 1781*

Das öffentliche Geheimnis [a German translation of Carlo Gozzi's *Il pubblico segreto*] is only endurable if one remembers that it is an Italian play, for the Princess's condescension to her servant is really too indecent and unnatural. . . . The Fischers [family acquaintances of the Mozarts] are living in the Tiefer Graben where I scarcely ever happen to go; but if my way does take me in that direction, I pay them a visit of a few minutes, since I really cannot endure for longer their tiny, overheated room and the wine on the table. I am well aware that people of their class consider this to be the greatest possible compliment, but I am no lover of such compliments and still less of people of that type. (A, 786)

▶ As for his outlook regarding society on a continental scale, Mozart cultivated a warm sense of nationalism. These parochial feelings were fed by two principal sources. First, he had personally experienced, abroad, and even in the German-speaking world, the professional disadvantages suffered by German artists in a milieu dominated by Italians. Second, and partly in consequence of the first, he enthusiastically welcomed the efforts to establish a German national theater and a German national opera. But the alien cultural and moral climate, such as he had encountered, for example, in Paris, lent intensity to his sense of German identity. ◀

To Leopold Mozart   *Paris, 1 May 1778*

I pray to God daily to give me grace to hold out here [Paris] with fortitude and to do such honor to myself and to the whole German nation as will redound to His greater honor and glory. (A, 533)

To Leopold Mozart   *Paris, 3 July 1778*

I always am and always will be happiest there [at home], or else in the company of some good, true, honest German who, if he is a bachelor, lives alone like a good Christian, or, if married, loves his wife and brings up his children properly. (A, 558)

▶ On the other hand, Mozart's patriotic loyalty was not free of ambivalence or even cynicism. ◀

To Leopold Mozart   *Vienna, 24 November 1781*

[Count Daubrawaick] said aloud to me: "I am proud of being your countryman. You are doing Salzburg great credit. I hope the times will change so that we shall have you back again, and then most certainly we shall not let you go." My reply was: "My own country will always have the first claim upon me." (A, 780)

To Leopold Mozart   *Vienna, 17 August 1782*

If Germany, my beloved fatherland, of which, as you know, I am proud, will not accept me, then in God's name let France or England become the richer by another talented German, to the disgrace of the German nation. You know well that it is the Germans who have always excelled in almost all the arts. But where did they make their fortune and their reputation? Certainly not in Germany! (A, 814)

To Anton Klein   *Vienna, 21 May 1785*

Were there but one good patriot in charge [of the German opera at the Kärntnerthor Theater in Vienna], things would take a different turn. But then, perhaps, the German national theater which is sprouting so vigorously would actually begin to flower; and of course that would be an everlasting blot on Germany, if we Germans were seriously to begin to think as Germans, to act as Germans, to speak German and, Heaven help us, to sing in German!! (A, 891)

A GOOD LIFE: HONOR, MORALITY, AND THE PURSUIT OF HAPPINESS

► Mozart, early on, was content to let Leopold put the following noble, if pretentiously expressed, sentiment into his mouth as to "why we live in this world." No doubt Mozart in fact endorsed the view. He well knew, after all, that he was in this world to compose and thus preordained to promote the fine arts. ◄

To Padre Martini, Bologna   *Salzburg, 4 September 1776*

We live in this world in order to learn industriously and, by interchanging our ideas, to enlighten one another and thus endeavor to promote the sciences and the fine arts [Italian]. (A, 266)

► Shortly thereafter, this world taught Mozart that the pursuit of happiness was closely connected to, and no less challenging than, the pursuit of such honorable ideals. The resignation expressed by the young man in the years 1777 and 1778 about the prospect of human happiness mirrored the professional frustrations and profound personal disappointments he experienced during his sojourns in Mannheim and Paris: most notably, the death of his mother, but also his unsuccessful love affair with Aloysia Weber. ◄

To Leopold Mozart   *Mannheim, 29 November 1777*

I am not careless, I am simply prepared for anything and am able, in consequence, to wait patiently for whatever may come, and endure it, provided that my honor and the good name of Mozart are not affected. Well, as it must be so, so let it be. But I must beg you at the outset not to give way prematurely to joy or sadness. For come what may, all is well, so long as a man enjoys good health. For happiness consists simply in imagination. (A, 396)

► Among the trials in Paris that Mozart was destined to endure was the evident sabotage of his efforts to arrange for a performance of his newly-composed sinfonia concertante for wind instruments. His stoicism on this occasion found expression in the cynical form of pride captured in the German proverb *Viel' Feind', viel Ehr'* (many enemies, much honor). ◄

To Leopold Mozart   *Paris, 1 May 1778*

There appears . . . to be a hitch with the sinfonia concertante, and I think that something is going on behind the scenes and that doubtless here too I have enemies. Where, indeed, have I not had them?—but that is a good sign. (A,532)

► By the end of his Paris sojourn, Mozart's pessimism, and his cynicism, were complete. ◄

To Leopold Mozart   *Paris, 7 August 1778*

To live respectably and to live happily are two very different things, and the latter I could not do without having recourse to witchcraft—indeed if I did, there would have to be something supernatural about it—and that is impossible, for in these days there are no longer any witches. (A, 594)

► Living happily, then, may have been impossible. But one always had one's honor. The greatest test of Mozart's, in his own opinion, was the break with Salzburg. The crisis erupted at the beginning of May 1781 when the Archbishop ordered Mozart to leave Vienna at once and return home. Mozart claimed that, unlike his colleagues, he had been given no advance notice of the day of departure. There were three interviews with the Archbishop, the last on May 9, when, according to Mozart, he was called "a scoundrel, a rascal, a vagabond," and was ordered out. Whether Mozart had been dismissed from the Salzburg service or just from the room is not entirely clear. At all events, Mozart decided to resign. He represented his decision to Leopold as a matter of honor. (A, 728) ◄

To Leopold Mozart   *Vienna, 19 May 1781*

Now more than ever—I can never abandon my resolve [to leave the Salzburg court]. Yet, because in certain passages[34] my honor and my character are most cruelly assailed, I must reply to these points. . . . You say that the only way to save my honor is to abandon my resolve. How can you perpetrate such a contradiction! When you wrote this you surely did not bear in mind that such a recantation would prove me to be the basest fellow in the world. All Vienna knows that I have left the Archbishop, and all Vienna knows the reason! Everyone knows that it was because my honor was insulted—and, what is more, insulted three times. And am I publicly to prove the contrary? Am I to make myself out to be a cowardly sneak and the Archbishop a worthy prince? (A, 734)

▶ Needless to say, Mozart regarded not only his personal conduct but his commitment to artistic quality to be a matter of honor as well. He invoked the virtue implicitly to justify the delay in completing the *Haffner* Symphony. ◀

To Leopold Mozart   *Vienna, 31 July 1782*

You see that my intentions are good—only what one cannot do one cannot! I am really unable to scribble off inferior stuff. (A, 811)

▶ The virtue of Honor, however, had its shadow: an urge to vindictiveness. Although Mozart evidently never acted upon the impulse, he yearned, in the aftermath of the ignominious kick in the arse he received on 6 June 1781 from the Archbishop's chamberlain, Count Arco, to have his revenge on its administrator. For weeks after the incident Mozart was obsessed with it and continued to refer to his need—not unlike some of his more buffonesque opera characters—to have his revenge. To quote Osmin, a character soon to be very much on Mozart's mind: "Ha! wie will ich triumphieren.!" ◀

To Leopold Mozart   *Vienna, 13 June 1781*

Enfin, . . . Count Arco hurls me out of the room and gives me a kick on my behind. Well, that means in our language that Salzburg is no longer the place for me, except to give me a favorable opportunity of returning the Count's kick, even if it should have to be in the public street. I am not demanding any satisfaction from the Archbishop, for he cannot procure it for me in the way in which I intend to obtain it myself. One of these days I shall write to the Count and tell him what he may confidently expect from me. (A, 743)

To Leopold Mozart   *Vienna, 16 June 1781*

That arrogant jackass will certainly get a very palpable reply from me, even if he has to wait twenty years for it. For to see him and to return his kick will be one and the same thing, unless I am so unlucky as to meet him first in some sacred place. (A, 746)

To Leopold Mozart   *Vienna, 20 June 1781*

As for Arco, . . . I intend at first to tell him quite reasonably how badly and clumsily he has played his part. But in conclusion I shall feel bound to assure him in writing that he may confidently expect from me a kick on his behind and a few boxes on the ear in addition. For when I am insulted, I must have my revenge; and if I do no more than was done to me, I shall only be getting even with him, and really I am too proud to measure myself with such a stupid booby. (A, 747)

To Leopold Mozart *Vienna, 4 July 1781*

I have not written to Count Arco and shall not do so, since you ask me to desist for the sake of your peace of mind. It is just as I suspected. You really are too timid. . . . For you, my father, need have no scruples in saying boldly . . . that you would be ashamed of having brought up a son who would allow himself to be so grossly insulted by such an infamous scoundrel as Arco; and you may asure them all that if I had the good fortune to meet him today, I should treat him as he deserves and he would certainly remember me as long as he lived. (A, 749)

▶ Honorable behavior, finally, embraced the delicate sphere of sexual morality. Mozart's attitude toward this central question reflected a considerable measure of personal insecurity—certainly with regard to Constanze. In general, his moral code seems to have been governed by a double standard. He was tolerant of, and mildly amused by, the frailties of his fellow men—whether colleagues or Kaiser. But he claimed to demand far more from himself, and certainly insisted on more from his wife. In denying an insinuation about the nature of his relationship with his early love and later sister-in-law, Aloysia Weber, Mozart protested: ◀

To Leopold Mozart *Mannheim, 22 February 1778*

There are people who think that no one can love a poor girl without having evil designs; and that charming word maîtresse, wh—e[35] in our tongue, is really much too charming! But I am no Brunetti! no Myslivecek! I am a Mozart, and a young and clean-minded Mozart. (A, 487)

▶ On the other hand, Mozart took a pragmatic, not to say opportunistic, view of a rumored liaison on the part of the Emperor. The Emperor's alleged affair was with Princess Elisabeth Wilhelmine Louise of Württemberg, whom Mozart had hoped to tutor. She was betrothed to Emperor Joseph's nephew, Franz, oldest son of the Emperor's brother, Leopold. Leopold, at the time, was the Grand Duke of Tuscany; he was to become Joseph's successor as Emperor. The Princess, incidentally, never became Mozart's pupil. ◀

To Leopold Mozart *Vienna, 5 December 1781*

It is quite true that, out of love for the Princess, *the Emperor* drove out to meet the Duke of Württemberg. This affair is an open secret in Vienna, but no one knows whether she is going to be a morsel for himself or for some Tuscan prince. Probably the latter. All the same the *Emperor* is far too *loving* with her for my taste. He is always kissing her hands, first one and then the other, and often both at once. I am really astonished, because she is, you might say, still a child. But if it be true, and what people predict does happen, then I shall begin to believe that in this case charity begins at home. For she is to remain here in a convent for two years and probably, if there is no hitch, she will become my pupil on the clavier [italicized words in code]. (A, 782)

► Soon thereafter Mozart revealed to Leopold his engagement to Aloysia Weber's sister, Constanze. He took the occasion to reiterate and elaborate upon the theme of his own sexual morality, proclaiming— shortly before his twenty-sixth birthday—his innocence of carnal knowledge. ◄

To Leopold Mozart   *Vienna, 15 December 1781*

The voice of nature speaks as loud in me as in others, louder, perhaps, than in many a big strong lout of a fellow. I simply cannot live as most young men do in these days. In the first place, I have too much religion; in the second place, I have too great a love of my neighbor and too high a feeling of honor to seduce an innocent girl; and, in the third place, I have too much horror and disgust, too much dread and fear of diseases and too much care for my health to fool about with whores. So I can swear that I have never had relations of that sort with any woman. Besides, if such a thing had occurred, I should not have concealed it from you; for, after all, to err is natural enough in a man, and to err *once* would be mere weakness—although indeed I should not undertake to promise that if I had erred once in this way, I should stop short at one slip. However, I stake my life on the truth of what I have told you. (A, 783)

► Whether Mozart was in fact telling the truth is uncertain. Months later he was begging his father to give his blessing to his betrothal, admitting that he had already gone "so far" with the girl that people already assumed they were married. ◄

To Leopold Mozart   *Vienna, 27 July 1782*

Dearest, most beloved father, I implore you by all you hold dear in the world to give your consent to my marriage with dear Constanze. Do not suppose that it is just for the sake of getting married. If that were the only reason, I would gladly wait. But I realize that it is absolutely necessary for my own honor and for that of the girl, and for the sake of my health and spirits. My heart is restless and my head confused; in such a condition how can one think and work to any good purpose? And why am I in this state? Well, because most people think that we are already married. Her mother gets very much annoyed when she hears these rumors, and, as for the poor girl and myself, we are tormented to death. (A, 810)

To Leopold Mozart   *Vienna, 31 July 1782*

Constanze is a respectable honest girl of good parentage, and I am able *to support her.* We love each other—and want each other. All that you have written and may possibly write to me on the subject can only be *well-meaning advice* which, however fine and good it may be, is no longer applicable to a man who has gone so far with a girl. In such a case nothing can be postponed. It is better for him to put his affairs in order and act like an honest fellow! God will ever reward that. I mean to have nothing with which to reproach myself. (A, 811)

▶ In contrast to his Emperor's moral behavior, that of his fiancée—like his own—could not be a matter of indifference, much less amusement. Flirtations and suggestive party games were hardly innocent and could not be tolerated. Moreover, appearances were almost as significant as deeds. ◀

To Constanze   *Vienna, 29 April 1782*

I entreat you . . . to ponder and reflect upon the cause of all this unpleasantness, which arose from my being annoyed that you were so impudently inconsiderate as to say to your sisters—and, be it noted, in my presence—that you had let a *chapeau* [a young gallant] measure the calves of your legs. No woman who cares for her honor can do such a thing. It is quite a good maxim to do as one's company does. At the same time there are many other factors to be considered—as, for example, whether only intimate friends and acquaintances are present—whether I am a child or a *marriageable girl*—more particularly, whether I am already betrothed— but, above all, whether only people of my own social standing or my social inferiors—or, what is even more important, my social superiors are in the company? If it be true that the Baroness [von Waldstätten] herself allowed it to be done to her, the case is still quite different, for she is already past her prime and cannot possibly attract any longer—and besides, she is inclined to be promiscuous with her favors. I hope, dearest friend, that even if you do not wish to become my wife, you will never lead a life like hers. If it was quite impossible for you to resist the desire to take part in the game (although it is not always wise for a man to do so, and still less for a woman), then why in the name of Heaven did you not take the ribbon and measure your own calves *yourself* (as *all self-respecting women* have done on similar occasions in my presence) and not allow a *chapeau* to do so?—Why, I myself *in the presence of others* would never have done such a thing to you. I should have handed you the ribbon myself. Still less, then, should you have allowed it to be done to you by a stranger—a man about whom I know nothing. But it is all over now; and the least acknowledgement of your somewhat thoughtless behavior on that occasion would have made everything all right again; and if you will not make a grievance of it, dearest friend, everything will still be all right. (A, 802–803)

► Mozart's concerns and insecurities about Constanze's flirtatiousness had still not subsided after eight years of marriage. ◄

To Constanze, Baden   *Vienna, August 1789*

I am glad indeed when you have some fun—of course I am—but I do wish that you would not sometimes make yourself so cheap. In my opinion you are too free and easy with N. N.[36] . . . and it was the same with N. N., when he was still at Baden. Now please remember that N. N. are not half so familiar with other women, as they are with you. Why, N. N. who is usually a well-conducted fellow and particularly respectful to women, must have been misled by your behavior into writing the most disgusting and most impertinent sottises which he put into his letter. A woman must always make herself respected, or else people will begin to talk about her. My love! Forgive me for being so frank, but my peace of mind demands it as well as our mutual happiness. Remember that you yourself once admitted to me that you were inclined to *comply too easily.* You know the consequences of that. Remember too the promise you gave to me. Oh, God, do try, my love! Be merry and happy and charming to me. Do not torment yourself and me with unnecessary jealousy. Believe in my love, for surely you have proofs of it, and you will see how happy we shall be. Rest assured that it is only by her prudent behavior that a wife can enchain her husband. (A, 933)

► In the final analysis, however, Mozart had no reservations at all about the state of marriage. His allusion to the "voice of nature" had been a prelude to his informing his father of his intention to marry. He justified this plan further on the most prosaic imaginable basis, concluding his transparent rationalization with a ringing endorsement of domesticity. ◄

To Leopold Mozart   *Vienna, 15 December 1781*

But owing to my disposition, which is more inclined to a peaceful and domesticated existence than to revelry, I who from my youth up have never been accustomed to look after my own belongings, linen, clothes, and so forth, cannot think of anything more necessary to me than a wife. I assure you that I am often obliged to spend unnecessarily, simply because I do not pay attention to things. I am absolutely convinced that I should manage better with a wife . . . than I do by myself. True, other expenses would have to be met, but—one knows what they are and can be prepared for them—in short, one leads a well-ordered existence. A bachelor, in my opinion, is only half alive. (A, 783)

► Six years later, on the occasion of the betrothal of his friend, Mozart was still prepared to argue the superiority of the marital state over the alternative. ◄

To Gottfried von Jacquin   *Prague, 4 November 1787*

You cannot fail to be happy, dearest friend, for you possess everything that you can wish for *at your age and in your position*, particularly as you now seem to be entirely giving up your former rather *restless way of living*. Surely you are becoming every day more convinced of the truth of the little lectures I used to inflict upon you? Surely the pleasure of a transient, capricious infatuation is as far removed as heaven from earth from the blessed happiness of a deep and true affection? Surely in your heart of hearts you often feel grateful to me for my admonitions? You will end up by making me quite conceited. But, jesting apart, you do owe me some thanks after all, if you have become worthy of Fräulein N——[37] for I certainly played no insignificant part in your reform or conversion. (A, 913)

Postscript: A Portrait of Constanze

▶ The object of Mozart's affections—and the main inspiration of his reflections upon love, marriage and morality—was, of course, his wife, Constanze. She also inspired him to a colorful portrait in which, like any conscientious portraitist, he attempted to capture both her appearance and her character. His success at this effort—at least with respect to the former—can be judged from a surviving picture (fig. 5.5). ◀

To Leopold Mozart   *Vienna, 15 December 1781*

The middle one[38] my good, dear Constanze, is the martyr of the family and, probably for that very reason, is the kindest hearted, the cleverest and, in short, the best of them all. She makes herself responsible for the whole household and yet in their opinion she does nothing right. Oh, my most beloved father, I could fill whole sheets with descriptions of all the scenes that I have witnessed in that house. . . . But before I cease to plague you with my chatter, I must make you better acquainted with the character of my dear Constanze. She is not ugly, but at the same time far from beautiful. Her whole beauty consists in two little black eyes and a pretty figure. She has no wit, but she has enough common sense to enable her to fulfill her duties as a wife and mother. It is a downright lie that she is inclined to be extravagant. On the contrary, she is accustomed to be shabbily dressed, for the little that her mother has been able to do for her children, she has done for the two others, but never for Constanze. True, she would like to be neatly and cleanly dressed, but not smartly, and most things that a woman needs she is able to make for herself; and she dresses her own hair every day. Moreover, she understands housekeeping and has the kindest heart in the world. I love her and she loves me with all her heart. Tell me whether I could wish myself a better wife?

One thing more I must tell you, which is that when I resigned the

FIGURE 5.5. Constanze Mozart

Archbishop's service, our love had not yet begun. It was born of her tender care and attentions when I was living in their house. (A, 784)

MEDICAL WISDOM

► Mozart's views on personal health and medical treatment are, for us, simply absurd—a pitiful, lingering remnant of medieval superstition and folklore. Enlightenment thought had not yet brought any significant practical benefits into this vital domain of human knowledge. On one occasion, when Leopold was suffering from a spell of dizziness, Mozart recommended a remarkable treatment that was indeed prevalent in Vienna at the time.[39] ◄

To Leopold Mozart   *Vienna, 6 October 1781*

And you, my dear father—get some cart-grease, wrap it in a bit of paper, and wear it on your chest. Take the bone of a leg of veal and wrap it up in paper with a kreuzer's worth of leopard's bane and carry it in your pocket. I am sure this will cure you. (A, 772)

► The Mozarts' first child, Raimund Leopold, was born on 17 June 1783, and was described by the composer as "a fine sturdy boy, round as a ball." Mozart's instructions regarding the proper feeding of the infant may have had tragic consequences. ◄

To Leopold Mozart   *Vienna, 18 June 1783*

I was quite determined that whether she should be able to do so or not, my wife was never to feed her child. Yet I was equally determined that my child was never to take the milk of a stranger! I wanted the child to be brought up on water, like my sister and myself. However, the midwife, my mother-in-law and most people have begged and implored me not to allow it, if only for the reason that most children here who are brought up on water do not survive, as the people here don't know how to do it properly. (A, 852)

► The child died two months later—on August 21—in the care of an acquaintance while Wolfgang and Constanze were in Salzburg. According to Peter J. Davies there was great distrust of breast feeding in Salzburg at this time, owing to concern about the health or habits of the mother or wet nurse. Newborns in Salzburg, however, were not given plain water. Mozart here doubtless has in mind a traditional pap made of barley or oats.[40] ◄

RELIGIOUS CONVICTIONS AND METAPHYSICAL MUSINGS

► Mozart was born, raised, and died a Roman Catholic. He attended church services with reasonable regularity, and evidently felt most comfortable in Catholic environments. One is inclined to believe his frequent reassurances to Leopold as to his faith. ◄

To Leopold Mozart   *Paris, 9 July 1778*

You know that there is nothing I desire more than a good appointment, good in its standing and good in money—no matter where—provided it be in a Catholic country. (A, 563)

► But this is not to say that Mozart was incapable of any irreverence regarding the Church. ◄

To Leopold Mozart   *Mannheim, 3 December 1778*

Although [the Imperial Abbot of Kaysersheim] is a priest and a prelate, he is a most amiable man. (A, 638)

► On the fundamental precepts, however, Mozart insisted that he was a believer. ◄

To Leopold Mozart   *Vienna, 5 December 1781*

You say that I must remember that I have an immortal soul. Not only do I think it, but I firmly believe it. If it were not so, wherein would consist the difference between men and beasts? (A, 782)

To Leopold Mozart   *Vienna, 17 August 1782*

Indeed for a considerable time before we were married we had always attended Mass and gone to confession and received Communion together; and I found that I never prayed so fervently or confessed or received Communion so devoutly as by her side; and she felt the same. In short, we are made for each other; and God who orders all things and consequently has ordained this also, will not forsake us. (A, 814)

► There was presumably a religious impulse—no doubt along with other motivations—behind Mozart's decision to become a Freemason, In December 1784 Mozart joined the Masonic lodge "Zur Wohltätigkeit" (Charity) and became a Master the following year. Masonic topics, however, are never explicitly mentioned by Mozart in any of his surviving letters. This may have been a consequence of the Masonic vows of secrecy. At most, the salutation of letters to fellow Masons refers to their shared membership. (See, for example, the letter to Puchberg, p. 158.) It is also possible that, owing to the later persecution of the Masons in Vienna, letters containing Masonic references were destroyed by Constanze. At all events, Mozart, as a Freemason, embraced the movement's tenets of self-perfection, tolerance, and enlightenment.

▶   The fullest expression of Mozart's religious sentiments are contained in his observations on death. These utterances, moreover, bear witness to his lifelong confrontation—and fascination—with this most universal and most painful human experience. They are informed by his Roman Catholic heritage, to be sure; but substantially colored as well by elements of Masonic philosophy and Enlightenment thought. Mozart had in fact confronted death early on. He informs us that he had witnessed public hangings on at least two occasions: in Milan at the age of fifteen, and evidently in Lyons, which he visited in 1766, that is, when he was ten. His reaction was unnervingly detached. ◀

To his Mother and Nannerl   *Milan, 30 November 1771*

I have seen four rascals hanged here in the Piazza del Duomo. They hang them just as they do in Lyons. (A, 207–208)

▶ His next documented encounter with death literally struck home. Among the most famous of Mozart's letters are his extraordinary reports—the first to his friend Joseph Bullinger, the second, after a week's delay, to Leopold—on the death of his mother (fig. 5.6.), disclosing, among other things, his tactful strategy to soften the blow for his father. The measure of sincerity in these almost clinically detailed, self-conscious, and rather artificial communications can be— and has been—questioned.[41] ◀

To Abbé Joseph Bullinger   *Paris, 3 July 1778*

Mourn with me, my friend! This has been the saddest day of my life—I am writing this at two o'clock in the morning [4 July 1778]. I have to tell you that my mother, my dear mother, is no more! God has called her to Himself. It was His will to take her, that I saw clearly—so I resigned myself to His will. He gave her to me, so He was able to take her away from me. Only think of all my anxiety, the fears and sorrows I have had to endure for the last fortnight. She was quite unconscious at the time of her death—her life flickered out like a candle. Three days before her death she made her confession, partook of the Sacrament and received Extreme Unction. During the last three days, however, she was constantly delirious, and today at twenty-one minutes past five the death agony began and she at once lost all sensation and consciousness. I pressed her hand and spoke to her—but she did not see me, she did not hear me, and all feeling was gone. She lay thus until she expired five hours later at twenty-one minutes past ten. No one was present but myself, Herr Heina (a kind friend whom my father knows), and the nurse. It is quite impossible for me to describe today the whole course of her illness, but I am firmly convinced that she was bound to die and that God had so ordained it. . . . Not only am I now comforted, but I have been comforted for some time. By the mercy of God I have borne it all with fortitude and composure. When her illness became

FIGURE 5.6. Mozart's
Mother: Anna Maria,
née Pertl

dangerous, I prayed to God for two things only—a happy death for her, and strength and courage for myself; and God in His goodness heard my prayer and gave me those two blessings in the richest measure. (A, 559–560)

To Leopold Mozart   *Paris, 9 July 1778*

I hope that you are now prepared to hear with fortitude one of the saddest and most painful stories; indeed my last letter of the 3rd will have told you that no good news could be hoped for. On that very same day, the 3rd, at twenty-one minutes past ten at night my mother fell asleep peacefully in the Lord; indeed, when I wrote to you, she was already enjoying the blessings of Heaven—for all was then over. I wrote to you during that night and I hope that you and my dear sister will forgive me for this slight and very necessary deception; for as I judged from my own grief and sorrow what yours would be, I could not indeed bring myself suddenly to shock you with this dreadful news! But I hope that you have now summoned up courage to hear the worst, and that after you have at first given way to natural, and only too well justified tears and anguish, you will eventually resign yourself to the will of God and worship His unsearchable, unfathomable, and all-wise providence. You will easily conceive what I have had to bear—what courage and fortitude I have needed to endure calmly as things grew gradually and steadily worse. And yet God in His goodness gave me grace to do so. I have, indeed, suffered and wept enough—but what did it avail? So I have tried to console myself: and please do so too, my dear father, my dear sister! Weep, weep your fill, but take comfort at last. Remember that Almighty God willed it thus—and how can we rebel against Him? Let us rather pray to Him, and thank Him for His goodness, for she died a very happy death. In those distressing moments, there were three things that consoled me—my entire and steadfast submission to the will of God, and the sight of her very easy and beautiful death which made me feel that in a moment she had become so happy; for how much happier is she now than we are! Indeed, I wished at that moment to depart with her. From this wish and longing proceeded finally my third source of consolation—the thought that she is not lost to us forever, that we shall see her again, that we shall live together far more happily and blissfully than ever in this world. We do not yet know when it will be—but that does not disturb me; when God wills it, I am ready. Well, His heavenly and most holy will has been fulfilled. Let us therefore say a devout Paternoster for her soul and turn our thoughts to other matters, for all things have their appropriate time. I am writing this in the house of Madame d'Épinay and M. Grimm, with whom I am now living. I have a pretty little room with a very pleasant view and, so far as my condition permits, I am happy. It will be a great help to restoring my tranquility to hear that my dear father and sister are submitting wholly and with calmness and fortitude to the will of God—are trusting Him with their whole heart in the firm belief that He orders all things for the best. My dearest father! Do not give way! Dearest sister! Be firm! . . . In the end, when God wills it, we shall all meet again in Heaven—for which purpose we were destined and created. (A, 561–562)

▶ Striking in connection with this event is Mozart's revelation that he had "often wished" to see someone die. Apparently, he had totally forgotten, at least for the moment, that he had witnessed those "rascals" hanged in Lyons and Milan. ◀

To Leopold Mozart   *Paris, 31 July 1778*

I have received yours [letters] of the 13th and 20th. The first brought tears of sorrow to my eyes because I was reminded of the sad death of my dear departed mother, and everything came back to me so vividly. As long as I live I shall never forget it. You know that I had never seen anyone die, although I had often wished to. How cruel that my first experience should be the death of my mother! . . . My dear departed mother *had to die.* No

FIGURE 5.7.
Leopold Mozart

doctor in the world could have saved her this time—for it was clearly the will of God; her time had come, and God wanted to take her to Himself. (A, 583–584)

► Mozart's most famous utterance on death and, understandably, the object of innumerable interpretations, is his final letter to Leopold Mozart, a document in which he attempts to console—or perhaps to taunt?—his father about the inevitable (fig. 5.7). The characterization of death as the "true goal" derives from Horace; the reflections in general are indebted to the Enlightened philosophy of Moses Mendelssohn,[42] as expounded in his treatise, *Phaedon* (a copy of which resided in Mozart's library). ◄

To Leopold Mozart   *Vienna, 4 April 1787*

As death, when we come to consider it closely, is the true goal of our existence, I have formed during the last few years such close relations with this best and truest friend of mankind that his image is not only no longer terrifying to me, but is indeed very soothing and consoling! And I thank my God for graciously granting me the opportunity (you know what I mean)[43] of learning that death is the *key* which unlocks the door to our true happiness. I never lie down at night without reflecting that—young as I am—I may not live to see another day. Yet no one of all my acquaintances could say that in company I am morose or disgruntled. For this blessing I daily thank my Creator and wish with all my heart that each one of my fellow creatures could enjoy it. (A, 907)

To Gottfried von Jacquin   *Vienna, May/June 1787*

I inform you that on returning home today I received the sad news of my most beloved father's death.[44] You can imagine the state I am in. (A, 908)

Part Two

On Music

6

A Short Introduction

I should like to write a book, a short introduction to music, illustrated by examples, but I need hardly add, not under my own name.

Vienna, 28 December 1782

AESTHETIC PREMISES

► When Mozart wrote to Leopold on 28 December 1782 of his desire to write a small book on music,[1] he was putting the finishing touches on the first of his string quartets dedicated to Haydn: the Quartet in G, K. 387, which bears the date "li 31 de decembre 1782" at the top of the autograph score.[2] As Mozart was to declare on the dedication page accompanying the publication of the quartets in 1785—and as the appearance of the surviving manuscripts abundantly confirms—these works were the "fruit of a long and laborious endeavor."[3] The long labor is evident as well in the exquisite refinement and technical sophistication of the finished compositions.

The G-major Quartet is Mozart's first outstanding masterpiece in the genre of the string quartet. Within the previous six months Mozart had completed two other "watershed" masterpieces in his career: the Piano Concerto in A, K. 414 (385p), the first of the mature Viennese piano concerti, and *Die Entführung aus dem Serail*, the work that had been his preoccupation for an entire year (from 30 July 1781, when he had received the libretto from Gottlieb Stephanie, until its premiere in the Burgtheater on 16 July 1782). It is easy to imagine that when Mozart reflected on what he had achieved in these works, he concluded that he had something of value to say, in words, on the subject of music.

Mozart was not at all a purely instinctive, intuitive artist. His remarks to the effect that he "loved to plan works, study, and meditate" and that he "preferred to work slowly and with deliberation" have been cited earlier on (Chapter 1). And it is apparent that working on major projects stimulated him to think *about* music, to ponder its nature and purpose. In particular, work on the first two major operatic efforts of his artistic maturity, *Idomeneo* (1780–1781) and *Die Entführung* (1781–1782), was accompanied by an invaluable series of letters in which Mozart was at pains to explain and clarify as much for himself as for his father the aesthetic premises that governed his musical and dramatic procedures.[4]

Most illuminating in this regard is Mozart's oft-quoted letter of 26 September 1781. This central document sets forth Mozart's aesthetic creed virtually in its entirety. And it is, of course, tempting to reproduce the letter in its entirety here. But doing so is hardly necessary, since, after all, it is readily available. It seems more helpful, therefore, to quote from the letter selectively (both here and in other chapters), amplifying Mozart's words, in accordance with his own intention, with examples. Moreover, the letter makes a number of points in such concise fashion that they often fail to be properly recognized as discrete, if closely related, articles of artistic faith. For that reason, a single sentence will be cited below, in varying degrees of completeness, in several different contexts.

On one level, Mozart's musical aesthetic is informed by three fundamental and closely related principles that can be designated Appeal, Propriety, Effect. It is axiomatic for him that music must please; and from this it follows not only that the composer must be reasonably cognizant of (but not pandering to) the taste of his audience but must ensure that his music not "excite disgust" or overstep the bounds of nature, that is, that it must observe propriety. Concern for propriety and naturalness in its turn informed, among other things, Mozart's insistence that harmonic modulations (changes of key) be executed in a smooth, "natural," manner.

Most striking, however, is Mozart's high esteem for what he calls Effect. Considerations of Effect seem in fact to have been a conscious concern for him when he was engaged in the act of composition. The rationale behind numerous changes and revisions visible in his manuscripts of otherwise perfectly correct and respectable readings can often best be understood as manifestations of the desire to create a "good" (or better) effect. To some extent Effect is synonymous with Originality and testifies to a desire to do the unexpected and to avoid the obvious. But the term also implies a concern for substantial dramatic impact and even enhanced surface sensuous appeal, at which point this particular aesthetic triangle is closed.

It would be vastly mistaken, however, to conclude from the above that Mozart was a "Formalist." Quite the contrary: for Mozart music was, above all, communication and expression; and what it communicated and expressed was the "thoughts and feelings" of the composer. Opera, clearly enough, had to develop the means of adequately—and "effectively"—representing the feelings and passions of the dramatic characters. But Mozart was convinced that instrumental music, too, was more than the play of abstract sounds. Indeed, instrumental music was not only capable of communicating feeling which (as we shall see in the following chapter) the performer was obliged to accomplish: it also possessed, to some significant degree, the capacity of representation— "tone painting," as it would be called by a later era. ◄

APPEAL

To Leopold Mozart   *Munich, 16 December 1780*

As for what is called the popular taste, do not be uneasy, for there is music in my opera [*Idomeneo*] for all kinds of people, but not for the long-eared. Apropos, what about *the Archbishop?* [in code]. (A, 690)

To Leopold Mozart   *Vienna, 26 September 1781*

Music . . . must never offend the ear, but must please the listener, or in other words must never cease to be *music* . . . The Janissary chorus [from *Die Entführung*] is . . . all that can be desired, that is, short, lively, and written to please the Viennese. (A, 769)

To Leopold Mozart   *Vienna, 13 October 1781*

If we composers were always to stick so faithfully to our rules (which were very good at a time when no one knew better), we should be concocting music as unpalatable as their [the poets'] libretti. (A, 773)

To Leopold Mozart   *Vienna, 27 July 1782*

I have composed my symphony in D major [i.e., the *Haffner* Symphony] because you prefer that key. (A, 810)

PROPRIETY

To Leopold Mozart   *Augsburg, 14 October 1777*

After many compliments [Graf] performed a concerto for two flutes. I had to play the first violin part. This is what I think of it. It is not at all pleasing to the ear, not a bit natural. He often plunges into a new key far too brusquely and it is all quite devoid of charm. . . . At last a clavichord . . . was brought in. . . . Herr Graf . . . stood there transfixed, like someone who has always imagined that his wanderings from key to key are quite unusual and now finds that one can be even more unusual and yet not offend the ear. (A, 316)

To Leopold Mozart   *Mannheim, 20 November 1777*

I went to the service, brand new music composed by Vogler. I had already been to the afternoon rehearsal the day before yesterday, but went off immediately after the Kyrie. I have never in my life heard such stuff. In many places the parts simply do not harmonize. He modulates in such a violent way as to make you think that he is resolved to drag you with him by the scruff of the neck; not that there is anything remarkable about it all to make it worth the trouble; no, it is all clumsy plunging. (A, 378)

To Leopold Mozart   *Vienna, 26 September 1781*

Passions, whether violent or not, must never be expressed to the point of exciting disgust, and as music, even in the most terrible situations, must never offend the ear. (A, 769)

To Leopold Mozart   *Vienna, 28 December 1782*

The golden mean of truth in all things is no longer either known or appreciated. In order to win applause one must write stuff which is so inane that a coachman could sing it, or so unintelligible that it pleases precisely because no sensible man can understand it. This is not what I have been wanting to discuss with you; but I should like to write a book, a short introduction to music, illustrated by examples, but I need hardly add, not under my own name. (A, 833)

EFFECT

To Leopold Mozart   *Paris, 5 April 1778*

Kapellmeister Holzbauer has sent a Miserere here, but . . . the choruses he has composed would not be effective [in Paris]. So M. Le Gros [Director of the Concert Spirituel] . . . has asked me to compose others . . . I have finished it and only trust that it will produce the desired effect. When he saw my first chorus, Mr. Gossec . . . said to Mr. Le Gros (I was not present) that it was charmant and would certainly produce a good effect, and that the words were well arranged and on the whole excellently set to music.[5] (A, 521)

To Leopold Mozart   *Mannheim, 3 December 1778*

Ah, if only we had clarinets too! You cannot imagine the glorious effect of a symphony with flutes, oboes, and clarinets. (A, 638)

To Leopold Mozart   *Vienna, 26 September 1781*

I have explained to Stephanie the words I require for the aria ["Solche hergelaufne Laffen" in act 1 of *Die Entführung*] . . . I am enclosing only the beginning and the end, which is bound to have a good effect . . . as Osmin's rage gradually increases, there comes (just when the aria seems to be at an end) the allegro assai, which is in a totally different meter and in a different key; this is bound to be very effective. [See ex. 6.2] (A, 769)

To Leopold Mozart   *Vienna, 15 February 1783*

My new *Haffner* Symphony [K. 385] has positively amazed me, for I had forgotten every single note of it. It must surely produce a good effect. (A, 840)

EXPRESSION AND REPRESENTATION

To Leopold Mozart   *Mannheim, 8 November 1777*

I cannot write in verse, for I am no poet. I cannot arrange the parts of speech with such art as to produce effects of light and shade, for I am no painter. Even by signs and gestures I cannot express my thoughts and feelings, for I am no dancer. But I can do so by means of sounds, for I am a musician. (A, 363)

To Leopold Mozart   *Mannheim, 6 December 1777*

[Cannabich's] daughter [Rosa] who is fifteen, his eldest child, is a very pretty and charming girl. She is very intelligent and steady for her age. She is serious, does not say much, but when she does speak, she is pleasant and amiable. Yesterday she again gave me indescribable pleasure; she played the whole of my sonata [Piano Sonata in C, K. 309 (284b), ex. 6.1)]—excellently. The Andante (which must *not be taken too quickly*) she plays with the utmost expression . . . Young Danner asked me how I thought of composing the Andante. I said that I would make it fit closely the character of Mlle. Rosa. When I played it, it was an extraordinary success. She is exactly like the Andante. (A, 408)

EXAMPLE 6.1. Piano Sonata in C, K. 309 (284b). Movement 2: Andante un poco adagio, mm. 1–46

▶ There is, not surprisingly, little agreement about the "character" of this music and, consequently, of Mlle. Rosa. According to Hermann Abert, the frequent forte-piano dynamic contrasts suggest that she must have been "quite a little rascal." Alfred Einstein argues that "since we know nothing of this young lady's character, we cannot judge whether the portrait is a faithful one or not." But he finds the movement "tender" and "sensitive," and remarks: "How little Mozart was concerned with realism may be inferred from the fact that the slow movement of the other Mannheim sonata [the D major, K. 311/284c]—an *Andante con espressione*, very child-like, very innocent—has also been taken to be the portrait of the young Rosa Cannabich." Perhaps, given Mozart's characterization of Rosa, we are obliged to find this movement "serious, pleasant, and amiable."[6] ◀

Osmin's rage (ex. 6.2) is rendered comical by the use of Turkish music [i.e., cymbals and bass drum].[7] . . . The passage "Drum beim Barte des Propheten" (ex. 6.2 b) is indeed in the same tempo, but with quick notes; and as Osmin's rage gradually increases, there comes (just when the aria seems to be at an end) the allegro assai (ex. 6.2c), which is in a totally different meter and in a different key; this is bound to be very effective. For just as a man in such a towering rage oversteps all bounds of order, moderation, and propriety and completely forgets himself, so must the music too forget itself. But since passions, whether violent or not, must never be expressed to the point of exciting disgust, and as music, even in the most terrible situations, must never offend the ear, but must please the listener, or in other words must never cease to be *music*, so I have not chosen a key foreign to F (in which the aria is written) but one related to it—not the nearest, D minor, but the more remote A minor.

EXAMPLE 6.2a *Die Entführung aus dem Serail:* "Solche hergelauf'ne Laffen," Beginning

EXAMPLE 6.2b. "Solche hergelauf'ne Laffen," mm. 120–130

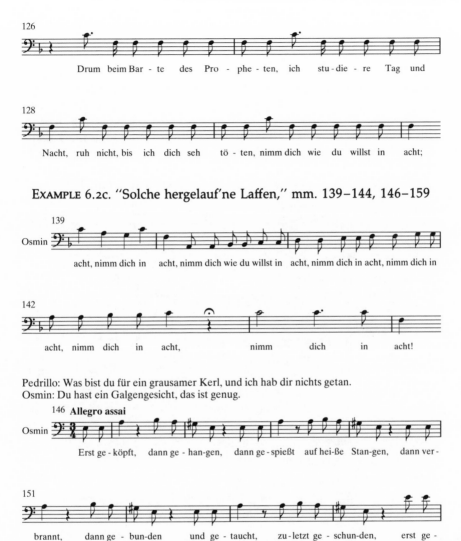

126

Drum beim Bar - te des Pro - phe - ten, ich stu - die - re Tag und

128

Nacht, ruh nicht, bis ich dich seh tö - ten, nimm dich wie du willst in acht;

EXAMPLE 6.2c. "Solche hergelauf'ne Laffen," mm. 139–144, 146–159

139

Osmin

acht, nimm dich in acht, nimm dich wie du willst in acht, nimm dich in acht, nimm dich in

142

acht, nimm dich in acht, nimm dich in acht!

Pedrillo: Was bist du für ein grausamer Kerl, und ich hab dir nichts getan.
Osmin: Du hast ein Galgengesicht, das ist genug.

146 **Allegro assai**

Osmin

Erst ge - köpft, dann ge - han-gen, dann ge - spießt auf hei-ße Stan-gen, dann ver -

151

brannt, dann ge - bun-den und ge - taucht, zu - letzt ge - schun-den, erst ge -

155

köpft, dann ge - han-gen, dann - ge - spießt auf hei-ße Stan-gen, dann ver - brannt, _

TRANSLATION: *Osmin:* These fops, standing around here, | Who just gape at the women, | I hate them more than the devil . . . I'm smart, too. | So, by the beard of the Prophet, | I'll study day and night | I won't rest, until I see you killed, | So, beware.

Pedrillo: What a cruel fellow you are, and I've done nothing to you.

Osmin: You have a gallows face, and that's enough. First beheaded, then hanged, |

Then impaled on hot poles, I Then burned, then bound, I Then drowned, and finally flayed.

Let me now turn to Belmonte's aria in A major, "O wie ängstlich, o wie feurig" (ex. 6.3a). Would you like to know how I have expressed it—and even indicated his throbbing heart? By the two violins playing octaves. This is the favorite aria of all those who have heard it, and it is mine also. I wrote it expressly to suit Adamberger's voice.

EXAMPLE 6.3a. *Die Entführung.* "O wie ängstlich," mm. 5–11

You see the trembling—the faltering—you see how his throbbing heart begins to swell; this I have expressed by a crescendo. You hear the whispering and the sighing—which I have indicated by the first violins with mutes and a flute playing in unison (ex. 6.3b).[8]

EXAMPLE 6.3b. "O wie ängstlich," mm. 29–45

TRANSLATION: Oh, how anxiously, how fervently, beats my loving heart . . . Already I tremble and shake, | hesitate and waver, | My swelling breast rises. | Is that her whispering? I'm so frightened.

I have sacrificed Constanze's aria a little to the flexible throat of Mlle. Cavalieri, "Trennung war mein banges Los und nun schwimmt mein Aug' in Tränen." I have tried to express her feelings as far as an Italian bravura aria will allow it (ex. 6.4). (A, 769)

EXAMPLE 6.4. "Doch wie schnell schwand meine Freude," mm. 10–18a, 36–49

nem Schoß, _ Kum-mer ruht in mei-nem _

Schoß, Kum-mer ruht_____ in mei

nem Schoß.

TRANSLATION: But how quickly my joy vanished. | Separation was my sad fate. Now my eyes swim in tears. | Grief rests in my breast.

THE CRAFT OF COMPOSITION

► In addition to the larger questions of musical aesthetics Mozart, of course, also had strong views about more technical matters connected with the "craft" of composition: the proper treatment of the constituent elements of a musical work—melody, harmony, sonority, the invention and working out of ideas, and so on. Unfortunately, we have very few specific remarks on such issues. The sparse information in the letters, however, is augmented somewhat by the comments and corrections he entered into the surviving exercises of his composition students—most notably, those of Thomas Attwood. The testimony of these documents, along with the letters and the reminiscences of others, sheds light not only on Mozart's opinions concerning the raw materials of music but on his pedagogical practice as well. ◄

The Reminiscences of Michael Kelly, 1826

"Melody is the essence of music," continued he; "I compare a good melodist to a fine racer, and counterpointists to hack post-horses; therefore be advised, let well alone, and remember the old Italian proverb— 'Chi sa più, meno sa—Who knows most, knows least.'" (Kelly, 1:225)

► That Mozart placed greatest value on the melodic interest of the parts (especially the top part), and on full sonority, is confirmed by his corrections and comments in Thomas Attwood's exercises in theory and composition. In one instance, Mozart corrected Attwood's harmonization of a bass line he had given him (ex. 6.5) with the remark: ◄

"In this way there is more melodic interest in the principal voice and the chords are fuller."[9]

EXAMPLE 6.5a. From Thomas Attwood's Harmony Exercises

[etc.]

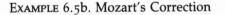

EXAMPLE 6.5b. Mozart's Correction

[etc.]

To Leopold Mozart   *Mannheim, 20 November 1777*

I will not say anything about the way in which the ideas are worked out. I will only say that it is impossible that a mass of Vogler's should please any composer who is worthy of the name. To put it briefly, if I hear an idea which is not at all bad—well—it will certainly not remain *not at all bad* for long, but will soon become—beautiful? God forbid!—bad and thoroughly bad; and that in two or three different ways. Either the idea has scarcely been introduced before another comes along and ruins it; or he does not round it off naturally enough to preserve its merit; or it is not in the right place; or, finally, it is ruined by the instrumentation. That's Vogler's music. (A, 378)

To Leopold Mozart   *Paris, 14 May 1778*

I think I told you in my last letter that the [Mlle.] de Guines . . . is my pupil in composition. . . . She is, however, extremely doubtful as to whether she has any talent for composition, especially as regards inventions or ideas. . . . If she gets no inspirations or ideas (for at present she really has none whatever), then it is to no purpose, for—God knows—I can't give her any. . . . I gave her her fourth lesson today and, so far as the rules of composition and harmony are concerned, I am fairly well satisfied with her. She filled in quite a good bass for the first minuet, the melody of which I had given her, and she has already begun to write in three parts. But she very soon gets bored, and I am unable to help her; for as yet I cannot proceed more quickly. It is too soon, even if there really were genius there, but unfortunately there is none. Everything has to be done by rule. She has no ideas whatever—nothing comes. I have tried her in every possible way. Among other things I hit on the idea of writing down a very simple minuet, in order to see whether she could not compose a variation on it. It was useless. "Well," I thought, "she probably does not know how she ought to begin." So I started to write a variation on the first bar and told her to go on in the same way and to keep to the idea. In the end it went fairly well. When it was finished, I told her to begin something of her own, only the treble part, the melody. Well, she thought and thought for a whole quarter of an hour and nothing came. So I wrote down four bars of a minuet and said to her: "See what an ass I am! I have begun a minuet and cannot even finish the melody. Please be so kind as to finish it for me." She was positive she couldn't, but at last with great difficulty— something came, and indeed I was only too glad to see something for once. I then told her to finish the minuet, I mean, the treble only. But for *home work* all I asked her to do was to alter my four bars and compose something of her own. She was to find a new beginning, use, if necessary, the same harmony, provided that the melody should be different. (A, 538–539)

► Mozart's methods of teaching minuet composition are graphically demonstrated in Thomas Attwood's lessons. In example 6.6, Mozart wrote down the melody and bass parts for the first part of a minuet for string quartet; Attwood was to fill in the second violin and viola parts in the first half and compose a second half completely. In another assignment (ex. 6.7) Mozart entered only the melody for the first part of a minuet and only the bass for the second. Attwood was to complete the composition, again scored for string quartet.[10]

EXAMPLE 6.6. A Minuet Exercise for Attwood

EXAMPLE 6.7. A Minuet Exercise for Attwood

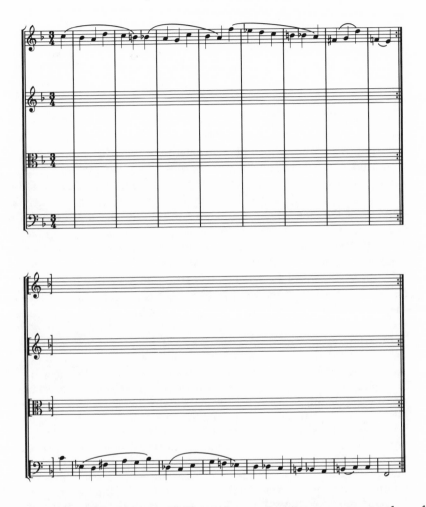

► The Attwood lessons reveal Mozart's conscientiousness as a teacher of theory and composition; but as to his convictions regarding the ultimate value of such instruction, or at least the value of musical theory, consider his comment on Vogler's book: ◄

To Leopold Mozart   *Mannheim, 13 November 1777*

I see from Papa's letter that he has not seen Vogler's book [*Tonwissenschaft und Tonsetzkunst*, (The Science of Harmony and the Art of Composition) Mannheim, 1776]. I have just read it. . . . His book is more useful for teaching arithmetic than for teaching composition. He says he can turn out a composer in three weeks and a singer in six months, but so far no one has seen him do it.[11] (A, 369–370)

► Mozart was evidently convinced that the wrong kind of instruction—
namely, either abstract speculation, as in the case of Vogler, or, as
Michael Kelly reports below, partial and "dry study" of the rules
(especially if it was administered at the wrong time—that is, after the
normal formative period of apprenticeship) in fact could be worse than
useless. For it had the capacity to "perplex" and "disturb" a "natural
gift." ◄

The Reminiscences of Michael Kelly, 1826

I determined to devote myself to the study of counterpoint, and consulted
[Mozart] by whom I ought to be instructed. He said, "My good lad, you
ask my advice, and I will give it you candidly; had you studied composition when you were at Naples, and when your mind was not devoted to
other pursuits, you would perhaps have done wisely; but now that your
profession of the stage must and ought, to occupy all your attention, it
would be an unwise measure to enter into a dry study. You may take my
word for it, Nature has made you a melodist, and you would only disturb
and perplex yourself. Reflect, a little knowledge is a dangerous thing;
should there be errors in what you write, you will find hundreds of
musicians in all parts of the world, capable of correcting them; therefore
do not disturb your natural gift." (Kelly, 1:224–225)

► A little knowledge, no doubt, could be a dangerous thing. But Mozart
did not really doubt that composition could in fact be properly taught
and—assuming the presence of a natural gift—properly learned. He
had, after all, been willing to offer lessons in composition to Thomas
Attwood, Johann Nepomuk Hummel, and others. And he had even
contemplated writing that textbook on music—one very likely intended in the first instance for the instruction of aspiring composers. In the
end, however, Mozart believed that the most effective way to learn and
to perfect the art of composition was through the direct study of
outstanding examples of music. This, at all events, was his personal
method. Niemetschek reports that on the eve of the Prague premiere of
Don Giovanni in October 1787 Mozart made the following confession to
a fellow musician, one Johann Baptist Kucharz, who had been charged
with leading the rehearsals. ◄

Franz Xaver Niemetschek, Biography of Mozart, 1808

"People are mistaken, if they think that my art has come easy to me. I
assure you, dear friend, no one has devoted so much effort in the study of
composition as have I. There is scarcely a famous master in music whose
works I have not diligently, and often repeatedly, studied." (Niemetschek
1808, 88).

7

Performance

Wherein consists the art of playing prima vista? In this: in playing the piece in the time in which it ought to be played, and in playing all the notes, appoggiaturas, and so forth, exactly as they are written and with the appropriate expression and taste, so that you might suppose that the performer had composed it himself.

Mannheim, 17 January 1778

► These remarks, nominally concerned only about the relatively minor art of sight-reading and quoted before in that connection (Chapter 1), constitute in fact Mozart's definitive statement of principle on the entire art of musical performance. They enunciate, in an admirably concise formulation, the two cardinal principles that are invoked repeatedly in Mozart's comments on proper performance: Precision and Expression. Above all, Mozart insists on precision with respect to musical time: both "keeping time" (i.e., maintaining a regular beat) and observing the correct tempo—a tempo which, more often than not, should not be taken "too fast."

But precision also entails rendering all the notes—pitches and also ornaments—"exactly as they are written." Mozart would seem, then, to have tolerated at best a minimum of improvised embellishment, at least by others, in his own music. Precision, finally, in the sense of maximum clarity of execution, lay at the root of Mozart's enthusiastic admiration for the pianos of Johann Andreas Stein.

A merely "precise," technically perfect, performance, however, was utterly unacceptable to him. Both as a composer (as we have seen in Chapter 6) and as a performer Mozart expected a musical composition to embody and communicate "appropriate expression and taste."[1] Taste, of course, was a most respected attribute in the culture of the eighteenth century. One need only recall that this was the first (if not the highest) quality mentioned by Joseph Haydn in his famous confession to Leopold Mozart: "Before God and as an honest man, I tell you that your son is the greatest composer known to me either in person or by name. He has taste and, what is more, the most profound knowledge of composition."[2] ◄

201

FUNDAMENTALS

Time and Tempo

The most difficult and the chief requisite in music, which is, time.

Augsburg, 24 October 1777

To Leopold Mozart   *Munich, 6 October 1777*

[Charles Dupreille] could not play four bars in succession without going wrong. He could not find his fingering and he knew nothing whatever about short rests. (A, 300)

▶ Mozart uses the term *sospirs*. In Leopold Mozart's violin treatise we read: "One sort of rest is the 'Sospiro.' It is so called because it is of short duration." (A footnote informs us that the word is derived from the Italian *sospirare*, to sigh.)[3] To judge from Leopold's examples *sospiri* are isolated rests appearing as part of 1+3 or 1+1 patterns. His point about them is that they have to be played and counted with as much precision as notes of the same value (ex. 7.1).[4] ◀

EXAMPLE 7.1. Leopold Mozart. Treatise on Violin Playing. "Sospir"

To Leopold Mozart   *Augsburg, 24 October 1777*

[Nannette Stein] will never acquire the most essential, the most difficult and the chief requisite in music, which is, time, because from her earliest years she has done her utmost not to play in time. . . . Everyone is amazed that I can always keep strict time. (A, 340)

To Leopold Mozart   *Mannheim, 6 December 1777*

[Rosa Cannabich] played the whole of my sonata [in C, K. 309 (284b)] excellently. The Andante (which must *not be taken too quickly*) she plays with utmost expression.[5] (A, 408)

To Leopold Mozart   *Mannheim, 17 January 1778*

I should mention that before dinner [Vogler] had scrambled through my concerto [for piano in C, K. 246, ex. 7.2] at sight. . . . He took the first movement *prestissimo,* the Andante *allegro* and the Rondo, believe it or not, *prestississimo.* He generally played the bass differently from the way it was written, inventing now and then quite another harmony and even melody. Nothing else is possible at that pace, for the eyes cannot see the music nor the hands perform it. Well, what good is it? That kind of sight-reading and shitting are all one to me. . . .

EXAMPLE 7.2. Piano Concerto in C (*Lützow*), K. 246, Opening Themes

The listeners . . . can only say that they have *seen* music and piano playing. They hear, think and feel as little during the performance *as the player himself.* Well, you may easily imagine that it was unendurable. At the same time I could not bring myself to say to him, *Far too quick!* Besides, it is much easier to play a thing quickly than slowly; in passage work you can leave out a few notes without anyone noticing it. But is that beautiful? In rapid playing the right and left hands can be changed without anyone seeing or hearing it. But is that beautiful?

► Mozart's famous prescription for the proper tempo in a fugue is of interest not least on account of its rationale. For its emphasis on the clear projection of the theme at all times contradicts the practice of J. S. Bach, who in his fugues often took great delight in obscuring the entrances of the subject. ◄

To Nannerl   *Vienna, 20 April 1782*

I have purposely written above [the Fugue for Clavier in C, K. 394 (383a)] *Andante maestoso,* as it must not be played too fast. For if a fugue is not played slowly, the ear cannot clearly distinguish the theme when it comes in and consequently the effect is entirely missed.[6] (A, 801)

► It would be a mistake, however, to conclude that Mozart fundamentally disapproved of fast tempi. ◄

To Leopold Mozart   *Vienna, 7 August 1782*

The first Allegro [of the *Haffner* Symphony in D, K. 385, ex. 7.3] must be played with great fire, the last—as fast as possible.[7] (A, 813)

EXAMPLE 7.3. Symphony in D (*Haffner*), K. 385: Movements 1 and 4, Opening Themes

► But it seems safe to conclude that, in Mozart's view, performers were more likely to err on the side of haste. This was confirmed years later by Constanze with reference to opera performance. ◄

The Reminiscences of Constanze Mozart, 1829

Mozart particularly disliked the hurried manner in which some orchestras accompanied his operas. (Novello, 102)

► For Mozart even the expressive rhythmic freedom of *tempo rubato* (literally, "stolen time"), typically applied in many adagio movements, was governed by the "most essential requisite." ◄

To Leopold Mozart   *Augsburg, 24 October 1777*

In tempo rubato in an Adagio, the left hand should go on playing in strict time. (A, 340)

► Mozart's position was in accord with his father's discussion of the device. Leopold Mozart comments on tempo rubato as follows in a footnote in his treatise:
    "A skillful accompanist must . . . know how to judge a soloist. To a true virtuoso, the accompanist must certainly not yield [i.e., must

maintain the beat] for he would then spoil [the soloist's] tempo rubato. What this "stolen tempo" is, is more easily shown than described. But on the other hand, if the accompanist has to deal with a fancied virtuoso, then he may often, in an adagio cantabile, have to hold out many an eighth the length of half a bar, until perchance the latter recovers from his paroxysms; and nothing goes according to time, for he plays after the style of a recitative."[8]

It has been pointed out that some passages in Mozart's adagios seem to be notated in the style of "written-out" rubati. For example, compare m. 3 and m. 19 from the Adagio of the C-minor Piano Sonata, K. 457 (ex. 7.4). ◄

EXAMPLE 7.4. Piano Sonata in C minor, K. 457: Movement 2, Adagio, mm. 1–4, 17–19

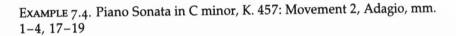

► Consider also the version of mm. 34–35 of the Adagio from the Piano Sonata in F, K. 332, as it appears in Mozart's autograph and in the first edition (ex. 7.5).[9] ◄

EXAMPLE 7.5. Piano Sonata in F, K. 332/300k: Movement 2, Adagio, mm. 33–35. Autograph and First Edition

► Rigorous adherence to strict time could be abandoned in the case of a single "peculiar kind of piece": the free keyboard prelude. ◄

To Leopold Mozart   *Paris, 20 July 1778*

I hope that you will be able to decipher the end of the prelude.[10] . . . You need not be very particular about the time. This is a peculiar kind of piece [*so eine gewisse sache*]. It's the kind of thing that may be played as you feel inclined. (A, 574)

INTERPRETATION: EXPRESSION AND ORNAMENTATION

► For Mozart an indispensable hallmark of a fine performance was that it conveyed "plenty of expression." But a properly expressive performance was not to be achieved at the expense of "proper precision." Mozart's close linguistic linkage of the two attributes—he rarely mentions the one without the other—suggests that he may have regarded proper expression as the logical, almost inevitable, consequence of a "precise," "accurate," rendering—at all events, assuming a properly marked score (and a player of taste). ◄

To Leopold Mozart   *Mannheim, 13 November 1777*

I should advise my sister . . . to play [Myslivecek's keyboard sonatas][11] with plenty of expression, taste, and fire, and to learn them by heart. For they are sonatas which are bound to please everyone, which are easy to memorize and very effective when played with the proper precision. (A, 371)

To Leopold Mozart   *Mannheim, 14 November 1777*

The Andante [of the Piano Sonata in C, K. 309 (284b)] will give us the most trouble, for it is full of expression and must be played accurately and with exact shades of forte and piano, precisely as they are marked. (A, 374)

► Did Mozart, then, tolerate no improvised embellishment at all? ◄

Leopold Mozart to Wolfgang   *Salzburg, 7 December 1780*

It was Herr Esser [visiting in Salzburg] whom we met in Mainz eighteen years ago [August 1763] and whose playing you criticized by telling him that *he played well, but that he added too many notes and that he ought to play music as it was written.* (A, 683)

► This remark, attributed to the seven-year-old Mozart by his father, is (along with the more general comment on playing the notes exactly as written, cited at the outset) the only statement by Mozart regarding improvised ornamentation. There can be little doubt, however, that Mozart expected and tolerated some degree of improvised embellishment in both his instrumental and vocal music. Moreover this expectation extended beyond the addition of cadenzas and *Eingänge*[12] in concertos and arias and included the embellishment of other soloistic passages as well. Mozart surely would have expected tasteful embellishments to be added to literal repetitions of themes, especially in slow movements (for example, that of the Piano Sonata in B-flat, K. 570), similar to those he had himself prescribed above in example 7.4, m. 17 (compared with m. 1) and example 7.5, m. 33 (the autograph compared with the first edition). (An example of the original embellishments for the vocal line of the aria "Ah, se a morir mi chiama" from *Lucio Silla* is reproduced in example 8.3.) ◄

ENSEMBLE SIZE

► One of the livelier controversies at the heart of modern discussions of "authentic performance" is the debate about proper orchestra size. Mozart described the orchestral forces at his disposal on several occasions. ◄

To Leopold Mozart   *Vienna, 11 April 1781*

You ask whether I have been to see [Giuseppe] Bonno? Why, it was at his house that we went through my symphony for the second time. I forgot to tell you the other day that at the concert the symphony went magnifique and had the greatest success. There were forty violins, the wind instruments were all doubled, there were ten violas, ten double basses, eight violoncellos and six bassoons. (A, 724)

► That is, perhaps some 96 players in all: 68 strings, 26 wind players (four each of flutes, oboes, clarinets, horns, trumpets, and six bassoons), timpani, and keyboard. There is a difference of opinion as to whether Mozart is referring here to the *Paris* Symphony in D, K. 297 (300a), or the Symphony in C, K. 338.[13] In his recent comprehensive study of Mozart's symphonies, Neal Zaslaw does not try to identify the work. He argues, however, that Mozart's statement does not necessarily imply that he favored large orchestras.[14] That Mozart was, at the least, favorably disposed toward large ensembles is clear also from his enthusiasm for the Mannheim orchestra which he described as follows: ◄

To Leopold Mozart   *Mannheim, 4 November 1777*

The orchestra is excellent and very strong. On either side there are ten or eleven violins, four violas, two oboes, two flutes and two clarinets, two horns, four violoncellos, four bassoons and four double basses, also trumpets and drums. They can produce fine music. (A, 355–356)

► Such an orchestra, comprising about 48–50 players (with 32 to 34 strings plus a keyboard player, not mentioned by Mozart), was approximately one and one-half times the size of the Salzburg court orchestra which in the late 1770s consisted of about 34 players with some 20 strings (6 + 6 violins, 2 violas, 2 cellos, 4 double basses), along with 5 oboes, 3 bassoons, 2 horns, and, presumably, 2 trumpets, 1 timpanist, and 1 keyboard player. (There were no flautists or clarinets.) On the other hand, we also read the following in the Mozart letters: ◄

To Nannerl   *Milan, 26 January 1770*

The opera at Mantua was charming. . . . The orchestra was not bad. In
Cremona it is good. (A, 110)

► The Mantua orchestra had six violins (3+3), the Cremona orchestra had
   ten (5+5). In short, the ultimate import of Mozart's various remarks
   about ensemble size is at best inconclusive.[15] ◄

SINGING

► Mozart's paramount concern for proper expression readily explains his
   impatience with mere bravura singing, his preference for the cantabile
   style (tastefully adorned with discreet vibrato, portamento, and messa
   di voce), the high value he placed on the ability of singers to act (i.e., to
   understand and convey—powerfully, but without exaggeration—the
   meaning and emotion of the music they sang) and, of course, his
   ridicule of singers who could not do so. ◄

STYLE

To Leopold Mozart   *Mannheim, 19 February 1778*

People soon get tired of coloratura passages. . . . Mlle. [Aloysia] Weber's
singing, on the other hand, goes to the heart, and she prefers to sing
cantabile. . . . If she goes to Italy, she will have to sing bravura arias.
Undoubtedly she will never forget how to sing cantabile, for that is her
natural bent. (A, 486)

To Leopold Mozart   *Paris, 12 June 1778*

[Anton] Raaff is too much inclined to drop into the cantabile. I admit that
when he was young and in his prime, this must have been very effective
and have taken people by surprise. I admit also that I like it. But he
overdoes it and so to me it often seems ridiculous. (A, 552)

► In August 1777, just a few weeks before he was to embark on his
   extended journey to Mannheim and Paris, Mozart composed a *scena* for
   soprano and orchestra, "Ah , lo previdi," K. 272 (ex 7.6). It was written
   for the Prague-born Josephine (or Josepha) Duschek, whose aquain-
   tance (along with that of her husband, Franz Xaver Duschek) Mozart
   had just made on the occasion of the Duscheks' visit to relatives in
   Salzburg. This ambitious and elaborate composition—in essence a
   four-movement solo cantata consisting of alternating recitatives and
   arias—represents, in the domain of operatic writing, as much of a
   watershed in the composer's artistic development as does the celebrated

"Jeunehomme" Piano Concerto in E-flat, K. 271, written the previous January, in the domain of instrumental music. The text is taken from the opera *Andromeda* by Giovanni Paisiello (librettist: Vittorio Amadeo Cigna-Santi) and captures the heroine's reaction upon learning from her betrothed, Eristeus, that her true lover, Perseus, was observed wandering about in a state of confusion carrying an unsheathed sword and is presumed to have killed himself. Mozart's setting is a *tour de force* of vivid musical representation: juxtaposing rage, despair, resignation, and transfigured grief. To this end he draws on some of the most effective dramatic and expressive resources available to an opera seria composer at the time: the formally and emotionally volatile *recitativo accompagnato* (ex. 7.6a, 7.6c) along with the diametrically contrasting aria styles marked, at the one extreme, by the passionate, violent, *aria parlante*, or *aria patetica* (ex. 7.6b) and, at the other, by the tender lyricism of the so-called *aria cantabile* (ex. 7.6d). About a year later Mozart explained to the singer Aloysia Weber (whom he had met in Mannheim in January 1778 and with whom he immediately fell deeply in love) what he expected her to consider when studying and performing the work. (Later in the same letter Mozart praises Aloysia's rendition of his "Non so d'onde viene," the aria inspired by Johann Christian Bach's setting and orginally conceived for the tenor Anton Raaff before it was recast for "Mlle. Weber.")

To Aloysia Weber, Mannheim   *Paris, 30 July 1778*

I shall be delighted if you will set to work as hard as you can at my Andromeda scena, "Ah, lo previdi," for I assure you that it will suit you admirably and that you will do yourself great credit with it. I advise you to watch the expression marks, to think carefully of the meaning and the force of the words, to put yourself in all seriousness into Andromeda's situation and position!—and to imagine that you really are that very person. . . .

► The aria text reads as follows: ◄

[Recitativo.] Ah, lo previdi! / Povero Prence, con quel ferro istesso / che me salvò, ti lacerasti il petto. / (Ad Eristeo:) Ma tu sì fiero scempio perchè non impedir? / Come, o crudele, d'un misero a pietà non ti movesti? / Qual tigre, qual tigre ti nodrì? / Dove, dove, dove nascesti? / Ah, t'invola, t'invola agli occhi miei!

TRANSLATION: [Recitative.] Ah, I foresaw it! / Poor Prince, with the very sword which saved me, you pierced your own breast. (To Eristeus:) But why did you not prevent such violent slaughter? / How, o cruel man, were you not moved to pity such a wretch? / What tiger nursed you? / Where were you born? / Ah, vanish from my sight!

EXAMPLE 7.6a *Scena:* "Ah, lo previdi," K. 272. Recitative, mm. 1–9

[Aria] Ah, t'invola agl'occhi miei, / alma vile, ingrato cor! / La cagione, oh Dio, tu sei / del mio barbaro, barbaro dolor. / Va, crudele! Va, spietato! / Va, tra le fiere ad abitar. (Eristeo parte)

[Aria.] Ah, vanish from my sight! / vile soul, ungrateful heart! / Oh God! You are the cause / of my cruel and brutal pain. / Go, cruel man! Go, ruthless one! / Go, dwell among the wild beasts. (Eristeus leaves.)

EXAMPLE 7.6b "Ah, lo previdi." Aria, mm. 28–42

[Recitativo.] Misera! Misera! Invan m'adiro, / e nel suo sangue intanto / nuota già l'idol mio. / Con quell'acciaro, ah Perseo, che facesti? / Mi salvasti poc'anzi, or m'uccidesti. Col sangue, ahi, la bell'alma, / ecco, già uscì dallo squarciato seno. / Me infelice! / Si oscura il giorno agli occhi miei, / e nel barbaro affanno il cor vien meno. Ah, non partir, ombra diletta, / io voglio unirmi a te. / Sul grado estremo, / intanto che m'uccide il dolor, / intanto fermati, fermati alquanto!

[Recitative.] Wretched woman that I am! In vain am I angered, / while my beloved lies in his own blood. / With that blade, ah Perseus, what have you done? / Not long ago you had saved me; now you have killed me. Alas! Here is the beautiful soul with blood / gushing forth from his wounded breast. / Unfortunate me! / Day becomes night to my eyes, / and my heart sinks in deepest sorrow. Ah, beloved spirit, do not leave, / I want to join you. / Upon the brink, / Until at last grief kills me, / Yet stay, stay awhile!

EXAMPLE 7.6c "Ah, lo previdi." Recitative, mm. 177–180, 194–198

[Aria. Cavatina.] Deh, no varcar quell'onda, / anima del cor mio. / Di Lete all'altra spondo, / ombra, compagna anch'io / voglio venir, venir con te. / Fermati!

> [Aria. Cavatina] Oh, do not cross that sea! / heart of my heart! / To Lethe's further shore / I too, your shadow, your companion, / want to come with you. Stay!

EXAMPLE 7.6d "Ah, lo previdi." Aria. Cavatina, mm. 217–234

To Aloysia Weber, Mannheim (continued)

In the aria "Non so d'onde viene" [K. 294],[16] which you learned by yourself, I found nothing to criticize or correct; you sang it to me with the interpretation, with the method and the expression I desired. . . . Please write to me . . . and tell me something about your study of stage acting— to which I urge you most warmly to apply yourself. (A, 581–582)

To Leopold Mozart Paris, 12 June 1778

I heard [Anton Raaff] for the first time [in Mannheim] in the rehearsal of Holzbauer's *Günther [von Schwarzburg]*. . . . When he was not singing he stood there like a child at stool: when he began to sing the first recitative, it went quite tolerably, but every now and then he gave a kind of shout, which I could not bear. He sang the arias in a way so obviously careless—and some notes he sang with too much emphasis—which did not appeal to me. (A, 551)

TECHNIQUE

► For Mozart the beauty (and expressivity) of a singer's performance depended—perhaps even more than in the case of instrumentalists— on the proper and tasteful execution of the ornaments, especially of those that affect the tone quality of individual notes and are, so to speak, "natural" to the human voice. These included the *messa di voce* (the controlled swelling and subsiding of volume on a sustained note), the *portamento* (a sliding connection from one note to another), and above all, the *vibrato*. It is worth observing that Mozart expected the effect of the vibrato, or something like it, to be emulated by all instrumentalists, even keyboard players. ◄

To Leopold Mozart Munich, 2 October 1777

When [Mlle. Kaiser] sustains her voice for a few bars, I have been astonished at the beauty of her *crescendo* and *decrescendo*.[17] She still takes her trills slowly and I am very glad. They will be all the truer and clearer when later on she wants to trill more rapidly, for it is always easier to do them quickly in any case. (A, 291)

To Leopold Mozart Mannheim, 19 February 1778

[Catterina Gabrielli] was not capable of *sustaining* a breve properly, and, as she had no *messa di voce*, she could not dwell on her notes. (A, 486)

To Leopold Mozart Mannheim, 7 March 1778

I only wish you could hear [Mlle. Weber] sing my new aria ["Non so, d'onde viene," K. 294] . . . it is absolutely made for her. A man like you, who really understands what portamento singing is, would certainly find complete satisfaction in her performance. (A, 506)

► Although portamento is possible on the violin as well as the voice, Leopold Mozart does not use the word in his treatise. But he does describe a bowing technique in which the finger slides between two notes on the same string.[18] A more-or-less contemporary definition of portamento appears in the *Musikalisches Lexikon* of Heinrich Christoph Koch: "Carrying the voice, understood as a certain flexibility in the intonation of the tones in cantabile movements, which is easier to hear or demonstrate than to describe."[19] ◄

To Leopold Mozart   *Paris, 12 June 1778*

The human voice trembles [zittert] naturally, but in its own way, and only to such a degree that the effect is beautiful. Such is the nature of the voice; and people imitate it not only on wind instruments, but on stringed instruments, too, and even on the clavier. But the moment the proper limit is overstepped, it is no longer beautiful because it is contrary to nature. It reminds me then of the organ when the bellows are puffing. (A, 552)

► Even more fundamental to competent singing than the correct rendition of the ornaments was the proper production of sound in the first place: a sound emanating from the chest, not the throat, that, in addition, would be in tune. ◄

To Leopold Mozart   *Munich, 30 December 1780*

[Vincenzo] Dal Prato . . . is utterly useless. His voice would not be so bad if he did not produce it in his throat and larynx. But he has no intonation, no method, no feeling, but sings—well, like the best of the boys who come to be tested in the hope of getting a place in the chapel choir. (A, 701)

► Further comments and verdicts on singers and the singer's art appear in Chapter 14. ◄

KEYBOARD PERFORMANCE

Style and Technique

► In the domain of keyboard performance, Mozart spoke with the authority and first-hand experience of a consummate virtuoso. As a pianist, and piano teacher, he did not fail to attend to the basics: insisting on correct posture and proper deportment, proper fingering, and systematic drill, one hand at a time, of passage work and ornaments. The ultimate objective was to play with "taste": that is, with an even and "natural lightness" of touch, and a *cantabile* (i.e., a singing) style. ◄

To Leopold Mozart   *Augsburg, 24 October 1777*

I do not make grimaces, and yet play with such expression that, as [Johann Andreas Stein] himself confesses, no one up to the present has been able to get such good results out of his pianofortes. (A, 340)

To Leopold Mozart   *Augsburg, 23 October 1777*

Anyone who sees and hears [Nannette Stein] play and can keep from laughing, must, like her father, be made of stone. For instead of sitting in the middle of the clavier, she sits right up opposite the treble, as it gives her more chance of flopping about and making grimaces. She rolls her eyes and smirks. When a passage is repeated, she plays it more slowly the second time. If it has to be played a third time, then she plays it even more slowly. When a passage is being played, the arm must be raised as high as possible, and according as the notes in the passage are stressed, the arm, not the fingers, must do this, and that too with great emphasis in a heavy and clumsy manner. But the best joke of all is that when she comes to a passage which ought to flow like oil and which necessitates a change of finger, she does not bother her head about it, but when the moment arrives, she just leaves out the notes, raises her hand and starts off again quite comfortably—a method by which she is much more likely to strike a wrong note, which often produces a curious effect. I am simply writing this in order to give Papa some idea of clavier playing and clavier teaching. (A, 339–340)

To Leopold Mozart   *Mannheim, 14 November 1777*

If I were [Rosa Cannabich's] regular teacher, I would lock up all her music, cover the keys with a handkerchief, and make her practice, first with the right hand and then with the left, nothing but passages, trills, mordents, and so forth, very slowly at first, until each hand should be thoroughly trained. I would then undertake to turn her into a first-rate clavierist. For it's a great pity. She has so much talent, reads quite passably, possesses so much natural facility, and plays with plenty of feeling. (A, 374)

To Leopold Mozart   *Mannheim, 17 January 1778*

[Abbé] Vogler's fingering too is wretched; his left thumb is just like that of the late Adlgasser and he does all the treble runs downwards with the thumb and first finger of his right hand. (A, 449)

To Leopold Mozart   *Paris, 24 March 1778*

[Rosa Cannabich] can now perform before anyone, and for a girl of fourteen and an amateur she plays quite well; and it is thanks to me, as all Mannheim knows. She now has taste and can play trills; her time is good and her fingering is much better; formerly she had nothing of this. (A, 517)

To Leopold Mozart   *Vienna, 27 June 1781*

The young lady [Josepha Auernhammer] is a fright, but plays enchantingly, though in cantabile playing she has not got the real delicate singing style. She clips [*verzupt*] everything.[20] (A, 748)

► Mozart was singularly unimpressed by mere technical brilliance when it exceeded or ignored the bounds of "appropriate expression and taste"; hence his contempt (once again) for excessively fast tempi and his scathing characterization of the piano virtuoso Muzio Clementi. ◄

To Leopold Mozart   *Vienna, 12 January 1782*

Clementi plays well, so far as execution with the right hand goes. His greatest strength lies in passages in thirds. Apart from this, he has not a kreuzer's worth of taste or feeling—in short he is simply a *mechanicus*.[21] (A, 792)

To Leopold Mozart   *Vienna, 7 June 1783*

Clementi's sonatas. . . . contain no remarkable or striking passages except those in sixths or octaves. And I implore my sister not to practice those passages too much, so that she may not spoil her quiet, even touch and that her hand may not lose its natural lightness, flexibility, and smooth rapidity. For after all what is to be gained by it? Supposing that you do play sixths and octaves with the utmost velocity (which no one can accomplish, not even Clementi)? You only produce an atrocious chopping effect and nothing else whatever.[22] (A, 850)

KEYBOARD INSTRUMENTS AND MAKERS

► It is hardly surprising that Mozart, who played all the keyboard instruments of his time—the clavichord, the harpsichord, the piano (which he generally referred to as "Pianoforte," written either as one or two words), and the organ—was thoroughly knowledgeable, and had strong views, about their musical capacities. From childhood on he had at his disposal in Salzburg both a clavichord and a large two-manual harpsichord (the latter built by Christian Ernst Friederici of the Thuringian town of Gera). In addition, he owned a portable clavier (*Clavierl*)— presumably a spinet (i.e., a small harpsichord) which he found helpful while composing.[23] ◄

To Leopold Mozart   *Augsburg, 14 October 1777*

I had the honor of playing for about three-quarters of an hour upon a good clavichord by [Johann Andreas] Stein. . . . an excellent instrument. (A, 315, 317)

To Leopold Mozart   *Nancy, 3 October 1778*

I should also like to have beside my writing-desk the little clavier [*das kleine Clavierl*] which Fischietti and Rust had, as it suits me better than Stein's small one [a portable clavier purchased by Leopold during the Mozarts' 1763 stay in Augsburg]. (A, 622)

To Leopold Mozart   *Vienna, 27 June 1781*

We have two harpsichords in the house where I am lodging, one for galanterie[24] playing and the other an instrument which is strung with the low octave throughout, like the one we had in London, and consequently sounds like an organ. So on this one I improvised and played fugues. (A, 748)

▶ Mozart was also keenly interested in the most recent technological developments and improvements—especially those regarding the piano. He presumably had heard, and perhaps even played on a piano, during his sojourn in London in 1764–1765. His first documented performance on the instrument took place in the winter of 1774–1775 at the home of his Munich acquaintance Franz Albert.[25] It is not clear when Mozart acquired a piano of his own. Despite his admiration for the pianos of Johann Andreas Stein, related below, and his familiarity with the instruments of Franz Jacob Späth, it seems that his first piano was one built by the Viennese maker Anton Walter, which Mozart had acquired sometime between 1782 and 1785. (This instrument, fig. 7.1, survives and is on display at the Mozart Museum in Salzburg.) ◀

FIGURE 7.1. Mozart's Pianoforte, built by Anton Walter, Vienna, ca. 1780

To Leopold Mozart   *Augsburg, 17 October 1777*

This time I shall begin at once with Stein's pianofortes. Before I had seen any of his, [Franz Jakob] Späth's claviers had always been my favorites. But now I much prefer Stein's, for they damp ever so much better than the Regensburg [i.e., Späth's] instruments. When I strike hard, I can keep my finger on the note or raise it, but the sound ceases the moment I have produced it. In whatever way I touch the keys, the tone is always even. It never jars, it is never stronger or weaker or entirely absent; in a word, it is always even. It is true that he does not sell a pianoforte of this kind for less than three hundred gulden, but the trouble and the labor which Stein puts into the making of it cannot be paid for. His instruments have this special advantage over others that they are made with escape action. Only one maker in a hundred bothers about this. But without an escapement it is impossible to avoid jangling and vibration after the note is struck. When you touch the keys, the hammers fall back again the moment after they have struck the strings, whether you hold down the keys or release them. He himself told me that when he has finished making one of these claviers, he sits down to it and tries all kinds of passages, runs, and jumps, and he shaves and works away until it can do anything. For he labors solely in the interest of music and not for his own profit; otherwise he would soon finish his work. He often says: "If I were not myself such a passionate lover of music and had not myself some slight skill on the clavier, I should certainly long ago have lost patience with my work. But I do like an instrument which never lets the player down and which is durable." And his claviers certainly do last. He guarantees that the sounding board will neither break nor split. When he has finished making one for a clavier, he places it in the open air, exposing it to rain, snow, the heat of the sun and all the devils in order that it may crack. Then he inserts wedges and glues them in to make the instrument very strong and firm. He is delighted when it cracks, for he can then be sure that nothing more can happen to it. Indeed he often cuts into it himself and then glues it together again and strengthens it in this way. He has finished making three pianofortes of this kind. Today I played on one again. . . . Here at Munich I have played all my six sonatas [K. 279–284 (189d–h, 205b)] by heart several times. . . . The last one in D [i.e., the "Dürnitz" Sonata, K. 284 (205b), ex. 7.7], sounds exquisite on Stein's pianoforte. The device, too, which you work with your knee is better on his than on other instruments. I have only to touch it and

EXAMPLE 7.7. Piano Sonata in D ("Dürnitz"), K. 284 (205b), Opening Themes

it works; and when you shift your knee the slightest bit, you do not hear the least reverberation. (A, 327–329)

► The salient technical characteristics of Johann Andreas Stein's pianos have been described as follows: "An important feature . . . is the extremely small and light hammers; their thin leather covering (instead of felt) is vital to these instruments' clavichord-like delicacy of articulation and nuance. Typically, the Stein action has either round hollow hammers . . . made of hazelwood, or short solid hammers usually made of pearwood. . . . The individual dampers are fitted into a rack above the strings, which the player can raise by means of knee levers under the keyboard. . . . Surviving Stein pianos (fig. 7.2) are usually double strung with the top octave or so triple strung. . . . The typical Stein compass is five octaves, F' to f'''."[26] ◄

To Leopold Mozart   *Vienna, 24 March 1781*

I should have extemporized and played a fugue and then the variations "Je suis Lindor" [K. 354 (299a)] on Countess Thun's beautiful Stein pianoforte.[27] (A, 718)

ORGANS

► The history of Mozart's relationship to the organ—from the time he taught himself the pedals at the age of seven until his performance at J. S. Bach's Thomaskirche in Leipzig in 1789—was reviewed earlier. (See Chapter 1.) His comments on specific instruments follow. (Unfortunately, his opinion of the Leipzig organ has not been recorded.) ◄

To Leopold Mozart   *Augsburg, 17 October 1777*

When I told Herr Stein that I should like very much to play on his organ, as that instrument was my passion, he was greatly surprised. . . . I noticed at once from what he said that he thought I would not do much on his organ; that I would play, for instance, in a thoroughly pianistic style . . . At first the pedal seemed a bit strange to me, as it was not divided [*gebrochen*]. It started with C, and then D and E followed in the same row. But with us D and E are above, as E-flat and F-sharp are here. But I soon got the hang of it. (A, 329)

FIGURE 7.2.
Pianoforte by
J. A. Stein,
Augsburg, 1773

► Mozart was accustomed to a pedal board with a "short octave," that is, one on which certain pitches were omitted from the lowest octave. This was not uncommon on keyboard instruments through the eighteenth century. Evidently the pitches E-flat and F-sharp were missing on the Salzburg organ. ◄

To Leopold Mozart   *Mannheim, 18 December 1777*

The organ in the Lutheran church which has just been tried today is very good, both in the full and in single stops. (A, 447–448)

To Leopold Mozart   *Strasbourg, 2 November 1778*

I have played here in public on the two best organs built by Silbermann, which are in the Lutheran churches—the New Church and St. Thomas's Church. (A, 629)

► Mozart is referring here not to the famous three-manual organ of the Strasbourg Minster, built in 1713/16 by Andreas Silbermann (1678–

1734) but rather to two instruments built by Andreas's son, Johann Andreas Silbermann (1712–1783). The organ at St. Thomas (1741) containing three manuals and 42 stops is still extant; the three-manual organ at the Neue Kirche (1749), with 45 stops, no longer exists. The Silbermanns, father and son, were members of the illustrious Alsatian family of organ builders whose most famous member was Andreas's brother, Gottfried (1683–1753). ◄

VIOLIN PLAYING

► Mozart, whose own tone on the violin won praise from his audiences (see Chapter 1), understandably placed great value on this quality in the playing of others. Less expected, perhaps, is his emphasis on the importance of good staccato technique—an asset that he stresses more than once. (The players mentioned by Mozart—Ignaz Fränzl, Paul Rothfischer, and Franz Lamotte—are identified and described more fully in Chapter 14. Heinrich Marchand was a pupil of Leopold's.) ◄

To Leopold Mozart   *Mannheim, 22 November 1777*

[Ignaz Fränzl] has . . . a most beautiful, round tone. He never misses a note, you can hear everything. It is all clear-cut. He has a beautiful staccato, played with a single bowing, up or down; and I have never heard anyone play a double trill as he does. (A, 384)

To Leopold Mozart   *St. Germain, 27 August 1778*

Rothfischer . . . plays well in his way (a little bit in the old-fashioned Tartini manner). (A, 607)

► Conceivably Mozart has in mind Tartini's highly embellished style of violin playing—as opposed to a more singing style—a trait for which he had been criticized by the famous theorist, Johann Joachim Quantz. On a more technical level, Tartini recommended using the second position to a far greater extent than did Leopold.[28] ◄

To Leopold Mozart   *Vienna, 6 December 1783*

Tell [Heinrich Marchand] too that he ought to concentrate hard on staccato playing, for it is just in this particular that the Viennese cannot forget Lamotte. (A, 862)

8

Opera: The Principal Categories

In the opera the chief thing is the music.

Vienna, 21 June 1783

► Operas can be classified in three ways: by dramatic genre—serious or comic—by national style, and by the relative importance of their components: the text, the voices, the music. Mozart had something to say about them all. ◄

DRAMATIC GENRE: SERIOUS OR COMIC

► Like all forms of drama, operas can be divided into the serious (or tragic) and the comic. This is certainly a most basic, and universal, division: a heritage of classical antiquity observed, at least in theory, in virtually all modern Western traditions of spoken and musical drama. In practice, however, the two genres were not always rigorously separated but were more typically and more realistically combined in varying mixtures. As far as eighteenth-century opera is concerned, the serious forms largely succeeded in preserving and protecting their purity (and dignity) throughout the century—to the point of petrification. The comic genres, however, increasingly absorbed elements of the serious, the sentimental, the magical (what have you) for the sake of vitality and theatrical effectiveness and in order to expand the expressive palette. This was emphatically the case with Mozart, especially in the operatic masterpieces of his maturity, all nominally comic operas. How ironic, then, that in his only comment directly addressing this issue (written as he was about to embark on the composition of *Die Entführung aus dem Serail*), Mozart—with considerable self righteousness, at that—advocates just the sort of strict separation of the dramatic genres that his infallible dramatic intuition knew would, in fact, be fatal. ◄

To Leopold Mozart   *Vienna, 16 June 1781*

I have not the slightest doubt about the success of the opera,[1] provided the text is a good one. For do you really suppose that I should write an opéra comique in the same style as an opera seria? In an opera seria there should be little frivolity and much seriousness and solidity, as in an opera buffa there should be little seriousness and all the more frivolity and gaiety. That people like to have a little comic music in an opera seria, I cannot help. (A, 746)

NATIONAL STYLES

Writing operas is now my one burning ambition, but they must be French rather than German, and Italian rather than either.

Mannheim, 7 February 1778

► With respect to the principal national styles, Mozart's preference for the Italian opera no doubt lay in his observation that in Italy music "reigned supreme." And, of course, Italian opera itself enjoyed supremacy throughout Europe. Moreover, the Italian stage was royally, indeed imperially, supported and hence commanded the best resources: above all, the most excellent and illustrious singers. On the other hand, Mozart respected the dramatic seriousness and power of the French opera and would have been attracted in particular to its sophisticated use of the chorus (his "favorite type of composition")—attracted enough, no doubt, to overcome his strong distaste for the French language. As for German opera, he was understandably drawn to it not only by patriotic impulse but, even more, by its very newness, that is, by its attendant openness to experiment and innovation and its untapped, seemingly boundless, potential. ◄

Italian Opera

Why do Italian comic operas please everywhere—in spite of their miserable libretti—even in Paris, where I myself witnessed their success? Just because there the music reigns supreme, and when one listens to it, all else is forgotten.

Vienna, 13 October 1781

I should dearly love to show what I can do in an Italian opera!

Vienna, 7 May 1783

Aria Forms and Styles

► The standard aria form in the eighteenth-century opera seria was the so-called da capo form, a symmetrical three-part design consisting of two poetic stanzas, generally of four lines each, set to two contrasting musical sections with the text and music of the first, or "A," part repeated in its entirety (with the vocal part typically ornamented) after the second, or "B," part. The repetition of the first part was not written out but simply indicated by the direction "D.C." or "da capo"—"from the beginning" (literally: "from the top" or "head"). Occasionally, the aria dispensed with the second strophe. Such a one-part aria (as well as other shorter aria forms) were referred to at the time as a "cavatina." Mozart refers to both the da capo and cavatina forms, but not by name, in the passage below. ◄

To Leopold Mozart   *Munich, 1 December 1780*

We should like at this point [act 3 of *Idomeneo*] to have a peaceful quiet aria. Even if it has only one part, so much the better; in every aria the second part must be kept for the middle section—and often indeed it gets in my way. (A, 678)

► Since the vast majority of opera seria arias shared the same basic da capo form, they were usually classified not by formal design but according to their vocal style and expressive character. The five categories described by the English writer John Brown (in his *Letters on the Italian Opera*, 1791) are typical: *aria cantabile* (songlike and lyrical), *aria di portamento* (sustained and dignified in expression), *aria di mezzo carattere* (serious and pleasing, and without pathos), *aria parlante* (violent, passionate), *aria di bravura* (a display of the singer's agility).[2] Largely synonymous terms used by other writers included *aria patetica* (evidently like the *aria parlante*) and *aria brillante* (like the *aria di bravura*).

Mozart was clearly familiar with this terminology, but he also chose to refer to (and, no doubt, to conceive of) arias according to more specifically musical qualities such as their tempo or scoring. ◄

Aria andantino

To Leopold Mozart   *Mannheim, 14 February 1778*

I only taught her [Aloysia Weber] the day before yesterday an Andantino Cantabile by [Johann Christian] Bach, the whole of it. (A, 482)

To Leopold Mozart   *Munich, 8 November 1780*

Ilia's aria in act 2, scene 2 [of *Idomeneo;* see ex. 8.1] . . . "Se il padre perdei, in te lo ritrovo" . . . we have agreed to introduce here an aria andantino[3] with obbligatos for four wind instruments, that is, a flute, oboe, horn, and bassoon. (A, 659–660)

TRANSLATION: If I have lost my father, my country, my peace, | Then you are now a father to me.

EXAMPLE 8.1. *Idomeneo,* K. 366. Ilia's Aria: "Se il padre perdei," Opening Theme

Aria di bravura

To Leopold Mozart   *Mannheim, 14 February 1778*

Yesterday there was a concert at Cannabich's . . . Mlle. Weber sang most charmingly the aria di bravura of De Amicis. (A, 482)

► Mozart is referring to Giunia's aria, "Ah, se il crudel" from act 2 of *Lucio Silla.* A sample of the vocal part is shown in example 8.2 (p. 230). ◄

Aria cantabile

To Leopold Mozart   *Mannheim, 14 February 1778*

There are also some cadenzas that I once jotted down and at least one aria cantabile with coloratura indications [ausgesetzten Gusto]. I should like that first of all, for it would be good practice for Mlle. Weber. (A, 482)

► In addition to a series of cadenzas for three different arias by J.C. Bach, Mozart prepared decorated versions for two cantabile arias: J. C. Bach's "Cara la dolce fiamma" and the aria for Cecilio, "Ah, se a morir mi

EXAMPLE 8.2. *Lucio Silla*, K. 135. Giunia's Aria: "Ah, se il crudel," Vocal Passages

TRANSLATION: Ah, if the cruel peril | Of my beloved I remember, . . . | Everything makes me freeze.

chiama" (ex. 8.3), from his own opera *Lucio Silla*.[4] It is notable that the embellished version of "Ah, se a morir" (which survives in Nannerl's hand) does not restrict the additional vocal embellishments to the final, da capo, section only but applies them throughout.[5] ◄

EXAMPLE 8.3. *Lucio Silla.* Cecilio's Aria: "Ah, se a morir mi chiama," Original and Embellished Versions of the Vocal Part

TRANSLATION: Ah, if my cruel fate calls me to death, | I shall always be with you as a faithful spirit.

Aria di licenza

▶ The *aria di licenza* was written for a particular occasion; its text contained specific references to the celebrated individual or occasion. ◀

To Leopold Mozart   *Munich, 30 December 1780*

In [Pietro Metastasio's] *Natal di Giove*, which I admit is very little known, Raaff has now found, I believe, an aria that is admirably suited to this situation.[6] I think it is the *aria di licenza*—Bell'alme al ciel dilette, si, ah! respirate ormai, . . . Well, he wants me to set this to music. (A, 702)

▶ Musically and dramatically, Mozart's vocal ensembles are surely his most sophisticated, original, and effective contributions to opera. Unfortunately, the only direct, general, observation about them in the letters is the following. ◀

To Leopold Mozart   *Munich, 27 December 1780*

In a quartet the words should . . . be spoken much more than sung. (A, 699)

Ballet

▶ Mozart's comments make clear that ballets were typically performed in conjunction with operatic productions not only in France (as is well known) but in Italy and Germany as well. ◀

To Nannerl   *Verona, 7 January 1770*

After each act [of an opera] there is a ballet. (A, 105)

To his Mother   *Munich, 14 January 1775*

After the opera [Mozart's *La finta giardiniera*, K. 196] was over and during the pause when there is usually silence until the ballet begins, people kept on clapping all the time and shouting "Bravo." (A, 259)

GERMAN OPERA

Every nation has its own opera and why not Germany? Is not German as singable as French and English? Is it not more so than Russian? Very well then!

                                                         Vienna, 5 February 1783

An Auspicious Birth and Troubled Infancy

▶ The 1770s saw the emergence of intense interest on the part of several enlightened monarchs of the German-speaking world to create both a German national theater and a German national opera. In the vanguard were the Electoral courts of Mannheim and Munich. From the beginning Mozart was fascinated by the prospect. ◄

To Leopold Mozart   *Munich, 2 October 1777*

I am *very popular* here. And how much more popular I should be if I could help forward the German national theater? And with my help it would certainly succeed. (A, 290–291)

To Leopold Mozart   *Mannheim, 14 November 1777*

There is a permanent German national theater here as in Munich. German singspiels are performed occasionally, but the singers in them are wretched. (A, 375)

► Emperor Joseph II soon followed suit and created a German-language musical theater called the Nationalsingspiel. Its first production, Ignaz Umlauf's *Die Bergknappen,* opened at the Burgtheater on 17 February 1778. The musicians of the Nationalsingspiel were relatively well paid, but its sixteen vocal soloists received far smaller salaries than their counterparts in the Italian-language Hofoper (court opera). Moreover, there were no outstanding resident composers or librettists attached to the enterprise. Despite some successes—most notably, Mozart's *Die Entführung,* first performed on 16 July 1782—the Nationalsingspiel never could maintain itself against the more popular Italian opera buffa and closed (for the first time) on 4 March 1783.[7] ◄

To Leopold Mozart   *Vienna, 5 February 1783*

On Friday, the day after tomorrow, a new opera is to be given, the music of which, a *galimathias,* [literally, gibberish; also a potpourri] is by a young Viennese.[8] . . . It will probably not be a success. Still, it is better stuff than its predecessor, an old opera by Gassmann, *La notte critica,* in German *Die unruhige Nacht,* which with difficulty survived three performances. This in its turn had been preceded by that execrable opera of Umlauf [*Welche ist die beste Nation?*], about which I wrote to you and which never got so far as a third performance. It really seems as if they wished to kill off the German opera before its time, which in any case is to come to an end after Easter; and Germans themselves are doing this—shame upon them! . . . I do not believe that the Italian opera will keep going for long, and besides, I hold with the Germans. I prefer German opera, even though it means more trouble for me. (A, 839)

► In October 1785 the Nationalsingspiel was revived. It managed to continue for about a year and a half until finally closing in February 1787. Mozart was skeptical, even cynical, about its chances, for reasons which he set forth in a letter to Anton Klein, the author of the libretto for Ignaz Holzbauer's important singspiel *Günther von Schwarzburg.* ◄

To Anton Klein, Mannheim   *Vienna, 21 May 1785*

At the moment I cannot send you any news about the coming German operatic stage, for at present, apart from the building operations at the Kärntnertor theater, which has been set apart for this purpose, things are progressing very slowly. They say that it is to be opened early in October. I for my part have no great hopes of its success. To judge by the preparations which have been made up to the present, it looks as if they were trying altogether to ruin German opera, which is probably only suffering a temporary eclipse, rather than to help put it on its legs again and keep it going. My sister-in-law Madame Lange is the only singer who is to join the German opera. Madame Cavalieri, Adamberger, Mlle. Teiber, all Germans of whom Germany may well be proud, have to stay at the Italian opera and compete against their own countrymen! At present it is easy to count up the German singers, male and female; and even if there really are as good singers as the ones I have mentioned, or even better ones, which I very much doubt, yet I am inclined to think that the directors of our theater are too niggardly and too little patriotically minded to offer large sums of money to strangers when they have on the spot better singers, or at least equally good ones, whom they can rope in for nothing. For the Italian company does not need them, as far as numbers go. The company can fill all the parts themselves. The idea at present is to carry on the German opera with actors and actresses who only sing when they must. Most unfortunately the directors of the theater and those of the orchestra have all been retained, and it is they who, owing to their ignorance and slackness, are chiefly responsible for the failure of their own enterprise. Were there but one good patriot in charge, things would take a different turn. But then, perhaps, the German national theater which is sprouting so vigorously would actually begin to flower; and of course that would be an everlasting blot on Germany, if we Germans were seriously to begin to think like Germans, to act as Germans, to speak German and, Heaven help us, to sing in German!! (A, 890–891)

▶ The German musical theater would ultimately triumph as a purely bourgeois, commercial enterprise under the aegis of Emanuel Schikaneder: the Freihaustheater auf der Wieden. ◀

Melodrama

▶ In contrast to the Italian opera which, whether seria or buffa, was set to music throughout, the eighteenth-century German singspiel typically made use of spoken dialogue rather than recitative between the musical numbers. Experimental forms, however, were developed, most notably the so-called melodrama (or duodrama, as Mozart calls it). As to the "German opera seria" mentioned by Mozart, it is not clear whether it was to make use of sung recitative in the manner of an Italian opera seria, or was to be a normal singspiel, but with a serious plot. ◀

To Leopold Mozart   *Munich, 2 October 1777*

When I heard the German singspiel [a German translation of Piccinni's *La Pescatrice*], I was simply itching to compose . . . They [the sponsors of a German national theater in Munich] would like to produce a German opera seria soon, and they are very anxious that I should compose it. (A, 290–291)

To Leopold Mozart   *Mannheim, 12 November 1778*

I have always wanted to write a drama of this kind [viz., a melodrama]. I cannot remember whether I told you anything about this type of drama the first time I was here. On that occasion I saw a piece of this kind performed twice and was absolutely delighted. Indeed, nothing has ever surprised me so much, for I had always imagined that such a piece would be quite ineffective! You know, of course, that there is no singing in it, only recitation, to which the music is like a sort of obbligato accompaniment to a recitative. Now and then words are spoken while the music goes on, and this produces the finest effect. The piece I saw was Benda's *Medea.*(A, 631)

EXAMPLE 8.4. Georg Benda: *Medea*, From scene 6

TRANSLATION: Medea (enraged): Cursed be Jason and Kreusa! Cursed the newly-weds! | Away! Shall they find you here and bind you together with the other slaves to their chariot? | Shall they drag your children to their deaths before your very eyes? | Shall the lovers' scornful laughter be your dirge? | You are still Medea! | Take your revenge and then die!

► Example 8.4, an excerpt from Georg Benda's *Medea*, is representative of this style. Mozart had planned at just this time to compose a duodrama called *Semiramis*, K. 315e (see below). He later set two numbers of his singspiel *Zaide*, K. 344 (336b), as *melodrame* and also employed the device in his incidental music for the heroic drama *Thamos, König von Aegypten*, K. 345 (336a). ◄

To Leopold Mozart   *Kaysersheim, 18 December 1778*

With regard to the monodrama or duodrama [*monodrame oder Duodrame*], a voice part is by no means necessary, as not a single note is sung; everything is spoken. In short, it is a recitative with instruments, only the actor speaks his words instead of singing them. If you could but hear it once, even with the clavier, it could not fail to please you; and if you could hear it performed, you would be swept off your feet, I warrant you. At the same time it requires a good actor or actress. (A, 641–642)

FRENCH OPERA

► Mozart never had an opportunity to compose a French opera. Had he done so, he would have found the experience technically and aesthetically challenging. On the one hand, he would have had to struggle with a language which he not only disliked but considered (as have other composers) to be less than ideally suited for musical setting. Moreover, neither great singing nor great vocal writing was particularly valued in French opera. On the other hand, the emphasis was on drama, spectacle, and dance; and this entailed not only music for the ballet, but also—to a far greater extent than was the case in Italian or German opera—music for chorus: an idiom that Mozart loved, calling it his "favorite type of composition." ◄

To Leopold Mozart   *Mannheim, 28 February 1778*

I am looking forward most particularly to the Concert Spirituel in Paris, for I shall probably be asked to compose something for it. The orchestra is said to be so excellent and strong, and my favorite type of composition, the chorus, can be well performed there. I am indeed glad that the French value choruses highly. The only fault found with Piccinni's new opera *Roland*, is that the choruses are too meager and weak . . . To be sure, they are accustomed to Gluck's choruses in Paris. (A, 498)

To Leopold Mozart   *Paris, 3 July 1778*

As for the opera, matters are as follows. It is very difficult to find a good libretto. The old ones, which are the best, are not adapted to the modern style and the new ones are all quite useless. Poetry, the only thing of which the French have had reason to be proud, becomes worse every day—and yet the poetry is the one thing that must be good here, for they do not understand music. There are now two operas in aria which I might compose. One, en deux actes, and the other en trois . . . the one en trois is a translation of *Demofoonte* (by Metastasio) interspersed with choruses and dances and altogether adapted to the French stage. (A, 558–559)

To Leopold Mozart   *Paris, 31 July 1778*

I assure you that if I am commissioned to write an opera, I shall have no fears whatever. True, the devil himself must certainly have invented the language of these people—and I fully realize the difficulties with which all composers have had to contend. But in spite of this I feel I am as well able to overcome them as anyone else. Au contraire, when I fancy, as I often do, that I have got the commission, my whole body seems to be on fire and I tremble from head to foot with eagerness to teach the French more thoroughly to know, appreciate, and fear the Germans. For why is a grand opera never entrusted to a Frenchman? Why must it always be a foreigner? For me the most detestable part of the business would be the singers. Well, I am ready. (A, 587–588)

To Leopold Mozart   *Vienna, 12 September 1781*

The translator of *Iphigenie* [by Gluck] into German is an excellent poet,[9] and I would gladly have given him my Munich opera [i.e., *Idomeneo*] to translate . . . I would have made several other alterations and arranged it more in the French style. (A, 765)

The Memoirs of Joseph Frank, 1852

As I always found him busy studying the scores of French operas, I was bold enough to ask him if he would not do better to devote his attention to Italian scores. "With respect to melody, yes, but with respect to dramatic effectiveness, no. Moreover, the scores which you see here are, apart from those of Grétry, by Gluck, Piccinni, Salieri, and there is nothing French about them but the words." (DDB, 561)

AUTEUR OR HAUTEUR?: COMPOSER'S OPERA VERSUS SINGER'S OPERA

► Particularly illuminating are Mozart's views on what should be the proper hierarchy among the principals concerned in the creation and execution of an opera: the poet, the composer, the singer. A venerable aesthetic posture dating back almost to the very beginnings of opera held that (in the famous phrase of an apologist for Claudio Monteverdi) "the words are the mistress of the harmony." This noble sentiment was periodically renewed during the course of operatic history—most recently, in Mozart's day, by the celebrated reformer Christoph Willibald von Gluck and his collaborator, the librettist, Raniero de Calzabigi. In radical contrast, and with no less eloquence, Mozart declared that "in an opera the poetry must be altogether the obedient daughter of the music." But while he was emphatic in asserting the supremacy of the composer's domain over that of the poet, Mozart, often enough, was more than willing to defer to the will, and even to the whim, of his singers. On more than one occasion he employed the sartorial metaphor: "I like an aria to fit a singer as perfectly as a well-made suit of clothes." When it came to the vocal ensemble, however—the hallmark and unequalled triumph of Mozartean opera—he insisted that "the composer must have a free hand." ◄

COMPOSER'S OPERA

To Leopold Mozart *Vienna, 13 October 1781*

I should say that in an opera the poetry must be altogether the obedient daughter of the music . . . Why, an opera is sure of success when the plot is well worked out, the words written solely for the music and not shoved in here and there to suit some miserable rhyme (which, God knows, never enhances the value of any theatrical performance, be it what it may, but rather detracts from it)—I mean, words or even entire verses which ruin the composer's whole idea . . . The best thing of all is when a good composer, who understands the stage and is talented enough to make sound suggestions, meets an able poet, that true phoenix; in that case no fears need be entertained as to the applause even of the ignorant. Poets almost remind me of trumpeters with their professional tricks! If we composers were always to stick so faithfully to our rules (which were very good at a time when no one knew better), we should be concocting music as unpalatable as their libretti. (A, 772–773)

To Leopold Mozart *Vienna, 21 June 1783*

Why, I consider it a great insult to myself that Herr Varesco is doubtful about the success of the opera [the planned opera buffa, *L'oca del Cairo*]. Of one thing he may be sure: that his libretto will certainly not go down if the music is no good. For in the opera the chief thing is the music. If then the opera is to be a success and Varesco hopes to be rewarded, he must alter and recast the libretto as much and as often as I wish and he must not follow his own inclinations, for he has not the slightest knowledge or experience of the theater. You may even give him to understand that it doesn't much matter whether he writes the opera or not. I know the story now; and therefore anyone can write it as well as he can. (A, 853)

To Leopold Mozart *Munich, 27 December 1780*

As far as trios and quartets are concerned, the composer must have a free hand. (A, 699)

SINGER'S OPERA

To Leopold Mozart *Mannheim, 28 February 1778*

I like an aria to fit a singer as perfectly as a well-made suit of clothes. (A 497)

▶ Mozart's eagerness to accommodate the desires and abilities of his singers is particularly well documented in his letters home chronicling the composition of *Idomeneo* (1780–1781) and *Die Entführung aus dem Serail* (1781–1782). The pertinent passages follow. ◄

Idomeneo

► Since Mozart was living in Munich during much of the composition of *Idomeneo*, it was Leopold's task to relay his desires for changes in the text to the Salzburg-based librettist, Abbate Giambattista Varesco. Of the singers mentioned here, the tenor, Anton Raaff (then sixty-six years old) sang the title role; Domenico de Panzacchi, also a tenor, sang the role of Arbace, Idomeneo's confidant. ◄

To Leopold Mozart   *Munich, 15 November 1780*

There is still one more alteration, for which Raaff is responsible. He is right, however, and even if he were not, some courtesy ought to be shown to his grey hairs . . . As he has no aria in act 3 . . . he wishes to have a pretty one to sing . . . after his last speech. (A, 664)

To Leopold Mozart   *Munich, 1 December 1780*

As I heard first from a reliable source and now from his own lips, [Raaff] said . . . : "Hitherto both in recitatives and arias I have always been accustomed to alter my parts to suit me, but here everything remains as written, for I cannot find a note which does not suit me . . . " *Enfin*, he is as happy as a king. (A 677)

To Leopold Mozart   *Munich, 5 December 1780*

I also wrote about Panzacchi; we must do what we can to oblige this worthy old fellow. He would like to have his recitative in act 3 lengthened by a couple of lines, which owing to the *chiaro e oscuro*[10] and his being a good actor will have a capital effect. (A, 682)

To Leopold Mozart   *Munich, 27 December 1780*

It is very difficult to compose for [Raaff], but very easy if you choose to compose commonplace arias, as for instance, the first one, "Vedrommi intorno" [act I, no. 6]. When you hear it, you will say that it is good and beautiful; but if I had written it for Zonca, it would have suited the words much better.[11] (A, 698)

► As mentioned later on in the same letter, however, a singer's prerogative had its limits, namely, at the threshold of an ensemble number. Mozart reports that Raaff had objected to his part in the great act 3 quartet, "Andró ramingo e solo:" ◄

To Leopold Mozart   *Munich, 27 December 1780*

The more I think of this quartet, as it will be performed on the stage, the more effective I consider it; and it has pleased all those who have heard it played on the clavier. Raaff alone thinks it will produce no effect whatsoever. He said to me when we were by ourselves: *"You can't let yourself go in it* [in Italian]. *It gives me no scope"* [emphasis in original]. As if in a quartet the words should not be spoken much more than sung. That kind of thing he does not understand at all. All I said was: "My very dear friend, if I knew of one single note which ought to be altered in this quartet, I would alter it at once . . . But so far there is nothing in my opera with which I am so pleased as with this quartet; and when you have once heard it sung as a whole, you will talk very differently.[12] I have taken great pains to serve you well in your two arias; I shall do the same with your third one, and shall hope to succeed. But as far as trios and quartets are concerned, the composer must have a free hand." (A, 699)

Die Entführung aus dem Serail

► The musical examples referred to here are reproduced in Chapter 6. See also the comments on the individual singers cited in Chapter 14. ◄

To Leopold Mozart   *Vienna, 26 September 1781*

As we have given the part of Osmin to Herr Fischer, who certainly has an excellent bass voice . . . we must take advantage of it, particularly as he has the whole Viennese public on his side. But in the original libretto [by C. F. Bretzner] Osmin has only this short song and nothing else to sing, except in the trio and the finale; so he has been given an aria in act 1, and he is to have another in act 2. I have explained to Stephanie the words I require for the aria ["Solche hergelaufne Laffen" in act 1]—indeed I had finished composing most of the music for it before Stephanie knew anything whatever about it. . . . In working out the aria I have . . . allowed Fischer's beautiful deep notes to glow. . . . I have sacrificed Constanze's aria a little to the flexible throat of Mlle. Cavalieri, "Trennung war mein banges Los und nun schwimmt mein Aug' in Tränen." I have tried to express her feelings, as far as an Italian bravura aria will allow it. (A, 769)

9

Opera as Drama

I have looked through at least a hundred libretti and more, but I have hardly found a single one with which I am satisfied.

Vienna, 7 May 1783

THE SEARCH FOR LIBRETTI—AND LIBRETTISTS

To Nannerl   *Rome, 21 April 1770*

[The castrato Giovanni] Manzuoli is negotiating with the Milanese to sing in my opera. . . . The libretto has not yet been chosen. I recommended . . . a text by Metastasio. (A, 130–131)

▶ The opera ultimately chosen was *Mitridate*, with a libretto by the Turin poet Vittorio Amedeo Cigna-Santi, based on a work of Racine. It is significant that the composer was engaged before the libretto or librettist was chosen and that the young composer's choice for a text did not prevail. In the future, however, Mozart's influence over the choice of librettists and the selection and preparation of texts would be decisive.

Mozart's criteria for a librettist were set out in a letter home describing both the personal vices and professional virtues of Gottlieb Stephanie the younger, the soon-to-be librettist (more precisely, the adaptor) of the text of *Die Entführung aus dem Serail*. ◀

To Leopold Mozart   *Vienna, 16 June 1781*

Well, I must now explain why we were suspicious of Stephanie. I regret to say that the fellow has the worst reputation in Vienna, for he is said to be rude, false, and slanderous, and to treat people most unfairly. But I pay no attention to these reports. There may be some truth in them, for everyone abuses him. On the other hand, he is in great favor with the Emperor. He was most friendly to me the first time we met, and said: "We are old friends already and I shall be delighted if it be in my power to render you any service." I believe and hope too that he himself may write an opera libretto for me. Whether he has written his plays alone or with the help of others, whether he has plagiarized or created, he still understands the stage, and his plays are invariably popular. I have only seen two new pieces of his, and these are certainly excellent. (A, 746)

► Following the immense success of *Die Entführung*, Mozart greatest desire—one in which he was encouraged by influential individuals at court—was to repeat the achievement by composing another opera. The first challenge was finding a satisfactory libretto. ◄

To Leopold Mozart   *Vienna, 21 December 1782*

Count Rosenberg himself spoke to me at Prince Galitzin's and suggested that I should write an Italian opera. I have already commissioned someone to procure for me from Italy the latest opere buffe texts to choose from, but as yet I have not received any. (A, 832)

To Leopold Mozart   *Vienna, 7 May 1783*

I have looked through at least a hundred libretti and more, but I have hardly found a single one with which I am satisfied; that is to say, so many alterations would have to be made here and there, that even if a poet would undertake to make them, it would be easier for him to write a completely new text—which indeed it is always best to do. . . . I should dearly love to show what I can do in an Italian opera! So I have been thinking that unless Varesco is still very much annoyed with us about the Munich opera [*Idomeneo*], he might write me a new libretto for seven characters. (A, 847–848)

► Varesco finally produced an opera buffa libretto: *L'oca del Cairo* [The Goose of Cairo], K. 422, a work destined to remain unfinished, but one that provoked a number of observations from Mozart on dramaturgical topics—especially concerning comic plot structure—that will be presented in due course. At precisely the same time that Mozart makes the above proposal to Varesco, he reports making the acquaintance of another poet with whom future artistic collaborations would prove to be infinitely more fruitful. ◄

To Leopold Mozart   *Vienna, 7 May 1783*

Our poet here is now a certain Abbate da Ponte. He has an enormous amount to do in revising pieces for the theater and he has to write *per obbligo* an entirely new libretto for Salieri [*Il ricco d'un giorno*], which will take him two months. He has promised after that to write a new libretto for me. But who knows whether he will be able to keep his word—or will want to? For, as you are aware, these Italian gentlemen are very civil to your face. Enough, we know them! If he is in league with Salieri, I shall never get anything out of him. (A, 848)

To Leopold Mozart   *Vienna, 5 July 1783*

An Italian poet here has now brought me a libretto which I shall perhaps adopt if he agrees to trim and adjust it in accordance with my wishes.[1] (A, 855)

► In the spring of 1785, Anton Klein, the librettist for Ignaz Holzbauer's *Günther von Schwarzburg* (an opera whose music Mozart admired while disparaging the text), had sent Mozart his drama *Kaiser Rudolf von Habsburg* and requested that he set it as an opera. Mozart put him off (permanently, as it turned out) with a response that sheds further light on the seriousness with which Mozart approached the selection of a libretto. ◄

To Anton Klein   *Vienna, 21 May 1785*

As for the opera . . . My hands are so full that I scarcely ever find a minute I can call my own. A man of such great insight and experience as yourself will know even better than I that a libretto of this kind has to be read through with all possible attention and deliberation, and not once only, but several times. So far I have not had time to read it through even once without interruption. All that I can say at the moment is that I should not like to part with it yet. So I beg you to leave the play with me for a little longer. (A, 890–891)

► In his memoirs, published in New York, where he ultimately settled and became a professor of Italian at Columbia University, Lorenzo Da Ponte relates the origin of the idea to write an opera on the subject of Figaro. ◄

The Memoirs of Lorenzo Da Ponte, 1830

I returned in all peace of mind to my search for subjects to be written for my two dear friends Mozart and Martini [i.e., Vicente Martín y Soler].

As for the former, I could easily see that the sweep of his genius demanded a subject of great scope, something multiform, sublime. In conversation with me one day in this connection, he asked me whether I could easily make an opera from a comedy by Beaumarchais—*Le Mariage de Figaro*. I liked the suggestion very much, and promised him to write one. (Da Ponte, 149–150)

DRAMATURGY

▶ Mozart's views on the fundamental aesthetic issues of expression and representation in opera were presented earlier, in Chapter 6. The topics discussed here are more specific: problems of length, plausibility, effect, plot, poetry. Once again, Mozart's most thoughtful and illuminating comments on these concerns were written in connection with his work on *Idomeneo* (1780–1781), *Die Entführung* (1781–1782), and also the abortive opera buffa, *L'oca del Cairo* (1783). As it happens, all but the last of the following passages bearing on the subjects of Length, Plausibility, and Effect, concern *Idomeneo*. ◀

LENGTH

▶ The problem of length, it seems, was always a problem of "too long." Mozart, typically, was concerned about boring his audience. It is also not surprising that the problem of excessive length stood in inverse relation to the acting ability of the singers. ◀

To Leopold Mozart   *Munich, 8 November 1780*

Some slight alterations will have to be made here and there, and the recitatives will have to be shortened a bit. (A, 659)

To Leopold Mozart   *Munich, 24 November 1780*

Do ask the Abbate Varesco if we may not break off at the chorus in act 2, "Placido è il mar," after Elettra's first verse when the chorus has repeated—or, failing that, after the second, for it is really far too long! (A, 672).

To Leopold Mozart   *Munich, 19 December 1780*

The scene between father and son [Idomeneo and Idamante] in act 1 and the scene in act 2 between Idomeneo and Arbace are both too long. They would certainly bore the audience, particularly as in the first scene both the actors [Raaff and Vincenzo Dal Prato] are bad, and in the second, one of them is; besides they only contain a narrative of what the spectators have already seen with their own eyes. These scenes are being printed as they stand. But I should like the Abbate to indicate how they may be shortened—and as drastically as possible—for otherwise I shall have to shorten them myself. These two scenes cannot remain as they are—I mean, when set to music. (A, 693)

To Leopold Mozart   *Munich, 18 January 1781*

The rehearsal of act 3 went off splendidly. It was considered much superior to the first two acts. But the libretto is too long and consequently the music also (an opinion which I have always held). . . . The speech of the oracle is still far too long and I have therefore shortened it; but Varesco need not know anything of this because it will all be printed just as he wrote it. (A, 708)

PLAUSIBILITY

To Leopold Mozart   *Munich, 13 November 1780*

To act 1, scene 8, [stage designer, Lorenzo] Quaglio has made the same objection that we made originally—I mean, that it is not fitting that the king should be quite alone in the ship. If the Abbé thinks that he can be reasonably represented in the terrible storm, forsaken by everyone, without a ship, quite alone and exposed to the greatest peril, then let it stand; but please cut out the ship, for he cannot be alone in one; but if the other situation is adopted, a few generals, who are in his confidence, must land with him. Then he must address a few words to his people and desire them to leave him alone, which in his present melancholy situation is quite natural. (A, 662–663)

To Leopold Mozart   *Munich, 3 January 1781*

After the mourning chorus the king and all his people go away; and in the following scene the directions are, *"Idomeneo in ginocchione nel tempio"* [Idomeneo, kneeling in the temple]. That is quite impossible. He must come in with his whole suite. A march must be introduced here, and I have therefore composed a very simple one for two violins, viola, cello, and two oboes, to be played a *mezza voce*. While it is going on, the King appears and the priests prepare the offerings for the sacrifice. Then the King kneels down and begins the prayer.

In Elettra's recitative, after the subterranean voice has spoken, there ought to be an indication—*Partono* [they leave]. . . . It seems to me very silly that they should hurry away so quickly for no better reason than to allow Madame Elettra to be alone. (A, 703–704)

EFFECT

To Leopold Mozart   *Munich, 8 November 1780*

Ilia's aria in act 2, scene 2, should be altered slightly to suit what I require. "Se il padre perdei, in te lo ritrovo"; this verse could not be better. But now comes what always seemed unnatural to me—I mean, in an aria—and that is *a spoken aside*. In a dialogue all these things are quite natural, for a few words can be spoken aside hurriedly; but in an aria where the words have to be repeated, it has a bad effect, and even if this were not the case, I should prefer an uninterrupted aria. (A, 659–660)

To Leopold Mozart   *Munich, 13 November 1780*

The second duet [in act 3] is to be omitted altogether—and indeed with more profit than loss to the opera. For, when you read through the scene, you will see that it obviously becomes limp and cold by the addition of an aria or a duet, and very gênant [embarrassing] for the other actors who must stand by doing nothing; and besides, the noble struggle between Ilia and Idamante would be too long and thus lose its whole force. . . . (A, 662)

To Leopold Mozart   *Munich, 15 November 1780*

[Raaff] wishes to have a pretty [aria] to sing (instead of the quartet) after his last speech, "O Creta fortunata! O me felice!" Thus, too, a useless piece will be got rid of—and act 3 will be far more effective.[2] In the last scene of act 2 Idomeneo has an aria or rather a sort of cavatina[3] between the choruses. Here it will be *better* to have a mere recitative, well supported by the instruments. For in this scene which will be the finest in the whole opera (on account of the action and grouping which were settled recently with Le Grand [master of the ballet]), there will be so much noise and confusion on the stage that an aria at this particular point would cut a poor figure—and moreover there is a thunderstorm, which is not likely to subside during Herr Raaff's aria, is it? The effect, therefore, of a recitative between the choruses will be infinitely better. (A, 664)

To Leopold Mozart   *Munich, 3 January 1781*

The accompaniment to the subterranean voice consists of five instruments only, that is, three trombones and two French horns, which are placed in the same quarter as that from which the voice proceeds. At this point the whole orchestra is silent. (A, 703)

► See also Mozart's comparison of the appearance of the subterranean voice in *Idomeneo* with that of the Ghost in *Hamlet*, cited in Chapter 4. ◄

To Leopold Mozart   *Vienna, 24 December 1783*

Abbate Varesco has written in the margin [of the libretto for *L'oca del Cairo*] beside Lavina's cavatina: *"for which the music of the preceding cavatina will do"* [Italian], that is, Celidora's cavatina. But that is out of the question, for in Celidora's cavatina the words are very disconsolate and despairing, whereas in Lavina's they are most comforting and hopeful. Besides, for one singer to echo the song of another is a practice which is quite out of date and is hardly ever made use of. (A, 864)

PLOT

▶ Lorenzo Da Ponte credited Mozart with having suggested the idea of writing an opera on Beaumarchais' *Le mariage de Figaro*—testimony enough not only to Mozart's desire for sensation but also to his flawless intuition regarding effective opera plots and to his often decisive role in their selection. How Mozart would suit a plot, like the music, to the singer (or singers) at hand, is suggested in the following altogether facetious and sarcastic plot proposal—one inspired by the desperate situation in Salzburg. ◀

A Modest Mozartean Proposal

To Abbé Joseph Bullinger   *Paris, 7 August 1778*

So you see how superfluous a new singer is [in Salzburg]![4] But just let me argue from an extreme case. Suppose that, apart from our weeping Magdalene [Haydn], we had no other female singer, which, of course, is not the case; but suppose that one were suddenly confined, the second were imprisoned, the third were whipped to death, the fourth had her head chopped off, and the fifth were perhaps whisked off by the devil, what would happen? Nothing!—For we have a castrato. . . . Let Ceccarelli be sometimes man, sometimes woman. Finally, because I know that in Salzburg people like variety, changes, and innovations, I see before me a wide field, the cultivation of which may make history. . . . I have no doubt (and I would even venture to arrange it) that we could get Metastasio to come over from Vienna, or that we could at least make him an offer to write a few dozen opera texts in which the primo uomo and the prima donna would never meet. In this way the castrato could play the parts of both the lover and the mistress and the story would be even more interesting—for people would be able to admire that virtue of the lovers which is so absolute that they purposely avoid any occasion of speaking to one another in public. (A, 595–596)

L'Oca del Cairo, K. 422

To Leopold Mozart   *Vienna, 7 May 1783*

I have been thinking that unless Varesco is still very much annoyed with us about the Munich opera, he might write me a new libretto for seven characters. . . . The most essential thing is that on the whole the story should be really *comic*; and, if possible, he ought to introduce *two equally good female parts*, one of these to be *seria*, the other *mezzo carattere*,[5] but both parts equal in *importance and excellence*. The third female *character*, however, may be entirely *buffa*, and so may all the male ones, if necessary. (A, 848)

► Varesco's libretto turned out to be a variation on the abduction opera and presumably was intended to capitalize on the success of *Die Entführung*. Mozart and Varesco began work on the project during Mozart's visit to Salzburg in the summer and autumn of 1783. Work continued by correspondence after the composer returned to Vienna in November. Mozart makes it abundantly clear in the course of his correspondence that the plot was too silly for his taste, but yet— significantly enough—he was prepared to accept its fundamental premise. Even more significantly, he was unable to finish it.

The plot, briefly, is this: The ruler of Ripasecca, Don Pippo, in love with Lavina, has exiled his wife Donna Pantea. Lavina is the companion of Celidora, who is the daughter of Pippo and Pantea. Pippo has imprisoned both young girls in a fortress and has offered Celidora's lover, Biondello, permission to marry her if he can penetrate the fortress. Lavina's beloved, Calandrino, has invented a mechanical goose which Donna Pantea, disguised as a Moorish woman, will bring to Ripasecca and persuade Don Pippo to allow into the fortress. Biondello will hide inside the goose, and thereby gain entry into the fortress.[6] ◄

To Leopold Mozart   *Vienna, 6 December 1783*

Neither you nor Abbate Varesco nor I have noticed that it will have a very bad effect and even cause the entire failure of the opera if neither of the two principal female singers appears on the stage until the very last moment, but they both keep walking about on the bastions or on the ramparts of the fortress. The patience of the audience might hold out for one act, but certainly not for a second one; that is quite out of the question. This first occurred to me at Linz [on the road back to Vienna from Salzburg], and it seems to me that the only solution is to contrive that some of the scenes in the second act shall take place in the fortress. . . . The scene could be so arranged that when Don Pippo gives orders for the goose to be brought into the fortress, the stage should represent a room where Celidora and Lavina are. Pantea comes in with the goose and Biondello slips out. They hear Don Pippo coming and Biondello again becomes a goose. At this point a good quintet would be very suitable, which would be the more comic as the goose would be singing along with the others. I must tell you, however, that my only reason for not objecting to this goose story altogether was because two people of greater insight and judgment than myself have not disapproved of it; I mean yourself and Varesco. But there is still time to think of other arrangements. Biondello has vowed to make his way into the tower; how he manages to do so, whether in the form of a goose or by some other ruse, does not really matter. I should have thought that effects far more natural and amusing might be produced, if he were to remain in human form. For example, the news that in despair at not being able to make his way into the fortress he has thrown himself into the sea, could be brought in at the very beginning of act 2. He might then disguise himself as a Turk or anyone he chose and bring Pantea with him as a slave (a Moorish girl, of course). Don Pippo is willing to purchase the slave for his bride. Therefore the slave dealer and the Moorish girl must enter the fortress in order to be inspected. In this way Pantea has an opportunity of bullying her husband and addressing all sorts of impertinent remarks to him, which would greatly improve her part, for the more comic an Italian opera is the better. (A, 861–862)

▶ Mozart's suggestion to have the lover gain access to his imprisoned beloved disguised as a Turk has elements in common, on the one hand, with *Die Entführung,* and on the other, with *Così fan tutte* where the lovers pretend to go off to war but then return disguised (as Albanians) to test the fidelity of their fiancees. ◀

POETRY

▶ For all his protestations about the supremacy of the music, Mozart was acutely sensitive to and demanding about the poetic values of the texts he was to set: their imagery, sentiment, syntax, and, above all, their "music," that is, their qualities of sound and rhythm. ◀

Idomeneo

To Leopold Mozart   *Munich, 8 November 1780*

Ilia's aria in act 2, scene 2 . . . "Se il padre perdei, in te lo ritrovo" [If I have lost my father, I have found him again in you];[7] this verse could not be better. . . . The poem is charming and, as it is absolutely natural and flowing and therefore as I have not got to contend with difficulties arising from the words, I can go on composing quite easily. (A, 659–660)

▶ As mentioned in the discussion of the "Singer's Opera," Anton Raaff wished to have a "pretty" aria to sing at the end of the opera. This proved to be a considerable stumbling block. No fewer than three different versions were necessary until a satisfactory one was found.[8] The first text supplied by Varesco (and sent on by Leopold along with his letter of 25 November 1780) began with the words: *Il cor languiva ed era | Gelida massa in petto.* (The heart languished and was | a frozen lump in the breast.) The reaction of both Mozart and Raaff was negative: ◀

To Leopold Mozart   *Munich, 29 November 1780*

The aria for Raaff which you have sent me pleases neither him nor myself. I shall not say anything about *era,* for in an aria of this kind that is always a mistake. . . . Besides, the aria is not at all what we wished it to be; I mean it ought to express peace and contentment, and this it indicates only in the second part [now lost]. For we have seen, heard, and felt sufficiently throughout the whole opera all the misfortune which Idomeneo has had to endure; but he can certainly talk about his present condition. (A, 674)

► The first objection was to the incomplete quality of the first line, ending as it did with the words *ed era* (i.e., "and was") which made it difficult to repeat in isolation. A week later Mozart restates the same objections. ◄

To Leopold Mozart   *Munich, 5 December 1780*

In regard to the *ultima aria* for Raaff, I mentioned that we both wished to have more pleasing and gentle words. The *era* is forced. The beginning would do quite well, but *gelida massa*—again is hard. In short, far-fetched or unusual words are always unsuitable in an aria that ought to be pleasing. (A, 682)

► On 11 December 1780 Leopold sent on a completely new text for Raaff's last aria. The first stanza read: *Sazio è il Destino al fine* | *Mostrami lieto aspetto.* | *Spirto novello in petto* | *Vien mi a rinvigorir.* (Destiny is satisfied at last. | It shows me a pleasant face. | A new spirit in my breast | Comes to invigorate me.) The faults with this new aria were discussed in Mozart's next letters. ◄

To Leopold Mozart   *Munich, 27 December 1780*

The other day [Raaff] was very much annoyed about some words in his last aria—*rinvigorir*—and *ringiovenir* [to rejuvenate]—and especially *vienmi a rinvigorir*—five i's!—It is true that at the end of an aria this is very unpleasant. (A, 698–699)

To Leopold Mozart   *Munich, 30 December 1780*

I am now in a difficulty in regard to his last aria, and you must help me out of it. He cannot stomach the *"rinvigorir"* and *"ringiovenir"*—and these two words make the whole aria distasteful to him. It is true that *mostrami* and *vienmi* are also not good, but the two final words are the worst of all. To avoid the shake [trill] on the *i* in the first *rinvigorir*, I really ought to transfer it to the *o*.[9] (A, 702)

► In the end Varesco submitted a completely new text for the final aria, "Torna la pace al core" (peace returns to my heart) which, with its euphonious "o's" and "a's" (instead of pinched "i's"), along with its soothing sentiment, proved to be altogether acceptable. ◄

Die Entführung aus dem Serail

To Leopold Mozart   *Vienna, 26 September 1781*

I have changed the "Hui" to "schnell," so it now runs thus: "Doch wie schnell schwand meine Freude." [But how quickly my joy vanished.] I really don't know what our German poets are thinking of. Even if they do not understand the theater, or at all events operas, yet they should not make their characters talk as if they were addressing a herd of swine. Hui, sow![10] (A, 769)

To Leopold Mozart   *Vienna, 13 October 1781*

Now as to the libretto of the opera. . . . The poetry is perfectly in keeping with the character of stupid, surly, malicious Osmin. I am well aware that the verse is not the best, but it fitted in and it agreed so well with the musical ideas which already were buzzing in my head, that it could not fail to please me; and I would like to wager that when it is performed, no deficiencies will be found. As for the poetry which was there originally, I really have nothing to say against it. Belmonte's aria, "O wie ängstlich" could hardly be better written for music. Except for "Hui" and "Kummer ruht in meinem Schoß" [sorrow rests in my heart] (for sorrow—cannot rest), the aria is not too bad, particularly for the first part. Besides, I should say that in an opera the poetry must be altogether the obedient daughter of the music. . . . Verses are indeed the most indispensable element for music—but rhymes, solely for the sake of rhyming, the most detrimental. (A, 772–773)

STAGING

To Nannerl   *Milan, 23 January 1773*

The first orchestral rehearsal of the second opera [Paisiello's *Sismano nel Mongol*] *took place yesterday evening, but I only heard the first act, since, as it was late, I left at the beginning of the second. In this opera there are to be twenty-four horses and a great crowd of people on the stage, so that it will be a miracle if some accident does not happen* [Italian]. (A, 227)

10

Opera and
Dramatic Music:
Individual Compositions

► In addition to the topical observations collected in the last two chapters, Mozart's letters contain numerous comments on individual works that shed light on their origin, composition, production, or later destiny. We learn, for example, that Mozart often began the composition of an opera by setting the recitatives and, sensibly enough, postponed composing the arias until he became familiar with the abilities of the particular singers.

For the early operas, while Mozart was busy composing, we are mostly dependent on Leopold's progress reports home from Italy. As we have already seen, Mozart's most extensive remarks were connected with the composition of *Idomeneo, Die Entführung aus dem Serail,* and *L'oca del Cairo.* Unfortunately, we have no such firsthand documentation for the later masterpieces—*Le nozze di Figaro, Don Giovanni, Così fan tutte, La clemenza di Tito, Die Zauberflöte*—since, in contrast to the situation with *Idomeneo* and *L'oca del Cairo,* Mozart was normally able to negotiate with his librettist in person. Moreover, following both the premiere of *Die Entführung* and his wedding in the summer of 1782, Mozart's principal confidante was no longer Leopold, but Constanze.

In consequence, by no means all of Mozart's operas will be represented in the following chronological review. The introductory commentary to each work will be limited to identifying the librettist, providing the date and place of composition and other basic historical information bearing on the work's origin and reception. ◄

OPERAS

Mitridate, Rè di Ponto, K. 87 (74a)

► Text by Vittorio Amadeo Cigna-Santi, based on a play by Racine. Composed in Italy between 29 September and December 1770. Composition began with the recitatives. First performance: Milan, Teatro Regio Ducale, 26 December 1770. *Mitridate* was Mozart's first opera seria. He conducted the first three performances from the keyboard. ◄

To Nannerl   *Rome, 21 April 1770*

Manzuoli is negotiating with the Milanese to sing in my opera. With that in view he sang four or five arias to me in Florence, including some which I had to compose in Milan, in order that the Milanese, who had heard none of my dramatic music, should see that I am capable of writing an opera. . . . I should like [De Amicis] and Manzuoli to take the parts. Then we should have two good acquaintances and friends. The libretto has not yet been chosen. I recommended . . . a text by Metastasio. (A, 130–131)

► Mozart ultimately got his wish neither with respect to the librettist nor the singers. Three months later Leopold reported on the outcome of the arrangements: ◄

Leopold Mozart to his Wife   *Bologna, 28 July 1770*

We received yesterday the libretto and the list of the singers. The title of the opera is *Mitridate, Rè di Ponto,* and the text is by a poet of Turin, Signor Vittorio Amadeo Cigna-Santi. It was performed there in 1767. The characters are

Mitridate, Rè di Ponto. . . . . Il Signor Guglielmo d'Ettore
Aspasia, promessa sposa di Mitridate . . . . Signora Antonia Bernasconi,
                                                prima donna. (A, 151)

Leopold Mozart to his Wife   *Bologna, 29 September 1770*

Wolfgang began the recitatives for the opera today. (A, 163)

To Nannerl   *Milan, 12 January 1771*

I have not written for a long time, for I was busy with my opera. . . . The opera, God be praised, is a success, for every evening the theater is full, much to the astonishment of everyone, for several people say that since they have been in Milan they have never seen such crowds at a first opera. . . . Yesterday the copyist called on us and said that he had orders to transcribe my opera for the court at Lisbon. (A, 180)

► Leopold Mozart supplies more detail about the work of the copyist. ◄

Leopold Mozart to his Wife   *Venice, 1 March 1771*

As for the opera, we shall not be able to bring it with us, for it is still in the hands of the copyist and he, like all opera copyists in Italy, will not let it out of his hands, as long as he can make his profit. When we left Milan, he had to make five copies, one for the Impresa [i.e., the Milan opera management], two for Vienna, one for the Duchess of Parma and one for the Lisbon court, to say nothing of individual arias. And who knows whether the copyist has not received some more orders in the meantime. Even then he told me that I must not expect to see it before Easter, by which time I hope to be in Salzburg; but it will be sent home from Milan. (A, 184)

Lucio Silla, K. 135

► Text by Giovanni de Gamerra, revised by Metastasio. Composed between October and December 1772. Composition began in Salzburg with the recitatives. First performance: Milan, Teatro Regio Ducale, 26 December 1772. ◄

Leopold Mozart to his Wife   *Milan, 14 November 1772*

Wolfgang has got much amusement from composing the choruses, of which there are three, and from altering or partly rewriting the few recitatives which he composed in Salzburg. (A, 215–216)

To Nannerl   *Milan, 5 December 1772*

I still have fourteen numbers to compose and then I shall have finished. But indeed the trio and the duet might well count as four. (A, 219)

La finta giardiniera, K. 196

► Text presumably by Giuseppe Petrosellini.[1] Mozart's second opera buffa (after *La finta semplice*, K. 51/46a). Composed between September 1774 and January 1775. First performance: Munich, Salvator Theater, 13 January 1775. In 1779/1780 Mozart recast the work as a German singspiel to words by Franz Joseph Stierle. This version, *Die verstellte Gärtnerin*, was apparently premiered in Augsburg on 1 May 1780. ◄

To Leopold Mozart   *Munich, 11 January 1775*

I am off this very moment to a rehearsal of my opera. Tomorrow we are having the dress rehearsal and the performance takes place on Friday, the 13th. (A, 258)

To his Mother   *Munich, 14 January 1775*

Thank God! My opera was performed yesterday, the 13th, for the first time and was such a success that it is impossible for me to describe the applause to Mamma. . . . In the first place, the whole theater was so packed that a great many people were turned away. . . . After the opera was over and during the pause when there is usually silence until the ballet begins, people kept on clapping all the time and shouting "bravo"; now stopping, now beginning again and so on. . . . Next Friday my opera is being performed again and it is most essential that I should be present. Otherwise my work would be quite unrecognizable—for very strange things happen here. (A, 259)

Thamos, König in Ägypten, K. 345 (336a)

▶ Text by Tobias Philipp von Gebler. Mozart composed the incidental music—choruses and interludes—for this "heroic drama" over the years from 1773 to 1779–1780. The chronology of this work is particularly complicated. The first two choruses were originally composed in 1773, the interludes in 1777, a second version of the choruses in 1779–1780.[2] ◀

To Leopold Mozart   *Vienna, 15 February 1783*

I am extremely sorry that I shall not be able to use the music of *Thamos,* but this piece, which failed to please here, is now among the rejected works that are no longer performed.[3] For the sake of the music alone it might possibly be given again, but that is not likely. Certainly it is a pity! (A, 840)

Zaide, K. 344 (336b)

▶ A serious singspiel with text by Johann Andreas Schachtner. In the period 1779–1780 Mozart composed fifteen numbers, including two set in the style of the melodrama, that is, accompanied recitative with spoken text. But the work remained unfinished, presumably interrupted by the commission for *Idomeneo* and then never resumed. It is clear, though, that Mozart did not willingly abandon the work. During the final rehearsals for the *Idomeneo* premiere he wrote home for the score. Both the plot and setting of *Zaide* anticipate *Die Entführung aus dem Serail.* ◀

To Leopold Mozart   *Munich, 18 January 1781*

I should like you to bring Schachtner's operetta, too. There are some people who come to the Cannabich's who might just as well hear a thing of this kind. (A, 709)

To Leopold Mozart   *Vienna, 18 April 1781*

As for Schachtner's operetta, there is nothing to be done—for the same reason which I have often mentioned. Stephanie junior is going to give me a new libretto, a good one, he says; and, if in the meantime I have left Vienna, he is to send it to me. I could not contradict *Stephanie.* I merely said that save for the long dialogues, the piece was very good, but not suitable for Vienna, where people prefer comic pieces [italicized words in code]. (A, 725)

► On July 30, Stephanie delivered a libretto: *Bellmont und Constanze, oder: Die Entführung aus dem Serail,* by Christoph Friedrich Bretzner. Over the ensuing months Stephanie would rework Bretzner's book in accordance with Mozart's instructions. ◄

Idomeneo, Rè di Creta, K. 366

► Text by Giambattista Varesco. Composed between October 1780 and January 1781. First performance: Munich, Cuvilliés Theater, 29 January 1781. Mozart revised the work in Vienna for a concert performance there on 13 March 1786 in the Auersperg-Palais. ◄

To Leopold Mozart   *Munich, 30 December 1780*

I have not quite finished the third act and, as there is no extra ballet, but only an appropriate divertissement in the opera, I have the honor of composing the music for that as well; but I am glad of it, for now all the music will be by the same composer. The third act will turn out to be *at least* as good as the first two—in fact, I believe, infinitely better—and I think that it may be said with truth, *finis coronat opus* [the end crowns the work]. (A, 701)

To Leopold Mozart   *Vienna, 12 September 1781*

The translator of [Gluck's] *Iphigenie* into German [Johann Baptist von Alxinger] is an excellent poet, and I would gladly have given him my Munich opera to translate. I would have altered the part of Idomeneo completely and changed it to a bass part for Fischer.[4] In addition I would have made several other alterations and arranged it more in the French style. Mme. Bernasconi, Adamberger, and Fischer would have been delighted to sing it. (A, 765)

To Leopold Mozart   *Vienna, 6 December 1783*

Please send me as soon as possible my *Idomeneo.* . . . I require *Idomeneo* because during Lent I am going to give as well as my concert in the theater six subscription concerts, at which I should like to produce this opera. (A, 862)

The Reminiscences of Constanze Mozart, 1829

But one air in the *Idomeneo* he preferred to hear [me] sing and on that account [I] prefer it also, "se il Padre perdei." . . . The most happy time of his life was while in Munich during which he wrote *Idomeneo* which may account for the affection he entertained toward the work. (Novello, 94)

Die Entführung aus dem Serail, K. 384

► Text by Christoph Friedrich Bretzner, revised by Gottlied Stephanie Junior. Composed between 30 July 1781 and 29 May 1782. First performance: Vienna, Burgtheater, 16 July 1782. In addition to affording the numerous insights into his aesthetic concerns related in earlier chapters, the references to *Die Entführung* in Mozart's letters reveal, among other things, that he had expected to have to compose the work—which he mistakenly (and perhaps significantly) refers to at its first mention as *Die Verführung* (i.e., the seduction) *aus dem Serail*—in about six weeks, not ten months (letter of 1 August 1781). We learn, too, that the composer was determined to enhance the musical importance of the role of Osmin, in comparison to the original Bretzner version by providing him with more solo numbers. (See the excerpt from the letter of 26 September 1781 at the end of Chapter 8.) Among the more significant formal changes vis-à-vis the original text was Mozart's decision to move a quintet from the beginning of Bretzner's act 3 to the end of act 2 and thus have it serve as a regular act finale (26 September). (Ultimately a completely new finale had to be written for this purpose: the quartet, "Ach Belmonte! ach mein Leben").[5] ◄

To Leopold Mozart   *Vienna, 1 August 1781*

Well, the day before yesterday Stephanie junior gave me a libretto to compose. . . . The libretto is quite good. The subject is Turkish and the title is *Belmonte und Konstanze*, or *Die Verführung aus dem Serail.* . . . Mlle. Cavalieri, Mlle. Teiber, M. Fischer, M. Adamberger, M. Dauer, and M. Walter[6] are to sing in it. . . . The time is short, it is true, for it is to be performed in the middle of September,[7] but the circumstances connected with the date of performance and, in general, all my other prospects stimulate me to such a degree that I rush to my desk with the greatest eagerness and remain seated there with the greatest delight. The Grand Duke of Russia [Paul Petrovich] is coming here, and that is why Stephanie entreated me, if possible, to compose the opera in this short space of time. (A, 755)

To Leopold Mozart   *Vienna, 29 August 1781*

I have now finished the first act of my opera. (A, 761)

To Leopold Mozart   *Vienna, 26 September 1781*

As the original text [by C. F. Bretzner] began with a monologue, I asked Herr Stephanie to make a little arietta out of it—and then to put in a duet instead of making the two chatter together after Osmin's short song. . . .

Now for the trio at the close of act 1. Pedrillo has passed off his master as an architect—to give him an opportunity of meeting his Constanze in the garden. Bassa Selim has taken him into his service. Osmin, the steward, knows nothing of this, and being a rude churl [*Flegel:* a lout] and a sworn foe to all strangers, is impertinent and refuses to let them into the garden. It opens quite abruptly—and because the words lend themselves to it, I have made it a fairly respectable piece of real three-part writing (ex. 10.1).

EXAMPLE 10.1. *Die Entführung.* "Marsch, marsch, marsch," Opening Measures

TRANSLATION:
Osmin: March, march, march! | Out of here! | Otherwise the club | will be there to
     serve you.
Belmonte, Pedrillo: Hey, hey, hey! | That would be too bad | To deal with us like that.
Osmin: Just don't come closer!
Belmonte, Pedrillo: Away from the door!

Then the major key begins at once pianissimo—it must go very quickly—
and winds up with a great deal of noise, which is always appropriate at the
end of an act.

I have sent you only fourteen bars of the overture (ex. 10.2), which is very
short with alternate fortes and pianos, the Turkish music always coming in
at the fortes. The overture modulates through different keys; and I doubt
whether anyone, even if his previous night has been a sleepless one, could
go to sleep over it.

EXAMPLE 10.2. *Die Entführung.* Overture, Opening Measures

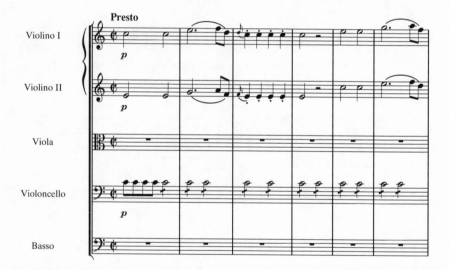

Now comes the rub! The first act was finished more than three weeks ago, as was also one aria in act 2 and the drunken duet ["Vivat Bacchus, Bacchus lebe"] (*per i signori viennesi*) (ex. 10.3) which consists entirely of *my Turkish tattoo.*

EXAMPLE 10.3. *Die Entführung.* "Vivat Bacchus," Opening Theme

TRANSLATION:
Pedrillo: Long live, Bacchus; Bacchus live! | Bacchus was a good man!
Osmin: Will I dare? Will I drink it? Will Allah be able to see it?

But I cannot compose any more, because the whole story is being altered—and, to tell the truth, at my own request. At the beginning of act 3 there is a charming quintet or rather finale ["Ach Belmonte! ach—mein Leben!"], but I should prefer to have it at the end of act 2. In order to make this practicable, great changes must be made; in fact, an entirely new plot must be introduced. (A, 768–770)

To Leopold Mozart   *Vienna, 30 January 1782*

My opera has not gone to sleep, but has suffered a setback on account of Gluck's big operas [*Iphigenie in Tauris, Alceste, Orfeo*] and owing to many very necessary alterations which have to be made in the text. It is to be performed, however, immediately after Easter. (A, 796)

To Leopold Mozart   *Vienna, 29 May 1782*

We are to have our first rehearsal next Monday. I must confess that I am looking forward with much pleasure to this opera. (A, 807)

To Leopold Mozart   *Vienna, 20 July 1782*

I hope that you received safely my last letter informing you of the good reception of my opera. It was given yesterday for the second time . . . I was relying on the closing trio ["Marsch, marsch, marsch!" in act 1], but, as ill luck would have it, Fischer went wrong, which made Dauer (Pedrillo) go wrong too; and Adamberger alone could not sustain the trio, with the result that the whole effect was lost and that this time *it was not repeated.* I was in such a rage (and so was Adamberger) that I was simply beside myself and said at once that I would not let the opera be given again without having a short rehearsal for the singers. In the second act both duets were repeated on the first night, and in addition Belmonte's rondo "Wenn der Freude Tränen fliessen." The theater was almost more crowded than on the first night and on the preceding day no reserved seats were to be had, either in the stalls or in the third circle, and not a single box. My opera has brought in twelve hundred gulden in the two days. (A, 807–808)

To Leopold Mozart   *Vienna, 27 July 1782*

My opera was given yesterday for the third time in honor of all the Nannerls [26 July, St. Anne's Day] and won the greatest applause; and again, in spite of the frightful heat, the theater was packed. It was to be given again next Friday, but I have protested against this, for I do not want it to become hackneyed. I may say that people are absolutely infatuated with this opera. Indeed it does one good to win such approbation. (A, 810)

Le nozze di Figaro, K. 492

► Text by Lorenzo Da Ponte, after Beaumarchais. Presumably composed between October 1785 and 29 April 1786. First performance: Vienna, Burgtheater, 1 May 1786. ◄

The Reminiscences of Michael Kelly, 1826

In the sestetto ["Riconosci in questo amplesso", ex. 10.4], in the second [i.e., third] act (which was Mozart's favorite piece of the whole opera), I had a very conspicuous part, as the Stuttering Judge. All through the piece I was to stutter; but in the sestetto, Mozart requested I would not, for if I did, I should spoil his music. I told him, that although it might appear very presumptuous in a lad like me to differ with him on this point, I did; and was sure, the way in which I intended to introduce the stuttering, would not interfere with the other parts, but produce an effect; besides, it certainly was not in nature, that I should stutter all through the part, and when I came to the sestetto, speak plain; and after that piece of music was over, return to stuttering; and, I added, (apologizing at the same time, for my apparent want of deference and respect in placing my opinion in

EXAMPLE 10.4. *Le nozze di Figaro.* Sextet: "Riconosci in questo amplesso,"
Opening Measures

TRANSLATION:
Marcellina: Recognize in this embrace | A mother, beloved son!
Figaro: My father, do the same, | Don't let me blush any more.
Bartolo: My conscience forbids | Me to deny your wish.
Curzio: He's his father, . . . she's his mother? The marriage . . . cannot take place!
Count: I'm lost . . . confused . . . I'd better leave.

opposition to that of the great Mozart), that unless I was allowed to perform the part as I wished, I would not perform it at all.

Mozart at last consented that I should have my own way, but doubted the success of the experiment. Crowded houses proved that nothing ever on the stage produced a more powerful effect; the audience were convulsed with laughter, in which Mozart himself joined. . . . When the opera was over, Mozart came on the stage to me, and shaking me by both hands, said, "Bravo! young man, I feel obliged to you; and acknowledge you to have been in the right, and myself in the wrong." (Kelly, 1:256–258)

To Gottfried von Jacquin   *Prague, 15 January 1787*

At six o'clock I drove . . . to the so-called Breitfeld ball. . . . I looked on . . . with the greatest pleasure while all these people flew about in sheer delight to the music of my *Figaro*, arranged for contredanses and German dances. For here they talk about nothing but *Figaro*. Nothing is played, sung or whistled but *Figaro*. No opera is drawing like *Figaro*. Nothing, nothing but *Figaro*. Certainly a great honor for me! (A, 903)

To Gottfried von Jacquin   *Prague, 15 October 1787*

A few of the leading ladies here, and in particular one very high and mighty one, were kind enough to find it very ridiculous, unsuitable, and Heaven knows what else that the Princess [Archduchess Maria Theresa] should be entertained with a performance of *Figaro*, the *Crazy Day* [the subtitle of Beaumarchais' comedy], as the management were pleased to call it. It never occurred to them that no opera in the world, unless it is written especially for it, can be exactly suitable for such an occasion and that therefore it was of absolutely no consequence whether this or that opera were given, provided that it was a good opera and one which the Princess did not know; and *Figaro* at least fulfilled this last condition. In short, by her persuasive tongue the ringleader brought things to such a pitch that the government forbade the impresario to produce this opera on that night. So she was triumphant! *"Ho vinto"* [I have conquered], she called out one evening from her box. No doubt she never suspected that the *ho* [I have] might be changed to a *sono* [I am]. But the following day [the actor] Le Noble appeared, bearing a command from His Majesty to the effect that if the new opera [*Don Giovanni*] could not be given, *Figaro* was to be performed! (A, 911)

The Reminiscences of Constanze Mozart, 1829

"Non so più" in *Figaro* was a great favorite with Mozart; also "Riconosci a questo amplesso." (Novello, 94)

Don Giovanni, K. 527

► Text by Lorenzo Da Ponte. Composed between March and October 1787. Completed on 28 October 1787. First performance: Prague, National Theater, 29 October 1787. ◄

To Gottfried von Jacquin   *Prague, 15 October 1787*

You probably think that my opera is over by now. If so, you are a little mistaken. In the first place, the stage personnel here are not as smart as those in Vienna when it comes to mastering an opera of this kind in a very short time. Second, I found on my arrival that so few preparations and arrangements had been made that it would have been absolutely impossible to produce it on the 14th, that is, yesterday. So yesterday my *Figaro* was performed in a fully lighted theater and I myself conducted. . . . *Don Giovanni* has now been fixed for the 24th.

October 21st. It was fixed for the 24th, but a further postponement has been caused by the illness of one of the singers. As the company is so small, the impresario is in a perpetual state of anxiety and has to spare his people as much as possible, lest some unexpected indisposition should plunge him into the most awkward of all situations, that of not being able to produce any show whatsoever!

So everything dawdles along here because the singers, who are lazy, refuse to rehearse on opera days, and the manager, who is anxious and timid, will not force them. (A, 911–912)

To Gottfried von Jacquin   *Prague, 4 November 1787*

My opera *Don Giovanni* had its first performance on October 29th and was received with the greatest applause. It was performed yesterday for the fourth time, for my benefit. . . . Perhaps my opera will be performed in Vienna after all! I hope so. (A, 912–913)

► The Viennese performance took place just a half–year later, in revised form, on 7 May 1788. ◄

The Reminiscences of Constanze Mozart, 1829

Madame confirmed the truth of her sitting up all night with him while he wrote the overture to *Don Giovanni*. (Novello, 95–96)

Die Zauberflöte, K. 620

► Text by Emanuel Schikaneder. Mostly composed in June/July 1791. The priests' march and overture were completed on September 28. First performance: Vienna, Theater auf der Wieden, 30 September 1791. ◄

To Constanze, Baden   *Vienna, 11 June 1791*

From sheer boredom I composed today an aria for my opera. . . . I kiss you a thousand times and say with you in thought: "Death and despair were his reward!"[8] (A, 953–954)

To Constanze, Baden   *Vienna, 7 October 1791*

I have this moment returned from the opera, which was as full as ever. As usual the duet "Mann und Weib" and Papageno's glockenspiel in act 1 had to be repeated and also the trio of the boys in act 2. But what always gives me most pleasure is the *silent approval!* You can see how this opera is becoming more and more esteemed. (A, 966–967)

To Constanze, Baden   *8/9 October 1791*

During Papageno's aria with the glockenspiel I went behind the scenes, as I felt a sort of impulse today to play it myself. Well, just for fun, at the point where Schikaneder [Papageno] has a pause, I played an arpeggio. He was startled, looked behind the wings and saw me. When he had his next pause, I played no arpeggio. This time he stopped and refused to go on. I guessed what he was thinking and again played a chord. He then struck the glockenspiel and said, *"Shut up."* Whereupon everyone laughed. I am inclined to think that this joke taught many of the audience for the first time that Papageno does not play the instrument himself. By the way, you have no idea how charming the music sounds when you hear it from a box close to the orchestra; it sounds much better than from the gallery. (A, 969)

To Constanze, Baden   *Vienna, 14 October 1791*

At six o'clock [yesterday, Thursday the 13th], I called in the carriage for Salieri and Madame Cavalieri and drove them to my box. . . . You can hardly imagine how charming they were and how much they liked not only my music, but the libretto and everything. They both said that it was an *operone*, worthy to be performed for the grandest festival and before the greatest monarch, and that they would often go to see it as they had never seen a more beautiful or delightful show. Salieri listened and watched most attentively and from the overture to the last chorus there was not a single number that did not call forth from him a bravo! or bello! It seemed as if they could not thank me enough for my kindness. They had intended in any case to go to the opera yesterday. . . . When it was over I drove them home. (A, 970)

The Memoirs of Ignaz Franz Castelli, 1861

The late bass singer Sebastian Meyer[9] told me that Mozart had originally written the duet where Papageno and Papagena first see each other quite differently from the way in which we now hear it. Both originally cried out "Papageno!" "Papagena!" a few times in amazement. But when Schikaneder heard this, he called down in to the orchestra, "Hey, Mozart: That's no good, the music must express greater astonishment. They must stare dumbly at each other, then Papageno must begin to stammer: 'pa-papapa-pa-pa'; Papagena must repeat that until both of them finally get the whole name out." Mozart followed the advice, and in this form the duet always had to be repeated. (DDB, 568)

La clemenza di Tito, K. 621

▶ Text by Caterino Mazzolà, after Metastasio. Composed between July and September 1791. Completed 5 September 1791. First performance: Prague, National Theater, 6 September 1791, for the coronation of Emperor Leopold II. ◀

To Constanze, Baden   *Vienna, 7 October 1791*

On the very evening when my new opera [*Die Zauberflöte*] was performed for the first time with such success, *Tito* was given in Prague for the last time with tremendous applause. [The castrato Domenico] Bedini [in the role of Annio] sang better than ever. The little duet in A major which the two maidens sing [No. 7, "Ah, perdona al primo affetto"] was repeated; and had not the audience wished to spare Madame Marchetti[-Fantozzi, as Vitellia], a repetition of the rondo [No. 23, "Non più di fiori"] would have been very welcome. Cries of "Bravo" were shouted at Stodla [Anton Stadler] from the parterre and even from the orchestra.[10] (A, 967)

ARIAS AND SONGS

K. 294 "Non so, d'onde viene"

▶ Dated Mannheim, 24 February 1778. This aria was inspired by Johann Christian Bach's setting of the same Metastasio text. On Mozart's first intentions concerning his own setting, see the discussion of the process of composition in Chapter 1. ◀

To Leopold Mozart   *Mannheim, 28 February 1778*

I decided to write it for Mlle. Weber . . . and made up my mind to compose
it exactly for Mlle. Weber's voice. It's an andante sostenuto (preceded by a
short recitative); then follows the second part, *Nel seno a destarmi,* and then
the sostenuto again. . . . This is now the best aria she has, and it will
ensure her success wherever she goes. (A, 497)

To Leopold Mozart   *Paris, 24 March 1778*

Thursday there was an afternoon concert at Cannabich's. . . . Mlle. Weber
sang two arias of mine, the "Aer tranquillo" from *Il Ré pastore* and my new
one, "Non so d'onde viene." With the latter my dear Mlle. Weber did
herself and me indescribable honor, for everyone said that no aria had ever
affected them as did this one; but then she sang it as it ought to be sung. As
soon as it was over, Cannabich called out loudly: "Bravo! Bravissimo,
maestro! *Truly written by a master!*" [Italian.] It was the first time I had heard
it with orchestral accompaniment. . . . The members of the orchestra
never ceased praising the aria and talking about it. (A, 517)

To Leopold Mozart   *Mannheim, 3 December 1778*

I assume that you received the trunk. . . . You will find in it the aria I wrote
for Mlle. Weber. You have no idea what an effect it produces with
instruments; you cannot judge of it by the score, for it must be rendered by
a singer like Mlle. Weber. (A, 638)

K. 295 "Se al labbro mio non credi"

► Dated Mannheim, 27 February 1778. ◄

To Leopold Mozart   *Mannheim, 28 February 1778*

I was at Raaff's yesterday and brought him an aria which I composed
for him the other day. The words are: *"Se al labbro mio non credi, bella
nemica mia,"* and so on (ex. 10.5a). I don't think that Metastasio wrote
them.[11] . . . I chose those words on purpose because I knew that he
already had an aria on them: so of course he will sing mine with greater
facility and more pleasure. . . . After he had sung the second part, he took
off his spectacles, and looking at me with wide-open eyes, said: "Beautiful!
Beautiful! That is a charming *seconda parte.*" And he sang it three times.
When I took leave of him he thanked me most cordially, while I assured
him that I would arrange the aria in such a way that it would give him
pleasure to sing it. For I like an aria to fit a singer as perfectly as a
well-made suit of clothes.[12] (A, 496–497)

EXAMPLE 10.5 a. K. 295: "Se al labbro:" Opening Theme

► The charming *seconda parte* is in 3/8 meter and Allegretto (ex. 10.5b). As Daniel Heartz has pointed out, the entire aria is in the old-fashioned style of Johann Adolph Hasse and perhaps modeled on Hasse's setting of the same text—a setting that Raaff had sung at Naples in 1760–1761 —some twenty-eight years earlier.[13] ◄

EXAMPLE 10.5 b. "Se al labbro:" Beginning of Second Part

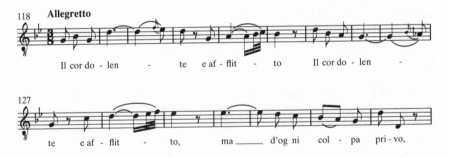

K. 316 (300b) "Popoli di Tessaglia"

► Dated Munich, 8 January 1779. The text for this scena was taken from Gluck's opera *Alceste*. Since Mozart refers to the aria six months earlier as "half finished," the date on the autograph score reveals an interruption before the composition received the final touches. ◄

To Aloysia Weber   *Paris, 30 July 1778*

I shall send in the same parcel the "Popoli di Tessaglia," which is already half finished. If you are as pleased with it as I am, I shall be delighted. Meanwhile until I have had the pleasure of hearing from you whether you really like this scena—for, since I have composed it for you alone, I desire no other praise than yours—I can only say that of all my compositions of this kind this scena is the best I have ever composed. (A, 581)

LOST AND UNFINISHED WORKS

A Scena for Giustino Tenducci, K. 315b

▶ The male soprano, Guistino Ferdinando Tenducci (1736–1790) was a close friend of Johann Christian Bach. The Mozarts had met him in London in 1764. ◀

To Leopold Mozart   *St. Germain, 27 August 1778*

The Maréchal de Noailles lives here. Tenducci is a great favorite of his, and because Tenducci is *very* fond of me, he was anxious to procure me this acquaintance. . . . I am composing a scena for Tenducci, which is to be performed on Sunday; it is for pianoforte, oboe, horn, and bassoon, the performers being the Maréchal's own people—Germans, who play very well. (A, 607)

▶ Mozart evidently completed this work. The final version, now lost, also included two clarinets, two supplementary horns, and strings.[14] ◀

Semiramis: A Declaimed Opera, K. 315e

To Leopold Mozart   *Mannheim, 3 December 1778*

To please Herr von Gemmingen and myself I am now composing the first act of the declaimed opera (which I was commissioned to write) and I am also doing this *for nothing;* I shall bring it with me and finish it at home. You see how strong is my liking for this kind of composition. Herr von Gemmingen is the poet, of course, and the duodrama is called *Semiramis.* (A, 638)

An Aria for Emanuel Schikaneder

To Leopold Mozart   *Munich, 8 November 1780*

My greetings to Herr Schikaneder and ask him to forgive me for not yet sending him the aria but I have not been able to finish it completely. (A, 660)

▶ This, Mozart's first written reference to the librettist of *Die Zauberflöte,* suggests he had already known him for some time. The aria was intended for Schikaneder's Salzburg production of Carlo Gozzi's drama *Le due notti affannose,* in German translation with the title *Peter der Grausame oder Die zwei schlaflosen Nächte.* ◀

An Ode, K. 386d

To Leopold Mozart   *Vienna, 28 December 1782*

I am engaged in a very difficult task, the music for a bard's song by [J. N. C. Michael] Denis about Gibraltar. But this is a secret, for a Hungarian lady wishes to pay this compliment to Denis. The ode is sublime, beautiful, anything you like, but too exaggerated and pompous for my fastidious ears. (A, 833)

► It is, at the least, most uncharacteristic for Mozart to declare that any musical task is "very difficult." As in the case of *L'oca del Cairo*, the text's failings evidently made it impossible for Mozart to finish the composition. In the end he managed to sketch a setting for three of the eleven strophes of this thankless poem. J. N. C. Michael Denis (1729–1800), a Viennese professor, was the translator of the notorious "Ossian" epic by James Macpherson. Denis's ode to Gibraltar celebrates Admiral Richard Howe's liberation of the rock from a Spanish blockade in 1782. As an example of the style that so frustrated Mozart the text for the opening strophe follows.

O Calpe! Dir donnert's am Fuße,
Doch blickt dein tausendjähriger Gipfel ruhig auf Welten umher.
Siehe! Dort wölket sich hinauf über die westlichen Wogen her,
Wölket sich breiter und ahnender auf.
Es flattert, o Calpe! Segelgewölk! Flügel der Hilfe!
Wie prächtig wallet die Fahnen Brittaniens, deiner getreuen
Verheisserin!
Calpe! Sie wallt! aber die Nacht sinkt!

O Calpe! It thunders at thy foot,
But your thousand-year summit looks around at whole worlds.
Behold! There, over the western waves, clouds gather,
They gather ever thicker and ever more suspecting.
They flutter, O Calpe! Clouds of sails! Wings of help!
How splendidly waves Brittania's flag, thy loyal Protector!
Calpe! It waves! But the night sinks!

Il servitore di due padroni, K. 416a

To Leopold Mozart   *Vienna, 5 February 1783*

I am now writing a German opera for myself. I have chosen [Carlo] Goldoni's comedy *Il servitore di due padroni* [The Servant of Two Masters] and the whole of the first act has now been translated. Baron Binder is the translator. But we are keeping it a secret until it is quite finished. (A, 839)

► Mozart, then, in response to the invitation of Count Rosenberg a month earlier to compose an Italian opera, and before he had plunged himself into the task of looking through "at least a hundred libretti" (see Chapter 9), had hoped to write an opera on the most successful text by the most successful opera buffa librettist of the eighteenth century, Carlo Goldoni (1707–1793). The opera was never finished, although two surviving German arias "Müßt ich auch durch tausend Drachen" and "Männer suchen stets zu naschen," K. 416b and 416c, may have been conceived as part of it. ◄

11

Church Music

Salieri . . . has never devoted himself to church music, whereas from my youth up I have made myself completely familiar with this style.

Vienna, May 1790

► That Mozart cultivated a lifelong interest in and enthusiasm for church music is amply attested. Constanze claimed that "church music was his favorite genre,"[1] and she apparently related to Franz Xaver Niemetschek that "if [she] wanted to give [Mozart] a special surprise at a family festivity, she would secretly arrange a performance of a new church composition by Michael or Joseph Haydn."[2] Until recently, however, it seemed that Mozart had virtually abandoned church composition once he had settled in Vienna in 1781. The only sacred works associated with the Vienna years were the monumental torsos: the Mass in C minor of 1783 and the Requiem, as well as the miniature masterpiece, the motet, *Ave verum corpus*, K. 618, dated 17 June 1791. It turns out, however, that several unfinished church compositions—settings of Kyrie and Gloria texts—which had always been assumed to belong to the Salzburg period, actually date from late in the Vienna years: the period after 1787.[3] Moreover, in addition to his own (abandoned) compositional efforts, Mozart, at this same time had taken the trouble of copying out a number of church pieces by the former court and cathedral Kapellmeister, Georg Reutter. Although the full biographical import of these discoveries has yet to be ascertained, it is clear in any event that by 1790 (as we read above) Mozart was emphasizing his skills as a church composer in support of a petition for an appointment as second court Kapellmeister and just one year later would be offering his services to the municipal council of Vienna as an unpaid assistant to the ailing Kapellmeister of St. Stephen's Cathedral.[4]

The passages that follow testify among other things to Mozart's dismay about declining standards both in the performance and in the composition of church music—the latter, for him, evidently tantamount to an abandonment of a noble and venerable musical tradition and, we may presume, of a cherished religious heritage. His conservative taste with respect to church music is in stark contrast to his modern predilections in most other musical matters. His characterizations, for example, of the otherwise respected composer Jommelli and of the "Tartini" school of violin playing as "old fashioned" were clearly not intended as praise. ◄

THE CURRENT STATE: DECLINE AND FALL?

True church music is to be found only in attics and in a worm-eaten condition.

Vienna, 12 April 1783

To Padre Martini   *Salzburg, 4 September 1776*

[The following passage is in Italian.] Our church music is very different from that of Italy, since a mass with the whole Kyrie, the Gloria, the Credo, the Epistle sonata, the Offertory or Motet, the Sanctus, and the Agnus Dei must not last longer than three-quarters of an hour. This applies even to the most Solemn Mass said by the Archbishop himself. So you see that a special study is required for this kind of composition. At the same time, the mass must have all the instruments—trumpets, drums, and so forth. (A, 266)

► This letter, although signed by Wolfgang, is in the hand of Leopold Mozart and may well reflect the father's views more than those of the son. While earlier interpreters of these comments concluded that the Salzburg Archbishop Colloredo had instituted a prohibition of both operatic-style arias and of fugal choruses in settings of the mass, there is no documentary evidence of any official restriction. On the other hand, the time limits that had been set did effectively preclude the composition of elaborate arias or fugues. In any case, the compositional challenge was to keep a mass setting within the modest temporal dimensions of a *Missa brevis* but scored in the fashion of a *Missa solemnis*, that is, with trumpets and drums. But this was nothing very new in Salzburg. Masses of this kind had been written by Mozart's predecessors even before the accession of Archbishop Colloredo.[5] ◄

To Leopold Mozart   *Mannheim, 4 November 1777*

[The Mannheimers] can produce fine music, but I should not care to have one of my masses performed here. Why? On account of their shortness? No, everything must be short here [i.e., in Salzburg], too. Because a different style of composition is required? Not at all. But because, as things are at present, you must write principally for the instruments, as you cannot imagine anything worse than the voices here.[6] (A, 356)

To Leopold Mozart   *Vienna, 12 April 1783*

Musical taste is continually changing, and *what is more* . . . this extends even to church music, which ought not to be the case. Hence it is that true church music is to be found *only* in attics and in a worm-eaten condition. (A, 845)

INDIVIDUAL COMPOSITIONS

To Nannerl   *Naples, 19 May 1770*

Go regularly to Mirabell[7] to hear the Litanies and to listen to the Regina Coeli or the Salve Regina and sleep soundly and do not have any bad dreams. (A, 138)

▶ It is tempting to assume that Mozart was particularly fond of the liturgical items he mentions here. The Salve regina and the Regina coeli are two of the four Marian antiphons (along with the Alma Redemptoris mater and the Ave regina coelorum) which are sung, each at a different season, at the end of the liturgical day. Although no Salve regina by Mozart survives, there are three settings of the Regina coeli, all for soloists, chorus, and orchestra and all composed in Salzburg.[8] Mozart also set Litany texts on at least four occasions during the Salzburg period, all for soloists, chorus, and orchestra. There are two settings of the five-movement "Lauretana" Litany in Veneration of the Virgin, and two settings of the longer Litany in Veneration of the Sacrament.[9] ◀

Motet: Exsultate jubilate, K. 165 (158a)

▶ Completed January 1773 ◀

To Nannerl   *Milan, 16 January 1773*

I for have the primo a uomo [Rauzzini] motet compose which to tomorrow at Church the Theatine performed be will.[10] (A, 226)

Misericordias Domini, in D minor, K. 222 (205a)

▶ Composed January/February 1775 ◀

To Padre Martini   *4 September 1776*

[The following passage is in Italian.] A few days before my departure [from Munich, in March 1775] the Elector expressed a desire to hear some of my contrapuntal compositions. I was therefore obliged to write this motet in a great hurry, in order to have time to have the score copied for His Highness and to have the parts written out and thus enable it to be performed during the Offertory at High Mass on the following Sunday.

Most beloved and esteemed Signor Padre Maestro! I beg you most
earnestly to tell me, frankly and without reserve, what you think of it. (A,
265–266)

► Padre Martini responded (on 18 December 1776) that the motet "has all
the qualities which modern music demands, good harmony, rich
modulation, moderate movement of the violins, natural and good voice
leading"[11] That Mozart himself continued to think highly of the work is
evident from the letter of 20 November 1777 cited next. ◄

Litany de Venerabili in E-flat, K. 243

► Composed March 1776 ◄

To Leopold Mozart   *Mannheim, 20 November 1777*

I left with [the Holy Cross Monastery at Augsburg] my mass in F [K. 192
(186f)], the first of the short masses in C [K. 220 (196b)] and my
contrapuntal Offertory in D minor [i.e., the Misericordias Domini, K. 222
(205a)]. . . . I have got back safely the Offertory, which I asked to be
returned first. Now they have all plagued me, including the Abbot, to give
them a litany de Venerabili. I told them that I hadn't one with me, and as a
matter of fact I was not quite sure whether I had. I looked for it, but
couldn't find it. But they wouldn't leave me in peace; they thought I was
just trying to put them off. So I said: "Look here, I haven't got it with me,
it's at Salzburg. Write to my Papa. It's for him to decide. If he sends it to
you, well and good. If not, I can do nothing." So I expect that a letter from
the Dean to Papa will soon make its appearance. Do just as you like. If you
want to send them one, send them my last one, in E-flat. (A, 378–379)

LOST AND UNFINISHED COMPOSITIONS

► Among Mozart's surprisingly numerous unfinished works—there is
about one musical "fragment" for every four finished compositions—
church music is not only disproportionately represented, but it includes
two of the most extraordinary compositions Mozart ever conceived: the
Mass in C minor, K. 427 (417a) and the Requiem, K. 626. The reason the
Requiem was never finished is abundantly obvious. Why Mozart failed
to complete many of the other works in this and other genres has
numerous explanations. In most cases, however, the occasion for which
a composition was planned simply failed to materialize. ◄

A Mass[12]

To Leopold Mozart   *Mannheim, 10 December 1777*

I have an idea of writing a new grand mass and presenting *it to the Elector*
[Karl Theodor] [in code]. (A, 415)

To Leopold Mozart   *Mannheim, 14 February 1778*

As a diversion [from working on the flute compositions commissioned by Ferdinand De Jean] I compose something else, such as duets for clavier and violin[13] or I work at my mass. . . . If only the Elector were here, I should very quickly finish the mass.[14] (A, 482)

To Leopold Mozart   *Mannheim, 28 February 1778*

Ah, if only *the Elector of Bavaria had not died!* [in code]. I would have finished the mass and produced it and it would have made a great sensation here [Mannheim]. (A, 499)

Miserere "Pasticcio," K. 297a

► Composed March/April 1778 ◄

To Leopold Mozart   *Paris, 5 April 1778*

Kapellmeister Holzbauer has sent a Miserere here, but as the choruses at Mannheim are weak and poor, whereas in Paris they are powerful and excellent, the choruses he has composed would not be effective. So M. Le Gros (Director of the Concert Spirituel) has asked me to compose others, Holzbauer's introductory chorus being retained. "Quoniam iniquitatem meam," an Allegro, is my first one. The second is an Adagio, "Ecce enim in iniquitatibus"; then an Allegro, "Ecce enim veritatem dilexisti" as far as "ossa humiliata"; then an Andante for soprano, tenor, and bass soli— "Cor mundum crea" and "Redde mihi laetitiam," but allegro as far as "ad te convertentur." I have also composed a recitative for a bass singer, "Libera me de sanguinibus," because a bass aria by Holzbauer follows "Dominus labia mea." Now because "Sacrificium Deo spiritus" is an aria andante for Raaff with an oboe and bassoon solo accompaniment, I have added a short recitative, "Quoniam si voluisses," also with oboe and bassoon obbligatos, for recitatives are now very popular here. "Benigne fac" as far as "Muri Jerusalem" is Andante moderato. A chorus. Then "Tunc acceptabis" as far as "Super altare tuum vitulos," Allegro and tenor solo (Le Gros) and a chorus all together. Finis. I may say that I am very glad to have finished that hackwork, which becomes a curse when one cannot compose at home and when in addition one is pressed for time. Thanks and praise be to God; I have finished it and only trust that it will produce the desired effect.[15] (A, 521)

To Leopold Mozart   *Paris, 1 May 1778*

My work on those choruses turned out in fact to be useless, for Holzbauer's Miserere in itself was too long and did not please. Thus they only performed two of my choruses instead of four, and left out the best. But that was of no consequence, for few people knew that I had composed some of the music and many knew nothing at all about me. However, there was great applause at the rehearsal and I myself (for I attach little value to Parisian praises) am very well satisfied with my choruses. (A, 532)

A French oratorio

To Leopold Mozart   *Paris, 9 July 1778*

For next Lent I have to compose a French oratorio which is to be performed at the Concert Spirituel. (A, 564)

► The work never materialized. ◄

A Mass[16]

To Leopold Mozart   *Munich, 29 December 1778*

I am going to compose a mass here (I am just telling you this as a tremendous secret). All my good friends are advising me to do so. (A, 646)

Mass in C minor, K. 427 (417a)

To Leopold Mozart   *Vienna, 4 January 1783*

The score of half of a mass, which is still lying here waiting to be finished, is the best proof that I really made the promise. (A, 834)

► This is Mozart's only reference to the C-minor Mass. The nature of Mozart's promise is not known.[17] Although the work was already half-finished in January 1783, it was still unfinished ten months later when it was performed in Salzburg on 26 October 1783 at the Church of the Benedictine Monastery of St. Peter's (with Constanze singing one of the soprano solos). Mozart had succeeded in completing only the Kyrie and Gloria movements, along with the Sanctus and Benedictus. Of the Credo he had managed to draft only the two opening movements extending through the words of the Et incarnatus est. That is, there is no setting of the Credo text from the Crucifixus on, nor is there any music for the closing Agnus Dei and Dona nobis pacem. Most likely Mozart had interrupted work on the Mass to turn his attention to two major opera buffa projects: *L'Oca del Cairo*, K. 422, and *Lo sposo deluso*, K. 430 (424a). Ironically, those compositions were never completed, either.[18] ◄

Requiem in D minor, K. 626

To Constanze, Baden   *Vienna, 8 October 1791*

This morning I worked so hard at my composition that I went on until half past one. . . . After lunch I went home and composed again until it was time to go to the opera [i.e., *Die Zauberflöte*]. (A, 969)

► This is the only written reference by Mozart himself to the Requiem. At the time of his death Mozart had managed to finish entirely only the first of the fifteen projected movements of the work. He had almost completed the second, the Kyrie eleison (only the doubling instruments, as well as the trumpet and timpani parts, were left blank), and had also entered the principal parts of seven further movements into his working score. (The principal parts were those of the chorus, vocal soloists, and instrumental bass as well as any instruments that had important melodic or motivic material.) In this manner he had outlined (and indeed essentially composed) the first five of the six movements of the Sequence: Dies Irae, Tuba mirum, Rex tremendae, Recordare, Confutatis (i.e., all but the Lacrimosa), and the two movements of the Offertorium: Domine Jesu and Hostias. He had also notated the first eight measures of the Lacrimosa, whereupon his manuscript breaks off. ◄

Constanze Mozart to Breitkopf & Härtel, Leipzig   *Vienna, 27 March 1799*

When [Mozart] foresaw his death, he spoke to Mr. Süssmayr . . . and told him that if he were really to die without finishing it, then he should repeat the first fugue, as is customary in any case, for the final movement. He also told him how he should work out the ending which for the most part had already been worked out here and there in the parts. (MBA, 4:234)

Sophie Haibel to Georg Nikolaus Nissen, 1825:

I ran back as fast as I could to my inconsolable sister. Sissmaier was there at M's bedside; and the well-known Requiem lay on the coverlet, and Mozart was explaining to him how he thought he should finish it after his death. . . . The last thing he did was to try to mouth the sound of the timpani in his Requiem; I can still hear it now. (DDB, 525)

► The work was completed in the following months by others. No fewer than three hands, in addition to Mozart's own, are visible in the remaining portions of his manuscript: those of his students and friends Franz Xaver Süssmayr, Franz Jakob Freystädtler, and Joseph Eybler. The last five movements of the work, however, from the Sanctus to the end, are exclusively in Süssmayr's hand. The concluding sections—the Lux aeterna and Cum sanctis tui—in accordance with Mozart's instructions, make use of the music of the opening movements. Whether any of the musical substance of the Sanctus, Osanna, Benedictus, and Agnus Dei movements derives from Mozart has been a matter of controversy for the past two hundred years.[19] ◄

12

Instrumental Music

These concertos are very brilliant, pleasing to the ear, natural, without being vapid. There are passages here and there from which the connoisseurs alone can derive satisfaction, but these passages are written in such a way that the less learned cannot fail to be pleased, though without knowing why.

Vienna, 28 December 1782

▶ Mozart expounded very little on the nature, or the potential, of instrumental music. He penned no central, thoughtful statements in this domain analogous to the dissertations on operatic drama contained in his letters to Salzburg of September and October 1781. The reason for this, perhaps, is that in the realm of instrumental music Mozart was autonomous: the sole agent in its creation—and often enough, the sole (or at least the principal) executive agent in its performance as well. Since he did not have to argue his points and prevail over other collaborators—librettists, singers, designers—when composing an instrumental work, he evidently felt little need to set down in words and thus clarify his understanding of, say, the aesthetic premises of sonata form.

More's the pity. It is hard to imagine anything that could have been more enlightening than Mozart's considered views on the tonal or formal strategies of a sonata movement, on scoring for wind instruments, on the treatment of counterpoint in chamber music, the relationship between soloist and ensemble in a concerto, or among the movements of a symphony. Mozart does comment on general stylistic matters, but unfortunately, his remarks mostly concern relatively external, even superficial, points: a cliché of the French symphony, the tempo and rhythm differences between the German and the Italian minuet, the difference between concertos orchestrated in the grand or the chamber style. On the other hand, it is obviously instructive to note the stylistic categories or details Mozart bothered to identify and to observe in his own work.

At times, in fact, his remarks are more illuminating than they appear to be on first reading. And he sometimes casually articulates an aesthetic point of profound importance. The passage cited above, for example, referring to the first piano concertos Mozart had written for Vienna, clearly reaffirms the basic tenets of his aesthetic credo. The attributes of "brilliant," "pleasing," and "natural" can readily be identified with the qualities of Effect, Appeal, and Propriety discussed earlier. But another consideration has been introduced—one perhaps even more telling. It is Mozart's observance in his own work of a careful balance between the Popular and the Subtle. Mozart's achievement of this highly elusive equilibrium of immediate appeal and sophisticated craftsmanship is no doubt the source not only of his universal appeal but of his artistic supremacy as well. ◄

THE CONCERTO

STYLISTIC OPTIONS

► Of the major instrumental forms, Mozart had by far the most to say about the concerto. His remarks reveal that the concerto allowed for a range of stylistic options. It is amusing to learn that the four-year-old Mozart (like more than one adult composer of a later generation) understood the concerto to be primarily an ordeal of technical difficulties imposed on the soloist: a piece that was seemingly (perhaps literally) impossible to play. By the time he had embarked on his double career in Vienna as both a composer and player of concertos, Mozart had learned that technical difficulty, like everything else in art, was a matter of propriety dictated by the particular circumstances. At times the object was to achieve "a happy medium" between the "too easy and the too difficult"; at others it was "to make the performer perspire." ◄

Johann Andreas Schachtner to Nannerl Mozart   *Salzburg, 24 April 1792*

I once went with your father to the house . . . we found the four-year-old Wolfgängerl busy with his pen:
Papa: What are you writing?
Wolfgang: A clavier concerto, the first part is nearly finished.
Papa: Show me.
Wolfgang: It's not ready yet.
Papa: Show me, it's sure to be interesting.
His father took it from him and showed me a smudge of notes, most of which were written over ink-blots which he had rubbed out. . . .
At first we laughed at what seemed such a galimatias [nonsense], but his father then began to observe the most important matter, the notes and music; he stared long at the sheet, and then tears, tears of joy and wonder, fell from his eyes. Look, Herr Schachtner, [he] said, see how correctly and properly it is all written, only it can't be used, for it is so very difficult that no one could play it. Wolfgängerl said: That's why it's a concerto, you must practice it till you can get it right, look, that's how it goes. He played, and managed to get just enough out of it for us to see what he intended. At that

time he had the notion that to play a concerto and work a miracle must be one and the same. (DDB, 452)

To Leopold Mozart   *Vienna, 28 December 1782*

There are still two concertos wanting to make up the series of subscription concertos. These concertos are a happy medium between what is too easy and too difficult; they are very brilliant, pleasing to the ear, and natural, without being vapid. There are passages here and there from which the connoisseurs alone can derive satisfaction; but these passages are written in such a way that the less learned cannot fail to be pleased, though without knowing why. (A, 833)

► Mozart is referring to the concertos in A, K. 414 (385p) (ex. 12.1); in F, K. 413 (387a); in C, K. 415 (387b), which he offered for sale for the subscription price of four ducats. The first of the three concertos to be composed was the A major, which is also the most well known of the three. ◄

EXAMPLE 12.1. Piano Concerto in A, K. 414 (385p), Opening Themes

► Mozart's interest in finding a public to purchase copies of these concertos no doubt explains his concern that they be playable by the amateur and thus strike "a happy medium between what is too easy and too difficult." The same motivation—relative accessibility—lay behind the alternative scoring options available for these concertos, as described below; pp. 288–289.

    The style of a concerto was determined not only by the degree of difficulty of the soloist's part but by the character of the orchestral scoring as well. On the one hand was the "grand concerto" for full orchestra. Mozart distinguishes this "category" from another, more intimately scored type, one that can be reasonably described as a "chamber concerto." ◄

To Leopold Mozart   *Vienna, 26 May 1784*

The concerto Herr [Georg Friedrich] Richter praised to her [Nannerl] so warmly is the one in B-flat [K. 450], the first one I composed [dated 15 March 1784] and which he praised so highly to me at the time. I really cannot choose between the two of them, but I regard them both as concertos which are bound to make the performer perspire. From the point of view of difficulty the B-flat concerto beats the one in D [K. 451, dated 22 March 1784]. Well, I am very curious to hear which of the three in B-flat, D, and G [K. 453, 12 April 1784] you and my sister prefer. The one in E-flat [K. 449, 9 February, 1784] does not belong at all to the same category. It is one of a quite peculiar kind, composed rather for a small orchestra than for a large one. So it is really a question of only three grand concertos. (A, 877)

► The concertos in B-flat, K. 450, and G, K. 453, both call for an accompaniment of 1 flute, 2 oboes, 2 bassoons, 2 horns, and strings; the D-major concerto, K. 451, adds trumpets and timpani to the scoring. In contrast, the Concerto in E-flat, K. 449, calls only for a string accompaniment, along with *ad libitum,* that is, optional, pairs of oboes and horns.

Mozart's concern, in the following passages, about excessive length —especially, in his letter of 4 April 1787, his declared disdain for overly long ritornelli—is as close as he ever comes to addressing directly a major issue of instrumental form. ◄

To Leopold Mozart   *Paris, 11 September 1778*

If I have time, I shall rearrange some of my violin concertos, and shorten them. In Germany we rather like length, but after all it is better to be short and good. (A, 615)

To Leopold Mozart   *Vienna, 4 April 1787*

The oboist from London [Johann Christian Fischer] came here this Lent. . . . And then his concertos! His own compositions! Why, each ritornello lasts a quarter of an hour, and then our hero comes in. (A, 907)

PERFORMANCE OPTIONS

► The instrumentation of Mozart's concertos—that is, the division into the "grand style," on the one hand, and "chamber style," on the other—was not always rigidly fixed. The option was sometimes available of realizing the same piano concerto in effect as either a piece of chamber music—a piano quintet—or as a relatively heroic work for soloist and orchestra. Mozart exploited this possibility in the case of the piano concertos, K. 413–415, which he offered for sale to the public on subscription, in manuscript copies.[1] His hope was obviously to make the pieces commercially more attractive. He placed the following announcement in the *Wiener Zeitung* of 15 January 1783. ◄

Herr Kapellmeister Mozart herewith apprises the highly honored public of the publication of three new, recently finished pianoforte concertos. These three concertos . . . may be performed either with a large orchestra with wind instruments or merely *a quattro,* viz. with two violins, one viola, and violoncello. (DDB, 212)

► A year later, Mozart made the same point in offering the concertos to the publisher Sieber. This time, the number of performance options had grown to three: ◄

To Jean Georges Sieber, Paris   *Vienna, 26 April 1783*

Well, this letter is to inform you that I have three piano concertos ready, which can be performed with full orchestra, or with oboes and horns, or merely *a quattro.* (A, 846)

► Mozart also raised the issue of performance options with respect to his concertos of the 1784 season, and, with a twist, with reference to the A-major Piano Concerto, K. 488—a work completed in 1786 but now known to have been begun one or two years earlier (see below). ◄

To Leopold Mozart   *Vienna, 15 May 1784*

I formed the opinion, which I still hold, that the music would not be of much use to you, because except for the E-flat concerto [K. 449], which can be performed *a quattro* without wind instruments, the other three concertos [K. 450, K. 451, K. 453] all have wind instrument accompaniment; and you very rarely have wind instrument players at your house. (A, 877)

To Sebastian Winter, Donaueschingen   *Vienna, 30 September 1786*

There are two clarinets in the A-major concerto [K. 488, completed 2 March 1786]. Should His Highness not have any clarinets at his court, a competent copyist might transpose the parts into the suitable keys, in which case the first part should be played by a violin and the second by a viola. (A, 900)

► It is striking that Mozart, in offering a copy of this radiantly scored concerto to Prince von Fürstenberg, suggests substituting a single violin and a viola—rather than, say, two oboes—for the clarinets. The concerto, incidentally, was begun in 1784 or 1785. In its incipient form it called in fact for two oboes, not clarinets.[2]

Given Mozart's phenomenal abilities as an improviser, along with the prevailing convention at the time of improvising cadenzas, it is surprising that he frequently wrote out both the full-scale cadenzas as well as the brief cadenza-like passages called "lead-ins" (*Eingänge*), for his concertos. Indeed, it seems that he sometimes performed the same precomposed cadenzas more than once. Occasionally, as the following citations reveal, these prepared cadenzas were shared with others, but apparently only with pupils or with his sister. Mozart evidently was willing as well to take the trouble of writing out for Nannerl ornamental passagework that he himself would normally have improvised in performance. ◄

To Leopold Mozart   *Vienna, 3 November 1781*

Please forgive me for not having acknowledged by the last post the receipt of the cadenzas for which I thank you most submissively. . . . I shall add the second piano part to the cadenzas and return them to you. (A, 776)

► On 27 June, 1781 Mozart had requested copies of his concertos for two pianos, that is, the concertos in E-flat, K. 365 (316a), composed in 1779, and in F, K. 242 (the *Lodron* Concerto, originally composed in 1776 for three pianos but later arranged for two). His intention was evidently to perform them with his pupil, Josepha Auernhammer. The precomposed cadenzas which Mozart acknowledges receiving here, belonged to the E-flat Concerto, K. 365. ◄

To Leopold Mozart   *Vienna, 22 January 1783*

I shall send the cadenzas and lead-ins [for the concertos, K. 413–415] to my dear sister at the first opportunity. I have not yet altered the lead-ins in the rondo,[3] for whenever I play this concerto, I always play whatever occurs to me at the moment. (A, 837)

To Leopold Mozart   *Vienna, 15 February 1783*

Herewith I send my sister the three cadenzas for the concerto in D [K. 175, with the new Finale, K. 382] and the two lead-ins for the one in E-flat [K. 271]. (A, 840)

To Leopold Mozart   *Vienna, 9 June 1784*

Please tell my sister that there is no adagio in any of these concertos [K. 449–451, K. 453], only andantes. She is quite right in saying that there is something missing in the solo passage in C in the [G-major] Andante of the concerto in D [K. 451]. I will supply the deficiency as soon as possible and send it with the cadenzas. (A, 880)

► What was missing was the ornamentation of the phrase in mm. 56–63, which Mozart presumably improvised when he performed the concerto himself (ex. 12.2). ◄

EXAMPLE 12.2. Piano Concerto in K. 451, Andante, mm. 56–63, Plain and Ornamented Versions

KEYBOARD MUSIC

► Given Mozart's total silence regarding the preeminent instrumental form of the late eighteenth century, the sonata, it is no small irony that he rather frequently mentions the keyboard forms most closely associated with the previous epoch of musical history: preludes and fugues. Counter to our expectations, however, he typically discusses preludes and fugues independently of one another. For Mozart the keyboard prelude was either an exercise in harmonic adventurousness, in modulation, or an indulgence in formal and interpretative freedom. In either case, the prelude (or capriccio) was, in spirit, an improvisation. The fugue, by contrast, "the most artistic and beautiful of all musical forms," was a demonstration of compositional rigor and interpretative discipline. ◄

PRELUDES

To Leopold Mozart   *Munich, 11 October 1777*

I enclose four praeambula for [Nannerl]. She will see and hear for herself into what keys they lead. (A, 308)

► Previously thought to be lost, these four praeambula have recently been identified as the four sections of the so-called Capriccio in C, K. 395 (300g), which should now be redated from 1778 to 1777 (and renumbered K. 284a). One of the harmonically more unstable portions is the following. It is not altogether clear whether they were intended to be played in direct succession (ex. 12.3).[4] ◄

EXAMPLE 12.3. "Capriccio" [i.e., Four Praeambula] for Piano, K. 395 (284a), mm. 14–29

▶ As a consequence of Wolfgang Plath's association of the Capriccio with the four preludes of 1777, the work referred to in the following letters of July 1778 must now be considered lost. But Mozart's comments on the different types of keyboard preludes remain valuable. ◀

To Leopold Mozart   *Paris, 20 July 1778*

I wanted to present my sister with a little praeambulum. The manner of playing it I leave to her own feeling. This is not the kind of prelude which passes from one key to another, but only a sort of capriccio, with which to test a clavier. . . . This is a peculiar kind of piece. It's the kind of thing that may be played as you feel inclined. (A, 573–574)

To Nannerl   *Paris, 31 July 1778*

I trust that you will be quite satisfied with my little prelude. It isn't exactly what you asked for, I admit—I mean, a prelude modulating from one key into the next and in which the performer can stop when he likes. But I hadn't sufficient time to write a prelude of that kind, for that sort of composition requires more work. As soon as I have time, I shall present you with one. (A, 589)

FUGUES

To Nannerl   *Vienna, 20 April 1782*

This most artistic and beautiful of all musical forms. (A, 801)

To Leopold Mozart   *Augsburg, 24 October 1777*

Then the others whispered to the Dean that he should just hear me play something in the organ style [i.e., a fugue].[5] I asked him to give me a theme. He declined, but one of the monks gave me one. I put it through its paces and in the middle (the fugue was in G minor) I started off in the major key and played something quite lively, though in the same tempo; and after that the theme over again, but this time arseways. Finally it occurred to me, could I not use my lively tune as the theme for a fugue? I did not waste much time in asking, but did so at once. (A, 339)

To Leopold Mozart   *Mannheim, 18 December 1777*

[Abbé Vogler] then began a fugue, in which one note was struck six times and presto. (A, 428)

► Mozart obviously found Vogler's monotone fugue subject (a not-uncommon thematic formula in the baroque era) monotonous. Mozart's paramount concern about the melodic interest of parts emerges from his comments and corrections in the exercises of his composition pupil Thomas Attwood, discussed in Chapter 6. ◄

To Leopold Mozart   *Vienna, 27 June 1781*

We have two harpsichords in the house where I am lodging, one for galanterie playing and the other an instrument which is strung with the low octave throughout, like the one we had in London, and consequently sounds like an organ. So on this one I improvised and played fugues. (A, 748)

To Nannerl   *Vienna, 20 April 1782*

I have purposely written above [the fugue in C, K. 394 (383a)] *Andante maestoso*, as it must not be played too fast. For if a fugue is not played slowly, the ear cannot clearly distinguish the theme when it comes in and consequently the effect is entirely missed. Learn it by heart and play it. It is not so easy to pick up a fugue by ear.[6] (A, 801)

► In his letters of October 1777 and June 1781 just cited Mozart of course reports doing precisely that—improvising, that is, picking up a fugue by ear. ◄

ORCHESTRAL MUSIC

INSTRUMENTATION

► An immediate hallmark of Mozart's orchestral writing is his imaginativeness and resourcefulness as a colorist, especially his "effective" use of wind instruments (alone and in combination)—and most notably, his sophisticated writing for horns and clarinets. According to Nannerl, Mozart's fascination with wind instruments began in childhood. ◄

The Memoirs of Nannerl Mozart, 1800

In London, where our father lay dangerously ill, we were forbidden to touch a piano. And so, in order to occupy himself, Mozart composed his first symphony for all the instruments of the orchestra, but especially for trumpets and kettledrums. I had to copy it out as I sat at his side. While he composed and I copied he said to me: remind me to give the horn something worthwhile to do. (DDB, 494)

► One would like to think that Nannerl's anecdote in fact refers to Mozart's first known symphony: the Symphony in E-flat, K. 16, composed in London in 1764 or 1765 (ex. 12.4). If it was written during Leopold's illness, then it would date from the four-week period beginning 8 July 1764. There are, however, no trumpet and drum parts in the E-flat symphony—at least not in its present form. (Conceivably, such parts had been written out on separate sheets that have not survived.) But the work does have a good horn part—especially in the Andante, where the horns discreetly intone the famous four-note motif that would find its most famous and triumphant expression in the final movement of the *Jupiter.*

EXAMPLE 12.4. Symphony in E-flat, K. 16. Andante, mm. 7–14

► Mozart's exposure to the brilliant Mannheim orchestra undoubtedly provided a new and powerful stimulus to his perennial interest and enthusiasm for instrumental color and effect. ◄

To Leopold Mozart   *Mannheim, 3 December 1778*

Ah, if only we had clarinets too! You cannot imagine the glorious effect of a symphony with flutes, oboes, and clarinets. (A, 638)

► There were no clarinets in the Salzburg court orchestra at that time. On the other hand, Salzburg had at least one rather exotic orchestral resource not readily available elsewhere which, when the appropriate artistic circumstance dictated, Mozart persistently endeavored to appropriate. ◄

To Leopold Mozart   *Munich, 29 November 1780*

For the march in act 2 [of *Idomeneo*, ex. 12.5] which is heard in the distance, I require mutes for the trumpets and horns, which it is impossible to get here. Will you send me one of each by the next mail coach, so that I may have them copied? (A, 674)

To Leopold Mozart   *Munich, 5 December 1780*

I asked you for something which I urgently require for my opera and that is to send me a *trumpet mute* of the kind we had made in Vienna, and also one for the *horn*, which you can get from the watchmen. I need them for the march in act 2. (A, 682)

EXAMPLE 12.5. *Idomeneo*. March from Act 2, Opening Measures

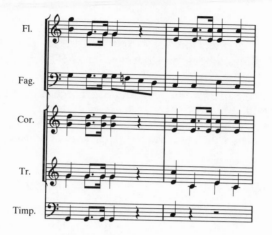

The Symphony in Italy, France, and Mannheim

▶ The history of the eighteenth-century symphony is normally related in terms of regional styles and traditions. Mozart, evidently, was quite aware of these distinctions, too. But while he occasionally uses national and geographic designations when referring to symphonies he has either heard or composed, he rarely bothers to provide descriptions specific enough to enable us to know what exactly he has in mind. For example, he writes to his sister from Italy: ◀

To Nannerl   *Bologna, 4 August 1770*

In the meantime I have composed four Italian symphonies. (A, 153)

▶ Mozart presumably has in mind the brilliant, light-textured, homophonic works, in three movements (i.e., without a minuet), and in the major mode—usually in the key of D—and with relatively modest employment of the wind instruments characteristic of the Italian style. It is possible, however, that he meant only symphonies that he had written in Italy. In any event, the identities of the four works referred to are not known for certain.[7] Similarly, we find the following reference in a letter from Paris written some eight years later: ◀

To Leopold Mozart   *Paris, 11 September 1778*

As for the symphonies [i.e., Mozart's earlier symphonies, written in Salzburg and taken along to Paris], most of them are not in the Parisian taste. (A, 615)

▶ A symphony written according to the Parisian taste typically consisted, once again, of three—rather than four—movements and was cast, once again, in the major mode, was rather lavishly orchestrated and made considerable noise.[8] But it also boasted a special feature that drew Mozart's attention: *le premier coup d'archet.* The *premier coup d'archet,* which is the topic of conversation in the following passages, literally means "the first bow stroke." But its use at the time in France and elsewhere referred to the popular convention of beginning a symphony with a powerful passage, normally in unison. ◄

To Leopold Mozart   *Mannheim, 20 November 1777*

What Mamma and I noticed at once about the symphonies here is that they all begin in the same manner, always with an introduction in slow time and in unison. (A, 378)

► Mozart himself had actually used this device, that is, a unison forte for the orchestra—but in an allegro tempo, as early as 1772: in the Overture to *Il Sogno di Scipione,* K. 126 (composed in Salzburg, March 1772).[9] ◄

To Leopold Mozart   *Paris, 12 June 1778*

I brought along the new symphony which I have just finished [the *Paris Symphony,* K. 297 (300a)]. . . . I have been careful not to neglect *le premier coup d'archet* (ex. 12.6)—and that is quite sufficient. What a fuss the oxen here make of this trick! The devil take me if I can see any difference! They all begin together, just as they do in other places. It is really too much of a joke. Raaff told me a story of Abaco's about this. He was asked by a Frenchman at Munich or somewhere: *"Sir, have you been to Paris?" "Yes." "Have you by chance been to the Concert Spirituel?" "Yes." "What do you say about the premier coup d'archet? Have you heard the premier coup d'archet?" "Yes, I've heard the first* [premier] *and the last." "How so, the last? What do you mean by that?" "Yes, indeed, the first and the last—and the last one gave me even more pleasure"* [French]. (A, 553)

THE MINUET IN ITALY AND GERMANY

► Just as the presence or absence of a minuet movement served to associate a symphonic work with a particular national school—Viennese symphonies typically had them, French and Italian symphonies typically did not—minuets themselves manifested national characteristics. This is hardly surprising, since minuets are dances, and every national tradition has its national style of dance. In addition, however, the style—especially the performance style and tempo—of a minuet (like that of other dance forms) could vary according to its function: on the one hand as a purely social dance, on the other, as an artistic or staged dance. Mozart, of course, was aware of these distinctions. ◄

EXAMPLE 12.6. Symphony in D (*Paris*), K. 297 (300a): *Premier coup d'archet*

To Nannerl   *Bologna, 24 March 1770*

I shall soon send you a minuet which Mr. Pick [Le Picq] danced in the theater and which everyone danced to afterwards at the feste di ballo in Milan, solely in order that you may see how slowly people dance here. The minuet itself is very beautiful. It comes, of course, from Vienna and was most certainly composed by Deller or Starzer. It has plenty of notes. Why? Because it is a stage minuet [theatralischer Menuett] which is danced slowly. The minuets in Milan, in fact the Italian minuets generally, have plenty of notes, are played slowly, and have several bars, for example, the first part has sixteen, the second twenty or twenty-four. (A, 121)

To Nannerl *Bologna, 22 September 1770*

We should like to be able to introduce the German taste in minuets into Italy, where they last nearly as long as the whole symphony. (A, 162)

► Examples 12.7 and 12.8 should illustrate the difference between the two minuet styles. The minuet from the Symphony in G, K. 124 (dated 21 February 1772, Salzburg), is typical of the German style: short and brisk, proceeding along smartly in quarters and eighths. The minuet from the late String Quartet in F, K. 589 (May 1790), perhaps represents the Italian style: marked "moderato," it is more lyric in character and has "plenty" of sixteenth-notes. Although the first section has only eight, rather than the sixteen, notated measures mentioned by Mozart, the minuet as a whole contains 37 measures, clearly compatible with the 36 to 40 (16 + 20/24) measures in Mozart's description of the Italian minuet. ◄

EXAMPLE 12.7. Symphony in G, K. 124. Minuet, First Part

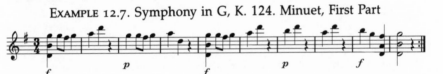

EXAMPLE 12.8. String Quartet in B-flat, K. 589. Minuet, First Part

FORMS OF FASHION

► Apart from the well-established instrumental genres—symphonies and concertos, as well as sonatas and chamber music for every combination of the familiar keyboard, stringed, and wind instruments—composers

active in the closing decades of the eighteenth century had to be willing
to cultivate a number of less lofty, more exotic forms of instrumental
music. Among the most popular (and profitable) of these in Josephine
Vienna were arrangements of complete operas for the *Harmonie*, that is,
for a woodwind octet consisting of pairs of oboes, clarinets, bassoons,
and horns. ◄

To Leopold Mozart   *Vienna, 20 July 1782*

Well, I am up to the eyes in work, for by Sunday week I have to arrange my
opera [*Die Entführung*] for wind instruments. If I don't, someone will
anticipate me and secure the profits. . . . You have no idea how difficult it
is to arrange a work of this kind for wind instruments, so that it suits these
instruments and yet loses none of its effect. Well, I must just spend the
night over it, for that is the only way.[10] (A, 808)

► In addition to the popularity of such exotic instrumental genres as the
woodwind arrangements of operas, there was also a rage at the time for
exotic instruments: for example, the baryton for which Joseph Haydn
was obliged to compose over a hundred works, or Benjamin Franklin's
glass harmonica, for which Mozart was evidently pleased to write the
Adagio, K. 356/617a, and the Adagio and Rondo, K. 617, or the
mechanical clockwork organ, for which he was far less pleased to
compose. ◄

To Constanze   *Frankfurt am Main, 3 October 1790*

I have now made up my mind to compose at once the Adagio for the clock
maker [in F minor, K. 594] and then to slip a few ducats into the hand of
my dear little wife. And this I have done, but it is a kind of composition
which I detest; I have unfortunately not been able to finish it. I compose a
bit of it every day, but I have to break off now and then, as I get
bored. . . . If it were for a large instrument and the work would sound like
an organ piece, then I might get some fun out of it. But, as it is, the works
consist solely of little pipes, which sound too high-pitched and too
childish for my taste.[11] (A, 943–944)

INDIVIDUAL COMPOSITIONS

► Mozart's comments about individual compositions (and sets of compositions) typically concern either the sometimes turbulent circumstances
surrounding their origins or, at the other end of their genesis, their early
reception. These narratives are not only invariably informative but quite
often amusing or even touching. At times they shed light as well on
matters of performance. The following review is organized by compositional genre, proceeding alphabetically from Ballet to Variations. ◄

A Ballet: *Le petits riens*, K. 299b

► During his sojourn in Paris Mozart had hoped to receive, through the good offices of the famous ballet master, Jean Georges Noverre, a commission for an opera. In the end, he was asked to compose no more than half a ballet. ◄

To Leopold Mozart   *Paris, 14 May 1778*

Noverre is also going to arrange a new ballet for which I am going to compose the music. (A, 539)

To Leopold Mozart   *Paris, 9 July 1778*

As for Noverre's ballet, all that I ever told you was that he might perhaps design a new one. He only needed half a ballet and for this I composed the music. Six pieces in it are composed by others and are made up entirely of wretched old French airs, while the overture and contredanses, about twelve pieces in all, have been contributed by me. This ballet has already been performed four times with the greatest applause. (A, 563 –564)

Chamber Music

Quintet for Piano and Winds in E-flat, K. 452

To Leopold Mozart   *Vienna, 10 April 1784*

I composed two grand concertos [K. 450, 451] and then a quintet (ex. 12.9), which called forth the very greatest applause.[12] I myself consider it to be the best work I have ever composed. It is written for one oboe, one clarinet, one horn, one bassoon, and the pianoforte. How I wish you could have heard it! And how beautifully it was performed! (A, 873)

EXAMPLE 12.9. Quintet for Piano and Winds, K. 452, Opening Themes

Six String Quartets Dedicated to Joseph Haydn

► These compositions, as Mozart declares in the dedication accompanying their publication (as opus X) by the Viennese publishing house Artaria & Co., were indeed the fruit of a long and laborious study. They were composed over a period of some two-and-a-half years: the Quartet in G major, K. 387, having been substantially completed by 31 December 1782, the Quartets in A major, K. 464, and C major, K. 465, bearing the dates 10 January and 14 January 1785, respectively, in the autograph scores. The genesis of the six quartets is a complicated one, marked by numerous interruptions and revisions.[13] ◄

[The following letter was written in Italian.]

To my dear friend Haydn,   *Vienna, 1 September 1785*

A father who had decided to send out his sons into the great world, thought it his duty to entrust them to the protection and guidance of a man who was very celebrated at the time and who, moreover, happened to be his best friend.

In like manner I send my six sons to you, most celebrated and very dear friend. They are, indeed, the fruit of a long and laborious study; but the hope which many friends have given me that this toil will be in some degree rewarded, encourages me and flatters me with the thought that these children may one day prove a source of consolation to me.

During your last stay in this capital you yourself, my very dear friend, expressed to me your approval of these compositions. Your good opinion encourages me to offer them to you and leads me to hope that you will not consider them wholly unworthy of your favor. Please then receive them kindly and be to them a father, guide, and friend! From this moment I surrender to you all my rights over them. I entreat you, however, to be indulgent to those faults which may have escaped a father's partial eye, and, in spite of them, to continue your generous friendship toward one who so highly appreciates it. (A, 891)

CONCERTOS

Concerto for Clarinet in A, K. 622

To Constanze, Baden   *Vienna, 7 October 1791*

Immediately after your departure I played two games of billiards with Herr von Mozart, the fellow who wrote the opera that is running at Schikaneder's theater; then I sold my nag for fourteen ducats; then I told Joseph to get Primus to fetch me some black coffee, with which I smoked a splendid pipe of tobacco; and then I orchestrated almost the whole of Stadler's rondo.[14] (A, 967)

► This is Mozart's only reference to the clarinet concerto. Although it reveals that Mozart completed the scoring of the final movement close to the end of his life, work on what was to become the clarinet concerto had actually begun years earlier. There is a sketch for the first 199 measures of a concerto in G major for basset horn (!) and orchestra that is virtually identical with the first movement of the clarinet concerto. Accordingly, it was given the number K. 621b in the most recent Köchel catalogue. In fact, the sketch dates from 1788 or 1789 or even earlier.[15] ◄

Concerto for Oboe in D, K. 314 (285d)

To Leopold Mozart   *Mannheim, 4 November 1777*

I have made [the oboist, Friedrich Ramm] a present of my oboe concerto, which is being copied in a room at Cannabich's, and the fellow is quite crazy with delight. I played this concerto to him today on the pianoforte at Cannabich's, and, although *everyone knew that I was the composer*, it was very well received. Nobody said that it was not *well composed*. (A, 355)

Concerto for Piano in D, K. 175 + Rondo, K. 382

► The Piano Concerto in D, K. 175, Mozart's first true piano concerto, was composed in Salzburg in December 1773. It remained one of Mozart's favorites; he played it numerous times in later years and, as the following passages reveal, continued to perform it in his Vienna period. When he performed the concerto at a Lenten concert on 3 March 1782 in the Burgtheater, he replaced the original finale with the Rondo, K. 382. ◄

To Leopold Mozart   *Vienna, 23 March 1782*

I am sending you at the same time *the last rondo* which I composed for my concerto in D major and which is making such a furore in Vienna. But I beg you to guard it like a *jewel* and not to give it to a soul to play. . . . I composed it *specially* for myself and no one else but my dear sister must play it. (A, 798)

To Baroness von Waldstätten   *Vienna, 28 September 1782*

I really do not want to let the concerto which I played in the theater go for less than six ducats. On the other hand I should undertake to pay for the copying. (A, 823)

► Mozart, then, was planning to publish the concerto in the form of a manuscript copy. Mozart's views on the copying and publication of his piano concertos—specifically, the concertos of 1782–1783, K. 413–415, and also those of the 1784 season, K. 449–451, 453—are cited and discussed in Chapter 3. ◄

DIVERTIMENTI

► Mozart used the terms *cassation, divertimento, serenade,* and *Nachtmusik* fairly interchangeably to designate a suite-like series of dances or other instrumental pieces arranged for a large or small ensemble. They were "occasional" pieces, intended not for concert performance but as an accompaniment for a particular occasion. Such music would be called "background music" today. A *Finalmusik,* for its part, was a Salzburg specialty: a serenade performed by the students for their teachers and the Prince-Archbishop, following their final examinations. It may be that the term *divertimento* was generally preferred for background music performed at parties by small ensembles of strings and/or wind instruments, whereas *serenades* were performed at more formal, cere-monial occasions calling for larger forces—an orchestra. But all such distinctions were not compelling. It is worth observing, for example, that two of the compositions Mozart refers to below as cassations in his letters—the F major, K. 247, and the B-flat, K. 287 (271h)—carry the heading *divertimento* in the surviving autograph scores. ◄

To Leopold Mozart   *Munich, 2 October 1777*

At Count Salern's . . . I played several things out of my head, and then the two cassations[16] I wrote for the Countess [Lodron] and finally the *Finalmusik* with the Rondo,[17] all from memory. (A, 289)

To Leopold Mozart   *Vienna, 4 July 1781*

I badly need the three cassations—those in F and B-flat [K. 247, K. 287] would do me for the time being—but you might have the one in D [K. 334 (320b)] copied for me sometime and sent on later. (A, 749)

Serenade for Winds in E-flat, K. 375

To Leopold Mozart   *3 November 1781*

I wrote it for St. Theresa's Day, for Frau von Hickel's sister, or rather the sister-in-law of Herr [Joseph] von Hickel, Court Painter, at whose house it was performed for the first time. . . . The chief reason I composed it was in order to let [the Imperial valet] Herr von Strack, who goes there every day, hear something of my composition; so I wrote it rather carefully.[18] (A, 776)

To Leopold Mozart   *Vienna, 27 July 1782*

I have had to compose in a great hurry a serenade but only for wind instruments. (A, 809)

► It is not certain whether this is a reference to the Serenade in C minor, K. 388 (384a) or to the revision of the E-flat Serenade, K. 375, into its more familiar form for eight instruments, that is, with the addition of two oboes. Mozart's reference to great haste might suggest that he was preparing the arrangement and not composing a new work of the seriousness and intensity of the C-minor Serenade. Yet he does say that he was composing. ◄

PRELUDE AND FUGUE IN C, K. 394 (383a)[19]

To Nannerl   *Vienna, 20 April 1782*

My dear Constanze is really the cause of this fugue's coming into the world. The Baron van Swieten, to whom I go every Sunday, gave me all the works of Handel and Sebastian Bach to take home with me (after I had played them to him.) When Constanze heard the fugues, she absolutely fell in love with them. Now she will listen to nothing but fugues, and particularly (in this kind of composition) the works of Handel and Bach. Well, as she had so often heard me play fugues out of my head, she asked me if I had ever written any down, and when I said I had not, she scolded me roundly for not recording some of my compositions in this most artistic and beautiful of musical forms, and never ceased to entreat me until I wrote down a fugue for her. So that is its origin.[20] (A, 800–801)

SONATAS

Six Sonatas for Piano, K. 279–284

► These six famous, "difficult" sonatas (ex. 12.10) were probably all composed in Munich during the first half of 1775.[21] Mozart's correspondence reveals that he performed them numerous times, especially during his travels in 1777–1778. It is notable that he explicitly mentions performing them both separately and as whole cycles of six, and also that he played them on both the pianoforte and the clavichord. ◄

EXAMPLE 12.10. Six Piano Sonatas, K. 279–284

Sonata in C, K. 279 (189d)

Sonata in F, K. 280 (189e)

Sonata in Bb, K. 281 (189f)

Sonata in Eb, K. 282 (189g)

Sonata in G, K. 283 (189h)

Sonata in D, K. 284 (205b)

To Leopold Mozart   *Augsburg, 17 October 1777*

Here and at Munich I have played all my six sonatas by heart several times.
I played the fifth, in G [K. 283 (189h)], at that grand concert in the Stube.
The last one in D [K. 284 (205b)], sounds exquisite on [Johann Andreas]
Stein's pianoforte. (A, 328)

To Leopold Mozart   *Mannheim, 4 November 1777*

I played all my six sonatas today at Cannabich's. (A, 355)

To Leopold Mozart   *Mannheim, 13 November 1777*

At [Ignaz van Beecke's] request I had to try his clavichord, which is a very
good one. . . . I improvised and played my sonatas in B-flat and D [K. 281
(189f), K. 284 (205b)]. (A, 368)

To Leopold Mozart   *Mannheim, 4 February 1778*

What surprises me most is [Aloysia Weber's] excellent sight-reading.
Would you believe it, she played my difficult sonatas at sight, *slowly* but
without missing a single note! On my honor I would rather hear my
sonatas played by her than by Vogler! (A, 460)

Sonata for Piano in C, K. 309 (284b)[22]

To Leopold Mozart   *Mannheim, 4 November 1777*

I am with Cannabich every day . . . He has a daughter who plays the clavier quite nicely; and in order to make a real friend of him I am now working at a sonata for her, which is almost finished save for the Rondo. When I had composed the opening Allegro and the Andante I took them to their house and played both to them. Papa cannot imagine the applause which the sonata won. (A, 355)

To Leopold Mozart   *Mannheim, 14 November 1777*

As soon as I can, I shall have the sonata which I have written for Mlle. Cannabich copied out on small paper and shall send it to my sister. I began to teach it to Mlle. Rosa three days ago. We finished the opening Allegro today. (A, 374)

To Leopold Mozart   *Mannheim, 29 November 1777*

I send [Nannerl] herewith the Allegro and Andante of the sonata for Mlle. Cannabich. The Rondo will follow next time. . . . You may have heard something of my sonata, for at Cannabich's it is sung, strummed, fiddled, or whistled at least three times a day! Only *sotto voce*, of course! (A, 397)

To Leopold Mozart   *Mannheim, 3 December 1777*

I hope you got the Allegro and Andante of my sonata! Here is the Rondo. (A, 401)

Sonatas for Piano, Four Hands

Sonata in B-flat, K. 358 (186c)   composed 1773–1774
Sonata in D, K. 381 (123a)   composed 1773–1774

To Leopold Mozart   *Mannheim, 17 January 1778*

Do you know what I should like to ask you to do? To send me whenever you have an opportunity, *but as soon as possible*, let us say, bit by bit, the two sonatas for four hands and the Fischer variations [K. 179 (189a)]!—For I could make good use of them in Paris. (A, 448)

SYMPHONIES

Symphony in D (*Paris*), K. 297 (300a)

► One of the livelier controversies of Mozart scholarship concerns the proper chronological ordering of the two surviving Andante movements for the *Paris* Symphony. ◄

To Leopold Mozart   *Paris, 9 July 1778*

The symphony was highly approved of, and Le Gros is so pleased with it
that he says it is his very best symphony. But the Andante has not had the
good fortune to win his approval; he declares that it has too many
modulations and that it is too long. He derives this opinion, however, from
the fact that the audience forgot to clap their hands as loudly and to shout
as much as they did at the end of the first and last movements. For indeed
the Andante is a great favorite with myself and with all connoisseurs,
lovers of music, and the majority of those who have heard it. It is just the
reverse of what Le Gros says for it is quite simple and short. But in order to
satisfy him (and, as he maintains, some others) I have composed a fresh
Andante; each is good in its own way for each has a different character.
But the last pleases me even more [ex. 12.11a, b]. (A, 565)

EXAMPLE 12.11a. *Paris* Symphony: Andante in 3/4

EXAMPLE 12.11b. *Paris* Symphony: Andante in 6/8

► The prevailing (but divided) view until fairly recently was that the
Andante in 3/4 meter was the later one, that is, the replacement, since it
is "shorter"—58 measures (or 84, counting the repeat) as against
98—and is the movement printed in the first edition of the work. The
current view, however, based on a careful study of the sources, is that
the Andante in 6/8 represents the later version.[23] ◄

Symphony in D (*Haffner*), K. 385

► The *Haffner* Symphony was originally written as a serenade: i.e., with
two minuets along with an introductory march. It was also written in
the greatest haste for the ceremonies attending the granting of a nobility
title to Mozart's Salzburg friend, Sigmund Haffner. The premiere of *Die
Entführung* had just taken place (on 16 July 1782), and Mozart had set
about immediately to make an arrangement of the opera for wind
instruments (see above), when he received the request from Leopold for
the serenade. ◄

To Leopold Mozart *Vienna, 20 July 1782*

And now you ask me to write a new symphony! How on earth can I do so? . . . You may rely on having something from me by every post. I shall work as fast as possible and, as far as haste permits, I shall turn out good work. (A, 808)

► The first movement was finished within the week. ◄

To Leopold Mozart *Vienna, 27 July 1782*

You will be surprised and disappointed to find that this contains only the first Allegro. . . . On Wednesday the 31st I shall send the two minuets, the Andante, and the last movement. If I can manage to do so, I shall send a march, too. . . . I have composed my symphony in D major because you prefer that key. (A, 810)

► The march was in fact soon provided, as the next letter reveals, along with the tempo suggestions for the outer movements. ◄

To Leopold Mozart *Vienna, 7 August 1782*

I send you herewith a short march [K. 408, No. 2 (385a)]. . . . The first Allegro must be played with great fire; the last, as fast as possible. (A, 813)

► A half-year later Mozart wished to perform the symphony at his March 23 concert, and asked for a copy of the score to be forwarded to him. ◄

To Leopold Mozart *Vienna, 4 January 1783*

It is all the same to me whether you send me the symphony of the last Haffner music which I composed in Vienna, in the original score or copied out, for, as it is, I shall have to have several copies made for my concert. (A, 835)

To Leopold Mozart *Vienna, 15 February 1783*

My new Haffner Symphony has positively amazed me, for I had forgotten every single note of it. It must surely produce a good effect. (A, 840)

► At the concert of March 23 the familiar four movements of the symphony were detached from one another and framed the other works on the program. (See Chapter 3.) ◄

Symphony in C (*Linz*), K. 425

► Mozart's next symphony, the *Linz* was written in even greater haste than the *Haffner*. ◄

To Leopold Mozart   *Linz, 31 October, 1783*

On Tuesday, November 4, I am giving a concert in the theater here and, as I have not a single symphony with me, I am writing a new one at breakneck speed, which must be finished by that time. (A, 859)

Four Salzburg Symphonies

► Mozart may have "forgotten every single note" of his recently composed *Haffner* Symphony, but he evidently well remembered other, considerably older, symphonies composed in Salzburg, during the early and mid 1770s: the D major, K. 204 (213a), dated 5 August 1775; the A major, K. 201 (186a), dated 6 April 1774; the B-flat, K. 182 (173dA), dated 3 October 1773, and the "little" G minor, K. 183 (173dB), dated 5 October 1773. Moreover, he thought well enough of them to perform them years later. ◄

To Leopold Mozart   *Vienna, 4 January 1783*

I should like to have the following symphonies (ex. 12.12.) as soon as possible. (A, 835)

EXAMPLE 12.12. Symphony Themes

Symphony in D, K. 204 (213a)

Symphony in A, K. 201 (186a)

Symphony in Bb, K. 182 (173dA)

Symphony in G minor, K. 183 (173dB)

VARIATIONS FOR PIANO ON A MINUET BY JOHANN CHRISTIAN FISCHER, K. 179 (189A)

► Despite his low opinion of Fischer's abilities—this is the same Fischer whose concerto ritornellos Mozart found absurdly long (see p. 288)—Mozart frequently performed his own variations on Fischer's theme. They are mentioned several times in his letters over a period of four years. ◄

To Nannerl   *Munich, 30 December 1774*

My sister must not forget to bring with her . . . my variations on Fischer's minuet. (A, 256)

To Leopold Mozart   *Mannheim, 29 November 1777*

I decided to take my six easiest variations on Fischer's minuet (which I had copied out here expressly for this purpose) *to the young Count* [Karl August, son of the Elector Karl Theodor] [italicized words in code].[24] (A, 397)

► Mozart's willingness to extract—at least for teaching purposes—the six easiest (of the twelve variations) suggests that he did not view the variation form as an integral work or "cycle," in the later sense. As we have already seen, Mozart requested the variations again (together with the sonatas for piano, four hands) on 17 January 1778 for "use" on his trip to Paris. ◄

LOST AND UNFINISHED COMPOSITIONS

Concerto for Piano, Violin, and Orchestra in D, K. 315f

► In November 1777 Mozart heard the Konzertmeister of the Mannheim court orchestra, Ignaz Fränzl, play a concerto and wrote an enthusiastic report home about Fränzl's playing.[25] Just one year later, on the journey home from Paris and after almost the entire court Kapelle had followed the Elector to Munich, Mozart proceeded not to Munich but, in defiance of his father's wishes, returned to his "beloved Mannheim." His various hopes for doing so all proved fruitless: among them, securing a position there, meeting the Webers, composing a duodrama on the story of *Semiramis*, and also writing a double concerto for the interesting combination of piano, violin, and orchestra. Mozart would have played the piano part; the violin part would have been for Fränzl, who had stayed behind. ◄

To Leopold Mozart   *Mannheim, 12 November 1778*

An Académie des Amateurs, like the one in Paris, is about to be started here. Herr Fränzl is to lead the violins. So at the moment I am composing a concerto for violin and clavier. (A, 631)

▶ In fact Mozart drafted 120 measures of a double concerto for violin, piano, and orchestra in D major. It was to be an ambitious work calling for a rich orchestration inspired by his experiences in Mannheim and Paris, including trumpets and drums along with flutes, oboes, horns, and strings. The last Köchel catalogue claims that "it is one of the greatest losses to art that Mozart did not complete this work."

Almost as poignant to contemplate as the unfinished compositions are those that were contemplated but never begun. ◀

Fugues

To Nannerl   *Vienna, 20 April 1782*

In time, and when I have a favorable opportunity, I intend to compose five more [i.e., fugues, in addition to K. 394] and then present them to the Baron van Swieten, whose collection of good music, though small in quantity, is great in quality. (A, 801)

Six Prussian String Quartets; *Six* Easy Clavier Sonatas

To Michael Puchberg, Vienna   *Vienna, 12 July 1789*

Meanwhile I am composing six easy clavier sonatas for Princess Friederike and six quartets for the King, all of which Kozeluch is engraving at my expense. At the same time the two dedications will bring me in something. (A, 930)

▶ Mozart completed only one of the six promised sonatas for the Prussian Princess: the Sonata in D, K. 576, and only three of the six promised string quartets for King Friedrich Wilhelm: the D major, K. 575; the B-flat, K. 589; and the F major, K. 590.[26] ◀

Sinfonia Concertante for Flute, Oboe, Horn, and Bassoon, K. 297B

▶ Mozart's sinfonia concertante for wind instruments, prominently mentioned in his letters from Paris, was never performed and may or may not be lost. At all events, no original sources for the work have survived. It is no exaggeration to say that its story is a tale of intrigue and controversy. The tale of intrigue originates with Mozart himself. According to the composer, the work fell victim to the machinations of an envious and threatened rival, Giuseppe Cambini, who succeeded in preventing its performance. The claim is altogether plausible, although its veracity cannot be independently ascertained. The controversy surrounding the work continues to the present. At its core is an anonymous *concertante* for oboe, clarinet, horn, and bassoon in E-flat that exists in a score copied in the nineteenth century. The central question is whether this frequently performed, attractive, and in many ways, "Mozartean" work has anything to do with Mozart's sinfonia concertante, and, if it does, can the authentic portion be retrieved and the rest reconstructed? The problem is not unlike that surrounding the Requiem—and, sorry to say, just as unlikely ever to be definitively resolved.[27] ◄

To Leopold Mozart   *Paris, 5 April 1778*

I am now going to compose a sinfonia concertante for flute, Wendling; oboe, Ramm; horn, Punto; and bassoon, Ritter. (A, 521–522)

To Leopold Mozart   *Paris, 1 May 1778*

I had to write the sinfonia in a great hurry and I worked very hard at it. The four performers were and still are quite in love with it. Le Gros kept it for four days to have it copied, but I always found it lying in the same place. The day before yesterday I couldn't find it—I searched carefully among the music—and discovered it hidden away. I pretended not to notice it, but just said to Le Gros: "Apropos. Have you given the sinfonia concertante to be copied?" "No," he replied, "I forgot all about it." As of course I could not command him to have it copied and performed, I said nothing; but when I went to the concert on the two days when it should have been performed, Ramm and Punto came up to me greatly enraged to ask me why my sinfonia concertante was not being played. "I really don't know," I replied. "It's the first I've heard of it. I know nothing about it." Ramm flew into a passion and in the music room he cursed Le Gros in French, saying it was a dirty trick and so forth. What annoys me most in the whole affair is that Le Gros never said a word to me about it—I alone was to be kept in the dark. If he had even made an excuse—that the time was too short or something of the kind—but to say nothing at all! I believe, however, that Cambini, an Italian maestro here, is at the bottom of the business. (A, 532–533)

To Leopold Mozart   *Paris, 9 July 1778*

You must know that, although I used to be with [Le Gros] every day, I have not been near him since Easter; I felt so indignant at his not having performed my sinfonia concertante. . . . It is really a pity that he did not perform it, as it would have made a great hit—but now he no longer has an opportunity of doing so, for where could four such players be found to perform it? (A, 564)

Variations on a Russian Song

To Leopold Mozart   *Vienna, 24 November 1781*

The Grand Duke [Paul Petrovich of Russia], the big noise, has arrived. . . . I have been looking about for Russian popular songs [*Russische favorit lieder*], so as to be able to play variations on them. (A, 780)

► It is odd imagining Mozart searching about for Russian popular songs. He had originally hoped to present *Die Entführung* on the occasion of the Russian crown prince's visit to Vienna, which had been expected to take place in September 1781. As it happened, the prince did not arrive until November 1781, and the opera was not to be ready until the following July. The prospect of composing and performing a set of variations on a Russian theme for the Duke was obviously a considerable compromise of Mozart's original plan for an opera production, and even so does not seem to have materialized. ◄

Part Three

On Musicians

13

Composers

I do not seek acquaintanceship . . . with any other composer. I understand my job—and so do they—and that is enough.

Paris, 9 July 1778

Mozart was very liberal in giving praise to those who deserved it but felt a thorough contempt for insolent mediocrity.

The Reminiscences of Michael Kelly, 1826

THE GOOD

► Judging by the written record, Mozart was very liberal indeed in his praise of other musicians. It is something of a surprise to ascertain, in fact, that more composers elicited kind words than contempt from his pen. Moreover, his ability (and willingness) to recognize the achievements of others embraced not only acknowledged (and lesser known) masters of the past and present but even extended to those of the future; the roster of composers to merit Mozart's high regard ranges from J. S. Bach and Handel to Beethoven and Hummel. Although his critical comments are often quite general, they usually succeed in making plain the aesthetic basis for his assessments of other composers' music. It is no surprise to discover that these judgments issue from the same premises (described in Chapter 6) that inform Mozart's own music.

To begin with the "music of the future," we only have second-hand testimony claiming to record Mozart's opinions about Hummel and Beethoven. It does not seem that Mozart had heard any of their necessarily youthful compositions. But it is significant that in both cases we are informed that he was less impressed with their ability to perform prepared pieces than with evidence of their natural, spontaneous musicality: Hummel's skills as a sightreader, Beethoven's as an improviser.

►   With regard to the music of the past, Mozart was quite familiar with music dating back at least to the mid-sixteenth century; he certainly was well acquainted with the church music of that period. The Miserere by Gregorio Allegri (1582–1652) that he had heard and copied out in the Sistine Chapel in 1770[1] was only one of many early church compositions he would have heard in Italy—and even before that, in Salzburg. Moreover, he had undertaken a systematic study of the principles of Renaissance counterpoint later that same year with the venerable Padre Martini in Bologna. But Mozart's active interest and enthusiasm about the music of the past evidently begins with the generation of Bach and Handel, that is, with music already composed according to the modern principles of tonality. What he most admires about the old masters (J. S. Bach, Handel, the older Bach sons) is their craftsmanship: their command of counterpoint in general and fugal writing in particular, but also their stunning accomplishments in choral writing. Mozart's esteem for well-written choral music is documented further in his high regard for the church music of Holzbauer and the two Haydns. And in the case of another venerable master, Christoph Willibald von Gluck, it was, once again, mainly the choral writing—impressive this time not so much for its contrapuntal sophistication as for its dramatic power and "effect"—that earned him Mozart's admiration. Gluck was not the only opera composer of the older generation whom Mozart respected. He greatly admired the works of Georg Benda who, like Gluck, was an imaginative innovator willing to challenge longstanding assumptions about the nature of musical drama. But Mozart also appreciated the most successful exponents of the traditional Metastasian school of opera seria—Johann Adolf Hasse and Nicolò Jommelli—although he felt obliged to add that Jommelli's music, for all its beauty, was "old fashioned."

Understandably, Mozart was most intensely interested in the music of his contemporaries. His enthusiasm for a number of works by lesser known composers—the church music of Holzbauer and di Maio, the piano sonatas of Myslivecek, Pleyel's string quartets, Schuster's duos for violin and piano—is highly intriguing, to say the least, and should stimulate efforts to make these and perhaps other works by the same composers more available to modern musicians and audiences.

Mozart's favorite composers, clearly, were Joseph and Michael Haydn and Johann Christian Bach—all personal acquaintances, all some twenty or so years older than himself. The influence of these masters on Mozart's artistic development was nothing less than profound. One by one, and with cumulative, continuing, impact—J. C. Bach's influence beginning as early as 1764 in London, Michael Haydn's during the apprentice years in Salzburg, Joseph Haydn's mostly during the Vienna period—they helped establish and transmit to him the essential hallmarks of the mature Viennese Classical style: immediacy of appeal, expressive power, subtlety of detail, formal elegance and refinement. ◄

Anton Cajetan Adlgasser (1729-1777)

► Mozart's predecessor as organist at the Salzburg cathedral, Adlgasser composed sacred and secular vocal music, keyboard works, and German stage works. In 1767 he collaborated with Michael Haydn and Mozart on the sacred drama *Die Schuldigkeit des ersten Gebots,* K. 35.[2] ◄

To Padre Martini   *Salzburg, 4 September 1776*

Meanwhile I am amusing myself by writing chamber music and music for the church, in which branches of composition we have two other excellent masters of counterpoint, Signori [Michael] *Haydn and Adlgasser* [Italian]. (A, 266)

Thomas Attwood (1765-1838)

► English composer, organist, and conductor, Thomas Attwood was Mozart's student in theory and composition from summer 1785 to February 1787. Attwood is never mentioned by Mozart in the surviving letters, but Michael Kelly reports the following: ◄

The Reminiscences of Michael Kelly, 1826

My friend Attwood (a worthy man and an ornament to the musical world) was Mozart's favorite scholar, and it gives me great pleasure to record what Mozart said to me about him; his words were, "Attwood is a young man for whom I have a sincere affection and esteem; he conducts himself with great propriety, and I feel much pleasure in telling you that he partakes more of my style than any scholar I ever had; and I predict that he will prove a sound musician." (Kelly, 1:225)

Carl Philipp Emanuel Bach (1714-1788)

► C. P. E. Bach was a prolific keyboard composer and author of an influential keyboard treatise; he served at the court of Frederick the Great from 1738 to 1768, and thereafter in Hamburg. In 1788 Mozart conducted a performance of Bach's oratorio, *Die Auferstehung und Himmelfahrt Christi.* ◄

To Leopold Mozart   *Vienna, 24 December 1783*

If you could have Emanuel Bach's fugues (there are six of them, I think) copied and sent to me sometime, you would be doing me a great kindness. (A, 865-866)[3]

Johann Christian Bach (1735-1782)

► Johann Christian, the "London" Bach was the youngest son of Johann Sebastian; he traveled to Italy where he soon became a successful organist and opera composer, and settled in London in 1762. He was important in the formulation of the early classic style. On the Mozart family's first meeting with Bach in London, May 1764, Nannerl recalled: ◄

The Reminiscences of Nannerl Mozart, 1792

Herr Johann Christian Bach, the Queen's teacher, took the son between his legs, the former played a few bars, and the other continued, and in this way they played a whole sonata, and someone not seeing it would have thought that only one man was playing it. (DDB, 456)

To Leopold Mozart   *Mannheim, 13 November 1777*

Bach has written two operas here, the first of which was more popular than the second, *Lucio Silla*. Now, as I too had composed a *Lucio Silla* in Milan, I wanted to see Bach's opera and I had heard from Holzbauer that Vogler possessed a copy. So I asked him for it. "Delighted," he said, "I shall send it to you tomorrow. But you will not make head nor tail of it." When he saw me a few days later, he asked me with an obvious sneer: "Well, do you find it beautiful? Have you learned anything from it? It has one fine aria. Let me see, what are the words?" He turned to somebody who happened to be standing beside him. "What sort of aria?" asked his companion. "Why, of course, that hideous aria by Bach, that filthy stuff—yes, yes, 'Pupille amate' [from *Lucio Silla*], which he certainly wrote in his cups [in Puntsch rausch, i.e., while drunk]." I thought I should have to seize his front hair and pull it hard, but I pretended not to hear him, said nothing and walked off. (A, 370)

To Leopold Mozart   *Mannheim, 14 February 1778*

I only taught her [Aloysia Weber] the day before yesterday an Andantino Cantabile by Bach, the whole of it.[4] (A, 482)

To Leopold Mozart   *St. Germain, 27 August 1778*

Mr. Bach from London has been here for the last fortnight. He is going to write a French opera, and has only come to hear the singers. He will then go back to London and compose the opera [*Amadis de Gaule*], after which he will return here to see it staged. You can easily imagine his delight and mine at meeting again; perhaps his delight may not have been quite as sincere as mine—but one must admit that he is an honorable man and willing to do justice to others. I love him (as you know) and respect him with all my heart; and as for him, there is no doubt but that he has praised me warmly, not only to my face, but to others also, and in all seriousness —not in the exaggerated manner which some affect. (A, 606)

To Leopold Mozart   *Paris, 12 June 1778*

When [Raaff] made his debut here in the Concert Spirituel, he sang Bach's scena "Non so d'onde viene" which, by the way, is a favorite of mine.[5] (A, 551)

To Leopold Mozart   *Vienna, 10 April 1782*

I suppose you have heard that the English Bach is dead? What a loss to the musical world! (A, 800)

Johann Sebastian Bach (1685–1750)

To Leopold Mozart   *Vienna, 10 April 1782*

I go every Sunday at twelve o'clock to the Baron van Swieten, where nothing is played but Handel and Bach. I am collecting at the moment the fugues of Bach—not only of Sebastian but also of Emanuel and Friede-mann. I am also collecting Handel's and should like to have the six I mentioned. I should like the Baron to hear Eberlin's, too. (A, 800)

To Nannerl   *Vienna, 20 April 1782*

The Baron van Swieten, to whom I go every Sunday, gave me all the works of Handel and Sebastian Bach to take home with me (after I had played them to him). When Constanze heard the fugues, she absolutely fell in love with them. Now she will listen to nothing but fugues, and particularly (in this kind of composition) the works of Handel and Bach. (A, 801)

To Leopold Mozart   *Vienna, 6 December 1783*

Please send me as soon as possible my *Idomeneo*, the two violin duets [K. 423, 424 for violin and viola] and Sebastian Bach's fugues.[6] (A, 862)

► Friedrich Rochlitz, founding editor of the influential Leipzig *Allgemeine Musikalishe Zeitung*, was a pupil at the Thomasschule at the time of Mozart's visit to Leipzig in April 1789. He later published the following account of Mozart's encounter with the music of Bach. ◄

Friedrich Rochlitz, 1799

On the initiative of the late Doles, then cantor of the Thomas-Schule at Leipzig, the choir surprised Mozart with the performance of the double chorus motet, "Singet dem Herrn ein neues Lied" [BWV 225], by Sebastian Bach. Mozart knew this master more by hearsay than by his works, which had become quite rare; at least his motets, which had never been printed, were completely unknown to him. Hardly had the choir sung a few measures when Mozart sat up startled; a few measures more and he called out: "What is this?" And now his whole soul seemed to be in his ears. When the singing was finished he cried out, full of joy: "Now, there is something one can learn from!" He was told that this School, in which Sebastian Bach had been cantor, possessed the complete collection of his motets and preserved them as a sort of sacred relic. "That's the spirit! That's fine!" he cried. "Let's see them!" There was, however, no score of these songs; so he had the parts given to him; and then it was for the silent observer a joy to see how eagerly Mozart sat himself down, with the parts all around him—in both hands, on his knees, and on the chairs next to him—and, forgetting everything else, did not get up again until he had looked through everything of Sebastian Bach's that was there. He requested a copy, valued it very highly, and, if I am not mistaken, no one who knows Bach's compositions and Mozart's Requiem will fail to recognize, particularly in the great fugue Christe [i.e., Kyrie] eleison, the study, the esteem, and the full comprehension of the spirit of the old contrapuntist achieved by Mozart's versatile and unlimited genius.[7]

Ludwig van Beethoven (1770–1827)

► According to Otto Jahn, author of the monumental nineteenth-century Mozart biography: ◄

Otto Jahn, 1891

Beethoven, who as a youth of great promise came to Vienna in the spring of 1787 [most likely, April 7–20] . . . was taken to Mozart and at that musician's request played something for him which he, taking it for granted that it was a show piece prepared for the occasion, praised in a rather cool manner. Beethoven, observing this, begged Mozart to give him a theme for improvisation. He always played admirably when excited and now he was inspired, too, by the presence of the master whom he reverenced greatly; he played in such a style that Mozart, whose attention and interest grew more and more, finally went silently to some friends who were sitting in an adjoining room, and said, vivaciously, "Keep your eyes on him; some day he will give the world something to talk about."[8]

Georg Benda (1722–1795)

► Benda was Kapellmeister at the court of Saxe-Gotha (Prussia). In 1775 he wrote his first stage works: the melodramas (i.e., spoken text with orchestral accompaniment): *Ariadne auf Naxos* and *Medea*. ◄

To Leopold Mozart   *Mannheim, 11 January 1778*

I know for a fact that *the Emperor* is proposing to *establish German opera in*

Vienna and that he is making every effort *to find a young Kapellmeister* who understands the *German language*, is talented and is capable of striking out a new line. *Benda of Gotha* is applying, but [Anton] *Schweitzer* is determined to get it [italicized words in code]. (A, 444)

To Leopold Mozart   *Mannheim, 12 November 1778*

The piece I saw was Benda's *Medea*. He has composed another one, *Ariadne auf Naxos*, and both are really excellent. You know that of all the Lutheran Kapellmeisters Benda has always been my favorite, and I like those two works of his so much that I carry them about with me.[9] (A, 631)

Christian Cannabich (1731–1798)

► Most renowned as the director of the Mannheim (later Munich) court orchestra, Christian Cannabich wrote compositions noted for their elegant orchestration. Mozart first met Cannabich in Paris in 1766 and later was a frequent guest of the Cannabichs during his sojourns in Mannheim and Munich. ◄

To Leopold Mozart   *Mannheim, 31 October 1777*

M. Cannabich . . . was exceedingly courteous. I played to him on his pianoforte, which is a very good one, and we went together to the rehearsal. . . . Herr Cannabich himself is taking me tomorrow to Count Savioli, the Intendant of the orchestra. (A, 350)

To Leopold Mozart   *Mannheim, 4 November 1777*

I am with Cannabich every day. Mamma too came with me today to his house. He is quite a different person from what he used to be and the whole orchestra says the same thing. He has taken a great fancy to me. (A, 355)

To Leopold Mozart   *Mannheim, 20 November 1777*

Cannabich is now a much better composer than he was when we knew him in Paris. (A, 378)

To Leopold Mozart   *Munich, 8 November 1780*

[The performance at] the Court Theater . . . began with an overture by Cannabich, which, as it is one of his latest, I did not know. I am sure, if you had heard it, you would have been as much pleased and excited as I was; and if you had not previously known it, you would never have believed it was by Cannabich. (A, 660)

Christoph Willibald von Gluck (1714–1787)

▶ Gluck's celebrated series of "reform" operas—*Orfeo ed Euridice* (1762), *Alceste* (1767), *Iphigénie en Aulide* (1774) and *Iphigénie en Tauride* (1779)—broke radically with the prevailing conventions of opera seria. In Paris during the 1770s, Gluck and Nicola Piccinni were cast as adversaries in an ideological battle of operatic styles. ◄

To Leopold Mozart   *Mannheim, 28 February 1778*

Piccinni's . . . music on the whole is a little monotonous; otherwise it was universally liked. To be sure, they are accustomed to Gluck's choruses in Paris. (A, 498)

To Leopold Mozart   *Vienna, 27 August 1781*

Gluck has had a stroke and his health is in a very precarious state. (A, 748)

To Leopold Mozart   *Vienna, 12 September 1781*

Gluck's *Iphigenie* [*in Tauris*] is to be given in German and his *Alceste* in Italian. If only one of the two were to be performed, I should not mind, but both—that is very annoying for me.[10] (A, 765)

To Leopold Mozart   *Vienna, 6 October 1781*

Nothing would be gained if the whole opera [*Die Entführung*] were finished, for it would have to lie there until Gluck's two operas were ready. (A, 771–772)

To Leopold Mozart   *Vienna, 24 October 1781*

The first performance of *Iphigenie* took place yesterday, but I wasn't there, for whoever wanted to get a seat in the parterre had to be at the theater by four o'clock, so I preferred to stay away. I tried to get a reserved seat in the third circle six days beforehand, but they were all gone. However, I was at nearly all the rehearsals. (A, 775)

To Leopold Mozart   *Vienna, 7 August 1782*

My opera [*Die Entführung*] was given again yesterday—and that too at Gluck's request. He has been very complimentary to me about it. I am lunching with him tomorrow. (A, 813)

To Leopold Mozart   *Vienna, 17 August 1782*

In regard to Gluck, my ideas are precisely the same as yours, my dearest father.[11] But I should like to add something. . . . You know well that it is the Germans who have always excelled in almost all the arts. But where did they make their fortune and their reputation? Certainly not in Germany! Take even the case of Gluck. Has Germany made him the great man he is? Alas no! (A, 814)

To Leopold Mozart   *Vienna, 12 March 1783*

Gluck had a box beside the Langes, in which my wife was sitting. He was loud in his praises of the symphony [the *Paris* Symphony, K. 297] and the aria ["Non so d'onde viene," K. 294] and invited us all four to lunch with him next Sunday. (A, 842).

To Leopold Mozart   *Vienna, 24 December 1783*

I have not yet been able to find the *Contessina* (or the *Countess*) [by Florian Leopold Gassmann]. If it is not to be had, would any of the following be suitable, *Das Irrlicht* by Umlauf, *Die schöne Schusterin* by the same, or *Die Pilgrimme von Mekka* [by Gluck]? The two latter operas especially would be very easy to perform. (A, 865)

Niemetschek, Biography of Mozart, 1808:

Mozart found a composer in Vienna whose genius was nearest to his own, I mean the famous creator of Alcestis and Iphigenia, the Ritter von Gluck, a Bohemian by birth. Intercourse with him and ceaseless study of his exalted works gave Mozart much sustenance and influenced his operas. (DDB, 504)

George Frideric Handel (1685–1759)

To Leopold Mozart   *Mannheim, 31 October 1777*

The oratorio, which is being rehearsed, is by Handel [*Messiah*, Part I], but I did not stay to hear it,[12] for before it came on, they rehearsed a Psalm—a Magnificat—by Vogler, the Deputy-Kapellmeister here, and it lasted almost an hour. (A, 350)

To Michael Puchberg   *Vienna, March/April 1790*

I am sending you Handel's life.[13] (A, 936)

The Reminiscences of Constanze Mozart, 1829

Mozart [was a] great admirer of Handel, well acquainted with his works especially his oratorios.[14] (Novello, 113)

Johann Adolf Hasse (1699–1783)

► Hasse was the leading composer of *opera seria* in both Italy and Germany. In Milan, in 1771, his *opera seria, Il Ruggiero*, and Mozart's serenata, *Ascanio in Alba*, K. 111, were composed and performed for the same occasion: the wedding of the Archduke Ferdinand of Austria to Maria Beatrice d'Este. ◄

To Nannerl   *Milan, 26 January 1770*

The opera at Mantua was charming. They played *Demetrio* [libretto by Metastasio, music by Hasse]. . . . The opera [at Cremona] was *La Clemenza di Tito* [by Hasse]. (A, 110)

To Nannerl   *Milan, 31 August 1771*

Hasse arrived yesterday and we are calling on him today. (A, 195)

To his Mother and Nannerl   *Milan, 2 November 1771*

There is a performance of Hasse's opera [*Ruggiero*] today, but as Papa is not going out, I cannot be there. Fortunately I know nearly all the arias by heart and so I can see and hear it at home in my head. (A, 205)

► As for Hasse's opinion of Mozart, Hasse provided Leopold with a letter of recommendation, dated 30 September 1769, for the Mozarts' upcoming trip to Italy. It is addressed to a friend in Bologna, the Abbé Giovanni Maria Ortes: "I have made the acquaintance here of a certain Herr Mozart . . . [His son], who cannot be older than twelve or thirteen, already bears the mark of a composer and Kapellmeister. I have seen the compositions that are supposed to be his; they are not bad at all, and betray nothing of a twelve-year-old. I do not doubt they are by him. I have tested him in various ways at the clavier, and he has demonstrated abilities that are incomprehensible at such an age and would even be admirable in a grown man. . . . The boy is attractive, lively, charming, and behaves so well that one cannot help liking him. One thing is certain: if his development continues to keep pace as he grows up, he will produce wonders. But his father must not drive him or spoil him with exaggerated praise. That is the only danger that I fear."[15] ◄

Joseph Haydn (1732–1809)[16]

To Michael Puchberg   *Vienna, December 1789*

I invite you, you alone, to come along on Thursday at 10 o'clock in the morning to hear a short rehearsal of my opera [*Così fan tutte.*] I am only inviting Haydn and yourself. (A, 935)

To Michael Puchberg   *Vienna, 20 January 1790*

We are having the first instrumental rehearsal [of *Cosi fan tutte*] in the theater tomorrow. Haydn is coming with me. (A, 935)

Niemetschek, Biography of Mozart, 1808:

Mozart also soon became the most devoted admirer of the great unforgettable Joseph Haydn, who was even then already the pride of music, and who now, after Mozart's death, remains our sole darling and our joy. Mozart often referred to him as his teacher. (DDB, 504)

Johann Michael Haydn (1737–1806)

► Konzertmeister at the Salzburg court from 1763, Michael Haydn succeeded Mozart as cathedral organist in 1781. In 1783, when illness prevented Haydn from fulfilling a commission, Mozart came to his assistance by composing the duets for violin and viola, K. 423, 424. ◄

To Nannerl   *Bologna, 24 March 1770*

Tell me also how you like Haydn's minuets and whether they are better than his earlier ones. (A, 121)

► Nannerl had evidently heard twelve minuets by Michael Haydn in Salzburg; she sent a copy of the first violin part to Mozart who thereupon arranged the dances for keyboard for her. In July Nannerl sent Mozart six more Haydn minuets presumably in the same manner and for the same purpose.[17] ◄

To Nannerl   *Naples, 19 May 1770*

When I have more time, I shall send you Herr Haydn's minuets. I have already sent you the first one [Italian]. . . . I very much like the twelfth minuet of Haydn, which you have sent me. (A, 136–137)

To Nannerl   *Rome, 7 July 1770*

Send me soon the other six minuets by Haydn. (A, 148)

To Nannerl   *Bologna, 22 September 1770*

I like Haydn's six minuets better than the first twelve. We have often had to perform them for the countess [Pallavicini]. (A, 162)

To Leopold Mozart   *Munich, 6 October 1777*

At our little concert in the afternoon. We first played Haydn's two quintets.[18] (A, 300)

To Leopold Mozart   Paris, 9 July 1778

I had to laugh heartily about Haydn's tipsy fit. . . . It is really disgraceful that such an able man should through his own fault render himself incapable of performing his duties—at a service instituted in honor of God—in the presence of the Archbishop and the whole court—and with the church full of people. How disgusting! (A, 562)

To Leopold Mozart   Paris, 18 July 1778

I preluded in the manner of Fischietti, played off a galanterie sonata in the style and with the fire, spirit, and precision of Haydn, and then played fugues with all the skill of a Lipp, Hülber, and Aman.[19] (A, 570)

To Leopold Mozart   Vienna, 4 January 1783

Then there are a few counterpoint works by Eberlin copied out on small paper and bound in blue, and some things of Haydn, which I should like to have for the Baron van Swieten. Tell me, are there any really good fugues in Haydn's last mass or vesper music, or possibly in both? I should be very much obliged to you if you would have them both scored for me bit by bit. (A, 835)

To Leopold Mozart   Vienna, 12 March 1783

Send me in the meantime the *Tres sunt* by Haydn, which will do until you can let me have something else of his. Indeed I should very much like them to hear the *Lauda Sion.* The full score of the *Tres sunt* copied out in *my own handwriting* must be somewhere at home. The fugue "In te Domine speravi" has won great applause and so have the "Ave Maria" and the "Tenebrae" and so forth.[20] (A, 842)

To Nannerl   Vienna, 2 August 1788

I should very much like Haydn to lend me for a short time his two Tutti masses and the Graduale which he has composed, all of them in the original scores. Tell him that I shall return them with many thanks. It is now exactly a year since I wrote to him and invited him to come and stay with me, but he has not replied. As a matter of fact, as far as answering letters is concerned, he seems, don't you think, to have a good deal in common with myself. So I urge you to arrange this for me in the following way. Invite him to your house at St. Gilgen and play to him some of my latest compositions. I am sure he will like the Trio and the Quartet.[21] (A, 918)

To Choirmaster Stoll, Baden   *Vienna, 12 July 1791*

I have a request to make, and that is, that you would be so kind as to send
me by the first mail coach tomorrow my mass in B-flat [K. 275 (272b)]
which we performed last Sunday, and Michael Haydn's Graduale in B-flat,
"Pax vobis," which we also performed. I mean, of course, the parts, not
the scores. I have been asked to conduct a mass in a church. (A, 965
–966)

Franz Xaver Niemetschek, Life of Mozart, 1798

If [Mozart's] wife wanted to give him a special surprise at a family festivity,
she would secretly arrange a performance of a new church composition by
Michael or Joseph Haydn. (p. 72)

The Reminiscences of Constanze Mozart, 1829

He frequently compared his married fate with that of . . . the two Haydns,
Joseph and Michael. "But no one is so happy as I am in a wife," he would
exclaim. (Novello, 98)

Ignaz Holzbauer (1711–1783)[22]

► From 1753 to 1778, Holzbauer was Kapellmeister in Mannheim. His
most important work, the opera *Günther von Schwarzburg* (1777),
initiated new interest in German opera. ◄

To Leopold Mozart   *Mannheim, 4 November 1777*

Today, Sunday, I heard a mass by Holzbauer, which he wrote twenty-six
years ago, but which is very fine. He is a good composer, he has a good
church style, he knows how to write for voices and instruments, and he
composes good fugues. (A, 355–356)

To Leopold Mozart   *Mannheim, 14 November 1777*

Now for the opera, but quite briefly. Holzbauer's music is very beautiful.
The poetry [by Anton Klein] doesn't deserve such music. What surprises
me most of all is that a man as old as Holzbauer should still possess
such spirit; for you can't imagine what fire there is in that music. (A,
374)

To Leopold Mozart   *Mannheim, 22 November 1777*

I hope I told you that Holzbauer's grand opera is in German? If not, I am
telling you now. It is entitled *Günther von Schwarzburg.* (A, 385)

To Leopold Mozart   *Mannheim, 3 December 1777*

I heard one [mass] of Holzbauer's recently and it is quite in our style. (A, 402)

Johann Nepomuk Hummel (1778–1837)

► A celebrated pianist and composer, Hummel studied with Mozart in 1785 or 1786 to 1787. He served as Kapellmeister in Stuttgart (1816–1818), then Weimar (from 1819). Mozart never mentions Hummel in his letters, but Hummel's father recalled their first interview as follows: ◄

Mozart: "You know, my dear friend, I don't much like taking on pupils; it takes up too much of my time and disturbs me in my work. But let's see and hear what the boy's like, and whether he's worth helping. Sit down at the piano, then, and show us what you can do," he said to Nepomuk. The latter came out with a few small pieces by Bach which he had carefully practiced, and spread them out. . . . Wolfgang had sat down . . . and listened with his arms crossed. He became ever more still . . . When my boy had finished the Bach, Mozart placed another and not exactly easy composition before him, one of his own this time, to see how good his sight-reading might be. . . . Suddenly, with a look that sparkled and twinkled for joy, he put his hand on my knee, pressed it gently, and whispered to me, "You must leave the lad here with me. I shan't let him out of my sight—something can be made of him!" . . . And to me he said, "It's agreed, then, I'll teach the lad, but he must live with me so that I can always have my eye on him. He shall have everything free, lessons, lodging, food. You will not have any of the cares of looking after him. Agreed?"[23] (DDB, 570)

► It seems that Hummel in fact lived with the Mozart family during the years he was Mozart's pupil. ◄

Nicolò Jommelli (1714–1774)

► Jommelli, a reform-minded opera composer, combined Italian melodic style with German harmonic and orchestral techniques. He held numerous musical posts including that of Oberkapellmeister in Stuttgart (1753–1770). Mozart first made his acquaintance in Ludwigsburg in 1763. ◄

To Nannerl   *Naples, 29 May 1770*

The day before yesterday we were at the rehearsal of Signor Jommelli's opera [*Armida abbandonata*] which is well composed and which I really like. He himself spoke to us and was very polite. (A, 141)

To Nannerl   *Naples, 5 June 1770*

The opera here is one of Jommelli's; it is beautiful, but too serious and old-fashioned [*viel zu gescheid, und zu altvätterisch*] for the theater. (A, 143)

▶ Mozart's reservations presumably referred not to the opera's musical style, which in fact was rather modern, but to the elaborate stage effects it called for, such as "battles (including two with monsters) . . . and a disappearing palace."[24] Jommelli's music, as Mozart observed, was not only "beautiful" but "well composed," that is, with richer orchestral textures and accompaniements and more subtle attention to detail (especially in recitatives) than was currently in vogue in Naples—a circumstance that (along with the old-fashioned staging) may also have contributed to Mozart's second thoughts about the work.[25] ◀

▶ Jommelli's judgment of the seven-year-old Mozart, as reported by Leopold, is worth quoting here: ◀

Leopold Mozart to Lorenz Hagenauer: *Ludwigsburg, 11 July 1763*

But not until the morning of the 10th was I able to see Chief Kapellmeister Jommelli. . . . Jommelli . . . was heard to say that it was amazing and hardly believable that a child of German birth could have such unusual genius and so much understanding and passion. (A, 23)

Francesco di Maio (1732–1770)

▶ Along with Jommelli and Tommaso Traetta (1727–1779) di Maio was one of the more progressive Italian composers of opera seria. ◀

To Nannerl   *Naples, 29 May 1770*

We have also been to a church to hear some music composed by Signor Ciccio di Maio, which was most beautiful [bellissima]. He too spoke to us and was most gracious. [Italian]. (A, 141)

Padre Giovanni Battista Martini (1706–1784)

▶ Venerated scholar, teacher, and composer, Martini was a resident of Bologna. Among his counterpoint pupils were J. C. Bach, Jommelli, and Mozart (1770). ◀

Salzburg, 4 September 1776

[The following passage is in Italian.] The regard, the esteem and the respect which I cherish for your illustrious person have prompted me to trouble you with this letter and to send you a humble specimen of my music, which I submit to your masterly judgment.[26] . . . Oh, how I have longed to be near you, most Reverend Father, so that I might be able to talk to and have discussion with you. . . . Alas, that we are so far apart, my very dear Signor Padre Maestro! If we were together, I should have so many things to tell you! I send my devoted remembrances to all the members of the Accademia Filarmonica [Bologna]. I long to win your favor and I never cease to grieve that I am far away from that one person in the world whom I love, revere, and esteem most of all. (A, 265–267)

To Leopold Mozart   *Paris, 18 July 1778*

Padre Martini's letter to Raaff, in which he praises me, must have gone astray. . . . Now since the Elector [Karl Theodor] rightly thinks a lot of the Padre Maestro's opinion, I believe it would be a very good thing if you would be so kind as to ask him to send another letter about me to Raaff. It would surely be of good use; and good Padre Martini would not hesitate to do me this kindness twice over, as he knows well that in so doing he might make my fortune. It is to be hoped that he will write in such a manner that Raaff can show the letter, if need be, to the Elector. (A, 572)

Joseph Myslivecek (1737–1781)

► Myslivecek, a Czech composer of opera, oratorio, and instrumental music, was a close friend of the Mozart family since their first meeting in Bologna in 1770. He died of syphilis at the age of forty-three. ◄

To Nannerl   *Milan, 22 December 1770*

Find out whether they have this symphony of Myslivecek's in Salzburg (ex. 13.1). If not, we shall bring it back with us.[27] (A, 176)

EXAMPLE 13.1. Joseph Myslivecek: Symphony in C, Theme

To Leopold Mozart   *Munich, 11 October 1777*

Was I to know that Myslivecek, so good a friend of mine, was in a town, even in a corner of the world where I was and was I not to see him, to speak to him? Impossible! So I resolved to go and see him. . . . Although everyone, even the doctors had assured me that there was no longer any danger of infection, I did not want to go to his room, as it was very small and smelt rather strongly. . . . If it were not for his face, he would be the same old Myslivecek, full of fire, spirit and life, a little thin, of course, but otherwise the same excellent cheerful fellow. All Munich is talking about his oratorio *Abramo ed Isacco,* which he produced here. He has now finished, except for a few arias, a cantata or serenata for Lent. When his illness was at its worst, he composed an opera for Padua. But nothing can help him. Even here they all say that the Munich doctors and surgeons have done for him. He has a fearful cancer of the bone. The surgeon, Caco, that ass, burnt away his nose. Imagine what agony he must have suffered. (A, 302–306)

To Leopold Mozart   *Manneheim, 13 November 1777*

I know what Myslivecek's sonatas are like, for I played them at Munich. They are quite easy and pleasing to the ear. I should advise my sister . . . to play them with plenty of expression, taste, and fire, and to learn them by heart. For they are sonatas which are bound to please everyone, which are easy to memorize and very effective when played with the proper precision.[28] (A, 371)

To Abbé Joseph Bullinger   *Paris, 7 August 1778*

Why were they so careless as to let Myslivecek give them the slip?—and he was so near, too! He would have been a fat morsel for them [to fill the position of Kapellmeister at Salzburg]. It would not be easy to get someone like him and someone, moreover, who has been discharged from the Duke Clemens Conservatorio [the hospital in Munich]. He would have been the man to terrify the whole court orchestra by his presence. (A, 594 –595)

Giovanni Paisiello (1740–1816)

► Paisiello, a highly successful Neapolitan composer, especially of opera buffa, could count Catherine the Great and Napoleon among his patrons. His most famous work, *Il barbiere di Siviglia,* based on the play by Beaumarchais, had its premiere in St. Petersburg in September 1782 and entered the repertory of the Viennese Court opera in 1783. Its success there presumably motivated Mozart's interest in an operatic version of Beaumarchais' *Le mariage de Figaro.* ◄

To Leopold Mozart   *Vienna, 16 January 1782*

The Grand Duchess [of Russia] produced some sonatas by Paisiello (wretchedly written out in his own hand), of which I had to play the Allegros and Clementi the Andantes and Rondos. We then selected a theme from them and developed it on two pianofortes.[29] (A, 793)

To Leopold Mozart   *Vienna, 8 May 1784*

Paisiello is in Vienna at the moment on his way back from Russia. He is
going to write an opera [*Il Ré Teodoro in Venezia*] here. (A, 876)

To Leopold Mozart   *Vienna, 12 June 1784*

Tomorrow Herr Ployer, the agent, is giving a concert in the country . . .
where Fraülein Babette is playing her new concerto in G [K. 453], and I am
performing the quintet [for piano and winds in E-flat, K. 452]; we are then
playing together the grand sonata for two claviers [in D, K. 448 (375a)]. I
am fetching Paisiello in my carriage, as I want him to hear both my pupil
and my compositions. (A, 880)

To Gottfried von Jacquin   *Prague, 15 January 1787*

We heard *Le gare generose* [by Paisiello]. In regard to the performance of
this opera I can give no definite opinion because I talked a lot; but that
quite contrary to my usual custom I chattered so much may have been due
to . . . Well, never mind![30] (A, 904)

The Reminiscences of Michael Kelly, 1826

Just at the same period [spring, 1784], the celebrated Paisiello arrived at
Vienna, on his way to Naples, from Petersburg . . . I had the pleasure of
seeing him introduced to Mozart; it was gratifying to witness the
satisfaction which they appeared to feel by becoming acquainted; the
esteem which they had for each other was well known. The meeting took
place at Mozart's house. (Kelly, 1:234–235)

Ignaz Joseph Pleyel (1757–1831)

► A prolific composer, music publisher, and piano manufacturer, Pleyel
was active in Paris. Best known today for his instruments, Pleyel's
chamber music, close to Joseph Haydn's in style, was celebrated during
his lifetime. ◄

To Leopold Mozart   *Vienna, 24 April 1784*

I must tell you that some quartets have just appeared, composed by a
certain Pleyel, a pupil of Joseph Haydn. If you do not know them, do try
and get hold of them; you will find them worth the trouble. They are very
well written and most pleasing to listen to [*sehr gut geschrieben und sehr
angenehm*]. You will also see at once who was his master. Well, it will be a
lucky day for music if later on Pleyel should be able to replace Haydn.[31] (A,
875)

Joseph Schuster (1748-1812)

▶ Dresden Kapellmeister and a pupil of Padre Martini, Schuster was successful as a composer of German and Italian opera as well as chamber music. ◀

To Leopold Mozart   *Munich, 6 October 1777*

I send my sister herewith six duets for clavicembalo and violin by Schuster, which I have often played here. They are not bad. If I shall stay on I shall write six myself in the same style, as they are popular here. My main object in sending them to you is that you may amuse yourselves à deux. Addio.[32] (A, 300)

▶ There have been several attempts to discern Schuster's influence in Mozart's violin sonatas. Hermann Abert suggests that Mozart absorbed elements of Schuster's melodic style and also emulated his approach to the relationship between the two instruments, a relationship in which the violin and keyboard are of equal importance and yet are each treated idiomatically. He cites the following melody from Schuster's Divertimento in G minor (ex. 13.2)[33] ◀

EXAMPLE 13.2. Joseph Schuster: Divertimento da camera in G minor, Theme

▶ Richard Engländer draws a specific connection between this passage and example 13.3 from Mozart's Violin Sonata in G, K. 301 (293a).[34] ◀

EXAMPLE 13.3. Sonata in G, K. 301 (293a), Opening Theme

Johann Baptist Vanhal (1739–1813)

▶ Born in Bohemia, Vanhal settled in Vienna as an independent artist; he was an important and prolific composer of instrumental music. ◀

To Leopold Mozart   *Augsburg, 23 October 1777*

[At the Holy Cross Monastery] I performed a symphony and played Vanhal's violin concerto in B-flat, which was unanimously applauded.[35] (A, 338)

▶ Other composers were briefly, but favorably, mentioned by Mozart:

Johann Georg Albrechtsberger (1736–1809). Composer and Kapell-meister of the Cathedral in Vienna; Beethoven's teacher.

Florian Deller (1729–1773). Viennese composer of ballet music.

Johann Gottfried Eckardt (1735–1809). German-born keyboard composer, active in Paris.

Johann Friedrich Edelmann (1749–1794). Strasbourg-born keyboard composer, active in Paris.

Nikolaus Joseph Hüllmandel (1751–1823). Keyboard player and composer, active in France and London.

Jean Joseph Rodolphe (1730–1812). Composer and horn player, active in Paris.

Benedikt Schack (1758–1826). Viennese singspiel composer and singer in Emanuel Schickaneder's troupe; was the first Tamino.

Johann Schobert (ca. 1735–1767). German-born keyboard player and composer, active in Paris.

Johann Samuel Schröter (1752–1788). German-born keyboard player and composer; active in London.

Joseph Starzer (1726–1787). Viennese violinist and composer of ballet music. ◀

THE BAD

▶ Mozart's invective needs little explanation or comment. It eloquently and delightfully speaks for itself, ranging in tone from scathing ridicule to moral indignation. He normally dispatches his target with a single annihilating adjective (which is typically even more pungent in the original—provided here in brackets—than in the English translation): "wretched," "worthless," "dumb," "shoddy." But at times his contempt evolved gradually. (It is particularly fascinating to trace Mozart's growing disillusionment with the music of Anton Schweitzer.)

For the most part Mozart's negative judgments have been sustained by history; with the notable exception of Clementi, the individuals skewered here have fallen into oblivion, at least as living presences in our concert life. To the extent that Mozart's criticisms become specific, they extend from matters of taste—the perceived empty virtuosity of

Clementi's piano writing—to aesthetic judgment—Fischer's overly long concerto ritornelli—to fundamental technique—Graf's unnatural, overly brusque modulations. But Mozart's judgments do not always rest on aesthetic considerations alone. His withering criticism of Abbé Vogler reflects moral outrage at Vogler's professional behavior as well as being a dispassionate dismissal of what Mozart regarded as technical incompetence. ◄

Ignaz von Beecke (1733–1803)

► Pianist and composer of instrumental music, Beecke was music director to Prince Krafft Ernst of Öttingen-Wallerstein. While in Munich in March 1775, Mozart engaged Beecke in a piano contest. ◄

To Leopold Mozart   *Augsburg, 17 October 1777*

There [at Johann Andreas Stein's] I just played at sight a sonata by Beecke, which was rather hard and *miserabile al solito* [wretched as usual]. (A, 328)

To Leopold Mozart   *Mannheim, 13 November 1777*

Well, would Papa like to know how Beecke received me? . . . In short, he was very polite and I was the same, but perfectly serious. We fell to talking of various things, among others of Vienna, and how the Emperor was no great lover of music. "That is true," he said; "he knows something about counterpoint, but that is all. I can still remember (here he rubbed his forehead) that when I had to play to him, I had not the least idea what to play. So I started to play fugues and such-like foolery, and all the time I played I was laughing up my sleeve." When I heard this, I was scarcely able to contain myself and felt that I should love to say to him: "Sir, I well believe that you laughed, but surely not as heartily as I should have done, had I been listening to you." (A, 368–369)

Muzio Clementi (1752–1832)

► Clementi (fig. 13.1) was a keyboard virtuoso and prolific composer of piano music as well as a publisher and piano manufacturer; he settled in England in 1774. Mozart met Clementi during the latter's continental tour. It is difficult to know which Mozart despised more: Clementi's compositions or his piano playing. ◄

To Leopold Mozart   *Vienna, 7 June 1783*

Well, I have a few words to say to my sister about Clementi's sonatas (ex. 13.4 a,b). Everyone who either hears them or plays them must feel that as compositions they are worthless [*nichts heist*]. They contain no remarkable or striking passages except those in sixths or octaves.[36] (A, 850)

EXAMPLE 13.4a. Clementi: Piano Sonata in C, Op. 7, No. 2: Movement 1, mm. 68–77

EXAMPLE 13.4b. Op. 7, No. 2: Movement 3, Opening Measures

FIGURE 13.1. Muzio Clementi

Johann Christian Fischer (1733–1800)

► Fischer was active in Dresden, later London (where he married the daughter of the painter Thomas Gainsborough). In 1774 Mozart wrote a set of variations on a minuet by Fischer (K. 179/189a). ◄

To Leopold Mozart   *Vienna, 4 April 1787*

Ramm and the two Fischers, the bass singer [J. I. Ludwig Fischer] and the oboist from London [Johann Christian], came here this Lent. The long and short of it is that he plays like a bad beginner . . . And then his concertos! His own compositions! Why, each ritornello lasts a quarter of an hour; and then our hero comes in, lifts up one leaden foot after the other and stamps on the floor with each in turn. (A, 907)

Johann Philipp Freyhold (dates unknown)

► Freyhold claimed to have been a flautist in the service of the Elector of
Mainz; he is known to have performed concerts in Frankfurt as well as
in Vienna. ◄

To Leopold Mozart   *Vienna, 20 February 1784*

Yesterday I was fortunate enough to hear Herr Freyhold play a concerto of
his own wretched composition.[37] . . . I was delighted that the Adagio,
which by the way he played at your house, was very short . . . The rondo
ought to be jolly, but it was the silliest stuff [*das dümmste zeug*] in the world.
As soon as I heard the first Allegro, I realized that if Herr Freyhold would
only learn composition properly, he would not be a bad composer. (A,
867)

Florian Gassmann (1729–1774)

► In 1764 Gassmann succeeded Gluck in Vienna as a composer of ballet
music; he was appointed Court Kapellmeister in 1772 and founded the
Vienna Tonkünstler-Societät. Gassmann recruited Antonio Salieri to
Vienna and provided for his education. ◄

To Leopold Mozart   *Vienna, 5 February 1783*

[*Liebe im Streit*] is to be given, the music of which . . . is by a young
Viennese [Johann Mederitsch (1752–1835)]. . . . It will probably not be a
success. Still, it is better stuff than its predecessor, an old opera by
Gassmann, *La notte critica*, in German, *Die unruhige Nacht*, which with
difficulty survived three performances. (A, 839)

Friedrich Hartmann Graf (1727–1795)

► A flute virtuoso and music director in Augsburg from 1772, Graf is best
known as a composer of chamber music, he was also active in
London. ◄

To Leopold Mozart   *Mannheim, 14 October 1777*

[Johann Andreas Stein] then talked a great deal about a certain composer,
called Graf, who, however, has only written flute concertos. He said,
"Now Graf is something quite exceptional," and all that kind of *exaggerated* talk. I was sweating with fright, my head, my hand, and my whole
body. . . . [Graf's] words are all on stilts and he generally opens his mouth
before he knows what he wants to say; and often it shuts again without
having done anything. After many compliments he performed a concerto
for two flutes. I had to play the first violin part. This is what I think of it. It

is not at all pleasing to the ear, not a bit natural. He often plunges into a
new key far too brusquely and it is all quite devoid of charm. When it was
over, I praised him very highly, for he really deserves it. The poor fellow
must have taken a great deal of trouble over it and he must have studied
hard enough. (A, 316–317)

Paul Grua (1753–1833)

▶ Grua was a violinist in the Mannheim orchestra and later Court
Kapellmeister in Munich. ◀

To Leopold Mozart   *Munich, 13 November 1780*

I have heard only one mass by Grua. Things like this one could easily turn
out at the rate of half a dozen a day. (A, 663–664)

Wenzel Müller (1767–1835)

▶ From 1786 to 1830 Müller was Kapellmeister at the Leopoldstädter-
Theater in Vienna; he was also a successful composer of singspiels for
the Volkstheater. ◀

To Constanze, Baden   *Vienna, 12 June 1791*

To cheer myself up I then went to the Kasperle Theater to see the new
opera *Der Fagottist* [*Kaspar der Fagottist,* by Wenzel Müller], which is making
such a sensation, but which is shoddy stuff [*gar nichts daran*]. (A, 954)

Johann Gottlieb Naumann (1741–1801)

▶ Naumann, although now obscure, was the most prominent Dresden
composer between Hasse and Weber. ◀

To Constanze   *Dresden, 16 April 1789*

On Monday, April 13th . . . we all went to the court chapel. The mass was
by Naumann, who conducted it himself, and very poor stuff [*sehr
Mittelmäßig:* i.e., mediocre] it was. (A, 922)

Anton Schweitzer (1735–1787)

▶ Active in Weimar and Gotha, Schweitzer was important in the establishment of German national opera, and possibly the originator of the
melodrama. ◀

To Leopold Mozart   *Mannheim, 22 November 1777*

During the next carnival *Rosemunde* will be performed, a new text by

Wieland with new music by Schweitzer. Both of them are coming here. I have already seen some of the opera and played it on the clavier, but I will not say anything about it yet. (A, 385)

To Leopold Mozart   *Mannheim, 3 December 1777*

Herr Kapellmeister Schweitzer is a good, worthy, honest fellow, dry and smooth like our [Michael] *Haydn* [code], but better spoken. There are some very beautiful passages in his new opera and I do not doubt that it will be a real success. His *Alceste* [1773], which is not half as fine as *Rosemunde*, was very popular. The fact that it was the first German singspiel had, of course, a lot to do with it.[38] It no longer makes so strong an impression on people who are only carried away by novelty. (A, 401)

To Leopold Mozart   *Mannheim, 10 January 1778*

Today there was a rehearsal of *Rosemunde* in the theater. It is—good, but *nothing more* [code]. If it were bad, they couldn't produce it, could they? (A, 444)

To Leopold Mozart   *Paris, 11 September 1778*

[Aloysia Weber] has one aria [in *Rosemunde*] where something good might be expected from the ritornello, but the voice part is alla Schweitzer, as if dogs were yelping [*als wenn die hund bellen wollten*]. She has only one song, a sort of rondo in the second act, where she has an opportunity of sustaining her voice a little and showing what she can do. Yes, unhappy indeed is the singer, male or female, who falls into Schweitzer's hands, for as long as he lives he will never learn how to write for the voice! (A, 616)

To Leopold Mozart   *Kaisersheim, 18 December 1778*

Well, that melancholy *Alceste* by Schweitzer is now being performed in Munich. The best part (besides some of the openings, middle passages, and the finales of a few arias) is the beginning of the recitative "O Jugendzeit" [act 4, scene 2]—and it was Raaff's contribution which *made this a success* . . . But the worst part of all (though most of it is bad) is undoubtedly the overture. (A, 642)

Anton Stamitz (1754–1809) and Karl Stamitz (1745–1801)

► Both Stamitz brothers were instrumental composers, violinists, and violists in the Mannheim orchestra; they moved to Paris together in 1770. ◄

To Leopold Mozart   *Paris, 9 July 1778*

Of the two Stamitz brothers only the younger one is here, the elder (the real composer à la Hafeneder) is in London. They indeed are two wretched scribblers [2 *Elende Notenschmierer*], gamblers, swillers, and adulterers— not the kind of people for me. The one who is here has scarcely a decent coat to his back. (A, 566)

Ignaz Umlauf (1746–1796)

► Viennese composer Umlauf was Kapellmeister of Joseph II's National Singspiel Theater from 1778, and, from 1782, assistant conductor of the Vienna court orchestra. His *Die Bergknappen* (1778) was the first work performed by the German National Singspiel. ◄

To Leopold Mozart   *Vienna, 6 October 1781*

Umlauf has been obliged to wait for his opera [presumably *Das Irrlicht*], which is ready and which took him a whole year to write. But (between ourselves) you must not believe that the opera is any good, just because it took him a whole year. I should have thought (again between ourselves) that it was the work of fourteen or fifteen days, particularly as the fellow must have learned so many operas *by heart*, and all he had to do was to sit down—and that is precisely how he composed it—you notice it at once when you hear it! (A, 772)

To Leopold Mozart   *Vienna, 21 December 1782*

A new opera, or rather a comedy with ariettas by Umlauf, entitled *Welche ist die beste Nation?* was performed the other day [December 13]—a wretched piece [*ein Elendes Stück*] which I could have set to music, but which I refused to undertake, adding that whoever should compose music for it without altering it completely would run the risk of being hooted off the stage; had it not been Umlauf's, it would certainly have been hooted; but being his, it was only hissed. Indeed it was no wonder, for even with the finest music no one could have tolerated such a piece. But, what is more, the music is so bad that I do not know whether the poet or the composer will carry off the prize for inanity.[39] To its disgrace it was performed a second time; but I think we may now say *Punctum satis*. (A, 832)

To Leopold Mozart   *Vienna, 5 February 1783*

. . . that execrable [*exegrable*] opera by Umlauf [*Welche ist die beste Nation?*], about which I wrote to you and which never got so far as a third performance. (A, 839)

Abbé Georg Joseph Vogler (1749–1814)

▶ Vice-Kapellmeister in Mannheim (later Kapellmeister in Munich and Darmstadt), Vogler (fig. 13.2) was famous as a virtuoso organist, clavier player, improviser, and theorist; his compositions, however, were considered pedantic. He was a pupil of Padre Martini and the teacher of Weber and Meyerbeer. ◀

To Leopold Mozart   *Mannheim, 31 October 1777*

They rehearsed a Psalm—a Magnificat—by Vogler, the Deputy-Kapell-meister here, and it lasted almost an hour. (A, 350–351)

To Leopold Mozart   *Mannheim, 4 November 1777*

Deputy-Kapellmeister Vogler, who had composed the mass which was performed the other day, is a dreary musical jester, an exceedingly

FIGURE 13.2. Abbé Vogler

conceited and rather incompetent fellow. The whole orchestra dislikes him. (A, 356)

To Leopold Mozart   *Mannheim, 13 November 1777*

Let me give you a short history of Vogler. He came here, absolutely down and out, performed on the clavier and composed a ballet. People took pity on him and the Elector [Karl Theodor] sent him to Italy [early 1773]. When the Elector happened to be in Bologna [1774], he asked Padre Vallotti about him and received this reply: *"Oh, Your Highness, he is a great man!"* [Italian]. He also asked Padre Martini, who informed him: *"Oh, Your Highness, he is good; and gradually, as he becomes older and surer of himself, he will improve. But he will have to change considerably"* [Italian]. When Vogler returned to Mannheim, he took orders and was immediately made court chaplain. He produced a Miserere which, everyone tells me, simply cannot be listened to, for it sounds all wrong. Hearing that his composition was not receiving much praise, Vogler went to the Elector and complained that the orchestra were playing it badly on purpose. In a word, he was so clever at pulling strings (he had had more than one naughty little affair with women, who were useful to him) that he was appointed Deputy-Kapellmeister. But he is a fool, who imagines that he is the very pitch of perfection. The whole orchestra, from A to Z, detest him. He has caused Holzbauer a great deal of annoyance . . . He disparages the great masters. Why, he has even belittled [Johann Christian] Bach to me.[40] (A, 369–370)

THE INDIFFERENT

▶ Finally, there are inevitably those composers whose talents, so far as we can tell, failed to elicit from Mozart a powerful response—positive or negative. He finds the fugues of Eberlin "trivial" when measured against the standard of Bach's or Handel's; but how many composers could fare much better? On others Mozart bestows his praise, but that praise is tepid—for example, his characterization of the music of Cambini, Fiala, and Righini as *recht Hübsch*, that is, "quite charming" or "pretty." Mozart obviously has a favorable opinion about some of his father's church music; but could he actually have considered Leopold to be anything more than a composer of quite limited talents? Could Mozart be expected to have rendered an objective judgment at all about his father's abilities as a composer? Conversely, could he have been perfectly (or even imperfectly) objective in assessing the talents of his serious rivals: Anfossi, or Martin, or Salieri? Can we justifiably conclude from his sharp description of Salieri's German opera *Der Rauchfangkehrer* [The Chimney Sweep] as "wretched" that Mozart actually regarded this clearly distrusted—but clearly formidable—rival with anything like the contempt he harbored for an Abbé Vogler? On balance one

suspects that Mozart would have been content to allow them all—
Leopold, Salieri, and the rest of the merely competent—to share this
lukewarm realm well to the south of Parnassus. ◄

Pasquale Anfossi (1727–1797)

► Anfossi was a prolific composer of operas and oratorios; among his
numerous positions was that of maestro di coro of the "Ospedale" in
Venice and Music Director of the King's Theatre, London. ◄

To Leopold Mozart   *Vienna, 2 July 1783*

Anfossi's opera *Il curioso indiscreto*, in which Madame Lange and Adamberger appeared for the first time, was performed the day before yesterday,
Monday, for the first time. It failed completely, with the exception of my
two arias. (A, 853–854)[41]

Giuseppe Maria Cambini (1746–1825)

► A violinist and prolific composer of instrumental music, Cambini was
best known for his string quartets and quintets, and his *sinfonie
concertanti;* he was a resident of Paris. ◄

To Leopold Mozart   *Paris, 1 May 1778*

I had to write the sinfonia [sinfonia concertante for wind instruments, K.
297B] in a great hurry and I worked very hard at it . . . When I went to the
concert on the two days when it should have been performed, . . . my
sinfonia concertante was not being played. . . . I believe . . . that Cambini,
an Italian maestro here, is at the bottom of the business. For in all
innocence, I swept the floor with him at our first meeting at Le Gros's
house. He has composed some quartets, one of which I heard at
Mannheim. They were quite pretty [*recht hüpsch*]. I praised them to him
and played the beginning of the one I had heard. But Ritter, Ramm, and
Punto, who were there, gave me no peace, urging me to go on and telling
me that what I could not remember I myself could supply. This I did, so
that Cambini was quite beside himself and could not help saying: "*What a
head!*" [Italian]. But I am convinced that he did not enjoy it. (A, 532–533)

Johann Ernst Eberlin (1702–1762)

► Eberlin was court and cathedral Kapellmeister in Salzburg and friend of
the Mozart family. In 1761 Mozart participated in a performance of one
of Eberlin's oratorios. ◄

To Leopold Mozart   *Vienna, 10 April 1782*

I have been intending to ask you . . . to enclose . . . Handel's six fugues and Eberlin's toccatas and fugues.[42] I should like the Baron [van Swieten] to hear Eberlin's, too. (A, 800)

To Nannerl   *Vienna, 20 April 1782*

If Papa has not yet had those works by Eberlin copied, so much the better, for in the meantime I have got hold of them and now I see (for I had forgotten them) that they are unfortunately far too trivial [*gar zu geringe*] to deserve a place beside Handel and Bach. With due respect for his four-part composition I may say that his clavier fugues are nothing but long drawn-out voluntaries [*versettl*]. (A, 801)

Joseph Fiala (1748/54?–1816)

► Fiala was an oboist, cellist, and composer, active in Munich, later (with the help of the Mozart family) Salzburg, then St. Petersburg, and finally Donaueschingen. ◄

To Leopold Mozart   *Munich, 3 October 1777*

About half past nine in the evening a small orchestra . . . came up to the house. . . . You can tell at once that Fiala has trained them. They played some of his compositions and I must say they were very pretty [*recht hübsch*] and that he has some very good ideas [*sehr gute gedancken*]. (A, 293)

François-Joseph Gossec (1734–1829)

► Opera and symphony composer Gossec was founder of the Concert des Amateurs in Paris (1769) and also served as co-director of the Concert Spirtuel and the Paris Opéra. ◄

To Leopold Mozart   *Paris, 5 April 1778*

Mr. Gossec . . . is a very good friend of mine and at the same time a very dull fellow [*sehr trockner Mann*]. (A, 521)

Leopold Kozeluch (1747–1818)

► Czech composer, pianist, and publisher, Kozeluch was Mozart's successor as chamber Kapellmeister and court composer, and allegedly his severe detractor in Prague. ◄

To Leopold Mozart   *Vienna, 4 July 1781*

The Archbishop secretly offered 1,000 gulden to Kozeluch, who, however, has declined, saying that he was better off in Vienna and that unless he could improve his position, he would never leave. But to his friends he added: "What deters me most of all is that affair with Mozart. If the Archbishop lets such a man go, what on earth would he not do to me?" So you see how he knows me and appreciates my talents. (A, 749)

Vicente Martín y Soler (1754–1806)

► Soler was active in Italy, Vienna, and St. Petersburg. His opere buffe were enormously successful, especially those written in Vienna to libretti of Lorenzo Da Ponte. Mozart quotes a tune from his most successful work, *Una cosa rara* (1786), in the banquet scene of *Don Giovanni*. ◄

To Constanze, Baden   *Vienna, 2 June 1790*

Yesterday I was at the second part of *Cosa rara*, but I did not like it as much as *Die Antons* [i.e., *Der dumme Gärtner oder Die zween Anton* by Benedict Schack]. (A, 940)

Leopold Mozart (1719–1787)

► Leopold Mozart was a violinist, teacher, and composer, active at the court of Salzburg since 1740, where he ultimately (1762) attained the position of Vice-Kapellmeister. Apart from his role in the life of his son, he is most famous as the author of the influential violin method, *Versuch einer gründlichen Violinschule* [A Treatise on the Fundamental Principles of Violin Playing] (Augsburg, 1756). He composed secular and sacred vocal works, but his most famous compositions are the "Musical Sleigh Ride," and the *Toy* Symphony, the latter long attributed to Haydn. ◄

To Padre Martini   *Salzburg, 4 September 1776*

My father is in the service of the Cathedral. . . . He has already served this court for thirty-six years and as he knows that the present Archbishop cannot and will not have anything to do with people who are getting on in years; he no longer puts his whole heart into his work, but has taken up literature, which was always a favorite study of his [Italian].[43] (A, 266)

To Leopold Mozart   *Vienna, 29 March 1783*

What we should like to have as well, my dearest father, is some of your best church music, for we like to amuse ourselves with all kinds of masters, ancient and modern. So I beg you to send us very soon some of your own compositions. (A, 844)

Niccolò Piccinni (1728–1800)

► Composer of French and Italian opera, Piccinni's comic opera *La buona figliuola* (Rome, 1762) was immensely successful. In 1776 he settled in

Paris and became the focus of a controversy on the relative merits of
Italian ("musical") and French ("dramatic") opera, the latter represented by Gluck. ◄

To Nannerl   *Milan, 26 January 1770*

Signor Piccinni, who is writing the next opera, is here. I have heard that his
is called *Cesare in Egitto*. (A, 111)

To Leopold Mozart   *Mannheim, 28 February 1778*

The only fault found with Piccinni's new opera *Roland* is that the choruses
are too meager and weak, and that the music on the whole is a little
monotonous [*zu einförmig*]; otherwise it was universally liked. (A, 498)

To Leopold Mozart   *Paris, 9 July 1778*

I spoke to Piccinni at the Concert Spirituel. He is most polite to me and I to
him when—by chance—we do meet. Otherwise I do not seek acquaintanceship, either with him or with any other composer. I understand my
job—and so do they—and that is enough. (A, 564)

To Leopold Mozart   *Paris, 11 September 1778*

I can do as well as Piccinni—although I am only a German. (A, 614)

Franz Xaver Richter (1709–1789)

► Composer mostly of church music and symphonies, Richter was active
at Mannheim and later Kapellmeister at Strasbourg Cathedral. ◄

To Leopold Mozart   *Strasbourg, 2 November 1778*

Kapellmeister Richter . . . now lives very economically, for instead of forty
bottles of wine a day he swills about twenty. (A, 629)

Vincenzo Righini (1756–1812)

► Composer, singing teacher, and conductor, Righini is most remembered
today owing to Beethoven's set of variations on a theme of his. In 1789
he was appointed director of the Italian Opera in Vienna; he was later
active in Mainz and Berlin. ◄

To Leopold Mozart   *Vienna, 29 August 1781*

I know nothing of Signor Righini's success. He makes a good deal of
money by teaching, and last Easter he was successful with his cantata [*La
sorpresa amorosa*], which was performed twice in succession and had good
receipts on both occasions. He composes *very charmingly* [*recht hüpsch*] and

he is not by any means superficial; but he is a monstrous thief. He offers his stolen goods in such superfluity, in such profusion, that people can hardly digest them. (A, 762)

Antonio Salieri (1750–1825)

► Salieri (fig. 13.3) was just five years older than Mozart. In 1774, at the age of 24, he succeeded Florian Gassmann as Court Composer and Conductor of the Italian Opera in Vienna. That is, he had been occupying one of the leading musical positions in Europe for seven years by the time Mozart moved to Vienna. In 1788 Salieri assumed the even loftier title of Court Kapellmeister—a position he held for the next thirty-six years, until a year before his death on 7 May 1825. In 1823, a rumor circulated that Salieri, who was suffering from a violent illness at the time and had expected to die, had confessed that he had poisoned Mozart. Whether he actually made the confession is not known. In any event the rumor made the rounds, and was even reported to the deaf Beethoven in one of his conversation books. It is clear that, with his influence at court, Salieri was in a position to help Mozart, had he chosen to. But he chose not to. There is no evidence, however, that Salieri ever actively plotted against Mozart, much less that he murdered him. Nonetheless, the dramatic potential of such a deed has attracted playwrights for more than a century: from Alexander Pushkin (whose play *Mozart and Salieri* was set to music by Rimsky-Korsakov) to Peter Shaffer (whose play *Amadeus* was made into a film by Milos Forman). ◄

To Leopold Mozart   *Vienna, 15 December 1781*

As for the Princess of Württemberg and myself, all is over. The Emperor has spoiled everything, for he cares for no one but Salieri. The Archduke Maximilian recommended *me* to her and she replied that had it rested with her, she would never have engaged anyone else, but that on account of her singing the Emperor had suggested Salieri.[44] (A, 782)

To Leopold Mozart   *Vienna, 8 May 1782*

Please write and tell me how Salieri's opera [*Semiramide*] in Munich went off. I am sure that you managed to hear it, but, if not, you are certain to know how it was received. (A, 804)

To Leopold Mozart   *Vienna, 31 August 1782*

You wonder how I can flatter myself that I shall be maestro to the Princess [of Württemberg]? Why, Salieri is not capable of teaching her the clavier! All he can do is try to injure me in this matter by recommending someone else, which quite possibly he is doing! (A, 818)

FIGURE 13.3. Antonio Salieri

To Leopold Mozart   *Vienna, 7 May 1783*

[Da Ponte] has to write *per obbligo* an entirely new libretto for Salieri [*Il ricco d'un giorno*], which will take him two months. He has promised after that to write a new libretto for me . . . If he is in league with Salieri, I shall never get anything out of him. (A, 848)

To Leopold Mozart *Vienna, 10 December 1783*

I am writing in the greatest haste to tell you that I have already bought the opera *Der Rauchfangkehrer* [music by Salieri] and have it at home. If the mail coach leaves for Salzburg next Sunday, I shall send it along with the two concertos. . . . Judging by your letter you seem to think that *Der Rauchfangkehrer* is an Italian opera! Not at all. It is a German and, what is more, a wretched work [*Elendes*], the author of which is Doctor Auernszucker [Josef Leopold Auenbrugger] in Vienna. You will remember that I told you about it and of how Herr Fischer [the basso] publicly damned it in the theater.[45] (A, 863)

Giuseppe Sarti (1729–1802)

► Sarti was a student of Padre Martini, active as a composer of operas and vocal music in Italy, St. Petersburg (as Paisiello's successor), and Vienna. Mozart quoted a tune from Sarti's *Fra i due litiganti* in *Don Giovanni.* ◄

To Leopold Mozart *Vienna, 8 May 1784*

Sarti is expected here any day on his way through to Russia. (A, 876)

To Leopold Mozart *Vienna, 12 June 1784*

Sarti is a good honest fellow! I have played a great deal to him and have composed variations on an air of his which pleased him exceedingly.[46] (A, 880)

► Mozart mentioned other composers in passing, with little or faint praise:

Giuseppe Bonno (1710–1788). Court Kapellmeister in Vienna since 1774.

Pasquale Cafaro (1706–1787). Neapolitan opera composer.

Ernst Eichner (1740–1777). Mannheim violinist, bassoonist, and composer.

Johann Mederitsch (1752–1835). Viennese composer of theater music.

Antonio Maria Gasparo Sacchini (1730–1786). Celebrated opera composer.

Franz Xaver Süssmayr (1766–1803).

Baron Gottfried van Swieten (1733–1803). ◄

14

Performers

► This chapter complements earlier discussions of performance and opera. It reaffirms Mozart's strong opinions and convictions on such matters as proper singing, acting, and playing, and above all, his insistence on precision and expression, and his disdain for empty virtuosity. Often enough, Mozart limits his comments to a concise, professional assessment of a performer—perhaps approving, perhaps annihilating. But the focus this time is not on principles alone, but on people. Mozart permits himself here to venture at times beyond the rendering of aesthetic judgments. The tone is often chatty and catty, amused and amusing.

Occasionally, we behold Mozart exercising his formidable dramaturgical talents (although, clearly enough, not in his preferred medium) and indulging his adroitness at observing and rendering human vanities and foibles, especially those of his fellow artists. A number of the amusing and poignant characters presented in this chapter are potentially as intriguing as the imaginary figures who strut upon Mozart's operatic stage. But this time they are real characters who played greater or lesser roles in the drama of Mozart's life—some of them by portraying the fictional characters who populate Mozart's operas. But unlike the rich, compelling portraits we encounter in Mozart's operatic masterpieces, those here, admittedly, are rarely more than incomplete sketches.

The entrance of the dramatis personae begins with the singers— separated (as far as it is possible to infer from Mozart's remarks) into the Good and the Tolerable, on the one hand, the Wanting and the Miserable, on the other.[1] ◄

SINGERS

THE MAGNIFICENT AND THE TOLERABLE

Johann Valentin Adamberger (1740–1804)

► Arguably Mozart's favorite tenor, the Munich-born Adamberger joined the Vienna Hofoper in 1780; the roles of Belmonte (*Die Entführung aus* dem Serail), Herr Vogelsang (*Der Schauspieldirektor*), and several arias were composed for him. According to a contemporary Viennese publication, the *Allgemeiner Theater Almanach vom Jahr 1782*, Adamberger played "leading young lovers, gentle and ardent."[2] ◄

To Leopold Mozart   *Vienna, 26 September 1781*

Let me now turn to Belmonte's aria in A major, "O wie ängstlich, o wie feurig" . . . This is the favorite aria of all those who have heard it, and it is mine also. I wrote it expressly to suit Adamberger's voice.[3] (A, 769)

To Anton Klein   *Vienna, 21 May 1785*

Madame Cavalieri, Adamberger, Mlle. [Thérèse] Teiber, all Germans of whom Germany may well be proud.[4] (A 890)

Maddalena Allegranti (1750–1802)

► Popular in Mannheim during the 1770s, Allegranti was also successful in Dresden in the 1780s and 1790s, especially in opera buffa roles. ◄

To Constanze   *Dresden, 16 April 1789*

We went to the opera, which is truly wretched . . . The leading woman singer, Madame Allegranti, is far better than Madame [Adriana] Ferraresi, which, I admit, is not saying very much. (A, 924)

"Bastardella" (Lucrezia Agujari) (1743–1783)

► An illegitimate child (hence her nickname) renowned for her passage work and her three-and-a-half octave range, Bastardella sang in the premiere of Paisiello's *Peleo e Teti* (1768) in Naples. ◄

To Nannerl   *Bologna, 24 March 1770*

In Parma we got to know a singer and heard her perform very beautifully in her own house—the famous Bastardella who has (1) a beautiful voice, (2) a marvelous throat, (3) an incredible range. While I was present she sang the following notes and passages (ex. 14.1).

Francesco Benucci (ca. 1745–1824)

► A celebrated basso buffo, Benucci sang in the premieres of three Mozart operas: Figaro in *Le nozze di Figaro*, Leporello in the Viennese production of *Don Giovanni*, and Guglielmo in *Così fan tutte*. ◄

EXAMPLE 14.1. Vocal Coloratura of "Bastardella" (A, 121)

To Leopold Mozart   *Vienna, 7 May 1783*

Well, the Italian opera buffa has started again here and is very popular.
The buffo is particularly good—his name is Benucci. (A, 847)

Antonia Bernasconi (1741–1803)

▶ Successful in both serious and comic roles, Bernasconi sang in the
premieres of Gluck's *Alceste* (1767) and *Iphigénie en Tauride* (1781), and
created the role of Aspasia in Mozart's *Mitridate* (1770). Mozart's
opinion of her was obviously mixed. ◀

To Leopold Mozart   *Vienna, 27 June 1781*

Madame Bernasconi is here and is drawing a salary of five hundred ducats
because she sings all her arias a good comma higher than others.[5] This is
really a great achievement, for she always keeps in tune. She has now
promised to sing a quarter of a tone higher still, but on condition that she
is paid twice as much. (A, 748)

To Leopold Mozart   *Vienna, 29 August 1781*

What is certain is that she was really forced on the Emperor. The great herd of the nobility are very much taken with her, but in his heart of hearts not the Emperor, who in fact is as little taken with her as he is with Gluck. Nor is she a favorite with the public. It is true that in great tragic parts she will always remain Bernasconi, but in operettas she is a total failure, as they no longer suit her. Moreover, as she herself admits, she is more Italian than German, and her accent on the stage is as thoroughly Viennese as it is in ordinary conversation. So now you can picture her to yourself. And when she occasionally tries to correct her accent, it is just as if you were to hear a princess declaim in a puppet show. Her singing too is now so bad that no one will compose for her. But that she may not draw her 500 ducats for nothing, the Emperor (with some difficulty) has been induced to have Gluck's *Iphigenie* and *Alceste* performed—the former in German, the latter in Italian. (A, 762)

Castrati

To Padre Martini   *Salzburg, 4 September 1776*

As for the theater [in Salzburg], *we are in a bad way for lack of singers. We have no castrati, and we shall never have them, because they insist on being handsomely paid; and generosity is not one of our faults* [Italian]. (A, 266)

▶ The castrato voice was no more fixed in range or quality than that of other singers, male or female. Among the quintet of castrati who enjoyed Mozart's favorable opinion (alphabetically: Giuseppe Aprile, Vincenzo Caselli, Francesco Ceccarelli, Giovanni Manzuoli, and Ludovico Marchesi), we encounter three sopranos, a mezzo-soprano, and an alto. ◀

Giuseppe Aprile (1731–1813)

▶ Aprile was an alto, celebrated for his phenomenal technique, especially his trills. ◀

To Nannerl   *Milan, 26 January 1770*

Aprile, primo uomo, sings well and has a beautiful even voice. We heard him in a church when there happened to be a great festival. (A, 111)

To Nannerl   *Naples, 5 June 1770*

The opera here is one of Jommelli's. . . . De Amicis sings amazingly well and so does Aprile, who sang in Milan. (A, 143)

Vincenzo [or Michele?] Caselli (dates unknown)

▶ Mozart designates Caselli as a "primo uomo"—a term normally applied at the time to castrati. According to Leopold Mozart, he was a soprano. (See MBA 1: 305). After his debut in Milan in 1733, Caselli enjoyed a long career in Italy. ◄

To Nannerl   *Milan, 26 January 1770*

The opera at Mantua was charming. They played *Demetrio* [libretto by Metastasio, music by Hasse]. . . . The primo uomo, il musico, sings beautifully, though his voice is uneven. His name is Caselli. (A, 110)

Francesco Ceccarelli (1752–1814)

► Ceccarelli was a soprano at the Salzburg court from 1778 to 1788; Mozart composed for him the recitative and aria "A questo seno deh vieni"—"Or che il cielo a me ti rende," K. 374 (1781). ◄

Nannerl to Wolfgang and Mother, Mannheim   *Salzburg, 27 October 1777*

A castrato who happened to be passing through sang yesterday at court. Papa was there and heard him, but he did not like his singing particularly, for he has a rather nasal voice and is a long-legged fellow with a long face and a low forehead. All the same, he sings far better than Madame Duschek. As the Archbishop is of the same opinion, perhaps he will take him into his service. (A, 342)

To Abbé Bullinger   *Paris, 7 August 1778*

We have a castrato. You know what sort of animal he is? He can sing high treble and can thus take a woman's part to perfection. The Chapter would interfere, of course. But, all the same, interference is better than intercourse; and they wouldn't worry him to any great extent. Meanwhile let Ceccarelli be sometimes man, sometimes woman.[6] (A, 595)

To Leopold Mozart   *Vienna, 6 October 1781*

As for Ceccarelli, I am quite sure that he will be appointed, for indeed I don't know where the Archbishop could find a better castrato *for the money.*[7] (A, 771)

Giovanni Manzuoli (1720–1782)

► Manzuoli was a soprano/mezzo soprano from whom Mozart took voice lessons in London in November/December 1764; he was celebrated for the power and sonority of his voice and for his dignified singing style. ◄

To Nannerl   *Rome, 21 April 1770*

Manzuoli is negotiating with the Milanese to sing in my opera [*Mitridate*] . . . [He] is demanding a thousand ducats.[8] (A, 130–131)

To Nannerl   *Milan, 24 November 1771*

Manzuoli, who up to the present has been generally looked upon as the most sensible of the castrati, has in his old age given the world a sample of his stupidity and conceit. He was engaged for the opera [viz., Hasse's *Ruggiero*] at a salary of five hundred cigliati, but, as the contract did not mention the serenata [viz., *Ascanio in Alba*, K. 111], he demanded another five hundred for that, that is, one thousand cigliati in all.[9] The court only gave him seven hundred and a fine gold snuffbox (quite enough, I think). But he like a true castrato returned both the seven hundred cigliati and the snuffbox and went off without anything. I do not know how it will all end—badly, I expect.[10] (A, 207)

Ludovico Marchesi (1754–1829)

► A soprano, acclaimed for his range, pure tone, and expressive acting, Marchesi sang in the premiere of Myslivecek's *Armida* (1779) at Milan. ◄

To Leopold Mozart   *Munich, 11 October 1777*

The primo uomo [for the next carnival season in Naples] is Marchesi, whom [Myslivecek] praises very highly and so does the rest of Munich. (A, 303)

To Leopold Mozart   *Munich, 30 December 1780*

You probably know that the worthy castrato Marchesi, or *Marquesius di Milano*, has been poisoned at Naples. And how? He was in love with a duchess, whose rightful lover became jealous and sent three or four fellows to give him his choice: either to drink poison out of a cup or to be assassinated. He chose the former, but being an Italian coward, he died *alone*, and allowed his murderers to live on in peace and quiet. Had it been myself and had it been absolutely necessary for me to die, I should have taken at least a couple with me into the next world. Such an excellent singer is a great loss.[11] (A, 702–703)

Catarina Cavalieri (1760–1801)

► Vienna-born (despite her Italianized stage name), Cavalieri, a pupil of Salieri, created the roles of Constanze in *Die Entführung* and Madame Silberklang in *Der Schauspieldirektor* (1786). She also sang Donna Elvira in the 1788 Vienna production of *Don Giovanni*. The 1782 *Almanach* reports that Cavalieri played "young lovers and girls' roles."[12] ◄

To Leopold Mozart   *Vienna, 26 September 1781*

I have sacrificed Constanze's aria a little to the flexible throat of Mlle.

Cavalieri, "Trennung war mein banges Los und nun schwimmt mein Aug' in Tränen." I have tried to express her feelings, as far as an Italian bravura aria will allow it.[13] (A, 769)

To Constanze   *Vienna, 14 October 1791*

At six o'clock I called in the carriage for Salieri and Madame Cavalieri—and drove them to my box [to see *Die Zauberflöte*].[14] (A, 970)

Anna Lucia De Amicis (ca. 1733–1816)

► Mozart first met De Amicis in Mainz in 1763; she was to create the role of Giunia in *Lucio Silla* (1772). Charles Burney lauded her technique (especially her staccato) and range (to E-flat); Metastasio admired her dramatic ability. ◄

To Nannerl   *Rome, 21 April 1770*

Some say that De Amicis will sing [in *Mitridate*]. We are to meet her in Naples. I should like her and Manzuoli to take the parts. Then we should have two good acquaintances and friends.[15] (A, 131)

To Nannerl   *Naples, 29 May 1770*

The day before yesterday we were at the rehearsal of Signor Jommelli's opera [*Armida abbandonata*] . . . Signora De Amicis sang marvelously well. (A, 141)

To Leopold Mozart   *Mannheim, 17 January 1778*

[Aloysia Weber] sings most excellently my aria written for De Amicis with those horribly difficult passages.[16] (A, 448)

To Leopold Mozart   *Paris, 11 September 1778*

If the Archbishop wants a new singer, by Heaven I do not know of a better one [than Aloysia Weber]. He will never get a[n Elisabeth] Teiber or a De Amicis; and the rest are certainly worse. (A, 616)

Johann Ignaz Ludwig Fischer (1745–1825)

► Fischer, a pupil of Anton Raaff, was the leading German basso of his time. In addition to the role of Osmin, Mozart composed two concert arias for him: "Aspri rimorsi atroci," K. 432 (421a), and a second setting of "Non so, d'onde viene," K. 512 (1787). ◄

To Leopold Mozart   *Vienna, 26 September 1781*

As we have given the part of Osmin to Herr Fischer, who certainly has an excellent bass voice (in spite of the fact that the Archbishop told me that he sang too low for a bass and that I assured him that he would sing higher next time), we must take advantage of it, particularly as he has the whole Viennese public on his side. . . . In working out the aria ["Solche herge-laufne Laffen," act 1] I have . . . allowed Fischer's beautiful deep notes to glow. (A, 768)

To Leopold Mozart   *Vienna, 5 February 1783*

Fischer, the bass singer, is with me and has just asked me to write about him to Le Gros in Paris, as he is going off there in Lent. The Viennese are making the foolish mistake of letting a man go who can never be replaced. (A, 839)

Maria Magdalena Haydn (née Lipp, 1745–1827)

► The wife of Michael Haydn, Maria Magdalena was a soprano who sang in Mozart's Salzburg church music as well as in the 1769 Salzburg performance of *La finta semplice*, K. 51 (46a). ◄

To Abbé Bullinger   *Paris, 7 August 1778*

It is true that Mme. Haydn is in poor health. She has overdone her austere mode of living. There are few of whom this can be said. I am surprised that she has not lost her voice long ago by her perpetual scourgings and flagellations, her hair shirt and her unnatural fasts and night prayers! But she will long retain her powers and, instead of becoming worse, her voice will improve daily. When at last God places her among the numbers of His saints, we shall still have five singers left [in Salzburg], each of whom can dispute the palm with the other. (A, 595)

Margarethe Kaiser

► Margarethe Kaiser was active in Munich from 1776 to 1784, and in Vienna in 1790. Mozart's admission, that his initial lavish praise for her singing was "a palpable lie," is both unique and puzzling. ◄

To Leopold Mozart   *Munich, 2 October 1777*

The leading soprano is called Mlle. Kaiser. She is the daughter of a cook by a count here and is a very attractive girl; pretty on the stage, that is; but I have not yet seen her near. She is a native of the town. When I heard her, it was only her third appearance. She has a beautiful voice, not powerful but by no means weak, very pure and her intonation is good. Valesi [Johann Evangelist Wallishauser] has taught her, and from her singing you can tell that he knows how to sing as well as how to teach. When she sustains her voice for a few bars, I have been astonished at the beauty of her *crescendo* and *decrescendo*. She still takes her trills slowly and I am very glad. They will be all the truer and clearer when later on she wants to trill more rapidly, for it is always easier to do them quickly in any case. People here are delighted with her . . . I was in the Brancas' box and I kept my opera glasses on Mlle. Kaiser and she often drew a tear from me. I kept on calling out "Brava, Bravissima," for I could not forget that it was only her third appearance on the stage. (A, 290–291)

To Leopold Mozart   *Mannheim, 19 February 1778*

As for your reproach about the little singer in Munich, I must confess that I was an ass to tell you such a palpable lie. Why, she does not yet know what *singing* means. It is true that for a person who had only been studying for three months, she sang surprisingly well, and she had, in addition, a very pleasing and pure voice. Why I praised her so much may well have been because I was hearing people say from morning to night: "There is no better singer in all Europe" and "Who has not heard her, has heard nothing." I did not dare to contradict them, partly because I wanted to make some good friends, and partly because I had come straight from Salzburg, where we are not in the habit of contradicting anyone; but as soon as I was alone, I never could help laughing. Why then did I not laugh at her when writing to you? I really cannot tell. (A, 485)

To Leopold Mozart   *Nancy, 2 October 1778*

I suppose that Piccinni's *Fishermaiden (La pescatrice)* or Sacchini's *Peasant girl at court (La contadina in corte)* will be the first of the Singspiele to be given [in Munich]. The prima donna will be Mlle. Kaiser, the girl I wrote to you about from Munich. I do not know her—I have only heard her sing. It was then her third appearance on the stage and she had only been learning music for three weeks. (A, 623)

Signor Otini

► Otini may be the same person as the composer Francesco Antonio Uttini (1723–1795), about whom little is known.[17] ◄

To Nannerl   *Milan, 26 January 1770*

The opera at Mantua [Hasse's *Demetrio*] was charming . . . As for the tenors, one is called Otini. He does not sing badly, but rather heavily like all Italian tenors, and he is a great friend of ours. (A, 110)

Domenico Panzacchi (1733–1805)

► Tenor at the Munich Hofkapelle, Panzacchi was also successful in Italy and Madrid; he sang the role of Arbace in the premiere of *Idomeneo*. ◄

To Leopold Mozart   *Munich, 22 November 1780*

Herr Panzacchi . . . has already paid me three visits and has just invited me to lunch on Sunday. I hope I shall not have the same experience as the two of us had with the coffee. He has enquired very meekly whether instead of "se la sa" he may not sing "se co la"—Well, why not "ut re mi fa sol la"?[18] (A, 669)

Anton Raaff (1714-1797)

▶ A student of Padre Martini, Raaff (fig. 14.1) enjoyed a long and successful career in Naples, Lisbon, Madrid, and Vienna. In Mannheim he sang the premieres of J. C. Bach's *Temistocle* (1772) and *Lucio Silla* (1776). He also created the title role in Mozart's *Idomeneo*. Mozart's letters discuss Raaff more than any other singer, with the exception of Aloysia Weber. But compared to his uniformly glowing assessments of

FIGURE 14.1. Anton Raaff

his beloved Aloysia, Mozart's views on Raaff's singing are infinitely complex, evolving over time from rather thorough contempt to considerable, if never unbounded, respect.[19] ◄

To Leopold Mozart *Mannheim, 14 November 1777*

On one occasion Raaff sang four arias, about 450 bars in all, in such a fashion as to call forth the remark that his voice was the strongest reason he sang so badly. Anyone who hears him begin an aria without at once reminding himself that it is Raaff, the once famous tenor, who is singing, is bound to burst out laughing. It's a fact. I thought to myself: "If I didn't know that this was Raaff, I should double up laughing." As it is, I just pull out my handkerchief and hide a smile. Moreover, he has never been, so people here tell me, anything of an actor; you'd only have had to hear him, without even looking at him; nor has he by any means a good presence. In the opera [Holzbauer's *Günther von Schwarzburg*] he had to die, and while dying sing a very, very, very long aria in slow time; well, he died with a grin on his face, and toward the end of the aria his voice gave out so badly that one really couldn't stand it any longer. I was sitting in the orchestra beside Wendling the flautist. He had objected beforehand that it was unnatural for a man to keep on singing until he had died, as it was too long to wait. Whereupon I remarked: "Have a little patience. He'll soon be gone, for I hear it." "So do I," he said, and laughed. (A, 374–375)

To Leopold Mozart *Mannheim, 28 February 1778*

I was at Raaff's yesterday and brought him an aria which I composed for him the other day ["Se al labbro mio non credi," K. 295.] . . . He liked it enormously. One must treat a man like Raaff in a particular way. I asked him to tell me candidly if he did not like it or if it did not suit his voice, adding that I would alter it if he wished, or even compose another. "God forbid," he said, "the aria must remain just as it is, for nothing could be finer. But please shorten it a little, for I am no longer able to sustain my notes."[20] (A, 496–497)

To Leopold Mozart *Paris, 12 June 1778*

I must now say something about our Raaff. You will remember, no doubt, that I did not write too favorably about him from Mannheim and was by no means pleased with his singing—enfin, that I did not like him at all. The reason, however, was that I scarcely heard him properly, as it were, at Mannheim. I heard him for the first time in the rehearsal of Holzbauer's *Günther*, when he was in his everyday clothes, with his hat on and a stick in his hand. . . . He sang the arias in a way so obviously careless—and some notes he sang with too much emphasis—which did not appeal to me. This has been a constant habit of his—and perhaps it is a characteristic of the Bernacchi school—for he was a pupil of Bernacchi's. At Court, too, he always sang arias which, in my opinion, by no means suited his voice; so that I did not like him at all. But when he made his debut here in the Concert Spirituel, he sang [Johann Christian] Bach's scena "Non so d'onde viene,"[21] which, by the way, is a favorite of mine. Then for the first time I really heard him sing, and he pleased me, that is, his particular style of singing, although the style itself—the Bernacchi school—is not to my taste. Raaff is too much inclined to drop into the cantabile. I admit that when he was young and in his prime, this must have been very effective and have taken people by surprise. I admit also that I like it. But he overdoes it and so to me it often seems ridiculous. What I do like is when he sings short pieces, as, for example, some andantinos; and he has also certain arias, which he renders in his peculiar style. Well, each in his own way. I fancy that his forte was bravura singing—and, so far as his age permits, you can still tell this from his manner; he has a good chest and a long breath; and then these andantinos. His voice is beautiful and very pleasant. If I shut my eyes and listen to him, he reminds me very much of Meissner, only that Raaff's voice seems to me even more pleasing. I am talking about their voices as they are at present, for I have never heard them in their prime. So all that I can discuss is their style or method of singing, which a singer always retains. Meissner, as you know, has the bad habit of making his voice tremble at times . . . and this I never could endure in him. . . . Now Raaff never does this—in fact, he cannot bear it. Yet, so far as real cantabile is concerned, I prefer Meissner to Raaff (though not quite unconditionally, for he too has mannerisms). In bravura singing, long passages, and roulades, Raaff is absolute master and he moreover has an excellent, clear diction which is very beautiful; and as I have already said, his andantinos or little canzonette are charming. (A, 551–552)

To Leopold Mozart   *Kaisersheim, 18 December 1778*

Well, that melancholy *Alceste* by Schweitzer is now being performed in Munich. The best part . . . is the beginning of the recitative "O Jugend-zeit" [act 4, scene 2]—and it was Raaff's contribution that *made this a success;* for he phrased it for [Franz Christian] Hartig (who sings the part of Admet) and by so doing introduced the *true expression* into the aria. (A, 642)

To Leopold Mozart   *Munich, 8 November 1780*

Raaff is like a statue. Well, just picture to yourself the scene in act 1 [of *Idomeneo*]. (A, 660)

To Leopold Mozart   *Munich, 27 December 1780*

Raaff is the best and most honest fellow in the world, but so tied to old-fashioned routine that flesh and blood cannot stand it. Consequently, it is very difficult to compose for him, but very easy if you compose commonplace arias . . . Raaff is too fond of everything that is cut and dried, and he pays no attention to expression.[22] (A, 698–699)

Therese Teyber (1760–1830)

► Soprano at the Vienna Hofoper beginning in 1778, Teyber sang Blonde in the premiere of *Die Entführung* and Zerlina in the Viennese production of *Don Giovanni*. In 1783, she and Mozart performed in benefit concerts for one another. ◄

To Leopold Mozart   *Vienna, 29 March 1783*

Our programme was as follows: . . .
(7) Mlle. Teiber sang the scena "Parto, m'affretto" out of my last Milan opera [i.e., Giunia's aria from *Lucio Silla*] . . .
Mlle. Teiber is giving a concert tomorrow, at which I am going to play. (A, 843)

To Anton Klein   *Vienna, 21 May 1785*

Madame Cavalieri, Adamberger, Mlle. Teiber, all Germans of whom Germany may well be proud. (A, 890)

Aloysia Weber (later Lange) (ca. 1760–1839)

► Soprano Aloysia Weber (fig. 14.2) was Mozart's voice pupil and his first love. They met in Mannheim in 1777. She made her debut with the German opera in 1779 in Vienna, where she later created the role of Mme. Herz in *Der Schauspieldirektor* and sang Donna Anna in the Viennese premiere of *Don Giovanni*. Mozart also composed numerous concert arias for her. ◄

To Leopold Mozart   *Mannheim, 17 January 1778*

She sings indeed most admirably and has a lovely, pure voice. The only thing she lacks is dramatic action; were it not for that, she might be the prima donna on any stage. She is only sixteen [sic]. Her father is a thoroughly honest German who is bringing up his children well, and for that very reason the girl is persecuted with attentions here. . . . She sings most excellently my aria written for De Amicis with those horribly difficult passages[23] and she is to sing it at Kirchheim-Bolanden. She is quite well able to teach herself. She accompanies herself very well and she also plays galanterie[24] quite respectably. What is most fortunate for her at Mannheim is that she has won the praise of all honest people of good will. Even the Elector and Electress are only too glad to receive her, provided it doesn't

FIGURE 14.2.
Aloysia Weber

cost them anything. She can go to the Electress whenever she likes, even daily; and this is due to her good behavior. (A, 447–448)

To Leopold Mozart   *Mannheim, 4 February 1778*

Saturday evening, we went to court, where Mlle. Weber sang three arias. I say nothing about her singing—only one word, excellent! I wrote to you the other day about her merits; but I shall not be able to close this letter without telling you something more about her, for only now have I got to know her properly and as a result to discover her great powers. . . . So now I should like you to write to our good friend Lugiati, the sooner the better, and enquire what are the highest terms given to a prima donna in Verona . . . perhaps too it would be possible to obtain the Ascensa[25] in Venice. As far as her singing is concerned, I would wager my life that she will bring me renown. Even in a short time she has greatly profited by my instruction, and how much greater will the improvement be by then! I am not anxious, either, about her acting. (A, 460–461)

To Leopold Mozart *Mannheim, 7 February 1778*

In my last letter I forgot to mention Mlle. Weber's greatest merit, which is her superb cantabile singing. Please do not forget about Italy. I commend this poor, but excellent little Mlle. Weber to your interest with all my heart, *caldamente*, as the Italians say. (A, 469)

To Leopold Mozart *Mannheim, 19 February 1778*

Mlle. Weber's singing . . . goes to the heart, and she prefers to sing cantabile. . . . If she goes to Italy, she will have to sing bravura arias. Undoubtedly she will never forget how to sing cantabile, for that is her natural bent. Raaff himself (who is certainly no flatterer), when asked to give his candid opinion, said "She sang, not like a student, but like a master."[26] (A, 486)

To Leopold Mozart *Mannheim, 28 February 1778*

I decided to write ["Non so d'onde viene," K. 294] for Mlle Weber . . . and made up my mind to compose it exactly for Mlle. Weber's voice.[27] It's an Andante sostenuto (preceded by a short recitative); then follows the second part, *Nel seno a destarmi* (ex. 14.2a),

EXAMPLE 14.2a. Aria, "Non so, d'onde viene," K. 294, Middle Section

TRANSLATION: To arouse in my breast |such fierce conflicts [cannot be only pity]

and then the sostenuto again. When it was finished, (ex. 14.2b),

EXAMPLE 14.2b. Aria, "Non so, d'onde viene," K. 294, Conclusion

TRANSLATION: This icy chill that flows |Through my veins

I said to Mlle. Weber: "Learn the aria yourself. Sing it as you think it ought to go; then let me hear it and afterwards I will tell you candidly what pleases and what displeases me." After a couple of days I went to the Webers and she sang it for me, accompanying herself. I was obliged to confess that she had sung it exactly as I wished and as I should have taught it to her myself. (A, 497)

To Leopold Mozart   *Mannheim, 3 December 1778*

I assume that you received the trunk. . . . You will find in it the aria I wrote for Mlle. Weber. You have no idea what an effect it produces with instruments; you cannot judge of it by the score, for it must be rendered by a singer like Mlle. Weber. Please do not give it to anyone, for that would be the greatest injustice, as it is written solely for her and fits her like a well-tailored garment. (A, 638)

To Anton Klein   *Vienna, 21 May 1785*

My sister-in-law Madame Lange is the only singer who is to join the German opera. Madame Cavalieri, Adamberger, Mlle. Teiber, all Germans of whom Germany may well be proud, have to stay at the Italian opera—and compete against their own countrymen![28] (A, 890)

► Here follow, for the sake of completeness, the names of other singers mentioned by Mozart in a generally favorable context: Giuseppe Afferi, Gaetano Caffarelli, Giacchino Caribaldi [i.e., Garibaldi], Tommaso Consoli, Franziska Danzi, Maria Antonia Girelli, Giuseppa Marchani [i.e., Maccherini], Clementine Piccinelli, Venanzio Rauzzini, Barbara Strasser, Giuseppe Ferdinando Tenducci, Johann Evangelist Wallishauser [Valesi], Augusta Wendling, Dorothea Wendling, Elisabeth Wendling, Giovanni Battista Zonca. ◄

THE WANTING AND THE MISERABLE

Adriana "Ferraresi" (Gabrieli) (ca. 1755–ca. 1799)

► Connected to Lorenzo da Ponte and possibly his mistress, Ferraresi created the role of Fiordiligi in *Così fan tutte,* and played Susanna in the 1789 revival of *Le nozze di Figaro.* ◄

To Constanze   *Dresden, 16 April 1789*

The leading woman singer, Madame Allegranti, is far better than Madame Ferraresi, which, I admit, is not saying very much. (A, 924)

To Constanze, Baden   *Vienna, 19 August 1789*

The little aria, which I composed for Madame Ferraresi ["Un moto di gioia," K. 579],[29] ought, I think, to be a success, provided she is able to sing it in an artless [*naiv*] manner, which, however, I very much doubt. She herself liked it very much. I have just lunched at her house. (A, 933–934)

Catterina Gabrielli (1730–1796)

► Gabrielli was a soprano famed for the light and brilliant quality of her voice. Mozart had first met her in Milan in October 1771. ◄

To Leopold Mozart   *Mannheim, 19 February 1778*

Everything you say about Mlle. [Aloysia] Weber is true, except one thing—that "she sings like a Gabrielli"; for I should not at all like her to sing in that style. Those who have heard Gabrielli are forced to admit that she was adept only at runs and roulades. She adopted, however, such an unusual interpretation that she won admiration, but it never survived the fourth time of hearing. In the long run she could not please, for people soon get tired of coloratura passages. Moreover, she had the misfortune of not being able to sing. She was not capable of *sustaining* a breve properly, and, as she had no *messa di voce,* she could not dwell on her notes; in short, she sang with skill but without understanding. (A, 486)

Gertrud Elisabeth Mara (1749–1833)

► Mara served Frederick the Great and later traveled throughout Europe; in London she specialized in the music of Handel and Haydn. ◄

To Leopold Mozart   *Munich, 13 November 1780*

Mara has not had the good fortune to please me. She has not the art to equal a Bastardella (for this is her peculiar style)—and has too much to touch the heart like a [Aloysia] Weber—or any sensible singer. (A, 663)

To Leopold Mozart   *Munich, 24 November 1780*

I want to tell you the whole story about [Johann Baptist] Mara. . . . When the first symphony was over, it was Madame Mara's turn to sing and I saw her husband come creeping up behind her with his violoncello. I thought that she was going to sing an aria with a cello obbligato. . . . Then the aria began, Giovanni Mara standing behind his wife, looking very sheepish and still holding his big fiddle. The moment they entered the hall, I had taken a dislike to both of them, for really you could not find two more insolent-looking people. . . . The aria has a second part [i.e., is in Da capo form]. Madame Mara, however, did not think it necessary to let the orchestra know beforehand that she was going to stop, but after the last ritornello, came down into the room with her usual *air d'effronterie* to pay respects to their Highnesses. (A, 670–671)

Joseph Meissner (d. 1795)

► Meissner became bass singer at the Salzburg court in 1747; Leopold Mozart greatly admired his enormous range, natural execution of passage work, and expressive power.[30] ◄

To Leopold Mozart   *Paris, 12 June 1778*

Meisner . . . has the bad habit of making his voice tremble at times, turning a note that should be sustained into distinct crotchets [quarter-notes], or even quavers [eighth-notes]—and this I never could endure in him. And really it is a detestable habit and one which is quite contrary to nature. (A, 552)

Vincenzo dal Prato (1756–1828)

► Dal Prato was a castrato (soprano), engaged in 1780 by the Hofkapelle and the Opera in Munich where he remained until 1805; he created the role of Idamante in *Idomeneo*. ◄

To Leopold Mozart   *Munich, 8 November 1780*

Now for a sorry story. I have not, it is true, the honor of being acquainted with the hero dal Prato; but from the description I have been given of him I should say that Ceccarelli is almost the better of the two. Most often in the middle of an aria his breath gives out, and, mark you, he has never been on any stage. (A, 660)

To Leopold Mozart   *Munich, 13 November 1780*

If I had known that this castrato was so bad, I should certainly have recommended Ceccarelli! (A, 664)

To Leopold Mozart   *Munich, 15 November 1780*

But to my molto amato castrato dal Prato I shall have to teach the whole opera [*Idomeneo*]. He has no notion how to sing a cadenza effectively, and his voice is so uneven! He is only engaged for a year and at the end of that time, next September, Count Seeau will get somebody else. (A, 664)

To Leopold Mozart   *Munich, 22 November 1780*

The day before yesterday dal Prato sang at the concert—most disgracefully. I bet you that fellow will never get through the rehearsals, still less the opera. Why, the rascal is rotten to the core. (A, 669)

To Leopold Mozart   *Munich, 27 December 1780*

Raaff and dal Prato spoil the recitative by singing it without any spirit or fire, and *so* monotonously. They are the most wretched actors that ever walked on a stage. (A, 698)

To Leopold Mozart   *Munich, 30 December 1780*

The day before yesterday we had a rehearsal of recitatives [from *Idomeneo*] at Wendling's and we went through the quartet together. We repeated it six times and now it goes well. The stumbling block was dal Prato; the fellow is utterly useless. His voice would not be so bad if he did not produce it in his throat and larynx. But he has no intonation, no method, no feeling, but sings—well, like the best of the boys who come to be tested in the hope of getting a place in the chapel choir. (A, 701)

French singers

To Leopold Mozart   *Paris, 5 April 1778*

And their singing! Good Lord! Let me never hear a Frenchwoman singing Italian arias. I can forgive her if she screeches out her French trash, but not if she ruins good music! It's simply unbearable. (A, 522)

To Leopold Mozart   *Paris, 9 July 1778*

And then the men and women singers! Indeed they hardly deserve the name, for they don't sing—they yell—howl—and that, too, with all their might, through their noses and throats. (A, 564)

Mannheim Chorus

To Leopold Mozart   *Mannheim, 4 November 1777*

I should not care to have one of my masses performed here . . . because, as things are at present, you must write principally for the instruments, as you cannot imagine anything worse than the voices here. Six sopranos, six altos, six tenors, and six basses against twenty violins and twelve basses is just like zero to one. They have only two castrati, who are already old and will just be allowed to die off. The soprano would actually prefer to sing alto, as he can no longer take the high notes. The few boys they have are miserable. The tenors and basses are like our funeral singers. (A, 356)

To Leopold Mozart   Paris, 5 April 1778

Kapellmeister Holzbauer has sent a Miserere here, but as the choruses at Mannheim are weak and poor, whereas in Paris they are powerful and excellent, the choruses he has composed would not be effective. (A, 521)

Mantua Soloists

To Nannerl   Milan, 26 January 1770

The opera at Mantua was charming. . . . The prima donna sings well, but very softly; and when you do not see her acting, but only singing, you would think that she is not singing at all. For she cannot open her mouth, but whines out everything. However, we are quite accustomed to that now. The seconda donna looks like a grenadier and has a powerful voice too, and, I must say, does not sing badly, seeing that she is acting for the first time. . . . Il secondo uomo is already old and I do not like him. (A, 110)

ORCHESTRAS AND CONDUCTORS

► The portrait gallery continues with the instrumentalists, divided into considerably less invidious categories this time, namely, according to their means of tone production, not their abilities. Nonetheless, it will not be very difficult to distinguish the saints from the sinners in this assembly. We begin with Mozart's opinions of the orchestras (and their conductors) he was destined either to enjoy or to endure.[31] ◄

Augsburg

To Leopold Mozart   Augsburg, 16 October 1777

The Augsburg orchestra is enough to give one a fit.[32] (A, 325)

To Leopold Mozart   Augsburg, 17 October 1777

The only thing I have to worry about now is how I shall be accompanied at my concert, for the orchestra here is execrable.[33] (A, 330)

To Leopold Mozart   Augsburg, 23 October 1777

In spite of their poor fiddling I prefer the [Holy Cross] monastery players to the Augsburg orchestra. (A, 338)

Cremona

To Nannerl   Milan, 26 January 1770

In Cremona [the opera orchestra] is good. The first violin is called Spagnoletto. (A, 110)

Mannheim, Christian Cannabich, Conductor

To Leopold Mozart   *Mannheim, 4 November 1777*

The orchestra is excellent and very strong. On either side there are ten or eleven violins, four violas, two oboes, two flutes and two clarinets, two horns, four violoncellos, four bassoons and four double basses, also trumpets and drums. They can produce fine music. (A, 355–356)

To Leopold Mozart   *Paris, 9 July 1778*

Ah, if only the [Salzburg] orchestra were organized as they are at Mannheim. Indeed I would like you to see the discipline that prevails there and the authority which Cannabich wields. There everything is done seriously. Cannabich, who is the best conductor I have ever seen, is both beloved and feared by his subordinates. Moreover, he is respected by the whole town and so are his soldiers. But certainly they behave quite differently from ours. They have good manners, are well dressed, and do not go to public houses and swill. (A, 562)

To Leopold Mozart   *Munich, 9 November 1780*

Do come soon, and hear and admire the orchestra. (A, 660)

Mantua

To Nannerl   *Milan, 26 January 1770*

The opera at Mantua was charming. They played *Demetrio.* . . . The orchestra was not bad. (A, 110)

Paris, Concert Spirituel, Joseph Le Gros, Conductor

► Le Gros (1739–1793) was a singer, composer, and conductor; in 1777, after a brilliant career as a tenor in the Paris Opéra, he assumed the post of director of the Concert Spirituel, one of the earliest public concert organizations. ◄

To Leopold Mozart   *Paris, 3 July 1778*

I have had to compose a symphony [K. 297] for the opening of the Concert Spirituel. . . . I was very nervous at the rehearsal, for never in my life have I heard a worse performance. You have no idea how they twice scraped and scrambled through it. (A, 557)

To Leopold Mozart   *Paris, 9 July 1778*

Le Gros is so pleased with it that he says it is his very best symphony. . . . Le Gros is now heart and soul for me.[34] (A, 564–565)

Salzburg

To Leopold Mozart   *Munich, 11 October 1777*

My greetings to all my good friends . . . and to my best friend Herr
Bullinger, whom I will get you to ask to be so good as to make at the eleven
o'clock concert next Sunday an authoritative pronouncement in my name,
presenting my compliments to all the members of the orchestra and
exhorting them to be diligent, lest I be proved a liar one of these days. For I
have extolled these concerts everywhere and shall continue to do so. (A,
308)

► See also the less than flattering comparison between the Mannheim and
Salzburg orchestra members in Mozart's letter of 9 July 1778 from Paris,
p. 375 above. ◄

Strasbourg

To Leopold Mozart   *Strasbourg, 26 October 1778*

I took in a little more money certainly, but the cost of the orchestra (who
are very bad but demand to be paid handsomely) . . . made up a
considerable sum. (A, 627)

KEYBOARD PLAYERS

PIANISTS

► Descriptions of Mozart's keyboard playing, along with his considered
views on proper keyboard performance, were presented earlier (Chapters 1 and 7). His verdicts on the playing of some of his students—and
some of his rivals—follow here. In the eighteenth century the term
"clavier" (literally, "keyboard") could apply in principle to any stringed
keyboard instrument: the clavichord, the harpsichord ("cembalo"), or
the pianoforte (alternatively called "fortepiano"). By the 1780s, however, "cembalo," too, had largely become a general term; moreover, both
"clavier" and "cembalo" by then often referred in the first instance to
the pianoforte. It is quite likely, then, that in the following comments—
certainly in those dating from the Vienna period—Mozart had pianists,
and pianoforte playing, foremost in mind. ◄

Muzio Clementi (1752–1832)[35]

To Leopold Mozart   *Vienna, 22 December 1781*

Another clavier player [*clavier spieller*], an Italian called Clementi, has
arrived here. He, too, had been invited to court. (A, 789)

► On 24 December 1781, at the behest of Emperor Joseph II, a keyboard playing contest took place in the Hofburg between Mozart and Clementi. Mozart referred to the event (more than once) and recorded his strong reaction to Clementi's playing.[36] ◄

To Leopold Mozart   *Vienna, 16 January 1782*

Now a word about Clementi. He is an excellent cembalo player [*ein braver Cembalist*], but that is all. He has great facility with his right hand. His star passages are thirds. Apart from this, he has not a farthing's worth of taste or feeling [*keinen kreutzer geschmack noch empfindung*]; he is a mere *mechanicus*.

After we had stood on ceremony long enough, the Emperor declared that Clementi ought to begin. "La Santa Chiesa Cattolica," he said, Clementi being a Roman. He improvised and then played a sonata. The Emperor then turned to me: "Allons, fire away." I improvised and played variations. The Grand Duchess produced some sonatas by Paisiello . . . of which I had to play the Allegros and Clementi the Andantes and Rondos. We then selected a theme from them and developed it on two pianofortes [2 Piano forte]. (A, 793)

To Leopold Mozart   *Vienna, 7 June 1783*

Clementi is a *ciarlatano*, like all Italians. He writes *Presto* over a sonata or even *Prestissimo* and *Alla breve*, and plays it himself *Allegro* in 4/4 time. I know this is the case, for I have heard him do so. What he really does well are his passages in thirds; but he sweated over them day and night in London. Apart from this, he can do nothing, absolutely nothing, for he has not the slightest expression or taste, still less, feeling [*nicht den geringsten vortrag, noch geschmack—viel weniger Empfindung.*] (A, 850)

► Clementi's impressions of Mozart's keyboard playing are cited in Chapter 1. It is also of interest to read his later assessment of his own playing at the time of the contest with Mozart, as reported in 1829 by the Berlin-based composer Ludwig Berger. ◄

At that early date [Clementi] took particular delight in great and brilliant dexterity, and especially in those double-chorded passages and extemporized ornaments that were not in common use before his time; . . . only subsequently did he come to favor the more melodious, nobler style of performance that he acquired through careful attention to then-famous singers, and also through the gradual perfecting of the English concert grand fortepiano in particular, the earlier faulty construction of which had practically excluded the possibility of a more singing, more legato style of playing.

Thus, it seems . . . must we explain Mozart's judgment that called him "tasteless and insensitive." (DDB, 542)

Maria Anna Josepha Aloysia von Hamm (b. 1765)

► No pertinent biographical information is available. ◄

To Leopold Mozart   *Augsburg, 16 October 1777*

All that I can say about the daughter of Hamm, the Secretary of War, is that she undoubtedly must have a gift for music, as she has only been learning for three years and yet can play several pieces really well. But I find it difficult to give you an idea of the impression she makes on me when she is playing. She seems to me so curiously affected. She stalks over the clavier [Clavier] with her long bony fingers in such an odd way. It is true that she has not yet had a really good teacher, and if she stays in Munich she will never, never become what her father is so anxious that she should be: and that is, a first-rate performer on the clavier. If she comes to Papa at Salzburg, her gain will be twofold, both in musical knowledge and in intelligence, which is not exactly her strong point at present. She has made me laugh a great deal already at her expense and you would certainly get plenty of entertainment for your pains. She would not eat much, for she is far too simple. You say that I ought to have tested her playing. Why, I simply could not do so for laughing. For whenever, by way of example, I played a passage with my right hand she at once exclaimed Bravissimo! in a tiny mouse-like voice. (A, 322)

Georg Friedrich Richter (ca. 1759–1789)

► Richter was a Dutch clavier virtuoso and teacher. ◄

To Leopold Mozart   *Vienna, 28 April 1784*

Herr Richter, the clavier player [*klavierspieller*], is making a tour on his way back to Holland, his native country. . . . He plays well as far as execution goes, but, as you will discover when you hear him, he is too rough and labored and entirely devoid of taste and feeling. Otherwise, he is the best fellow in the world and is not the slightest bit conceited. When I played to him he stared all the time at my fingers and kept on saying: "Good God! How hard I work and sweat—and yet win no applause—and to you, my friend, it is all child's play." "Yes," I replied, "I too had to work hard, so as not to have to work hard any longer." Enfin, he is a fellow who may be included among our good clavier players [*klavierspieller*] and I trust that the Archbishop will be more inclined to hear him, because he is a *clavierist* [*Clavierist*] (A, 875)

Johann Matthias Schreyer (ca. 1731–1808)

► Schreyer was a priest and organist at the Church of the Holy Spirit, Munich. ◄

To Leopold Mozart   *Munich, 11 October 1777*

Miss Simplicity von Hamm's teacher is a certain clergyman of the name of Schreier. He is a good organist, but no cembalist [*Cymbalist*]. . . . He is a dry sort of fellow, who does not say much: but he tapped me on the shoulder, sighed and said: "Yes—you are—you know—yes—that is true—you are first-rate." (A, 307)

Nanette Stein

To Leopold Mozart   *Augsburg, 23 October 1777*

Herr Stein is quite crazy about his daughter, who is eight and a half and who now learns everything by heart. She may succeed, for she has great talent for music. But she will not make progress by this method—for she will never acquire great rapidity, since she definitely does all she can to make her hands heavy.[37] (A, 339–340)

Johann Franz Xaver Sterkel (1750–1817)

► Sterkel was organist at the Electoral Court of Mainz until 1797, and Kapellmeister there from 1793. ◄

To Leopold Mozart   *Mannheim, 26 November 1777*

Herr Sterkel came here from Würzburg a few days ago. The day before yesterday, the 24th. . . . I spent the evening at Cannabich's *al solito* [as usual]. Sterkel came in. He played five duets, but so fast it was hard to follow them, and not at all clearly, and not in time. Everyone said the same. Mlle. Cannabich played the sixth and, to tell the truth, better than Sterkel. (A, 391)

Elisabeth Augusta ("Gustl") Wendling (1752–1794)

► Pianist and singer, Elisabeth Augusta was the daughter of the Mannheim musicians Johann Baptist and Dorothea Wendling. ◄

To Leopold Mozart   *Mannheim, 8 November 1777*

The daughter, *who was at one time the Elector's mistress*, plays the clavier very charmingly [italicized words in code]. (A, 362)

ORGANISTS

Johann Georg Albrechtsberger (1736–1809)

► Albrechtsberger was court organist in Vienna, later Kapellmeister of St. Stephen's Cathedral. He was a master contrapuntist and teacher of Beethoven and Hummel. See the entry below for Johann Wilhelm Hässler, to whom Albrechtsberger is favorably compared. ◄

Nikolaus Bayer and Anton Marxfelder

► No pertinent biographical information is available. ◄

To Leopold Mozart   *Mannheim, 4 November 1777*

They have two organists here who alone would be worth a special visit to Mannheim. I have had an opportunity of hearing them properly, for it is not the custom here to sing the Benedictus, but during that part of the service the organist has to play the whole time. On the first occasion I heard the second organist and on the second, the first organist. But in my opinion the second is even more distinguished than the first. For when I heard him, I enquired: "Who is playing the organ?" I was told, the second organist. He played abominably. When I heard the other one, I asked: "Who is playing now?" I was told, our first organist. He played even more wretchedly and I think that if they were thrown together, something even worse would be the result. To watch these gentlemen is enough to make one die of laughing. The second, when seated at the organ, is like a child at stool, for his face tells you what he can do. The first, at any rate, wears spectacles. I went and stood at the organ and watched him in the hope of learning something from him. At every note he lifts his hands right up in the air. His forte is to play in six parts, but chiefly in five and eight parts! He often leaves out the right hand for fun and plays with the left hand alone. In short, he can do just what he likes, for he is completely master of his instrument. (A, 356)

Johann Michael Demmler (1748–1785)

► Cathedral organist in Augsburg from 1774, Demmler in 1777 played the Concerto for Three Pianos in F, K. 242, with Mozart and Johann Andreas Stein. ◄

To Leopold Mozart   *Kaysersheim, 18 December 1778*

I commend to your kindness an organist—who is at the same time a good clavierist, Herr Demmler from Augsburg. I had entirely forgotten him and was very glad when I heard of him here. He is very talented, and an appointment in Salzburg might be extremely useful in promoting his further success, for all he needs is a good guide in music—and there I know of no one better than you, my dearest father; it would be really a pity if he were to leave the right path. (A, 642)

Johann Wilhelm Hässler (1747–1822)

► Organist, pianist, and composer, Hässler settled in Russia in 1792.

To Constanze   *Dresden, 16 April 1789*

A certain Hässler, who is organist at Erfurt, is in Dresden. . . . He is a pupil of a pupil of Bach's [Johann Christian Kittel]. His forte is the organ and the clavier (clavichord [*clavier: clavikord*]). Now people here think that because I come from Vienna, I am quite unacquainted with this style and mode of playing. Well, I sat down at the organ and played. Prince Lichnowsky, who knows Hässler very well, after some difficulty persuaded him to play also. This Hässler's chief excellence on the organ consists in his footwork, which, since the pedals are graded here [*stuffenweise gehen*, i.e., scalewise], is not so very wonderful. Moreover, he has done no more than commit to memory the harmony and modulations of old Sebastian Bach and is not capable of executing a fugue properly;[38] and his playing is not thorough. Thus he is far from being an Albrechtsberger. After that we decided to go back to the Russian Ambassador's, so that Hässler might hear me on the fortepiano [*forte piano*]. He played, too. I consider Mlle. Auernhammer as good a player on the fortepiano as he is, so you can imagine that he has begun to sink very considerably in my estimation. (A, 923–924)

Leopold Mozart[39]

To Leopold Mozart   *Munich, 11 October 1777*

The papa of the two beautiful young ladies whom I have mentioned [Franziskus Erasmus Freysinger] says he knows Papa quite well, and was a student with him. He still remembers particularly Wessobrunn, where Papa (this was news to me) played on the organ amazingly well. *"It was quite terrifying,"* he said, *"to see how rapid your Papa was with his feet and hands. Indeed he was absolutely amazing."* (A, 307)

Abbé Georg Joseph Vogler[40]

To Leopold Mozart   *Mannheim, 18 December 1777*

Vogler played [the organ in the Lutheran church]. He is, to put it bluntly, a trickster [*ein hexenmeister*] pure and simple. As soon as he tries to play maestoso, he becomes as dry as dust; and it is a great relief that playing upon the organ bores him and that therefore it doesn't last long. But what is the result? An unintelligible muddle. I listened to him from a distance. He then began a fugue, in which one note was struck six times and presto. Whereupon I went up to him. Indeed I would much rather watch him than hear him. (A, 428)

STRING PLAYERS

VIOLINISTS

Antonio Brunetti (ca. 1744–1786)

► Brunetti was violinist in the Salzburg court orchestra from 1771; in 1777 he succeeded Mozart as Konzertmeister. ◄

To Leopold Mozart   *St. Germain, 27 August 1778*

[Paul Rothfischer] conducts better than Brunetti, but is not so good at solo playing. He has better execution, and plays well in his way (a little bit in the old-fashioned Tartini manner)—but Brunetti's style is more pleasing.[41] (A, 607)

To Leopold Mozart   *Vienna, 11 April 1781*

Te Deum Laudamus that at last that coarse and dirty Brunetti has left, who is a disgrace to his master, to himself, and to the whole orchestra—or so say [the castrato] Ceccarelli and I.[42] . . . At the last concert . . . I composed *a new rondo for Brunetti* [code] [in C for Violin and Orchestra, K. 373]. (A, 722–723)

Charles Albert Dupreille (1728–1796)

► Dupreille was a violinist in the Munich court orchestra. ◄

To Leopold Mozart   *Munich, 6 October 1777*

The day before yesterday, Saturday, the 4th . . . we had a little concert here. M. Dupreille, whom Papa will probably remember, was also present. He was a pupil of Tartini. In the morning he was giving a violin lesson to Albert's youngest son Carl, when I happened to come in. I had never thought much of Dupreille, but I saw that he was taking great pains over the lesson, and when we started to talk of the fiddle as a solo and orchestral instrument, he made quite sensible remarks and always agreed with me, so that I went back on my former opinion and was convinced that I should find in him an excellent performer and a reliable orchestral player. I asked him therefore to be so good as to come to our little concert in the afternoon. We first played [Michael] Haydn's two quintets, but to my dismay I found that I could hardly hear him. He could not play four bars in succession without going wrong. . . . The best one can say about him is he was very polite and praised the quintets; apart from that—Well, I said nothing at all, but he kept on exclaiming: "I beg your pardon. I have lost my place again! It's ticklish stuff, but very fine." I kept on replying: "Do not worry. We are just among ourselves." I then played my concertos in C, B-flat and E-flat [for piano and orchestra, K. 246, 238, 271]. There indeed I had a fine accompaniment! In the Adagio I had to play his part for six bars. (A, 300)

Ignaz Fränzl (1736–1811)

► Fränzl was Konzertmeister at the Mannheim court orchestra until 1778; following the departure of the Electoral court to Munich, Fränzl remained in Mannheim and became director of the national theater there. ◄

To Leopold Mozart   *Mannheim, 22 November 1777*

At six o'clock today the gala concert took place. I had the pleasure of hearing Herr Fränzl (who is married to a sister of Mme. Cannabich) play a concerto on the violin. I like his playing very much. You know that I am no great lover of difficulties. He plays difficult things, but his hearers are not aware that they are difficult; they think that they could at once do the same themselves. That is real playing. He has, too, a most beautiful, round tone. He never misses a note, you can hear everything. It is all clear-cut. He has a beautiful staccato, played with a single bowing, up or down; and I have never heard anyone play a double trill as he does. In a word, in my opinion, he is no wizard, but a very sound fiddler. (A, 384)

► One year later Mozart, during his return visit to Mannheim, began a double concerto for piano, violin, and orchestra. Fränzl was the intended violin soloist. (See Chapter 12.) ◄

Franz Lamotte (ca. 1751–ca. 1781)

► First violinist in the court chapel of Empress Maria Theresa, Lamotte was renowned for his double stops, bowing technique, and staccato. ◄

To Leopold Mozart   *Vienna, 6 December 1783*

Tell [Heinrich Marchand, a pupil of Leopold's] too that he ought to concentrate hard on staccato playing, for it is just in this particular that the Viennese cannot forget Lamotte. (A, 862)

Zeno Franz Menzel (1756–1823)

► Menzel was violinist in the Vienna Hofkapelle from 1787. ◄

To Leopold Mozart   *Vienna, 10 April 1784*

As Hafeneder has died, Herr von Ployer has been commissioned to find a violinist. I recommended to him a certain Menzel, a handsome and clever young fellow. But I asked him not to say anything about me, as otherwise it might not work. He is now awaiting the decision. I think he has asked for and is to get four hundred gulden—and a suit of clothes. I have already scolded him about the suit of clothes, for it is a beggarly request. If anything comes of this, I shall give him a letter for you. . . . You will think him a charming violinist, and he is also a very good sight-reader. So far no one in Vienna has played my quartets [viz., the quartets dedicated to Haydn, K. 387, 421 (417b), 428 (421b)] so well at sight as he has. Moreover he is the kindest fellow in the world, and he will be delighted to play at your house whenever you want him to. I had him in the orchestra at my concert. (A, 874)

To Leopold Mozart   *Vienna, 12 June 1784*

Menzel is, and always will be an ass. The whole affair is as follows: Herr von Ployer asked me whether I knew of a violinist. I spoke to Menzel, who was much gratified. You can imagine that I as an honest man advised him not to accept anything but a permanent post. But he never came to see me until the last moment and Herr von Ployer told me that he was going off to Salzburg on trial for four hundred gulden and, mark you, *a suit of clothes.* But Menzel declared to me and to everyone here that he had actually been appointed. (A, 880)

Paul Rothfischer (1746–ca. 1785)

► Rothfischer was a violinist in the employ of the Princess of Nassau-Weilburg, later Konzertmeister and conductor of the German theater orchestra in Vienna. ◄

To Leopold Mozart   *Paris, 9 July 1778*

If by any chance Brunetti were to be dismissed, I should very much like to recommend a good friend of mine to the Archbishop as first violin; he is a most worthy fellow, and very steady. I should take him to be forty, and he is a widower. Rothfischer is his name. He is Konzertmeister at Kirchheim-Bolanden in the service of the Princess of Nassau-Weilberg. Between ourselves, he is dissatisfied—for the Prince does not like him, or rather, does not like *his music.* He has urged me most earnestly to do something for him—and indeed, it would give me real pleasure to help him, for he is one of the best fellows. (A, 566)

To Leopold Mozart   *St. Germain, 27 August 1778*

You really want a portrait of Rothfischer? He is an intelligent, hardworking conductor—not a great genius. But I was delighted with him—and, best of all, he is the kindest fellow, with whom you can do anything—of course, if you know how to set about it. He conducts better than Brunetti, but is not so good at solo playing. He has better execution, and plays well in his way (a little bit in the old-fashioned Tartini manner), but Brunetti's style is more pleasing. The concertos which he writes for himself are pretty, for playing now and then. They are always pleasant to listen to, and who can tell whether he may not please? Of course he plays ten million times better than Pinzger; and, as I have already said, he is a good conductor and very hardworking. I recommend him to you heartily, for he is the best fellow in the world. (A, 607)

Regina Strinasacchi (1764–1839)

► Active in Italy and Austria during the 1780s, Strinasacchi later toured extensively as a soloist but was also acclaimed as a chamber musician specializing in the string quartets of Haydn. ◄

To Leopold Mozart   *Vienna, 24 April 1784*

We now have here the famous Strinasacchi from Mantua, a very good violinist. She has a great deal of taste and feeling in her playing. I am this moment composing a sonata which we are going to play together on Thursday [29 April] at her concert in the theater.[43] (A, 875)

A CELLIST

Innocenz Danzi (ca. 1730–1798)

► Danzi was a cellist in the Mannheim orchestra and one of its highest paid musicians; he moved with the court to Munich in 1778. ◄

To Leopold Mozart   *Munich, 24 November 1780*

Old Danzi is the first violoncello here and accompanies very well. (A, 670)

A HARPIST

Mlle. de Guines

► Mlle. de Guines, the daughter of the Governor of Artois, is known only through her connection with Mozart. One can add to the following comments that Mozart's Concerto for Flute and Harp, K. 299 (297c) was written for Mlle. and her father. ◄

To Leopold Mozart   *Paris, 14 May 1778*

I think I told you in my last letter that the Duc de Guines, whose daughter is my pupil in composition, plays the flute extremely well, and that she plays the harp magnifique. She has a great deal of talent and even genius, and in particular a marvelous memory, so that she can play all her pieces, actually about two hundred, by heart.[44] (A, 538)

WIND PLAYERS

FLAUTISTS

Johann Philipp Freyhold[45]

To Leopold Mozart   *Vienna, 20 February 1784*

Yesterday I was fortunate enough to hear Herr Freyhold play a concerto of his own wretched composition. I found very little to admire in his performance and missed a great deal. His whole tour de force consists in double tonguing. Otherwise there is nothing whatever to listen to. (A, 867)

Johann Baptist Wendling (1723–1797)

► Principal flautist in the Electoral court orchestra of Mannheim (later Munich), Wendling first met the Mozarts in 1763 in Schwetzingen (the summer residence of the Mannheim court). Leopold described his flute playing as "admirable." ◄

To Leopold Mozart   *Mannheim, 4 February 1778*

Wendling is a thoroughly honest, excellent fellow, but unfortunately he has no religion whatever; and the whole family are the same. (A, 461)

OBOISTS

Johann Christian Fischer (1738–1800)

► Fischer was an oboist and composer of works for oboe or flute; he played in the Dresden court orchestra and at the court of Frederick the Great as well as at the English court. Mozart had first met him in The Hague in 1765. ◄

To Leopold Mozart   *Vienna, 4 April 1787*

Ramm and the two Fischers, the bass singer [J. I. Ludwig Fischer] and the oboist from London, came here this Lent. If the latter when we knew him in Holland played no better than he does now, he certainly does not deserve the reputation he enjoys. *But this is between ourselves.* In those days I was not competent to form an opinion. All that I remember is that I liked his playing immensely, as indeed everyone did. This is quite understandable, course, on the assumption that taste can undergo remarkable changes. Possibly he plays in some old-fashioned style? Not at all! The long and short of it is that he plays like a bad beginner. . . . His tone is entirely nasal, and his held notes like the tremulant on the organ. Would you ever have thought that his playing is like this? Yet it is nothing but the truth, though a truth that I should only tell to you.[46] (A, 907)

Friedrich Ramm (1744–1811)

► Ramm was principal oboist in the Mannheim and, later, the Munich court orchestra. Mozart's Oboe Quartet in F, K. 370 (368b), was written for Ramm. ◄

To Leopold Mozart   *Mannheim, 4 November 1777*

It so happened that some members of the orchestra were there [at Cannabich's], young Danner, a horn player called [Franz or Martin] Lang, and the oboist whose name I have forgotten [Friedrich Ramm], but who plays very well and has a delightfully pure tone. I have made him a present of my oboe concerto,[47] which is being copied in a room at Cannabich's, and the fellow is quite crazy with delight. (A, 355)

To Leopold Mozart   *Mannheim, 3 December 1777*

Ramm, the oboist, is a very good, jolly, honest fellow of about thirty-five, who has already traveled a great deal, and consequently has plenty of experience. (A, 401–402)

To Leopold Mozart   *Mannheim, 4 February 1778*

Ramm is a decent fellow, but a libertine. (A, 461)

To Leopold Mozart   *Mannheim, 14 February 1778*

Yesterday there was a concert at Cannabich's. . . . Herr Ramm (by way of a change) played for the fifth time my oboe concerto written for Ferlendis [K. 314 (285d)], which is making a great sensation here. It is now Ramm's cheval de bataille. (A, 482)

CLARINETISTS

Joseph Beer (1744–1812)

► Beer was clarinetist in the Concert Spirituel beginning in 1771, later at St. Petersburg (1782–1792) and thereafter at the court of Frederick Wilhlem II of Prussia. ◄

To Leopold Mozart   *Paris, 9 July 1778*

As for the letter of recommendation to Herr Beer, I don't think it is necessary to send it to me. So far I have not made his acquaintance; I only know that he is an excellent clarinet player, but in other respects a dissolute sort of fellow. I really do not like to associate with such people, as it does one no credit; and, frankly, I should not like to give him a letter of recommendation—indeed I should feel positively ashamed to do so— even if he could do something for me! But, as it is, he is by no means respected here—and a great many people do not know him at all. (A, 565–566)

Anton Stadler (1753–1812)

▶ Stadler was Mozart's close friend and fellow Mason, for whom he composed the Clarinet Quintet, K. 581, the Concerto, K. 622, the basset horn obbligatos in *La Clemenza di Tito,* and perhaps other works. In addition to his activities as a player, Stadler developed the so-called bassett-clarinet, which extended the normal clarinet range by four semitones. Unfortunately, Mozart left no description of Stadler's playing. ◀

To Michael Puchberg   *Vienna, ca. 8 April 1790*

Tomorrow, Friday, Count Hadik has invited me to perform for him Stadler's quintet [K. 581] and the trio I composed for you [the Divertimento for Violin, Viola, and Cello in E-flat, K. 563]. (A, 937)

To Constanze, Baden   *Vienna, 7 October 1791*

Then I orchestrated almost the whole of Stadler's rondo [from the Clarinet Concerto in A, K. 622]. (A, 967)

A BASSOONIST

Georg Wenzel Ritter (1748–1808)

▶ Ritter played bassoon in the orchestras at Mannheim, Munich, and Berlin, He also composed works for his instrument. ◀

To Leopold Mozart   *Mannheim, 3 December 1777*

Herr Ritter, a fine bassoon player, is off to Paris on December 12. Now if I had been alone, this would have been an excellent opportunity for me. He mentioned it to me himself. (A, 402)

HORN PLAYERS

▶ Following Mozart's sound advice regarding "good Effect," we shall abandon the stern order of the alphabet in introducing the final protagonists in this revue. ◄

Giovanni Punto (Johann Wenzel Stich) (1746–1803)

► A virtuoso horn player, Punto served Count Thun and the Mainz court (1769–1774) before traveling to Paris. He was the intended horn soloist for Mozart's sinfonia concertante for four wind instruments, K. 297B. Beethoven's horn sonata, op. 17, was written for Punto. ◄

To Leopold Mozart   *Paris, 5 April 1778*

Punto plays magnifique. (A, 522)

Joseph Leutgeb (1732–1811)

► Leutgeb was a close friend of the Mozart family and a horn player in the Salzburg court orchestra from about 1763. In 1770 he appeared as a soloist in the Concert Spirituel (demonstrating the recently developed technique of hand stopping); he moved to Vienna in 1777. Most of Mozart's works for the horn were written for Leutgeb, who was obliged to suffer as the butt of the composer's jibes and jokes. ◄

To Nannerl   *Milan, 28 November 1772*

Tell Herr Leutgeb to take the plunge and come to Milan, for he will certainly make his mark here. But he must come soon. Do not forget to tell him this, for I am very anxious that he should come [italicized words in code]. (A, 218)

To Nannerl   *Milan, 23 January 1773*

I am vexed that Leutgeb left Salzburg too late to see a performance of my opera [*Lucio Silla*]; and perhaps he will miss us, too, unless we meet on the way. (A, 227)

Leopold Mozart to Wolfgang   *Salzburg, 1 December 1777*

Herr Leutgeb, who has now bought in a suburb of Vienna a cheese-monger's shop (the size of a snail's shell), wrote to us both after your departure, promised to pay me in due course, and asked you for a concerto. But he must know by now that you are no longer in Salzburg. (A, 399)

► Leopold had evidently lent Leutgeb some money. ◄

To Leopold Mozart   *Vienna, 8 May 1782*

Please have a little patience with poor Leutgeb. If you knew his circumstances and saw how he has to muddle along, you would certainly feel

sorry for him. I shall have a word with him and I feel sure that he will pay
you, at any rate by installments. (A, 805)

To Constanze, Baden   *Vienna, 8 October 1791*

Leutgeb begged me to take him a second time [to *Zauberflöte*] and I did so.
(A, 969)

► Unfortunately, as with the clarinetist Stadler, Mozart left no verbal
description of Leutgeb's abilities—except, in Leutgeb's case, for some
outrageous comments inscribed in his scores. The most colorful example is found in the score of the Horn Concerto in D major, K. 412 (ex.
14.3), now known to have been composed, but left unfinished, during
the last year of Mozart's life.[48] It seems more than fitting that Mozart
have his final word here, and his final laugh, accompanied by music
written at about the same time as the Requiem. The sentiments
expressed by Mozart's parting words in the torso of the horn concerto
finale are rather less somber than those of the "Lacrimosa dies illa." But
they could hardly be more final: "Finished? Thank heaven! Enough,
enough!" ◄

EXAMPLE 14.3. Concerto for Horn in D, K. 412, Rondo Finale.
Annotated Version

APPENDIX I

Biographical Glossary

Abaco, Evaristo Felice dall' (1675–1742). Cellist in Munich court orchestra.

Abel, Karl Friedrich (1723–1787). Famous composer and performer on the viola da gamba. Close associate of Johann Christian Bach, with whom he co-founded the Bach–Abel concerts in London.

d'Affligio, Giuseppe (1719–1787). Impresario of the Burgtheater and the Kärnt-nertor-Theater in Vienna from 1767 to 1770. In 1768 d'Affligio was instrumental in preventing a Viennese performance of Mozart's *La finta semplice.*

Arco, Count Karl Joseph (1743–1830). Chamberlain to the Salzburg court.

Auernhammer, Josepha (1758–1820). A piano pupil of Mozart's in Vienna for whom he composed the Sonata for Two Pianos, K. 448/375a, and to whom he dedicated the six sonatas for piano and violin, K. 296, 376–80 (374d, 374e, 317d, 373a, 374f), which were published in 1781 by Artaria & Co.

Becke, Johann Baptist (1743–1817). Flautist in the Munich court orchestra.

Bernacchi, Antonio (1685–1756). Illustrious bel canto castrato and founder, in 1736, of a successful school for singing at Bologna.

Boisserée, Sulpiz (1783–1854). Member of the literary circle around Goethe; influential in the rivival of interest in medieval and Gothic art and architecture. His comments about Mozart, published posthumously in his *Selbstbiographie, Tagebücher und Briefe* (Stuttgart, 1862), were based on conversations in the year 1815 with Franz von Destouches, Kapellmeister to the court chapel of Prince Oettingen-Wallerstein,.

Bonno, Giuseppe (1710–1788). Court Kapellmeister in Vienna from 1774 until his death, whereupon he was succeeded by Antonio Salieri.

Bose, Baron Friedrich Karl von (b. 1751). Saxon councillor.

Bretzner, Christoph Friedrich (1746–1807). Author of the singspiel libretto *Belmont und Constanze,* that formed the basis for Gottlieb Stephanie's libretto for Mozart's *Die Entführung aus dem Serail.*

Bullinger, Abbé Joseph (1744–1810). Jesuit priest and close Salzburg friend of the Mozart family.

Cannabich, Rosa (b. 1764). Daughter of the composer Christian Cannabich. A talented piano pupil of Mozart's.

Casti, Giambattista (1724–1803). Well-traveled writer and poet, renowned especially for his opera buffa libretti. His comic libretti were set by Paisiello and Salieri.

Cobenzl, Count Johann Philipp von (1741–1810). Court and State Chancellor in Vienna, a close advisor to Emperor Joseph. Mozart made Cobenzl's acquaintance early on during his Viennese years and was a frequent guest at the Reisenberg, the count's country estate.

Colloredo, Hieronymus von (1732–1812). Reform-minded Prince-Archbishop of Salzburg, in which post he succeeded Sigismund von Schrattenbach in 1772. Mozart's difficulties with the Archbishop are legendary.

Dalberg, Baron Wolfgang Heribert von (1750–1806). Manager of the Mannheim National Theater.

Danner, Johann Georg (1722–1803). Mannheim violinist and old friend of the Mozart family. His son, Christian Franz, is also mentioned in the correspondence.

Da Ponte, Lorenzo (1749–1838). Poet and adventurer. Converted Jew, later a Roman Catholic priest; settled in Vienna in 1783 as Court Poet. Librettist for Mozart's *Le nozze di Figaro, Don Giovanni,* and *Così fan tutte.* Ultimately emigrated to New York where, among other activities, he taught Italian at Columbia University and wrote his memoirs.

Daubrawaick, Johann Anton Daubrawa von (1731–1810). Court Councillor in Salzburg.

Dauer, Johann Ernst (1746–1812). Tenor at the Burgtheater; sang the role of Pedrillo in the first production of *Die Entführung aus dem Serail.*

De Jean, Ferdinand (1731–1797). German-born Dutch surgeon and amateur flautist, whom Mozart met in Mannheim in 1777 through Johann Baptist Wendling. De Jean commissioned the three flute quartets, K. 285, 285a, 285b, the two flute concerti, K. 313/285c, and 314/285d, and, presumably, the Andante for flute and orchestra, K. 315/285e.

Deller, Florian (1729–1773). Viennese composer.

Dittersdorf, Carl Ditters von (1739–1799). Leading Viennese violinist and composer; principally known for his singspiels.

Doles, Johann Friedrich (1715–1797). Thomaskantor in Leipzig, pupil of J. S. Bach. Mozart met Doles on his visit to Leipzig in April 1789.

Dürnitz, Baron Thaddäus von (d. 1803). Amateur pianist, bassoonist, and patron of music.

Duschek, Franz Xaver (1731–1799). Prague music teacher and pianist. Duschek and his wife, Josephine (1753–1824), the soprano for whom Mozart, in 1777, composed the recitative and aria "Ah, lo previdi," K. 272, were close friends of the Mozart family.

d'Épinay, Madame Louise Florence (1726–1783). French writer and intellectual; friend of Diderot, Rousseau, and Voltaire. Madame d'Épinay lived with Melchior Grimm; cared for Mozart after the death of his mother.

Esser, Karl Michael, Ritter von (b. 1737–after 1791). Traveling violin virtuoso.

Eybler, Joseph (1765–1846). Pupil of Joseph Haydn and highly regarded friend and associate of Mozart; succeeded Salieri as Court Kapellmeister in 1824.

Ferlendis, Giuseppe (1755–ca. 1802). Oboist in the Salzburg court orchestra.

Firmian, Count Karl (Carlo) Joseph von (1716–1782). Governor General of Lombardy in Milan; was responsible for Mozart's obtaining the commission for the opera *Lucio Silla.*

Fischietti, Domenico (ca. 1725–ca. 1810). Neapolitan-born Kapellmeister at Dresden from 1765–1772. From 1772–1783 he was Kapellmeister, at least in title, at Salzburg.

Francis, Archduke of Austria (1768–1835). Son of Emperor Leopold II; later Emperor Francis II (from 1792).

Frank, Joseph. A Viennese physician who claimed to have become "intimate" with Mozart.

Freystädtler, Franz Jakob (1761–1841). Pupil of Mozart's in Vienna, nicknamed "Gaulimauli" in the canon, K. 232/509a.

Galitzin, Prince Dimitri Alexeivich (1721–1793). Russian ambassador in Vienna.

Gemmingen, Otto Heinrich von (1755–1836). Mannheim diplomat and man of letters; later a fellow lodge member of Mozart's in Vienna.

Grétry, André-Ernest-Modeste (1741–1813). French opera composer, celebrated for his command of melody and dramatic expression, important in the establishment of the opéra-comique. He had heard Mozart perform in Geneva in 1766. Around 1781 Mozart composed a set of variations on a theme of Grétry, K. 352 (374c).

Grimm, Friedrich Melchior (1723–1807). German-born Parisian man of letters. Founder of the prestigious *Correspondance Littéraire*. Grimm had been at first an enthusiastic champion of Mozart's talent (as well as that of his sister), but the relationship soured during the course of Mozart's 1778 sojourn in Paris.

Guines, Duc Adrien-Louis de (1735–1806). Governor of the County of Artois, and a fine flautist. His daughter, a talented harpist, was Mozart's pupil in composition. The Concerto for Flute and Harp, K. 299/297c, was composed for de Guines.

Hadik, Count Johann Karl. Hungarian Court Councillor.

Hafeneder, Joseph. Violinist in the Salzburg court orchestra; also a composer.

Hagenauer, Johann Lorenz (1712–1792). Salzburg merchant and the Mozart family's landlord until 1773. He was the recipient of numerous informative letters from Leopold describing young Wolfgang's early travel experiences and achievements. Among his sons, Ignaz (who founded an Italian branch of the family business) and Johann Nepomuk are mentioned in the correspondence.

Haibel, Jakob (1762–1826). Singer, and husband of Constanze Mozart's younger sister, Sophie.

Hofdemel, Franz (ca. 1755–1791). Attendant to the Viennese Supreme Court and the husband of Magdalena Pokorny Hofdemel, who is said to have been a pupil of Mozart's and with whom she is also rumored to have had an affair. The day after Mozart's death Hofdemel attempted to kill his wife and took his own life, adding fuel to the rumor.

Hofer, Franz de Paula (1755–1796). Violinist and husband of Constanze Mozart's eldest sister Josefa.

Hoffmeister, Franz Anton (1754–1812). Composer and publisher of several of Mozart's compositions, among them the Piano Quartet in G minor, K. 478, and the *Hoffmeister* String Quartet in D, K. 499.

Hofmann, Leopold (1738–1798). Kapellmeister of St. Stephen's Cathedral, Vienna.

Jacquin, Gottfried von (1767–1792). One of the composer's closest friends in Vienna, to whom most of Mozart's letters from Prague were addressed.

Jacquin's sister, Franziska (1769–1853), was a piano pupil of Mozart's. The *Kegelstatt Trio* for Piano, Clarinet, and Viola, K. 498, and the Sonata in C for Piano, four hands, K. 521, were written for the Jacquins.

Jeunehomme, Mademoiselle. French pianist, for whom Mozart composed the Piano Concerto in E-flat, K. 271, in January 1777.

Joseph II (1741–1790). Son of Francis I and Maria Theresa and Emperor of Austria from 1780. An Enlightened monarch, Joseph abolished serfdom and drastically reduced the power of both the Church and the aristocracy. In 1787 he appointed Mozart Imperial and Royal Chamber Composer.

Karl Theodor (1724–1799), Elector of Palatinate-Bavaria. Upon his succession to the Electoral seat of Bavaria in 1778, Karl Theodor moved his court from Mannheim to Munich. Under his enthusiastic patronage the Mannheim-Munich court opera, and especially the orchestra, ranked as perhaps the most outstanding in Europe. Karl Theodor also sponsored the creation of a national theater in both Mannheim and Munich.

Kaunitz, Count Wenzel Anton von (1711–1794). Austrian Chancellor and musical amateur.

Klein, Anton (1748–1810). Librettist and professor of philosophy and aesthetics. Author of the text of *Günther von Schwarzburg*, a singspiel set to music by Ignaz Holzbauer.

Kucharz, Johann Baptist (1751–1829). Prague organist and conductor; assisted at the rehearsals for the Prague premiere of *Don Giovanni* in 1787; later prepared vocal scores for several Mozart operas.

Lange, Joseph (1751–1831). Actor, painter, and husband of Constanze Mozart's sister, Aloysia.

Le Grand, Claude. Ballet master in Munich for the premiere of *Idomeneo*.

Lichnowsky, Prince Karl (1756–1814). Best known as a patron of Beethoven, chose Mozart as his traveling companion to Berlin, Leipzig, and Dresden in April/May 1789.

Lodron, Count Ernst Maria Joseph Nepomuk (1716–1779). Marshal of Salzburg. His wife was Countess Maria Antonia (1738–1786), for whose name day Mozart composed the divertimenti, K. 247 and 287 (271H). The Concerto for Three Pianos, K. 242, was intended for the Countess and her daughters, Aloysia and Josepha.

Lugiati, Pietro (1724–1788). Patron of music, and the Mozart's host in Verona.

Lützow, Countess Antonie. Wife of the Commandant of the Salzburg Fortress, for whom Mozart composed the Piano Concerto in C, K. 246, in 1776.

Marchand, Heinrich (b. 1769). For three years, from 1781 on, Marchand lived with Leopold Mozart as his pupil in clavier, violin, and composition. His sister, Margarethe ("Gretl") (1768–1800), became Leopold's pupil in clavier and voice in 1782.

Maximilian (1756–1801). Archduke of Austria, later Archbishop of Cologne.

Meissner, Joseph (ca. 1724–1795). A Salzburg bass, famous for his large vocal range.

Metastasio, Pietro (1698–1782). Imperial court poet in Vienna from 1740; preeminent Italian poet and librettist of the eighteenth century; his two-dozen opera seria texts had been set to music approximately 1,000 times by the end of the century.

Mozart, Maria Anna ("Nannerl") (1751–1829). Mozart's older sister. Later the wife of Johann Baptist Franz von Berchtold zu Sonnenburg.

Mozart, Maria Anna Thekla ("Bäsle") (1758–1841). Mozart's "little cousin," daughter of Leopold Mozart's brother.

Neumann, Johann Leopold (b. 1748). Secretary to the Saxon War Council and a librettist. His wife was a pianist.

Niemetschek, Franz Xaver (1766–1849). Czech professor of philosophy, made Mozart's acquaintance in Prague, presumably in 1787. His biography of Mozart was first published in 1798; it appeared in a revised edition in 1808.

Nissen, Georg Nikolaus (1761–1826). Second husband of Constanze Mozart and author of the first full-scale Mozart biography—published (posthumously) in 1828. It was based on materials provided by Constanze and other individuals close to the composer.

Noverre, Jean Georges (1727–1810). Famous dancer and choreographer; maître de ballet at the Paris opera; also active in Vienna (from 1767 to 1774).

Paradies, Domenico (1707–1791). Italian composer and teacher, settled in England in the mid 1740s. Leopold Mozart recommended that Nannerl practice Paradies's sonatas for harpsichord.

Picq, Carlo de (1749–1806). Dancer and ballet master, admired by the Mozarts.

Pierron, Mlle. Therese. Stepdaughter of Privy Court Councillor Serrarius in Mannheim, in whose residence Mozart and his mother temporarily roomed.

Pinzger, Andreas (ca. 1742–1817). Violinist and violist at the Salzburg court.

Ployer, Barbara. Mozart's pupil in piano and composition, for whom he composed the Piano Concertos in E-flat and G, K. 449 and 453. Her father was Gottfried Ignaz Ployer, Court Councillor in Vienna and agent of the Salzburg court there.

Puchberg, Michael (1741–1822). Wealthy Viennese dry goods merchant and a fellow Freemason to whom, over the course of three years, Mozart made numerous urgent appeals for money, and to whom he dedicated the String Trio, K. 563.

Quaglio, Lorenzo (1730–1804). Stage designer for the Munich premiere of *Idomeneo*.

Rauzzini, Venanzio (1746–1810). Internationally celebrated castrato. Sang the role of Cecilio in the Milan premiere of *Lucio Silla*, K. 135, December 1772.

Reutter, Georg (1708–1772). Kapellmeister of St. Stephen's Cathedral in Vienna from 1738 and First Court Kapellmeister from 1769. An early mentor of Joseph Haydn.

Rochlitz, Johann Friedrich (1769–1842). Former pupil at the Leipzig Thomasschule under Johann Friedrich Doles; later publisher of the influential musical journal, the Leipzig *Allgemeine Musikalische Zeitung*.

Rosenberg, Count Franz Xaver Wolfgang Orsini-Rosenberg (1723–1796). Director of the court theaters in Vienna.

Rumbeck [Rumbeke], Countess Marie Karoline Thiennes de (1755–1812). Mozart's first piano pupil in Vienna.

Rust, Jakob. Served as Kapellmeister in Salzburg in 1777–1778.

Sacchini, Antonio (1730–1786). Leading opera composer, active in Italy and Germany, London, and Paris.

Salern, Count Joseph von (1718–1805). Manager of the Munich opera.

Schachtner, Johann Andreas (1731–1795). Trumpeter at the Salzburg court and friend of the Mozart family. A librettist and translator, he may have provided the text for Mozart's *Zaide;* he certainly prepared the German translations of *La finta giardiniera* and *Idomeneo.*

Schikaneder, Emanuel (1751–1812). Actor, playwright, and man of the theater; made the acquaintance of the Mozarts during his sojourn in Salzburg in 1780–1781. The librettist for *Die Zauberflöte,* in which he played the role of Papageno in the first performance at the Theater auf der Wieden, of which he was the manager.

Seeau, Joseph Anton, Count von (1713–1799). The manager of the National Theater in Munich.

Sensheim [Seinsheim], Count Joseph Maria von (d. 1786). Minister for foreign affairs at the Munich court.

Seyler, Abel (1730–1800). Director of the Seyler traveling theatrical company.

Sieber, Jean Georges (1734–1816). Parisian music publisher. Published Mozart's violin sonatas, K. 301–306, in 1778, and the *Paris* Symphony, K. 297 (300a), in 1788.

Silbermann, Johann Andreas (1712–1783). Member of the illustrious Alsatian family of organ builders.

Späth, Franz Jakob (1714–1786). Piano maker in Regensburg, teacher of Johann Andreas Stein.

Stadler, Abbé Maximilian (1748–1833). Friend of the Mozart family, helped sort through Mozart's musical manuscripts after his death, also completed several of Mozart's unfinished compositions. No relation to the clarinetist Anton Stadler.

Starzer, Joseph (1726/27–1787). Viennese composer and violinist, one of the founders, in 1771, of the Tonkünstler-Societät of Vienna.

Stein, Johann Andreas (1728–1792). Famous Augsburg maker of pianos and organs.

Stein, Maria Anna ("Nannette") (1769–1833). Daughter of the above, inherited her father's firm which, after her marriage to the piano builder Johann Andreas Streicher, she transferred to Vienna.

Stephanie, Johann Gottlieb, the Younger (1741–1800). Translator and dramatist; director at the Vienna Court Opera since 1769; adapted the text for *Die Entführung aus dem Serail* from an original play by Christoph Friedrich Bretzner.

Stoll, Anton (1747–1805). Choirmaster at Baden.

Storace, Stephen (1762–1796). English-born friend and pupil of Mozart, and brother of the singer Nancy Storace (1765–1817). Nancy created the role of Susanna in Mozart's *Figaro.*

Strack, Johann Kilian (1724–1793). Imperial valet and an influential personage at court.

Süssmayr, Franz Xaver (1766–1803). Mozart's pupil and assistant from ca. 1790. After Mozart's death he became a pupil of Salieri; in 1794 he assumed the post of Kapellmeister of the German opera at the National Theater in Vienna. He is best known for having completed Mozart's *Requiem.*

Swieten, Baron Gottfried van (1733–1803). Prefect of the imperial library in Vienna; patron of music, amateur composer. Mozart participated in Swieten's Sunday musicales, at which the music of Bach and Handel was studied and performed. Swieten commissioned Mozart to arrange several of Handel's oratorios for performance.

Tartini, Giuseppe (1692–1770). Celebrated composer, was also one of the greatest violinists of his time. As a pedagogue of violin playing he was extremely influential, having founded the so-called School of Nations in Padua in 1728, and written a treatise which was extensively incorporated by Leopold Mozart into his own.

Tenducci, Giustino Ferdinando (1736–1790). Male soprano, resident in London and a close friend of J. C. Bach. The Mozarts met him in London in 1764.

Teyber, Elisabeth (1744–1816). Soprano, sister of Therese Teyber; pupil of Hasse; made her reputation in Italy and St. Petersburg.

Thun, Count Johann Josef Anton (1711–1788), music-loving patriarch of the Thun family, resident in Prague and Linz. His son, Franz Joseph (1734–1800) was the husband of Wilhelmine (1747–1800), a leading patroness of music in Vienna and close friend of Mozart's.

Trattner, Johann Thomas Edler von (1717–1798). Wealthy Viennese publisher and book dealer in whose luxurious home Mozart once roomed and often performed. His wife, Therese, was a piano pupil of Mozart's and the dedicatee of the Fantasia and Sonata in C minor for Piano, K. 475, 457.

Varesco, Abbate Giambattista (1735–1805). Italian-born priest, resident in Salzburg; the librettist for *Idomeneo* (1780–1781) and the unfinished opera buffa, *L'oca del Cairo* (1783).

Waldstätten, Baroness Martha Elisabeth von. (1744–1811). Mozart's friend and patroness in Vienna, and a fine pianist.

Wagenseil, Georg Christoph (1715–1777). Important Viennese composer of the preclassic period.

Walter, Anton (1752–1826). Austrian piano maker, resident in Vienna from 1780. Mozart owned a Walter piano. The instrument survives and is on display in the Mozart Museum in Salzburg.

Walter, Johann Ignaz. Actor at the Burgtheater.

Weber family. Fridolin (1733–1779). Singer and copyist; the father of Mozart's wife, Constanze (1762–1842), and her sisters: Josefa (Hofer, 1758–1819), the first Queen of the Night in *Die Zauberflöte*; Aloysia (Lange, ca. 1760–1839), and Sophie (Haibel, ca. 1763–1846).

Weigl, Anna Maria. Singer at the German National Theater in Vienna from 1769.

Wendling family: Johann Baptist (1723–1797). Principal flautist in the Electoral court orchestra of Mannheim (later Munich). Mozart was a close friend of the entire Wendling family in Mannheim. Johann Baptist's wife, Dorothea (1737–1811), singer, created the role of Ilia in *Idomeneo*. Elisabeth Augusta "Gustl" (1752–1794), their daughter, pianist and singer. Franz Anton (1729–1786), violinist, and brother of Johann Baptist. Elisabeth Augusta "Lisl" (1746–1786), singer, wife of Franz Anton, sang Elettra in *Idomeneo*.

Wetzlar von Plankenstern, Baron Raimund (1752–1810). Viennese banker. A converted Jew in whose house Mozart lived from December 1782 to February 1783, also the godfather of the Mozarts' first child, Raimund Leopold. Mozart first met Lorenzo Da Ponte in Wetzlar's home.

Winter, Sebastian (1743–1815). Salzburg friend of the Mozarts, later Chamberlain at the Donaueschingen court, for which he helped procure compositions from Mozart.

Wolfegg, Count Anton (1729–1821). Canon of Salzburg Cathedral.

Zichy, Count Karl (1753–1826). Court Councillor in Vienna. His wife was Countess Anna Maria Antonia (1759–1809), one of Mozart's pupils.

Zonca, Giovanni Battista (1728–1809). Bass singer at the Mannheim and, later, the Munich court.

APPENDIX II

Original German Texts

1. Acrostic from Letter to Leopold, 24 November 1780

wenn Nur der Esel welcher einen Ring Zereist, und durch die gewalt einen Bruch bekommet, daß ich ihn darüber scheissen höre wie einen Castraten mit hörner, und mit seinem langen ohr den fuchs-schwanz streicht, nicht so . . . . . . wäre.

(MBA, 3:31)

2. Postscript to Letter to Leopold, 31 October 1777

à Mad^selle^ Rosalie joli.
Ich sag dir tausend danck mein liebste Sallerl,
und trincke dir zur ehr ein ganzes schallerl,
Coffé und dann auch thée und limonadi,
und tuncke ein, ein stangerl vom Pomadi
und auch—auweh, auweh, es schlägt iust Sex,
und wers nit glaubt der ist—der ist—ein fex.
die fortsezung folgt nächstens.

(MBA, 2:95)

3. Letter to His Mother, 31 January 1778

Madame Mutter!
Ich esse gerne Butter.
Wir sind Gottlob und Dank
Gesund und gar nicht krank.
Wir fahren durch die Welt,
Haben aber nit viel Geld;
Doch sind wir aufgeräumt
Und keins von uns verschleimt.
Ich bin bei Leuten auch

die tragen den Dreck im Bauch,
doch lassen sie ihn auch hinaus
So wohl vor, als nach dem Schmaus.

Gefurzt wird allzeit auf die Nacht
Und immer so, daß es brav kracht.

Doch gestern war der fürze König,
deßen Fürze riechen wie Hönig,
Nicht gar zu wohl in der Stimme,
Er war auch selbsten voller Grimme.
Wir sind ietzt über 8 Täge weck
Und haben schon geschißen vielen Dreck.
Herr Wendling wird wohl böse seyn,
Daß ich kaum nichts geschrieben fein,
Doch wenn ich komm' über d' Rheinbrücke
So kom ich ganz gewiß zurücke
Und schreib die 4 Quartetti ganz
Damit er mich nicht heißt ein Schwantz.

Und das Concert spar ich mir nach Paris,
Dort schmier ichs her gleich auf den ersten Schiß.
Die Wahrheit zu gestehen, so möcht ich mit den Leuten
Viel lieber in die Welt hinaus und in die große Weiten,
Als mit der Tac-gesellschaft, die ich vor meiner seh,
So oft ich drauf gedenke, so thut mir der Bauch weh;
Doch muß es noch geschehen, wir müssen noch zusamm—
Der Arsch vom Weber ist mehr werth als der Kopf vom Ramm
Und auch von diesem Arsch ein Pfifferling
Ist mir lieber als der Mons: Wendling.
Wir beleidigen doch nicht Gott mit unserem Scheißen
Auch noch weniger, wenn wir in dreck nein beißen.
Wir sind ehrliche Leute die zusammen taugen,
Wir haben summa summarum 8 Augen
Ohne dem wo wir drauf sitzen.
Nun will ich mich nit mehr erhitzen
Mit meiner Poesie; nur will ich Ihnen sagen

Daß ich Montag die Ehre hab, ohne viel zu fragen,
Sie zu embrassiren und dero Händ zu küssen,
Doch werd' ich schon vorhero haben in die Hosen geschißen.
à dieu Mamma

Worms den 1778^{ten}Jenner
Anno 31.

Dero getreues Kind
ich hab' den Grind
Trazom.
(MBA, 2: 245–247)

4. Letter to Nannerl, 18 August 1784

Du wirst im Ehstand viel erfahren
was dir ein halbes Räthsel war;
bald wirst du aus Erfahrung wissen,
wie Eva einst hat handeln müssen
daß sie hernach den kain gebahr.

doch schwester, diese Ehstands Pflichten
wirst du vom Herzen gern verrichten,
denn glaube mir, sie sind nicht schwer;
doch Jede Sache hat zwo Seiten;
der Ehstand bringt zwar viele freuden,
allein auch kummer bringet er.
drum wenn dein Mann dir finstre Mienen,
die du nicht glaubest zu verdienen,
    in seiner üblen Laune macht:
So denke, das ist Männergrille,
und sag: Herr, es gescheh dein wille
beytag——und meiner bey der Nacht.

(MBA, 3:321)

5. Elegy on the Death of His Pet Starling
4 June 1787

Hier ruht ein lieber Narr,
Ein Vogel Staar.
Noch in den besten Jahren
Mußt er erfahren
Des Todes bittern Schmerz.
Mir blu't das Herz,
Wenn ich daran gedenke.
O Leser! schenke
Auch du ein Thränchen ihm.
Er war nicht schlimm;
Nur war er etwas munter,
Doch auch mitunter
Ein lieber loser Schalk,
Und drum kein Dalk.
Ich wett, er ist schon oben,
Um mich zu loben
Für diesen Freundschaftsdienst
Ohne Gewinnst.
Denn wie er unvermuthet
Sich hat verblutet,
Dacht er nicht an den Mann,
Der so schön reimen kann.
Den 4ten Juni 1787.

(MBA, 4: 49–50)

6. Letter to "Bäsle," 28 February 1778

Mademoiselle
    ma trés chére Cousine!

sie werden vielleicht glauben oder gar meynen ich sey gestorben!——ich
sey Crepirt—oder verreckt?—doch nein! meynen sie es nicht, ich bitte sie;
denn gemeint und geschissen ist zweyerley!—wie könnte ich denn so schön

schreiben wenn ich tod wäre?—wie wäre das wohl möglich?———wegen meinem so langen stillschweigen will ich mich gar nicht entschuldigen, denn sie würden mir so nichts glauben; doch, was wahr ist, bleibt wahr!— ich habe so viell zu thun gehabt, daß ich wohl zeit hatte, an das bäsle zu denken, aber nicht zu schreiben, mithin hab ichs müssen lassen bleiben.

Nun aber habe ich die Ehre, sie zu fragen, wie sie sich befinden und sich tragen?—ob sie noch offens leibs sind?—ob sie etwa gar haben den grind?——ob sie mich noch ein bischen können leiden—ob sie öfters schreiben mit einer kreiden?—ob sie noch dann und wan an mich ge- dencken?—ob sie nicht bisweilen lust haben sich aufzuhencken?—ob sie etwa gar bös waren? auf mich armen narrn; ob sie nicht gutwillig wollen fried machen, oder ich lass bei meiner Ehr einen krachen! doch sie lachen——victoria!——unsre arsch sollen die friedens-zeichen seyn!—ich dachte wohl, daß sie mir nicht länger wiederstehen könnten. ja ja, ich bin meiner sache gewis, und sollt ich heut noch machen einen schiss, obwohl ich in 14 Tägen geh nach Paris. wenn sie mir also wolln antworten, aus der stadt Augsburg dorten, so schreiben sie mir baldt, damit ich den brief erhalt, sonst wenn ich etwa schon bin weck, bekomme ich statt einen brief einen dreck. dreck!——dreck!—o dreck!—o süsses wort!—dreck!—schmeck!—auch schön!—dreck, schmeck!—dreck!—leck—o charmante!—dreck, leck!— das freüet mich!—dreck, schmeck und leck!—schmeck dreck, und leck dreck! . . .

an alle meine freünde mein Compliment, und wers nicht glaubt, der soll mich lecken ohne End, von nunan bis in Ewickeit, bis ich einmahl werd wieder gescheid. da hat er gwis zu lecken lang, mir wird dabey schier selbsten bang, ich fürcht der dreck der geht mir aus, und er bekommt nicht gnug zum schmaus. Adieu bäsle. ich bin, ich war, ich wär, ich bin gewesen, ich war gewesen, ich wär gewesen, o wenn ich wäre, o daß ich wäre, wollte gott ich wäre, ich wurde seyn, ich werde seyn, wenn ich seyn würde, o das ich seyn würde, ich wurde gewesen, ich werde gewesen seyn, o wenn ich gewesen wäre, o daß ich gewesen wäre, wolltegott ich wäre gewesen, was?—ein stockfisch.

addieu ma chére Cousine, wohin?—ich bin der nämlich wahre vetter

Mannheim den 28ten *feb^{ro}* 1778   Wolfgang Amadé Mozart

                                          (MBA, 2:307–310)

Notes

Chapter 1. The Musician

1. Arthur Hutchings, *Mozart: The Man, The Musician*, II: 12–14.
2. The Variations on a Minuet by J. C. Fischer, K. 179 (189a), were one of Mozart's favorite concert and teaching pieces at this time. See Chapter 12.
3. As reported by Ludwig Berger in *Cäcilia*, 10 (1829). See DDB, 542.
4. For Mozart's opinion of Clementi's playing on that and other occasions, see Chapters 7 and 14.
5. As reported by Carl Czerny in a communication to the Mozart biographer, Otto Jahn. See Elliot Forbes, *Thayer's Life of Beethoven*, I: 88.
6. Contrary to Kelly's implication, Dittersdorf was actually a virtuoso violinist.
7. Since the composer Paisiello is said to have been in the audience, this party must have taken place in May or June 1784.
8. Mozart is presumably referring to the Missa brevis in B-flat, K. 275 (272b), composed in 1777.
9. By 1777 Mozart had composed considerably more than three operas. He is presumably counting only the three operas written in Italy: *Mitridate*, K. 87 (74a) (1770), *Ascanio in Alba*, K. 111 (1771), and *Lucio Silla*, K. 135 (1772).
10. Mozart took the examination in Bologna, in the Accademia filarmonica, on 9 October 1770. The product of the examination was the four–part setting, "Quaerite primum regnum Dei," K. 86 (73v). See K6, 111–112.
11. The German original reads: "meinem genie—lust—wissenschaft und freüde." MBA, 2: 409.
12. The German original reads: "von superieren Talent." MBA, 2: 473.
13. See Alan Tyson, *Mozart: Studies of the Autograph Scores*, and especially Erich Hertzmann, "Mozart's Creative Process," *The Musical Quarterly*, 43 (1957): 187–200.
14. The reference is to the flute concertos and quartets commissioned by Ferdinand De Jean.
15. It is not clear whether the reference is to the Serenade in E-flat, K. 375, or the one in C minor, K. 388.
16. This was the *Linz* Symphony, K. 425.
17. The recitative and Aria, "Basta, vincesti,"—"Ah, non lasciarmi," K. 295a.
18. The variations were to be dedicated to the Grand Duke, Paul Petrovich of Russia. The work was never written. See Chapter 12.
19. The Bach aria is published in Johann Christian Bach, *12 Konzert- und Opernarien*, edited by Ludwig Landshoff (Leipzig, 1930). For a detailed and illuminating comparison of the Bach and Mozart settings see Stefan Kunze, "Die Vertonungen der Arie "Non sò d'onde viene" von J. Chr. Bach und W.A. Mozart," *Analecta Musicologica*, 2 (1965): 85-111; also Hermann Abert, *W.A. Mozart*, I, 509-512 On the Italian aria styles and forms, see Chapter 8.
20. As it happened, work on the opera, with interruptions and delays, would spread out over some ten months. See the various citations in Chapters 8–10.
21. From the dedication of the six string quartets, K. 387, 421, 428, 458, 464, 465. The rest of the famous dedicatory text appears in Chapter 12.
22. "Anekdoten. Noch einige Kleinigkeiten aus Mozarts Leben, von seiner Wittwe mitgetheilt," *Allgemeine Musikalische Zeitung*, I (1799), column 855, footnote.

Chapter 2. The Career

1. The contract for a singing engagement.
2. Padre Martini had written an enthusiastic testimonial for Mozart on 12 October 1770—three days after he had successfully passed the rigorous examination for admission to the Academia filarmonica of Bologna. See DDB, 127–28.
3. Presumably the *Coronation* Mass in C, K. 317, completed on 23 March 1779, and the Missa solemnis in C, K. 337, composed in March 1780.
4. Mozart's salary was actually 450 gulden.
5. On Colloredo's Enlightened social policies see Volkmar Braunbehrens, *Mozart in Vienna: 1781–1791*, pp. 22–29.
6. An Austro-Bohemian specialty, normally an octet consisting of two oboes, two clarinets, two horns, and two bassoons.
7. The two leading concert organizations in Paris: the oldest, the Concert Spirituel, was founded in 1725; the competing Concert des Amateurs was founded in 1769.
8. Excerpts appear in Chapters 4 and 11.
9. See MBA, 5: 281.
10. The most comprehensive description of Mozart's life in Vienna is found in Braunbehrens, *Mozart in Vienna.*
11. The casino building, a site for winter concerts, in the city square known as the Mehlmarkt (also as the Neuer Markt).
12. An elegant Viennese park where outdoor concerts were held.
13. *Galanterie:* Light-textured homophonic pieces in a popular style featuring a pleasant, song-like or dance-like melody and an unpretentious accompaniment. Thoroughbass, or figured bass: A system of indicating chords by numerals representing the intervals above the bass.
14. Vincenzo dal Prato, who sang Idamante in the premiere of *Idomeneo.*
15. Among other works Mozart had recently published the *Haffner* Symphony, K. 385, the six string quartets dedicated to Haydn, the piano concertos, K. 413–415 (387a, 385p, 387b), and the Fantasy and Sonata for Piano in C minor, K. 475, K. 457.

Chapter 3. The Profession

1. See below, Concert Life.
2. See DDB, 142.
3. With the exception of Mozart's signature, the letter is in the hand of Leopold Mozart.
4. An English translation of the original decree and related documents is published in DDB, 305–306.
5. See H. C. Robbins Landon, *Mozart: The Golden Years*, 213, and Braunbehrens, *Mozart in Vienna*, 347.
6. See Chapter 11.
7. See Chapter 13.
8. The six sonatas for violin and piano, K. 301–306, published in 1779 and dedicated to the Electoress Maria Elisabeth.
9. Only the Kyrie, apparently, was ever composed. It survives as K. 322 (296a).
10. The Quartet in A, K. 298, never mentioned in this connection, was formerly ascribed to Mozart's sojourn in 1778 in Paris. It was actually composed in 1786 or 1787. See Wolfgang Plath, "Beiträge zur Mozart-Autographie, II," *Mozart-Jahrbuch 1976/77*, 170.
11. See Wolf-Dieter Seiffert, "Schrieb Mozart drei Flötenquartette für Dejean? Neuere Quellendatierung und Bemerkungen zur Familienkorrespondenz," *Mozart-Jahrbuch 1987/88*, 267–275.
12. It is unclear which symphony is meant. The most likely candidates are assumed to be the Symphonies in D, K. 95 (73n) or K. 97 (73m). See MBA, 5: 251.
13. The offertory motet *Misericordias Domini*, K. 222 (205a), composed in Munich in January or February, 1775.
14. Mozart is presumably referring to the Divertimenti in F, K. 247, B-flat, K. 287 (271H), and D, K. 334 (320b).
15. See also the comments on the work of the copyists relating to the opera *Mitridate*, cited in Chapter 10.
16. K. 449, incidentally, has the distinction of being the first work entered by Mozart into his personal thematic catalogue, his *Verzeichnüss aller meiner Werke.*
17. Possibly Felix Hofstätter, a member of the Salzburg Court orchestra. See MBA, 6: 181.

18. According to MBA, this is presumably a reference to Joseph Haydn's Symphonies Nos. 76, 77, 78. See MBA, 6: 161. Landon, *Mozart: The Golden Years*, 85, on the other hand, claims that Mozart is referring to symphonies of Michael Haydn.
19. These were ultimately the sonatas K. 301–306 (293a–d, 300c, 3001). See above, p. 61.
20. For an informative study of Mozart's relations with publishers, along with a comprehensive catalogue of the first editions of his works, see Gertraut Haberkamp, *Die Erstdrucke der Werke von Wolfgang Amadeus Mozart.*
21. The sonatas, K. 304 (300c) and K. 306 (3001).
22. The sonatas were engraved and published by the Paris firm of J. G. Sieber in November 1778. See Haberkamp, *Die Erstdrucke,* I: 126–127.
23. Ibid., 1: 20, 26.
24. On the sonatas, see Chapter 12, p. 307–308.
25. The sonatas were announced for publication on 26 November 1778.
26. Haberkamp, *Die Erstdrucke,* 1: 15.
27. See DDB, 198.
28. The advertisement appeared in the *Wiener Zeitung;* it is reproduced in part in Chap. 12.
29. The sonatas, K. 296, 376–380. See above, p. 67.
30. The six string quartets dedicated to Haydn: K. 387, 421 (417b), 428 (421b), 458, 464, 465.
31. Both the piano concertos and the string quartets were ultimately published, in 1785, by Artaria—not Sieber—as opus 4 and opus 10, respectively. On the performance options for the concerto described by Mozart in this letter, see Chapter 12.
32. The reference is to the publication of Leopold Mozart's treatise on violin playing in 1756 by the Augsburg publisher J. J. Lotter.
33. Only the G-major Concerto, K. 453, was published during Mozart's lifetime: in 1787 by H. P. Bossler in Speyer. It appeared in the form of a set of parts—with numerous mistakes. See Haberkamp, *Die Erstdrucke,* I: 222–223.
34. A rival institution, the Concert des Amateurs, founded in 1769 by François-Joseph Gossec, is occasionally mentioned in Mozart's correspondence.
35. See Neal Zaslaw, "Mozart's Paris Symphonies," *The Musical Times,* 119 (1978): 753–757.
36. See the citations on both the *Paris* symphony and the Sinfonia Concertante in Chap. 12.
37. Landon, *Mozart: The Golden Years,* 28.
38. The number includes the chorus for the oratorio.
39. Actually 450 gulden.
40. The concert of March 16. See p. 71.
41. The concert took place at the home of Prince Rudolph Joseph Colloredo on April 8. The rondo for Antonio Brunetti was the Rondo in C for Violin and Orchestra, K. 373; the "new sonata for myself" presumably the Sonata for Piano and Violin in G, K. 379 (373a); the "new rondo" for the castrato Francesco Ceccarelli, the recitative and aria "A questo seno deh vieni," and "Or che il cielo a me ti rende," K. 374.
42. The Mozarts had moved into an apartment in the luxurious home of the wealthy book dealer and publisher Johann Thomas von Trattner about two months earlier.
43. It is unclear whether the reference is to John Abraham Fischer, the English violinist, or the celebrated Viennese bass singer, Johann Ignaz Ludwig Fischer.
44. The Piano Concerto in C, K. 246.
45. That is, a quartet in the guest room, presumably the Piano Quartet in E-flat, K. 493.
46. "Hammera" is a dialect contraction of "haben wir auch." See MBA, 6: 331. Mozart is saying, "and we also played the pretty Bandl Trio," namely, "Liebes Mandel, wo is's Bandel," for Soprano, Tenor, Bass, and String Quartet, K. 441, a work now known to have been composed no earlier than 1786, that is, not in 1783 as listed in the sixth edition of the Köchel catalogue. See Tyson, *Mozart: Studies,* 33.
47. Mozart, his Prague friend, the soprano Josephine Duschek, and the family of his Dresden host, one Johann Leopold Neumann.
48. According to Otto Erich Deutsch, the snuffbox contained 100 ducats. DDB, 339.
49. Joseph Hafeneder: one of the Salzburg court musicians.
50. The Emperor was said to be fond of fugues.
51. Mozart is referring to two concerts held at the home of Prince Rudolph Colloredo: on April 8 and 27.
52. The symphony is thought to be the one in C, K. 338, Mozart's last symphony composed in Salzburg (in August 1780). See MBA, 6: 108–109.
53. The *Paris* Symphony in D, K. 297 (300a).

54. See the musical excerpt in Chapter 8.
55. Mozart had met the Countess, Josepha Paumgarten, in Munich in November 1780. It is worth noting that the aria was originally composed for a soprano but sung here by a tenor.
56. Six Variations on "Salve tu, Domine" from Paisiello's *I filosofi immaginarii*.
57. The concert of the Wiener Tonkünstler-Societät took place on December 22 in the Burgtheater. It is not known which concerto Mozart performed. The aria was probably "Misero! o sogno," "Aura, che intorno," K. 431 (425b).
58. The date and place of these concerts are unknown.
59. The title of the opera was *Cora*. See MBA, 5: 572. It was never produced.
60. "Ah, conte, partite," K. 418, and "No, no, che non sei capace," K. 419.
61. "Per pietá, non ricercate," K. 420, for insertion into the opera.
62. It does not seem that Mozart ever used the aria.
63. Chapter 1, p. 8.
64. The *Paris* Symphony in D, K. 297 (300a).
65. It is not altogether clear which passage is meant. According to the most recent speculations, it is mm. 84–92. See the discussion of various attempts to identify this passage in Neal Zaslaw, *Mozart's Symphonies: Context, Performance Practice, Reception*, 311–314.

Chapter 4. The World

1. See Peter Branscombe, "Mozart and the Theatre of his Time," in H. C. Robbins Landon, *The Mozart Compendium*, 358.
2. Neither effort can be dated. Both are published in MBA, 4: 167–173.
3. *Die Haushaltung nach der Mode, oder Was soll man für eine Frau nehmen*, a comedy written in 1765 by Franz von Heufeld, who later became the director of the German theater in Vienna and one of its more successful dramatists.
4. *Die Gunst der Fürsten*, the German version by Christian Heinrich Schmidt of *The Unhappy Favorite* by the Earl of Essex.
5. *Peter der Grausame oder Die zwei schlaflosen Nächte*, J. G. Dyk's German translation of Carlo Gozzi's drama *Le due notti affannose*.
6. According to MBA, 6: 162
7. The dances were part of the performance of Mozart's *Ascanio in Alba*, K. 111, which, as Leopold Mozart claims in the same letter, is "really an azione teatrale" and not a serenata.
8. The folk theater featuring the Kasperl, or Lipperl, figure.
9. The translatable part of the title: "The Egg Produced by the Fairy girl . . ."
10. Antoine Dionys Crux had also danced in the ballet in the Munich production of *Idomeneo*.
11. The inventory, including an identification of the individual items, is published in DDB, 587–589, 601–602.
12. Presumably that of Christoph Martin Wieland published in Zurich, 1763–1766, in eight volumes. See DDB, 541.
13. The German original reads: "daß nehmlich der gottlose und Erz-spizbub voltaire so zu sagen wie ein hund—wie ein vieh crepiert ist." MBA, 2: 389.
14. See DDB, 59, 66.
15. See Landon, *The Mozart Compendium*, 149–150.
16. See Rudolph Angermüller, *W. A. Mozarts musikalische Umwelt in Paris (1778)*.
17. One Wenzel Andre Gilowsky.
18. A, 570 and MBA, 5: 539.
19. Mozart's original transcription is published in MBA, 2: 548. See also the comment in MBA, 5: 587.
20. The German reads: "eine lustige Nachricht," that is, an amusing piece of news. See MBA, 4: 199.
21. See Braunbehrens, *Mozart in Vienna*, 175–180.
22. See the discussion of the incident in Braunbehrens, 184–188.
23. See A, 440, n. 2; and MBA, 5: 467.
24. See Joseph Heinz Eibl, *Wolfgang Amadeus Mozart: Chronik eines Lebens*, 90–94.
25. Namely, of Konzertmeister and organist in Salzburg. Leopold Mozart had described this

prospect to Wolfgang in his letter of 11 June 1778 (A, 547). Six months later Mozart accepted the appointment of court organist.

26. See Mozart's letters on the Bavarian War, above.
27. See above, and also Chapters 3 and 8.
28. The reference is to the plan to write a comic opera—ultimately the aborted *L'Oca del Cairo*.
29. On the Wetzlar family see Braunbehrens, *Mozart in Vienna*, 112, 434.
30. The Concerto in E-flat for Two Pianos, K. 365 (316a), composed in 1779, and perhaps the Concerto in F for Three Pianos (the *Lodron* Concerto, K. 242), as arranged by Mozart for two pianos.
31. Raimund Leopold Mozart was born 17 June 1783; he died on August 19.

Chapter 5. The Man

1. See Joseph Heinz Eibl, ''Amadeus'? (Mozarts Vornamen),'' *Acta Mozartiana*, 19 (1972), 4–8.
2. Hermann Abert, *W. A. Mozart*, 2: 3.
3. The German form of the acrostic (which concludes with the same dots of elision shown here) appears in Appendix II.
4. "Di Wolfgang Amadé Mozart mp. Wien den 27t Jullius 1786 untern Kegelscheiben."
5. Unfortunately, Mozart's pantomime music, K. 446 (416d), survives as a fragment consisting of only the first violin part in an incomplete state. It is published in NMA II/6/2.
6. The original German versions of these rhymes appear in Appendix II.
7. The quartets and concerti referred to were compositions for flute commissioned from Mozart by Ferdinand de Jean. Mozart had hoped to travel to Italy with the Weber family.
8. "Joseph" is probably Joseph Preisinger, the proprietor of the inn, *Zur goldenen Schlange*. "Primus" was the nickname for Joseph Deiner, the waiter at the inn.
9. Retaining Mozart's own orthography, as reproduced in MBA, 2: 122. "Farewell. I hope that you will already have taken a lesson in the French language, and I do not doubt that—listen!—that you will soon know French better than I; for it has certainly been two years that I have not written a word in that language. Farewell for now. I kiss your hands, your face, your knees and your—in short, whatever you permit me to kiss. I am, with all my heart, your most affectionate nephew and cousin . . ."
10. NMA volume X/30/1. The examples below appear on pages 9, 44, 24, respectively.
11. The bracketed material is missing in the original, owing to paper damage. See the commentary volume of the NMA edition, p. 14.
12. See Eibl, *Wolfgang Amadeus Mozart: Chronik*, 70.
13. As translated in Marcia Davenport, *Mozart* (New York, 1932), 273. The German original is reproduced in Appendix II.
14. The German original is reproduced in Appendix II.
15. At one point Mozart indulges a pun on Bäsle-baiser. See the entry above under Languages: French, English.
16. See Michael Ochs, "Grace Notes," *Notes*, 47 (1991): 1326–1328; and Ochs, " 'L. m. i. a.': Mozart's Suppressed Canon Texts," *Mozart-Jahrbuch 1991* (forthcoming). I am indebted to Mr. Ochs for making these articles available to me before their publication and for allowing me to include the newly-discovered canon text here.
17. The proverbs are printed in DDB, 268. The translation of the riddles is reproduced from Maynard Solomon, "Mozart's Zoroastran Riddles," *American Imago*, 1985, 345–369, especially pp. 347–350. The German originals appear in MBA, 3: 506–507; 6: 713–715.
18. Ibid., 356.
19. Ibid., 353.
20. Ibid., 362.
21. See Braunbehrens, *Mozart in Vienna*, 383–384, and 450, n. 16.
22. Maynard Solomon calls attention to the sexual innuendo here. "Zoroastran Riddles," p. 352.
23. Ibid., 355.
24. On 14 February 1778 Mozart explained that he had not yet left for Paris because he first had to arrange for his mother to return to Augsburg and thence to Salzburg. In the end, his mother went along with Wolfgang to Paris.

25. The third encounter with Archbishop Colloredo was the final audience and the one during which Mozart resigned from his post at the Salzburg court.

26. See Peter J. Davies, *Mozart in Person*, Chapter 16. The description cited appears on page 145.

27. It has been suggested that Mozart chattered so much during this performance because he had heard Paisiello's opera a few months earlier in Vienna. See MBA, 6: 332. It is not difficult, however, to think of other reasons—for example, that he found it boring.

28. Nothing at all is known about this "person of ill repute."

29. Mozart attempted to publish three piano concertos, K. 413–415 under his own auspices. See Chapter 3.

30. The possibility that Mozart may have been an inveterate gambler is developed in Uwe Krämer, "Wer hat Mozart verhungern lassen?," *Musica* (1976): 203–211. For a systematic analysis of Mozart's finances, see Carl Bär, " 'Er war kein guter Wirth': Eine Studie über Mozarts Verhältnis zum Geld." *Acta Mozartiana* (1978): 30–53.

31. According to both Landon and Braunbehrens, the letter just cited was probably written not in June 1788, as commonly proposed, but rather some months later, and that the planned concerts in the Casino were to feature Mozart's last three symphonies, which were recently completed. See Landon, *Mozart: The Golden Years*, 198, and Braunbehrens, *Mozart in Vienna: 1781–1791*, 324.

32. While there are no vulgar sexual obscenities in the Bäsle letters, there are a very few mildly suggestive passages, as cited earlier. As for the possibility of additional sexual double entendres, see Joseph Heinz Eibl and Walter Senn, eds., *Mozarts Bäsle-Briefe*, 79–80.

33. According to Emily Anderson, each dot represents a word that has been obliterated in the original.

34. The reference is to Leopold's previous letter, now lost.

35. Mozart shows the same delicacy in the German original, where he writes: *h=re. [Hure]*.

36. The name has been obliterated in the original by a later hand.

37. Marianne von Natorp became Jacquin's betrothed.

38. Actually, Constanze was the third of the four Weber sisters: Josepha, Aloysia, Constanze, and Sophie.

39. Davies, *Mozart in Person*, 21.

40. Ibid., 39–40. See also MBA, 6: 145;

41. See Wolfgang Hildesheimer, *Mozart*, 78–81.

42. Ibid., 192–196.

43. Presumably a reference to his Masonic beliefs.

44. Leopold died on 28 May 1787.

Chapter 6. A Short Introduction

1. The German reads: "ein Buch—eine kleine Musicalische kritick mit Exemplen" (MBA, 3: 246). "Kritik," in eighteenth-century German usage, suggests a systematic study—as in Immanuel Kant's *A Critique of Pure Reason*.

2. Actually the finishing touches, a revision of a passage in the last movement, were probably added to the work several months later, presumably after completion of the D minor quartet, the following summer. See Tyson, *Mozart: Studies*, 85.

3. Reproduced more fully in Chapter 12.

4. Extensive excerpts appear in Chapter 9.

5. See also Mozart's remarks about "effect" in the *Paris* Symphony, K. 297, in Chapter 12.

6. The German description reads: "serios . . . mit anmuth und freundlichkeit." MBA, 2: 170. See Abert, *Mozart*, 1: 515, and Alfred Einstein, *Mozart: His Character, His Work*, 243–244.

7. Mozart's designation "Turkish music" usually includes a triangle, too, but not in this particular instance.

8. Contrary to Mozart's description of the passage here, the autograph score of the opera makes no mention of violin mutes. See the NMA edition: NMA II/5/12, xxvi.

9. "Così c'è più cantilena nella prima voce, e gli accordi sono più compietti. full." (The English "full" at the end of the comment is Mozart's.)

10. For an illuminating discussion of Mozart's teaching method, see Daniel Heartz, "Thomas Attwood's Lessons in Composition with Mozart," *Proceedings of the Royal Musical Association*, 100 (1975), 175–183.
11. For a comprehensive study of Vogler's theoretical system, see Floyd D. Grave and Margaret G. Grave, *In Praise of Harmony: The Teachings of Abbé Georg Joseph Vogler*.

Chapter 7. Performance

1. The German reads: "mit der gehörigen expreßion und gusto." MBA, 2: 228.
2. As reported from Vienna by Leopold in a letter to Nannerl, 16 February 1785 (A, 886).
3. Leopold Mozart, *A Treatise on the Fundamental Principles of Violin Playing*, Chapter 1, Section 3, paragraph 3. (English translation, 36)
4. Ibid., Chapter 1, Section 3, paragraphs 5, 6. (English translation, 38).
5. The Andante is reproduced in example 6.1.
6. The opening of the fugue is reproduced in example 1.5.
7. The final movement is in alla breve time and marked "Presto."
8. Leopold Mozart, *A Treatise*, Chapter 12, paragraph 20, footnote, as translated in David D. Boyden, *The History of Violin Playing*, 471.
9. See Eva and Paul Badura-Skoda, *Interpreting Mozart on the Keyboard*, 44–45.
10. The piece Mozart is referring to is apparently lost. It was previously considered to be the Capriccio in C, K. 395 (300g). But Wolfgang Plath, the editor of the pertinent volume of the NMA, has demonstrated that this cannot be so. See the foreword to NMA IX,27/2, xii–xv. In any event, Mozart must be referring to a composition with similar episodes in unmeasured time. See example 12.8.
11. Mozart may have had in mind Myslivecek's *Six Easy Divertimentos for the Harpsichord or Pianoforte* (London, 1777). See MBA, 5: 413, 430.
12. "Lead-ins," that is, brief cadenza-like passages inserted between phrases.
13. See MBA, 6: 61 and Eibl, *Chronik*, p. 54.
14. See Neal Zaslaw, *Mozart's Symphonies*, 368–369, 450ff.
15. Zaslaw provides a valuable table of statistics for all the orchestras Mozart conducted. (*Mozart's Symphonies*, 458–459).
16. An excerpt from the aria is reproduced in example 1.7.
17. Mozart is describing the *messa di voce*, an extremely important vocal—and instrumental —ornament in the eighteenth century. It consisted of increasing and diminishing the volume on virtually all relatively long notes.
18. See Boyden, *Violin Playing*, 381.
19. Heinrich Christoph Koch, *Musikalisches Lexikon* (Frankfurt, 1802), col. 1163.
20. In this connection, see Beethoven's description of Mozart's keyboard playing, cited in Chapter 1.
21. Mozart's indignation at Clementi's playing was great enough to prompt him to repeat his judgment, practically in the same words, a few days later. See Chapter 14.
22. A characteristic passage from one of Clementi's sonatas is reproduced in example 13.3. Chapter 13 contains as well the rest of Mozart's description of his playing.
23. On Mozart's keyboard instruments see Nathan Broder, "Mozart and the 'Clavier'"; also Badura-Skoda, *Interpreting Mozart*, 6–26.
24. Light-textured, homophonic pieces in a popular style featuring a pleasant, song-like or dance-like melody and an unpretentious accompaniment.
25. See Chapter 1.
26. Philip R. Belt, "History of the Piano: Germany and Austria," *The New Grove Musical Instrument Series: Piano* (New York, 1988), 15, 18.
27. Although he did not expect to be allowed to do so, Mozart in the end was able to play at the benefit concert of the Tonkünstler-Societät, which took place on 3 April 1781. It is not known for certain whether he fulfilled his intention as described here.
28. See Boyden, *Violin Playing*, 458, 378, and passim.

Chapter 8. Opera: The Principal Categories

1. The reference is to a projected opera to a libretto (on a subject as yet unknown) supplied by Gottlieb Stephanie. This was ultimately to be *Die Entführung aus dem Serail*.
2. See Donald J. Grout, *A Short History of Opera*, 3rd edition, p. 216.

3. In the score the aria carries the tempo indication "Andante ma sostenuto."
4. The cadenzas, along with the ornamented arias, share the number 293e in K6.
5. See K6, pp. 300–301, also the editor's commentary in NMA II/5/7, p. xlii.
6. A planned final aria for Idomeneo, peaceful in character. See the discussion of Poetry in Chapter 9.
7. See Braunbehrens, *Mozart in Vienna*, especially 77, 127–130, 170, 188.
8. Johann Mederitsch (1752–1835).
9. Johann Baptist von Alxinger (1755–1797).
10. *Chiaroscuro*, that is, light-dark, a painting term for the dramatic use of light and shadow. According to Abert, *Mozart*, I: 695, Mozart is referring here to the character Arbace's wavering between fear and hope.
11. Giovanni Battista Zonca was a bass. This passage implies that Mozart had originally planned to cast the role of Idomeneo for a bass, not a tenor. See Chapter 10; also MBA, 6: 44, and the commentary in NMA II/5/11, xxiv.
12. See the perceptive analysis of this quartet by Daniel Heartz, "The Great Quartet in Mozart's *Idomeneo*," *The Music Forum*, 5 (1980): 233–256.

Chapter 9. Opera as Drama

1. The Italian poet was presumably Lorenzo Da Ponte, the libretto presumably the text for the unfinished opera buffa, *Lo sposo deluso*, K. 430 (424a).
2. The "useless piece" was not the great quartet "Andrò rimango," but a different quartet altogether—a "*licenza* of the perfunctory type." See Daniel Heartz, "Raaff's Last Aria: A Mozartian Idyll in the Spirit of Hasse," *The Musical Quarterly*, 60 (1974): 519.
3. A short, simple aria generally consisting of one, sometimes two, strophes.
4. See the preceding passage from this letter, cited in Chapter 5 in the section "A Musician's Guide to Europe—Salzburg."
5. Neither purely serious nor purely comic. See also the description of the aria *di mezzo carattere*, in Chapter 8.
6. See the discussion of the work in William Mann, *The Operas of Mozart*, 322–330.
7. The text in the final version reads: "Se il padre perdei,/la patria, il riposo,/tu padre mi sei", that is, "If I have lost my father, my country, my rest, you are now a father to me."
8. See the informative discussion of the genesis of this aria in Heartz, "Raaff's Last Aria," 517–543.
9. The continuation of this letter, in which Mozart mentions Raaff's suggestion to use the text of the *aria di licenza* "Bell'alme al ciel dilette" (Beautiful Souls, Heaven's delight) from Metastasio's *Natal di Giove*, for the final aria of *Idomeneo* was cited in Chapter 8, under "Aria Forms."
10. *Hui* and *schnell* are completely synonymous and mean "quickly" or "fast."

Chapter 10. Opera and Dramatic Music: Individual Compositions

1. See Rudolph Angermüller, "Wer war der Librettist von 'La Finta Giardiniera,'" *Mozart-Jahrbuch 1976/77*: 1–20.
2. See Plath, "Beiträge zur Mozart-Autographie II," pp. 169, 172–173.
3. The play had been produced in Vienna in 1774.
4. Mozart's original intention, apparently, was to cast the role of Idomeneo for a bass, Giovanni Battista Zonca. See Chapter 8.
5. On the origin of *Die Entführung* and the relation between the Mozart-Stephanie version and that of Bretzner, see Bauman, *W. A. Mozart, Die Entführung aus dem Serail*, especially Chapter 2.
6. According to MBA, 6: 77, the actor Johann Ignaz Walter was presumably to take the part of Bassa Selim, a spoken role. At the first performance, however, it was played by another: Dominik Jautz
7. The premiere did not take place until the following July.
8. "Tod und Verzweiflung war sein Lohn." This is a quotation from the second act duet (No. 11) for the two priests.
9. The second husband of Mozart's sister-in-law, Josepha Hofer, née Weber.
10. The aria "Non più di fiori" features an elaborate obbligato part for the basset horn, which was played by Anton Stadler.

11. The words, although evidently not by Metastasio, appeared in Hasse's setting of Metastasio's *Artaserse*. They are thought to be by the poet Antonio Salvi. See NMA II/7/2, xiv–xv.
12. Mozart's description of the revisions made for Raaff's sake is reproduced in the section on revision in Chapter 1. See also the entry on Raaff in Chapter 14.
13. See Heartz, "Raaff's Last Aria," 534–539.
14. See K6, 329.

Chapter 11. Church Music

1. Letter of 31 May 1827 to Abbé Maximilian Stadler. MBA, 4: 491.
2. Franz Niemetschek, *Life of Mozart*, 72.
3. Tyson, *Mozart: Studies*, 26–28.
4. The pertinent citations are reproduced in Chapter 2.
5. See NMA I/1/1/2, viii–ix.
6. See also Mozart's description of his participation, as an organist, in a mass service in Mannheim, reproduced in Chapter 1.
7. The Mirabell palace and gardens in Salzburg were originally built by Prince Archbishop Wolf Dietrich in 1606.
8. K. 108 (74d) in C, from May 1771; K. 127 in B-flat, from May 1772—both in four movements—and a C-major setting, K. 276 (321b), dating from ca. 1779, cast as a single multisectional movement.
9. Litaniae de B.M.V. in B-flat, K. 109 (74e), May 1771; Litaniae Lauretanea in D, K. 195 (186d), May 1774; Litaniae de venerabili altaris sacramento in B-flat, K. 125, March 1772 (nine movements); Litaniae de venerabili altaris sacramento in E-flat, K. 243, March 1776 (ten movements).
10. The German original reads: Ich vor habe den primo eine homo motteten machen welche müssen morgen bey Theatinern den producirt wird (MBA, 1: 475).
11. See MBA 1: 534.
12. The fragment of a Kyrie in E-flat, K. 322 (296a), formerly thought to be part of the mass contemplated in the following series of exerpts, is now known to have been composed a year later. See Plath, "Beiträge zur Mozart-Autographie II," 170.
13. The six Sonatas for Violin and Piano, K. 301–306 (293a–c, 300c, 293d, 300l), composed in Mannheim and Paris (between January/February and Summer 1778) and published in Paris in November 1778.
14. Upon the death of Max III Joseph, Elector of Bavaria on 31 December 1777, Karl Theodor inherited the Bavarian throne and moved his court from Mannheim to Munich.
15. That is, Mozart composed a total of eight movements for Holzbauer's work: Movements 1–3: Choruses; Movement 4: Trio for Soprano, Tenor, and Bass; Movements 5–6; Recitatives; Movement 7: Chorus; Movement 8: Tenor Solo with Chorus.
16. Presumably the fragmentary Kyrie in E-flat, formerly considered to have been written the previous year, really belongs to this planned work. See above, note 12.
17. Earlier in the letter Mozart writes: "When I made [the promise] my wife was still single: yet, as I was absolutely determined to marry her soon after her recovery, it was easy for me to make it." This casts doubt on the explanation in Georg Nikolaus Nissen's Mozart biography that the oath had to do with the birth of the Mozarts' first child. See Nissen, *Biographie W. A. Mozart's*, 476.
18. See Chapter 9.
19. Among the most recent studies that summarize recent research (as well as include copious quotations from the writings of the early protagonists in the tumultuous posthumous history of this legendary work) are H. C. Robbins Landon, *1791: Mozart's Last Year* and Richard Maunder, *Mozart's Requiem: On Preparing a New Edition*.

Chapter 12. Instrumental Music

1. The publication history of these concertos is related in Chapter 3.
2. See Tyson, *Mozart: Studies*, 152.
3. The Concert Rondo in D, K. 382 written as a new finale for the Piano Concerto in D, K. 175, composed in Salzburg in 1773, but frequently performed by Mozart in his Vienna years.

4. See Wolfgang Plath's foreword to NMA IX/27/2, xii–xiv.
5. But on the clavichord. See the earlier excerpt from this letter reproduced in Chapter 1.
6. See example 1.7.
7. See Zaslaw, *Mozart's Symphonies*, 161–162.
8. Ibid., 334.
9. Ibid., 246.
10. Mozart's arrangement, long lost, was recently rediscovered and published. See Bastian Blomhert, *The Harmoniemusik of* Die Entführung aus dem Serail *by Wolfgang Amadeus Mozart: Study about its Authenticity and Critical Edition.*
11. See also the citations presented in Chapter 1 attesting to Mozart's distate for the flute, and—at least in his childhood—the trumpet, as well.
12. At its premiere at Mozart's first public concert at the Burgtheater on 1 April 1784.
13. A detailed study of the chronology of the quartets appears in Tyson, *Mozart: Studies*, 83–105.
14. Re Joseph and Primus, see Chapter 5, note 8.
15. See Tyson, *Mozart: Studies*, 35
16. The Divertimenti for Strings and Horns in F and B-flat, respectively, K. 247, and K. 287 (271H).
17. Possibly the *Haffner* Serenade in D, K. 250 (248b).
18. Other portions of this letter are cited in Chapter 3.
19. See example 1.7.
20. An earlier passage from the same letter concerning this composition is cited in Chapter 1 in the section on Composing.
21. See Wolfgang Plath, "Zur Datierung der Klaviersonaten KV 279–284," *Acta Mozartiana*, 21 (1974), 26–30.
22. In addition to the following citations, see the important references to this sonata in Mozart's letter of 6 December 1777 quoted in Chapters 6 (including an example) and 7.
23. See Tyson, *Mozart: Studies*, 106–113; and Zaslaw, *Mozart's Symphonies*, 323–329.
24. Earlier in the same letter, Mozart expresses his desire "to teach the young Count."
25. Cited in Chapter 7.
26. In the end, Kozeluch did not do the engraving of the quartets but rather Artaria & Co. See MBA, 6: 386.
27. See Robert D. Levin, *Who Wrote the Mozart Four-Wind Concertante?* for a comprehensive study of the historical and analytical problems surrounding the work.

Chapter 13. Composers

1. See Chapter 1.
2. The biographical information in this chapter is based on the standard musical reference works, above all *The New Grove Dictionary of Music and Musicians*, ed. Stanley Sadie, the commentary volumes (vols. 5 and 6) of MBA, also Nicolas Slonimsky, *The Concise Baker's Biographical Dictionary of Musicians.*
3. According to MBA, 6: 162, Mozart may have been referring to the *Six Fugues pour le Piano-forte*, (H. 99ff.), Bonn: N. Simrock, n.d. Another reference by Mozart to C.P.E. Bach appears below under J.S. Bach.
4. This work has not been identified. See MBA, 5: 494.
5. On the relationship between Bach's setting of this text and Mozart's, K. 294, see Chapter 1.
6. Mozart is presumably referring to his string quartet arrangements of five fugues (Nos. 2, 5, 7, 8, 9) from Book 2 of *The Well-Tempered Clavier*, K. 405.
7. *Allgemeine Musikalische Zeitung*, I (1799), 117, as translated in Hans David and Arthur Mendel, *The Bach Reader* (New York, 1966), 359–360.
8. Otto Jahn, *W. A. Mozart*, 3rd edition, II: 40, as cited in Forbes, *Thayer's Life of Beethoven*, I: 87.
9. An excerpt from Benda's *Medea* is reproduced as example 8.4.
10. Mozart's concern was that the Gluck performances would delay the premiere of *Die Entführung*. See below. See also the entry on the singer Bernasconi in Chapter 14.
11. It is not known what those "ideas" were. MBA, 6: 115 speculates that Mozart may have hoped to succeed Gluck, whose health was poor, as chamber composer, in the event of his death.

12. Mozart not only ultimately got to hear Handel's *Messiah:* he reorchestrated the work in March 1789 at the request of Baron van Swieten. Mozart's arrangement bears the K. number 572. On Mozart's interest in Handel, see also above under Johann Sebastian Bach.

13. Probably John Mainwaring's *Memoirs of the Life of the Late G. F. Handel* (1760) in the German translation of Johann Mattheson (1761).

14. In addition to *Messiah*, Mozart—again at the request of van Swieten—prepared arrangements of Handel's *Acis and Galathea*, K. 566 (November 1788), *Alexander's Feast*, K. 591 (July 1790) and *Ode for St. Caecilia's Day*, K. 592 (July 1790).

15. Cited in Abert, *Mozart*, I, 144.

16. Mozart's famous 1785 dedication of his six string quartets is reproduced in Chapter 12.

17. Mozart's arrangements of the first twelve are lost; it is not certain whether he ever made keyboard arrangements of the second six. MBA, 5: 238.

18. According to MBA, 5: 391, it is not known which of Haydn's six quintets were performed.

19. Mozart is being sarcastic. In the German original Mozart spells the names "Lips" = Franz Ignaz Lipp; "Hilber" = Joseph Hülber, Salzburg violinist; "Aman" = Corregent Ammand, about whom nothing is known. See MBA, 5: 539–540.

20. Tres sunt = *Offertory pro Festo SS: Trinitatis;* Ave Maria = *Offertory pro Domenica Adventus (quarta);* the Tenebrae = *Tenebrae factae sunt* by Eberlin. See MBA, 6: 135.

21. Presumably the Piano Trio in E, K. 542, and the Quartet for Piano and Strings in E-flat, K. 493.

22. See also Chapter 11, regarding Mozart's additions to Holzbauer's Miserere.

23. Johannes Hummel died in 1828; his reminiscences were published in 1873. See DDB, 570.

24. Niccolò Jommelli, *Armida abbandonata*. Introduction by Eric Weimer, p. [iii].

25. See Marita P. McClymonds, *Niccolò Jommelli: The Last Years, 1769–1774*, 85–86.

26. *Misericordias Domini*, K. 222 (205a). On this work—including Padre Martini's opinion of it—see Chapter 11.

27. The symphony is unknown. It carries the identifying number 2890 in Jan LaRue, *A Catalogue of 18th-Century Symphonies, Volume I. Thematic Identifier*, 56.

28. Mozart is presumably referring to Myslivecek's *Six easy divertimentos for the harpsichord or pianoforte* (London, 1777). See MBA, 5: 413.

29. The competition between Mozart and Clementi took place on 24 December 1781; see the entry for Clementi in Chapter 14.

30. According to MBA, 6: 332 Mozart may have chatted because he had already heard the opera in Vienna, where it had been performed in September 1786; but other explanations are conceivable.

31. Mozart presumably has in mind Pleyel's string quartets, op. 1 (1776), published in 1784 in Vienna. MBA, 6: 180.

32. According to MBA, 5: 391, Mozart is probably referring to the *VI Divertimenti da camera a Cembalo e Violino* (ca. 1777).

33. Abert, *Mozart*, I: 516–517.

34. See Richard Engländer, *Die Dresdner Instrumentalmusik in der Zeit der Wiener Klassik*, 78–81.

35. According to MBA, 5: 408, this concerto is apparently lost.

36. The remainder of this quote appears in Chapter 7. Since Clementi's op. 7 sonatas had recently been published in Vienna, it is likely that Mozart had one of the sonatas from that set specifically in mind.

37. Mozart writes "scomposition," that is, with the derogatory Italian s prefix

38. Mozart is mistaken here. There are several earlier examples of singspiel, for example, by Johann Standfuss (1752) and Johann Adam Hiller (1766). See Abert, *Mozart*, I: 748–750.

39. The libretto was by one Cornelius Hermann von Ayrenhoff (1733–1819). MBA, 6: 124.

40. The rest of this passage appears above under Johann Christian Bach. See also Chapter 6, for Mozart's opinions on Vogler's theory book, his mass, and his woeful command of compositional craft; also the remarks in Chapter 14 on his organ playing.

41. See Chapter 3 for a description of the intrigues surrounding Mozart's insertion arias.

42. Mozart is referring to Eberlin's publication *IX Toccate e Fughe per l'Organo* (Augsburg, 1747). See MBA, 6: 105.

43. This letter is in Leopold's hand, and presumably its content is his, as well.

44. Mozart had expected to become the Princess's teacher. See the quotation from his letter

of 5 December 1781 in Chapter 5. But as late as the following August he still was entertaining the hope that this might come to pass. See below.

45. Further references to Salieri appear in Chapter 10 (under *Die Zauberflöte*) and in Chapter 11 (letter to Archduke Francis).

46. Mozart is presumably referring to his variations on "Come un agnello" from *Fra i due litiganti*, K. 460 (454a), the same tune quoted in *Don Giovanni.*

Chapter 14. Performers

1. The biographical information in this chapter is based on the standard reference works: *The New Grove Dictionary of Music and Musicians*, the commentary volumes of MBA; also K. J. Kutsch and Leo Riemens, *Grosses Sängerlexikon*, and *Dizionario enciclopedico universale della musica e dei musicisti.*

2. As cited in Landon, *Mozart: The Golden Years*, 36.

3. The remainder of this passage (with musical examples) appears under the entry on Expression in Chapter 6.

4. Additional comments on Adamberger appear in the section on Intrigues in Chapter 3.

5. A comma is a small pitch interval, about a ninth of a whole tone, that is, slightly smaller than a quarter tone.

6. Further passages from this letter appear in Chapter 4, under Salzburg, and in Chapter 9, under Plot.

7. Ceccarelli had been in the Salzburg service since 1778; his contract was to expire on 1 November 1781, but was renewed. See MBA, 6: 87.

8. In the end the role of Mitridate went to the tenor Guglielmo D'Ettore.

9. Hasse's opera *Ruggiero*, and Mozart's serenata, *Ascanio in Alba*, K. 111, were commissioned for, and ultimately performed at, the same occasion: the wedding of the Archduke Ferdinand of Austria to the Princess Maria Ricciarda Beatrice of Modena. The performances took place in 1771 Milan on October 16 (Hasse) and October 17 (Mozart).

10. In the end Manzuoli sang the role of Ascanio in Mozart's serenata.

11. The story about Marchesi's death is a fabrication. See also under Dal Prato, below (Bad Singers).

12. See note 2 above.

13. See the musical examples in Chapter 6.

14. The remainder of this passage appears in Chapter 10 under *Die Zauberflöte*. See also the reference for 21 May 1785 cited above under Adamberger.

15. As with Manzuoli, De Amicis did not sing in *Mitridate*. The role of Aspasia was taken by Antonia Bernasconi.

16. Giunia's aria "Ah, se il crudel" from *Lucio Silla*. See the excerpt reproduced in example 8.2.

17. See MBA, 5: 223.

18. See also the references to Panzacchi in Chapter 8.

19. On Mozart's relations with Raaff, see Heartz, "Raaff's Last Aria," and Chapters 9–10.

20. The continuation of this letter appears in Chapter 10, under the aria, K. 295.

21. An excerpt from Bach's aria is reproduced in example 1.6.

22. See also the sections on "Singer's Opera," Chapter 8; also Chapter 9, "Opera as Drama."

23. Giunia's aria "Ah, se il crudel" from *Lucio Silla*. See the excerpt reproduced in example 8.2.

24. Keyboard music in a light-textured, melodious style.

25. The contract for the Venetian opera festival at Ascension time.

26. Additional excerpts from this letter are reproduced in Chapter 7.

27. See also the discussions of this aria and its origins in Chapters 1 and 10.

28. This is a reference to the recent upheavals at the Nationalsingspiel. See Chapter 3, Opera World.

29. A substitute aria replacing Aria No. 12 in *Figaro*: "Venite, inginocchiatevi."

30. See Leopold's favorable description of Meissner's voice as reproduced in MBA, 5: 63.

31. A discussion of Mozart's views on orchestral size appears in Chapter 7.

32. The German reads: "ein Orchestre zum frais kriegen." MBA, 2: 65. According to Neal Zaslaw the Augsburg orchestra had "no more than eight weak violinists." See Zaslaw, *Mozart's Symphonies*, p. 451.

33. The German of the final clause reads: "die musique ist hier vom ganzem herzen schlecht." MBA, 2: 68.
34. See also the discussion of the *Paris* Symphony, K. 297, and the lost Sinfonia Concertante for Winds, K. 297B, in Chapter 12.
35. See the entry on Clementi in Chapter 13, Composers (Bad).
36. See also the comments in Chapter 7.
37. The remainder of the quotation appears in Chapter 7.
38. Mozart's views on the proper execution of a fugue appear in Chapter 7.
39. See the biographical entry in Chapter 13.
40. See the biographical entry in Chapter 13.
41. See the discussion of violin playing in Chapter 7.
42. See also Mozart's characterization of Brunetti's morals in Chapter 5.
43. The composition referred to is the sonata in B-flat, K. 454. It is dated "21 April 1784," in Mozart's personal catalogue—that is, three days before this letter was written, and in which Mozart remarks that he was still working on it. At the time of the concert on the 29th, he had managed to write out only the violin part; Mozart himself played from a manuscript score in which the piano part was only partially sketched. See the commentary in the latest edition of the Köchel catalogue (K6).
44. Mozart's less flattering description of Mlle. de Guines's abilities as a composition pupil is reproduced in Chapter 6.
45. See the entry for Freyhold in Chapter 13, Composers (Bad).
46. Mozart's characterization of Fischer's meager abilities as a composer appears in Chapter 13, Composers (Bad).
47. The work survives as the Flute Concerto in D, K. 314 (285d). The original version for oboe, in C major, has been reconstructed and is frequently performed.
48. See Alan Tyson, *Mozart: Studies*, 246–261, especially 252.

Bibliography

Abert, Hermann. *W. A. Mozart. Neubearbeitete und erweiterte Ausgabe von Otto Jahns Mozart.* 7th edition. 2 vols. Leipzig: Breitkopf & Härtel, 1955.

Allegri, Gregorio. *Miserere (Psalm 51) für zwei Chöre.* Arranged and edited by Erwin Zillinger. *Die Motette, 539.* Neuhausen-Stuttgart: Hänssler-Verlag, 1970.

Anderson, Emily. *The Letters of Mozart and His Family.* Chronologically arranged, translated, and edited with an introduction, notes, and indexes. 3rd edition. London: Macmillan, 1985.

Angermüller, Rudolph. "Wer war der Librettist von 'La Finta Giardiniera,'" *Mozart-Jahrbuch 1976/77:* 1–20.

———· *W. A. Mozarts musikalische Umwelt in Paris (1778). Eine Dokumentation. Musikwissenschaftliche Schriften, 17.* Munich-Salzburg: Musikverlag Emil Katzbichler, 1982.

Bach, Johann Christian. *12 Konzert- und Opernarien.* Piano score. Edited by Ludwig Landshoff. Leipzig: C. F. Peters, 1930.

Badura-Skoda, Eva and Paul. *Interpreting Mozart on the Keyboard.* London: Barrie and Rockliff, 1962.

Bär, Carl. "'Er war kein guter Wirth': Eine Studie über Mozarts Verhältnis zum Geld," *Acta Mozartiana,* (1978): 30–53.

Bauman, Thomas. *W. A. Mozart Die Entführung aus dem Serail. Cambridge Opera Handbooks.* Cambridge: Cambridge University Press, 1987.

Benda, Jiri (Georg). *Medea. Melodram. Partitura.* Edited by Jan Trojan. Prague: Editio Supraphon, 1976.

Blomhert, Bastiaan. *The Harmoniemusik of* Die Entführung aus dem Serail *by Wolfgang Amadeus Mozart: Study About its Authenticity and Critical Edition.* The Hague: Bastiaan Blomhert, 1987.

Boyden, David D. *A History of Violin Playing from its Origins to 1761.* London: Oxford University Press, 1965.

Braunbehrens, Volkmar. *Mozart in Vienna: 1781–1791.* Translated from the German by Timothy Bell. New York: Grove Weidenfeld, 1990.

Broder, Nathan. "Mozart and the 'Clavier,'" *The Musical Quarterly,* 27 (1941): 422–432 (also published in Paul Henry Lang, ed., *The Creative World of Mozart.* New York: W. W. Norton, 1963).

Buchner, Alexander, Karel Koval, et al. *Mozart and Prague.* Translated by Daphne Rusbridge. Prague: Artia, 1962.

Clementi, Muzio. *Complete Works for Piano Solo. Published From 1771 to 1783.* Edited with an Introduction by Nicholas Temperley. *The London Pianoforte School 1766–1860.* Volume 1. New York: Garland Publishing, 1987.

Davenport, Marcia. *Mozart.* New York: Charles Scribner's Sons, 1932.

Davies, Peter J. *Mozart in Person: His Character and Health*. Foreword by Stanley Sadie. New York: Greenwood Press, 1989.

Da Ponte, Lorenzo. *Memoirs of Lorenzo Da Ponte*. Translated from the Italian by Elisabeth Abbott. Edited and annotated by Arthur Livingston. New York, 1929. Reprint edition, with a new preface by Thomas G. Bergin. New York: Dover Publications, 1967.

David, Hans and Arthur Mendel, *The Bach Reader*. New York: W. W. Norton, 1966.

Deutsch, Otto Erich. *Mozart: A Documentary Biography*. Translated by Eric Blom, Peter Branscombe, and Jeremy Noble. Stanford, Calif.: Stanford University Press, 1965.

Dizionario enciclopedico universale della musica e dei musicisti. Edited by Alberto Basso. Torino: UTET, 1983–1988.

Eibl, Joseph Heinz. *Wolfgang Amadeus Mozart: Chronik eines Lebens*. Kassel: Bärenreiter-Verlag, 1965.

———. "'Amadeus'? (Mozarts Vornamen)," *Acta Mozartiana*, (1972): 4–8.

Einstein, Alfred. *Mozart: His Character, His Work*. Translated by Arthur Mendel and Nathan Broder. London: Cassel, 1946.

Engländer, Richard. *Die Dresdner Instrumentalmusik in der Zeit der Wiener Klassik*. Uppsala: Lundequistska Bokhandeln, 1956.

Forbes, Elliot. *Thayer's Life of Beethoven*. Princeton, N.J.: Princeton University Press, 1967.

Grave, Floyd D. and Margaret G. *In Praise of Harmony: The Teachings of Abbé Georg Joseph Vogler*. Lincoln: University of Nebraska Press, 1987.

Haberkamp, Gertraut. *Die Erstdrucke der Werke von Wolfgang Amadeus Mozart*. 2 vols. Tutzing: Hans Schneider, 1986.

Heartz, Daniel. "Raaff's Last Aria: A Mozartian Idyll in the Spirit of Hasse," *The Musical Quarterly*, 60 (1974): 517–543.

———. "Thomas Attwood's Lessons in Composition with Mozart," *Proceedings of the Royal Music Association*, 100 (1975): 175–183.

———. "The Great Quartet in Mozart's *Idomeneo*," *The Music Forum*, 5 (1980): 233–256.

Hertzmann, Erich. "Mozart's Creative Process," *The Musical Quarterly*, 43 (1957): 187–200 (also published in Paul Henry Lang, ed., *The Creative World of Mozart*. New York: W. W. Norton, 1963.

Hildesheimer, Wolfgang. *Mozart*. New York: Farrar Straus Giroux, 1982.

Hirt, Franz Josef. *Stringed Keyboard Instruments 1440–1880*. Boston: Boston Book and Art Shop, 1968.

Hutchings, Arthur. *Mozart: The Man, The Musician*. New York: Schirmer Books, 1976.

Jommelli, Niccolò. *Armida abbandonata*. Introduction by Eric Weimer. *Italian Opera 1640–1770*. New York & London: Garland Publishing, 1983.

Kelly, Michael. *Reminiscences of Michael Kelly of the King's Theatre and Theatre Royal Drury Lane*. London, 1826. Facsimile reprint with an introduction by A. Hyatt King. New York: Da Capo Press, 1968.

Kerst, Friedrich. *Mozart: The Man and the Artist Revealed in His Own Words*. Translated by Henry Edward Krehbiel. London: Geoffrey Bles, 1926. Reprint edition. New York: Dover Publications, 1965.

Koch, Heinrich Christoph. *Musikalisches Lexikon*. Frankfurt, 1802. Facsimile reprint. Hildesheim: Georg Olms Verlag, 1985.

Kraemer, Uwe. "Wer hat Mozart verhungern lassen?," *Musica* (1976): 203–211.

Kunze, Stefan. "Die Vertonungen der Arie 'Non sò d'onde viene' von J. Chr. Bach and W. A. Mozart," *Analecta Musicologica*, 2 (1965): 85–111.

Kusch, Eugen. *Nürnberg: Lebensbild einer Stadt.* Nuremberg: Verlag Nürnberger Presse, 1951.

Kutsch, K. J., and Leo Riemens, *Grosses Sängerlexikon*, Berne and Stuttgart: Francke Verlag, 1987.

Landon, H. C. Robbins. *Mozart: The Golden Years, 1781–1791.* New York: Schirmer Books, 1989.

——— · *1791: Mozart's Last Year.* New York: Schirmer Books, 1988.

——— · (ed.). *The Mozart Compendium: A Guide to Mozart's Life and Music.* New York: Schirmer Books, 1990.

LaRue, Jan. *A Catalogue of 18th-Century Symphonies.* 2 vols. Bloomington: Indiana University Press, 1988.

Levin, Robert D. *Who Wrote the Mozart Four-Wind Concertante?* Stuyvesant, N.Y.: Pendragon Press, 1988.

Mann, William. *The Operas of Mozart.* London: Cassell, 1977.

Maunder, Richard. *Mozart's Requiem: On Preparing a New Edition.* Oxford: Clarendon Press, 1988.

McClymonds, Marita P. *Niccolò Jommelli: The Last Years, 1769–1774.* Ann Arbor: UMI Research Press, 1980.

Mozart, Leopold. *Versuch einer Gründlichen Violinschule.* Augsburg, 1756. English edition: *A Treatise on the Fundamental Principles of Violin Playing.* Translated by Editha Knocker with a preface by Dr. Alfred Einstein. 2nd edition. London: Oxford University Press, 1951.

Mozart Briefe und Aufzeichnungen. Complete edition. Published by the Internationale Stiftung Mozarteum, Salzburg. 7 vols. Volumes 1–4: text, edited by Wilhelm A. Bauer and Otto Erich Deutsch; volumes 5–7: commentary and index, prepared by Joseph Heinz Eibl. Kassel: Bärenreiter-Verlag, 1962–1975.

Mozart, Wolfgang Amadeus. *Neue Ausgabe sämtlicher Werke (Neue Mozart-Ausgabe).* Edited by the Internationale Stiftung Mozarteum, Salzburg, in cooperation with the Mozart cities Augsburg, Salzburg, and Vienna. Kassel: Bärenreiter-Verlag, 1954–1991.

Mozart, Wolfgang Amadeus, *Twenty-One Concert Arias for Soprano.* 2 Volumes. New York: G. Schirmer, 1952.

The New Grove Dictionary of Music and Musicians. Edited by Stanley Sadie. London: Macmillan, 1980.

The New Grove Musical Instrument Series: Piano. New York: W. W. Norton, 1988.

Niemetschek, Franz. *Life of Mozart (Leben des K. K. Kapellmeisters Wolfgang Gottlieb Mozart, 1798).* Translated by Helen Mautner with an introduction by A. Hyatt King. London: Leonard Hyman, 1956.

——— · *Lebensbeschreibung des k. k. Kapellmeisters Wolfgang Amadeus Mozart.* Reprint of the Prague 1808 edition with an afterword, corrections, and additions by Peter Krause. Leipzig: Deutscher Verlag für Musik, 1978.

Nissen, Georg Nikolaus. *Biographie W. A. Mozart's.* Leipzig, 1828. Facsimile reprint with a foreword by Rudolph Angermüller. Hildesheim: Georg Olms Verlag, 1972.

Novello, Vincent and Mary. *A Mozart Pilgrimage: Being the Travel Diaries of Vincent & Mary Novello in the Year 1829.* Edited by Nerina Medici di Marignano and Rosemary Hughes. London: Eulenberg, 1955.

Ochs, Michael. "Grace Notes, *Notes,* 47 (1991): 1326–1328.

———. " 'L. m. i. a.': Mozart's Suppressed Canon Texts," *Mozart-Jahrbuch 1991.*

Plath, Wolfgang. "Zur Datierung der Klaviersonaten KV 279–284," *Acta Mozartiana,* 21 (1974): 26–30.

———. "Beiträge zur Mozart-Autographie II: Schriftchronologie 1770–1780," *Mozart-Jahrbuch 1976/77:* 131–170.

Seiffert, Wolf-Dieter. "Schrieb Mozart drei Flötenquartette für Dejean? Neuere Quellendatierung und Bemerkungen zur Familienkorrespondenz," *Mozart-Jahrbuch 1987/88:* 267–275.

Slonimsky, Nicolas. *The Concise Baker's Biographical Dictionary of Musicians.* New York: Schirmer Books, 1988.

Solomon, Maynard. "Mozart's Zoroastran Riddles," *American Imago,* (1985): 345–369.

Tyson, Alan. *Mozart: Studies of the Autograph Scores.* Cambridge, Mass.: Harvard University Press, 1987.

Valentin, Erich. *Lübbes Mozart Lexikon.* Bergisch Gladbach: Gustav Lübbe Verlag, 1983.

Zaslaw, Neal. "Mozart's Paris Symphonies," *The Musical Times,* 119 (1978): 753–757.

———. *Mozart's Symphonies: Context, Performance Practice, Reception.* Oxford: Clarendon Press, 1989.

Index

The following is a single, comprehensive, alphabetical index of names, works, and topics. Mozart's compositions are integrated alphabetically by title (in the case of operas) or work category (concerto, sonata, etc.), not as a subheading under the composer's name, nor by "K." (i.e., "Köchel") number. With the exception of Mozart's immediate family (his father Leopold, his mother Maria Anna, his sister "Nannerl," and his wife Constanze), for whom such an itemization would have been impractical, page references for recipients of the family correspondence are included here and their role as addressees identified in a subheading under their names. Page references for place names in the datelines of letters ("Paris, 31 July 1778"; "Vienna, 5 October 1782") have been omitted.

Biographical information appears variously in Chapter 4 (for writers), Chapter 13 (composers), and Chapter 14 (performers). For all other individuals (except the most obscure), brief identifications are included in Appendix I (Biographical Glossary). Page references for these biographical entries appear below in italics, as do page references for basic historical information on Mozart's operas.

A